JOSEPH CHAMBERLAIN

Joseph Chamberlain about the time of his third marriage in 1888

Peter Fraser

JOSEPH CHAMBERLAIN

Radicalism and Empire, 1868—1914

South Brunswick
New York: A. S. Barnes and Co.

Library of Congress Catalogue Card Number: **67-13131**

First American Edition 1967

A. S. Barnes and Co., Inc.
Cranbury, New Jersey 08512

6641

Printed in the United States of America

Contents

Illustrations

Acknowledgments

For permission to consult and use unpublished documents and for other helpful facilities I am indebted to the Chamberlain Trustees and to Mr K. W. Humphreys, Librarian of the University of Birmingham, and his staff: the Passfield Trustees and Mr G. Woledge (Librarian) and Mr. C. G. Allen of the British Library of Political and Economic Science: the Trustees of the British Museum: the Controller of H.M. Stationery Office: the Duke of Devonshire and Mr T. S. Wragg, Librarian at Chatsworth: the Marquess of Salisbury: the Dowager Countess of Westmorland: Earl St Aldwyn: Sir George Trevelyan, Bt.: the late Sir Winston Churchill: Mr C. A. Gladstone: the late Warden of Ashburne Hall, Manchester: Miss Viola G. Garvin: and for drawing my attention to papers of R. W. Dale, Miss Valerie Cromwell.

Throughout the book superior figures refer to Source Notes listed at the back of the book commencing on page 312.

Introduction

THE existing biographies of Joseph Chamberlain have been more or less works of contemporary history by people who knew him at first hand. Even the full and valuable work by J. L. Garvin and Julian Amery is set out on the plan of the chronicler rather than the critic, and written in the spirit of the apologist rather than the historian. As editor of *The Observer* and confidant of Chamberlain in his last years, Garvin was a passionate spokesman for tariff reform, seeing in this policy of Chamberlain's the only way to national salvation in the dangerous years after 1906. Garvin rightly strove to rescue Chamberlain's reputation from the falsehoods and calumnies which stuck like burrs to this most controversial of statesmen. Enormously informed, meticulous and discriminating, the three volumes which he lived to write established Chamberlain incontrovertibly as a man of personal as well as political greatness, and redeemed his policies from any taint of shallowness or opportunism. But Garvin steered clear of the larger questions of interpretation which were more strictly historical. He did not attempt to analyse the broader movements or to define the influential creeds of the time. He uses terms such as Liberalism, Radicalism, Whiggism, Cobdenism, Unionism, Collectivism or Socialism, Nonconformity, or Imperialism, and scores of lesser party labels and classifications at their face value, seen from a viewpoint common to himself and his earlier readers.

The Chamberlain age—spanning the period from 1868 to 1914—has now receded into historical perspective. Its assumptions concerning democracy, class, race, public morality, empire, the social system, and other fundamentals, can now be seen as distinct and special. No account of Chamberlain's career may now avoid some attempt to interpret and explain his action in relation to its distinct intellectual background. The task is a daunting one, for his career runs through complicated and epic struggles, while the political environment changes rapidly from the relatively parochial affairs of the 1870's to the alarming confusion of Edwardian times. The present work does not pretend to do more than sketch a new approach to Chamberlain's career. It concentrates on his political technique and the broad strategy behind his policies, venturing at times further in attempting to relate party politics to the governing ideological movements. An overriding aim has been to re-establish the political episodes dealt with in their contemporaneous setting and meaning: to show from the documents the immediate reasonings of the participants. Too much emphasis, admittedly, can be placed on the gamesmanship of politics. Yet it is necessary for the historical student to know what game is being played to extract the utmost sense out of speech and action. Chamberlain was a superb tactician, and is worth following in detail. And if further excuse is needed for quoting liberally from the wealth of unpublished papers which have recently become available, it might be pleaded that the best insights into historical figures, as into the character of personal acquaintances, are often gathered from incidental details, casual remarks or minor gestures.

If Chamberlain was the first middle-class politician to reach the highest rank, he was also in a sense the first 'professional' politician. In contrast to those of the older school who, like Balfour, could boast that they never read the newspapers or thought about politics in bed, Chamberlain lived with his whole being in the political element. His private life was not detached. As may be seen from his heavy-handed courtship of Beatrice Potter (later Mrs Sidney Webb), even the society of women was for him an exercise in political debate. Nor did he bring personal preferences to bear on his decisions. He pursued one idea, the extension of democracy and the betterment of the working classes. At the outset of his career the most popular leaders, such as John Bright or Gladstone, fell short of being democrats. The patrician values of the old landed and aristocratic polity still predominated even in Liberal circles, in the London clubs, at Court, in the parliamentary lobby and Whitehall. Against this system Chamberlain deliberately pitted the growing confidence and egalitarian spirit of the provincial towns. Earlier democrats had been outsiders and had not carried the middle classes with them. Chamberlain enjoyed social respectability while preaching political heresy. The very pattern of the energetic, pragmatic and successful bourgeois, he was able to build up a popular front which skilfully allied the Nonconformist congregations with the urban artisans. Taking advantage of the 1867 Reform Act, he brought issues into national prominence calculated to divide the provincial press, pulpit and platform from the circles of power in London. He violated the convention which restrained politicians from denouncing the upper classes or offering the electorate practical rather than moral choices. The precedents he set throughout his career were the most potent influence in establishing the conventions of British democracy. The National Liberal Federation became the model for all later party machines. His Radical Programme was the prototype of later party programmes and campaign handbooks. He insisted on decision by majority, doing much to establish the parliamentary closure and to defeat proportional representation. Modern forms of party discipline, electioneering, party conferences, propaganda, and a lot else, owe as much to him as to any other. He never lost his faith in the democratic process, and his final movement for tariff reform was an ambitious attempt to transform the Unionist party, including the Conservatives, into a popular organization with a more progressive programme.

It is a common belief that Chamberlain began his career as a 'socialist' Radical, and ended it as an 'imperialist' Conservative. Here we encounter a difficulty of terminology. Chamberlain certainly called himself a socialist in his early years and later became a determined opponent of Marxism and even of the Fabian socialists. He remained, however, throughout a consistent disciple of John Stuart Mill in matters of social and economic doctrine. That Mill and Chamberlain could call themselves 'socialists' (in the indigenous English sense of the word) is testimony to the almost complete ascendancy of individualist beliefs among Radicals before the 1870's. To contradict Herbert Spencer's social Darwinism, to plead for a sense of social responsibility while still accepting the generalities of *laissez-faire*, was 'socialism'. Thus Chamberlain always believed in self-reliance, competition, free enterprise, and private capitalism. He always favoured municipal as against state control; never supported a graduated income tax with the idea of redistributing wealth; and never countenanced the idea of economic class war. When varieties of Marxist socialism appeared to gain ground in the last decades of the century, Chamberlain was bound to oppose them.

xiii

His imperialism is not so easily accounted for. The word itself is a snare and delusion to students of the period. It started its career as a pejorative term for Disraeli's autocratic and chauvinistic style of handling the Turkish crisis. Soon its usual application was to the Empire proper, and by 1900 almost all British politicians, Conservatives, Fabians, and Liberals, proudly acknowledged themselves as 'imperialists'. The Marxist socialists were practically the only serious dissentients. But there were many varieties of imperialism, and fierce disputes between the various schools. The Liberals of Chamberlain's generation divided mainly into two camps, those who like John Morley or Sir Charles Dilke wished to promote the global interests and collective amity of the English-speaking peoples of British descent, and those like Rosebery for whom underdeveloped territories, markets and subject peoples were the stuff of empire. The former, whom we may call the 'Anglo-Saxon' imperialists, viewed with suspicion the empire of trade and the flag. The Rosebery school, on the other hand, were sceptical if not hostile to Imperial Federation—the knitting together of the 'white' empire by constitutional links with the mother country. Here they were in agreement, though for a different reason, with Dilke and his disciples, for whom Imperial Federation meant excluding the U.S.A. and splitting the Anglo-Saxon world. For all these complicated and contradictory reasons the Liberals as a whole were able to unite in opposing Chamberlain's scheme for imperial preferential tariffs, which was conceived as a stepping stone towards Federation.

Chamberlain had always been opposed to John Bright and the policy of 'Little England'. His imperialism was a judicious mixture of the policies of the Liberal schools mentioned, save for the one particular that he was prepared as Colonial Secretary to push towards Imperial Federation at a time when the major British parties and the self-governing colonies themselves were very tepid and distrusting. His policy of imperial preference was however an integral part of his larger conception of tariff reform, designed to meet domestic as well as imperial exigencies.

Seen from the broadest viewpoint, Chamberlain's politics evolved from an aggressive to a defensive strategy. The theme of his career was popular control, popular institutions, appeal to the people: but he had always presupposed leadership, standards, and an aristocracy of merit, applying to himself Gambetta's title of *Radical autoritaire*. In the 1890's he encountered popular leaders who could outbid him, appeal to class hatred, and openly aim to subvert the social order. Accused of demagogy himself, he became convinced that democratic forms were being abused and exploited by rabble-rousers, nihilists, self-seeking and ignorant imposters. Shortly before taking office under Lord Salisbury in 1895 he wrote a play satirizing with transparent feeling the 'New Radicals' who travestied his own methods. To his close friend Jesse Collings he confided: 'As I grow older my doubts increase. Of course there has been great indirect progress, but with it there has disappeared much that was lovable in the past and that made men happier and better. Faith, reverence, self-sacrifice were potent factors in the lives of men; and science and democracy and the struggle for existence seem to me to leave something wanting.' For him as for so many of his generation the cult of duty, self-sacrifice and service to the community, nation or empire, became increasingly the antidote for waning religious belief and growing materialism. His desire to associate imperialism with some tangible and popular programme, his sense of the urgent need to rouse the people from apathy or domestic quarrels to some larger purpose, was the initial motive behind his last and greatest campaign in favour of tariff reform.

It boots little to speculate where Chamberlain's ultimate niche will be in the hagiography of party. As an advocate of social reform and 'ransom' he might be claimed as a harbinger of the welfare state. As a believer in private enterprise and opponent of bureaucratic centralization the Liberals may still claim him. While as his reputation now stands he is classed as an imperialist and a Conservative. His policies however belong to his own age and mean nothing outside it. His real legacy is his methods in their widest aspect, which are now the stock-in-trade of all parties.

CHAPTER ONE

The 'Party of Progress'

He [Chamberlain] *is a man worth watching and studying: of strong self-consciousness under most pleasing manners and I should think of great tenacity of purpose: expecting to play an historical part, and probably destined to it.*

Gladstone–Lord Granville, 1 June 1877

THE year 1868 is rightly regarded as the turning-point in the fortunes of nineteenth-century Liberalism. Before that date it was not at all clear who or what the Liberals were. The name itself was useful for covering up the gulf between the two sections of the 'party of progress', the Whigs and the Radicals. For decades the Whig element had kept the upper hand by its mastery of a political system still essentially aristocratic. But the Radicals were strong in the country, and theirs was the distinctive creed of the middling and commercial classes, the creed of *laissez-faire*. Through Richard Cobden they had won a symbolic victory over the landed class with the success of the Anti-Corn Law League. Whigs, equally with Tories, were obliged to swallow the leek in being forced to abandon the doctrine that the landed interest deserved a paramount place in the constitution. While the patricians scoffed at the idea that Cobden might become Prime Minister, the episode of the repeal of the Corn Laws produced a convert to Cobdenism with impeccable social credentials in the person of Gladstone. Gladstone created Liberalism by combining the seeming incompatibles of Whiggery and Radicalism. From the time when he threw in his lot with Palmerston's Whig government of 1859–1865, it began to be possible to distinguish who the Liberals were. They were the men in sympathy with Mr Gladstone.

But Gladstone was then still 'muzzled'. He was kept in check by Palmerston, who prophesied that after Gladstone's liberation there would be 'strange doings'. Shortly after Palmerston's death in 1865 the strange doings began. Reform came first—the extension of the parliamentary franchise to householders in the boroughs—but in this Gladstone was out-manœuvred by the Whigs and outbidden by Disraeli, who unexpectedly accepted a Radical amendment to his Reform Bill of 1867 granting what neither he nor Gladstone had dared to suggest. The amended Bill conferred the vote on all householders without any devices for excluding the poorest classes.

The introduction of democracy into the urban constituencies seemed to offer the Radicals just the leverage they needed to oust the Whigs, and great expectations were entertained when after the election of 1868 Gladstone took office for the first time as Prime Minister, with a triumphant majority at his back. Here at last was a Liberal, not merely a Whig-liberal, administration. Gladstone had received the enthusiastic support of the Radicals and Nonconformists of the provincial towns after he chose for his electioneering cry the policy of 'justice for Ireland' and the disestablishment of the Irish Church. These supporters expected that the same principles would be applied to England.

The most immediate concern of the Radicals was national education. The establishment of some overall system of popular elementary schools had been declared by John Bright to be the first obligation of a Liberal government. The existing system of state-aided denominational schools—mostly Church of England —had been promoted by the Whigs and had stood in the way of a truly national system. Nonconformists had reacted to it by resisting the theory of state aid, or by advocating undenominational or even secular teaching. Meanwhile, half the nation's children ran wild in the streets or were employed scaring crows in the fields.

Yet education was the fetish of the Radicals or 'advanced Liberals'. The Nonconformists were passionately involved in the question on religious grounds. The secular Liberals viewed popular education as the key to social improvement. The Radical 'left' was a house of many mansions. Utilitarians of the persuasion of John Stuart Mill, Comtists and Positivists following the 'religion of humanity', system-building materialists like Herbert Spencer, exponents of 'evolutionary ethics', Cobdenites, and Owenite or Millite socialists, constituted a very diverse array of creeds. One myth, however, they shared in common. They believed that human intelligence, rationality and moral improvement depended upon education. The tradition of human 'perfectibility' and educational optimism which may be traced from the eighteenth-century rationalists through Godwin, Robert Owen and the Benthamites into the general stream of Liberalism was still predominant among intellectuals of secular or scientific outlook. Lamarckian views concerning the transmission of acquired characters had not been upset, but rather reinforced, by the popularity of Darwin's theory of evolution, and lent a scientific cachet to the notion of progress through 'cultivation'. Writing in 1867, Walter Bagehot stated a very common assumption about the environmental derivation of human intellectual abilities:

The special laws of inheritance are indeed as yet unknown. All which is clear . . . is, that there is a tendency, a probability . . . that the descendants of cultivated parents will have, by born nervous organisation, a greater aptitude for cultivation than the descendants of such as are not cultivated; and that this tendency augments, in some enhanced ratio, for many generations. . . .

There is, by this doctrine, a physical cause of improvement from generation to generation . . . playing upon the nerves of men, and, age after age, making nicer music from finer chords. . . .[1]

From this characteristically Liberal viewpoint the mass of the people were sunk in a morass of ignorance, apathy and superstition, perpetuating the irrational habits from which improvidence, intemperance, vice and crime had their origin. What was called 'the social problem' had thus a holistic explanation and might be mitigated by a holistic remedy—namely, education.

The tendency, indeed, of scientific Liberalism was to simplify all political and social problems and to search for the operation of large monolithic causes. Parliamentary reform was regarded as a complete remedy for the defects of the 'corrupt' old régime of grinding taxation and dynastic wars which, in Cobden's phrase, made millions party to the 'family squabbles' of the European monarchies. When the Reform Act of 1832 failed to yield dramatic results, other panaceas had to be looked for. In the eyes of the Cobdenites, international free trade and a cheap popular press became the guarantees of peace and goodwill between nations. For the Radical land reformers, the system of primogeniture and entail which prevented the free sale of land became a complete explanation for the impoverishment of the urban working classes. But for all sections of advanced Liberalism the prime cause of the political apathy and social improvidence of the urban population was their ignorance and illiteracy.

In these matters the Whigs were thought of as being on the side of the enemy. They were great landed proprietors who had very tardily consented to the repeal of the Corn Laws and who still opposed Bright's demand for 'free trade in land'. They upheld the established church and the denominational schools and called free education 'socialism'. They opposed democracy at home and non-intervention abroad. They were in brief a nexus of landed families who thought they had a prescriptive right to be regarded as the natural leaders of the people. They traded upon popular ignorance and their established position in Parliament. So long as the traditional ruling class dominated the House of Commons, the Whigs might be deemed useful in providing the respectability and education indispensable to high office. But surely, the Radicals thought, a popularly-supported Liberal government could afford to defy them.

The lesson of Gladstone's first ministry was that it could not be so. The parliamentary forces of the advanced Liberals remained feeble and disunited, while the domination of the 'classes' remained unshaken. In such circumstances the legislative reforms of the ministry represented a far more considerable achievement than their scale in the broad perspective of later developments would suggest. To have disturbed the interests of the Irish landlords, the church, the universities, the army and the publicans was a courageous course for which Gladstone's large majority in the Commons hardly proved sufficient. The case of Gladstone's educational measures is somewhat different. Here he deliberately set out to preserve and indeed to fortify the denominational schools as part of his great Act of 1870, while also creating the basis of a national system by permitting the establishment of local school boards dispensing rates for the building and upkeep of non-denominational schools. He carried this compromise in the teeth of the Nonconformists and Radicals on his own side by enlisting the votes of Conservatives and churchmen opposite. His solution may have been necessary, just, and successful in the long run: but it flew in the face of Liberalism in the country. It

4

was seen as a Whig-Liberal measure from a man who had posed as a disciple of Cobden.

The mantle of Cobden had fallen on John Bright, M.P. for Birmingham. Bright, however, had no fight left in him, and played no part in the struggle except to condemn the Education Bill privately. He was a chronic invalid, perhaps a hypochondriac,* and he deprecated any rupture in the Liberal party. But Birmingham, the time-honoured home of provincial Radicalism, had seen the emergence of two institutions designed to discipline the scattered forces of the left, the Birmingham Liberal Association and the National Education League. The Association had successfully thwarted the intention of the 'minority clause' of the 1867 Reform Act by contriving through its ward committees to secure such an even distribution of the Liberal vote that all three seats in the constituency fell to the party. Its pyramidal organization of committees and sub-committees and its thoroughly democratic constitution were copied in other urban constituencies, and from it grew the Liberal 'Caucus' which gained great notoriety a decade later. The National Education League was by no means just an educational pressure group. Under the guidance of the chairman of its executive committee, Joseph Chamberlain, it was the spearhead of militant Radicalism in the country from the outset.

In his early thirties, Chamberlain had established himself as an agent, soon to become a partner, in the manufacturing firm of Nettlefold and Chamberlain which, using methods of mass production and automatic machinery patented in the U.S.A., had swallowed up the scattered workshops of Birmingham where iron wood-screws were made. The task of negotiating further business mergers called for judgment and organizing ability, but it was executed without ruthlessness, for Chamberlain had acquired a social conscience. Of a serious and somewhat gloomy temperament, his sense of humour rarely escaped from social realities or rose above the sardonic. In a local debating

---

* Bright excused himself from participation by explaining to the Rev. R. W. Dale: 'I cannot write much, and scarcely write any letter yet . . . writing wearies me, as indeed does any mental labour . . . after so long a period of illness, and so many drawbacks, I sometimes lose my confidence and almost despair of recovering my normal health.' (Dale papers, 5 March 1871)

society he had made his mark as an advanced Liberal and a speaker of unshakeable effrontery, without the slightest respect for persons or institutions whose authority could not be justified on rational grounds. Having helped to organize the Liberal victory in the general election, he became a town councillor and joined the League in 1869. In his earliest speeches he appeared as an orthodox Cobdenite who referred for ultimate guidance to the works of John Stuart Mill. He preached economy, spoke of the need to emancipate the people from the economic and social oppression of the aristocracy and established church, and viewed the House of Commons as a preserve of 'sinister interests' inimical to government for the good of the majority. But Chamberlain differed from the other self-appointed tribunes of the people in one important particular. Believing that it was his mission to forestall a violent clash between the rich who were growing richer and the degraded urban masses, he was prepared to appeal to the special interests of the working classes and to form a popular front for direct action against official Liberals.

A crisis in the schools system, unavoidable if any scheme for compulsory attendance were to be advanced, had long been anticipated by educationalists. School inspectors had begun to advocate compulsion. The National Education League turned the matter into an acrimonious political squabble. For this Chamberlain was largely responsible. He toured the country speaking to Radical and working-class gatherings, and represented the question as one of party politics and class interest.

In preparation for the coming parliamentary session the League, modelling itself upon Cobden's great national organization, founded branches all over the country. By January 1870 it had 9,000 enrolled members including 50 members of parliament and, more significantly, nearly 500 ministers of religion. Its well-subscribed funds were to be called up over a period of ten years, and having already 63 branches formed and 72 in progress, it was well on the way to achieving its aim of a branch in every borough of England and Wales 'both ready and able to influence the votes' of parliamentary candidates and members. A draft Bill was circulated proposing the setting up of school boards in every district, and also undenominational teaching in terms almost identical to those stated later in the famous Cowper-Temple clause.[2]

When the government announced the terms of its own measure, it was apparent that the denominational schools were to be preserved within the national system. Forster seemed to go out of his way to meet the demands of the powerful interests which had rallied to the defence of the church schools. He offered them a year's grace in which to build new schools, eligible for the state grant, before school boards could be elected, and (as later transpired) he intended to increase the state grant. This was hire and salary, not revenge, and the evident intention to revive the denominational system was made more galling to Nonconformists by Forster's refusal to set up universal school boards or make schooling compulsory or free. Worse still, the Bill as originally cast allowed the school boards to authorize denominational teaching in the new rate-supported schools.

The League's executive committee, Chamberlain presiding, met on 24 February and decided to appeal over Forster's head to Gladstone against this attempt to 'rivet an intensely sectarian and party system upon the country'. As the main fighting issue Chamberlain chose the 'religious point' of the threat of sectarian teaching on the rates. Carrying the war into the enemy's camp, he demanded that religious teaching in denominational schools should be set apart from other instruction, out of school hours. His report to George Dixon, the League's spokesman in Parliament, reveals his initiative in the situation:

Chamberlain–Dixon, 26 February 1870: I think we have anticipated your suggestions. . . . We have sent out an inflammatory circular to all branches, urging large delegation [i.e. to Gladstone on 9 March] —also public meetings and petitions. . . .
The fight will be on the religious question. Separate religious teaching is not enough unless you mean by this the scheme of our Bill, viz. in new schools, education to be practically secular, in existing schools to be at a distinct time before or after school hours. My hope is that we may make such a show as will justify you in talking out the Bill. I don't believe Forster will give way on the religious point, and we will fight tooth and nail against the Bill if this clause is preserved.[3]

There would be no question of compromise. Indeed Chamberlain had already determined to make Forster the symbol of the trimming Liberalism which had kept the democratic Radicals for so

7

long as mere hewers of wood and drawers of water for the Whigs and whips at Westminster.

He saw that the religious issue in education could be used to rouse the Nonconformists to bring forward their demand that the Church of England be disestablished. The principle of religious equality implicit in Gladstone's abolition of the privileged position of the Irish Church pointed alike to English disestablishment and undenominational schools. The Ulster Protestants were fearful that anything short of secular education would obliterate their religion in the Catholic south of Ireland. In England where the duality of Church and Dissent had become a stalemate, the religious issue in education needed to be carefully dramatized. Chamberlain sought to effect this by 'rate martyrs' refusing to pay for religious teaching, and by representing Forster's Bill as an attack on Nonconformity in the interests of the Church. Encouraged by the spirit shown by Birmingham Nonconformists, who sent out an appeal to every dissenting minister in the country, he wrote to screw Dixon up to the mark:

Chamberlain–Dixon, 3 March 1870: If Forster forces his Bill through the House there will be a tremendous revival of the agitation for the disestablishment of the English Church. Very strong feeling was expressed against Mr Forster, who was accused of gross ingratitude to the Dissenters who assisted so greatly in securing the present government majority, and it was asserted amidst cheers that the present education Bill was a distinct betrayal and contradiction of the principle involved in the Irish Church Bill. I am bound to add that strong exception was taken to the first paragraph in your speech . . . in which you are alleged to have said that the country would receive the Bill with satisfaction.[4]

The deputation which filed into No. 10 Downing Street the following week was one of the largest on record, and its arguments may well have persuaded Gladstone that amendments in the Bill were imperative.

Organic changes were made in Forster's original measure during the course of the stormy session of 1870. But, as so often happened to Bills when the ministers in charge of them attempted major alterations in committee, the chapter of accidents bedevilled their intentions. Mr Cowper-Temple, whose amending clause is usually associated with the interests of Nonconformity, was in fact an evangelical Churchman and the chairman of a hostile organization, the National Education Union. While his amendment copying the formula of the League for undenominational teaching disarmed the opposition of Nonconformists, its effect was to exclude the voluntary schools from the rate aid which Forster had proposed to extend to them. Gladstone accepted this amendment in preference to a Radical one tabled by Harcourt and in doing so offered to compensate the Church schools by an increase in the state grant. In this way these schools, whose interests Cowper-Temple had at heart, were relieved from the control of the ratepayer and also largely of the subscriber, and fortified against the financial pressures which the Nonconformists hoped would squeeze them out of existence. The net result of the Cowper-Temple transaction was an unforeseen bonus for the denominational system, and the arrangement was supported by the votes of 132 Conservatives and only 121 Liberals, while 132 Liberals voted against ministers and a further 133 Liberals walked out.* Another amendment transferring the election of the proposed school boards to ratepayers (including women) was nullified in the eyes of Radicals by the system of 'cumulative' voting and the government's hesitation to give a decisive support to the ballot.

Thus 'betrayed' by the government, the Nonconformists broke into open revolt. For Chamberlain the whole episode was a display of the inherent lack of solidarity in the Liberal party and he resolved to plunge the League into a winter campaign for a complete revision of the Education Act in the next session. 'The Bill', he commented, 'is so detestably bad that I for one could do nothing in a movement which would infer that it was worth amendment. The whole thing is a farce, and meant to be so.' He would prefer a Tory ministry in power to this 'Liberal government truckling to Tory prejudices'.[5]

The most vulnerable part of Forster's Act was its 25th clause, empowering school boards to pay the fees of necessitous children attending voluntary schools. This clause had passed unopposed as part of the original plan of rate aid to the voluntary schools,

---

* For an account of the struggle in the Commons, see Francis Adams, *History of the Elementary School Contest.*

and should logically have been excised. It became symbolically important when the school boards which were set up in many of the large boroughs in 1871 were seen to be dominated, through the anomalies of the cumulate voting procedure, by Church representatives. The Birmingham school board, for instance, contained six Liberals—Chamberlain among them—and eight Conservatives and Churchmen, although there had been 14,709 Liberal voters and only 10,247 Conservative ones. A Catholic headed the poll, with the smallest number of voters and the largest number of votes. The Liberals had overreached themselves by grasping at too many seats. The Manchester school board had also a majority of Churchmen, and it was this body which embarked on a major exploitation of the 25th clause. It had no schools under its control, not choosing to build any, and for some years it did not ask for the right to inspect the voluntary schools it was relieving out of the rates. The sums involved were minute, even over the whole country, but here was a matter of principle which the Nonconformist conscience could not stomach.

For Chamberlain the clause was a godsend, and he led the opposition in the country against it, making it the spearhead of the revolt against the official leaders. In Birmingham the Liberal minority on the school board used their party control of the town council to resist any application of the 25th clause. In October 1870 the revived Central Nonconformist Committee, with Chamberlain in the chair, formally demanded nothing less than the gradual but total withdrawal of the state grant. At its annual meeting the following week the League representatives were inclined to demand outright secular education, but were dissuaded by Chamberlain, who considered that the general body of subscribers were not prepared for it. Keeping the contest centred on the favourable ground of the 25th clause, Chamberlain moved on the school board a resolution that its adoption would be 'an infringement of the rights of conscience, and would delay the establishment of free schools'. It was becoming apparent that in country districts the voluntary adoption of school boards would come about piecemeal and very slowly, and the clause would enable these Church-dominated boards to become an adjunct to the voluntary school system. The menace to Nonconformity was therefore real, though remote. It should be countered, Chamberlain felt, by a demand to abolish the voluntary schools.

To get up steam for such an enterprise it was necessary to keep the question at boiling point and to bring the working classes into the agitation. This was Chamberlain's first great work, a feat of dynamic leadership which bore fruit when in 1877 the League had become comprehensive and popular enough to form the nucleus of the National Liberal Federation. If he failed in his educational objectives he succeeded in the broader aim of welding the fragments of popular Radicalism into something approaching a party, and above all he set Radicalism on the road to democracy. The essential novelty of his approach may be seen in its contrast to that of John Bright. Chamberlain was prepared to smash the Liberal party, believing it to be a 'sham' standing in the way of democracy. Any grievance against it was grist to his mill. He maintained that, when the privileged classes exploited popular delusions and ignorance, it was legitimate for democrats to exploit popular enthusiasms where they found them. Bright, by contrast, could not entertain ulterior designs of this kind, and looked only to the immediate problems and exigencies of the Liberal party. Faced with the threat of a Nonconformist revolt, he rallied to Gladstone, and condemned the attitude of the League as factious.

At its third annual meeting in October 1871, the League upheld the decision to withdraw support from any Liberal candidate in parliamentary elections who refused to pledge himself to the repeal of the offensive provisions of the Education Act.* In January 1872 the executive committee of the League recast its objectives, coming out boldly for universal school boards controlling all existing schools and providing secular instruction, leaving religious instruction to be given out-of-hours by any denomination caring to provide it. The Church schools were not going to be starved out, but taken over.

At this point Bright roused himself from his sick bed and pleaded in favour of a compromise. One of the most influential of the Birmingham Nonconformists, the Rev. R. W. Dale, had

---

* During the summer the League had formed 109 new branches, making 300 in all, and it now employed visiting agents. See *Birmingham Daily Post*, 14 September 1871.

spoken in favour of the direct action of the League. Bright sent him an appeal for moderation:

Bright–Dale, 1 January 1872: As to the revolt of the Nonconformists, I don't think they are likely to break with the Liberal party; but acting with wisdom and moderation, they may bring the party to their course. To me it seems that your friends lay far too much stress on the one grievance found in the payment out of the rate to sectarian schools. If compulsion is to be used . . . before Board Schools exist, they can only go to sectarian schools. . . .

If you clamour about the 25th clause . . . you will do little to remedy the whole mischief of this unfortunate Act. In my opinion you ought to protest against any increase of the parliamentary grant; and you should condemn in the strongest manner the mode of election by which public opinion is hampered and effectually thwarted. Unless you take hard ground, you will not get the support of the working classes, who will consider the dispute as one, as they will describe it, 'between Church Parsons and Dissenting Parsons', and in which they have little real interest. . . .

I write as a 'looker on'—as one of the Nonconformists, as I have always been, and as a friend of the Administration of which for a time I was a member. . . .[6]

Bright may have been correct in his conclusion that the Non-conformists alone could not do much in the House of Commons. '. . . they may', he told Dale, 'perhaps destroy the government— which is not certain—and that might be only mischief, and would do themselves no good.' But what if other popular grievances were tacked on to the educational one?

Chamberlain himself was well aware of the narrowness of the educational issue, viewed as a popular cry. A year later he confessed that he had 'long felt that there is not force in the education question to make it the sole fighting issue for our friends. . . . Education for the Ignorant cannot have the same meaning that belonged to Bread for the Starving.' He now set himself to popularize a more comprehensive programme by weaving together the separate strands of three chief Radical grievances, the Church, the land, and education. The occasion on which he chose to promulgate the programme, under the slogan 'Free schools, free land and free church', was a Birmingham meeting held in connection with John Stuart Mill's Land Tenure Reform

Association. As always, he strove to show that the three freedoms he demanded were interconnected and called for a general attack on the citadel of class privilege:

Chamberlain at Temperance Hall, 19 February 1872: . . . Without discussing which of these ['free schools', 'free land' and 'free church'] was the most important, he would say that all these things were more or less interwoven. All class privileges had a tendency to herd together; you could not tread on the foot of any vested interest, but the corns of all the others began to ache.

If the working classes should be induced to continue the connection of Church and State, they would find the political power they were maintaining used, as it always had been, against their interests and in favour of the landed and territorial aristocracy.

So again with education, they could not hope to gain the result they hoped for from the reforms now being urged till the labourers were thoroughly educated; and when they asked for national education and claimed that every child should be educated they were met continually with the reply that the agricultural labourers receive such a miserable pittance that they could not do without the labour of their children. Therefore the children's chance of raising themselves above the misery of their parents was to be taken away, or the parents . . . must necessarily . . . become the recipients of pauper relief.

Illiteracy, pauperism, religious inequality and political disfranchisement were maintained in the deep shires by a sinister 'Quadrilateral' made up of the landowner, the farmer, the parson and the publican. But the insuperable difficulty remained the habitual placidity and deference which the rural Hodge unfailingly displayed in the presence of his masters.

Unknown to Chamberlain, the day of his address to the Land Tenure Association was also the first day of the strike of the Wellsbourne agricultural labourers. Less than a fortnight earlier Joseph Arch had delivered his historic speech under the chestnut tree. Somewhat precipitantly the men had served their demand for a sixteen shilling-a-week wage upon the farmers and, on refusal, come out on strike. 'Men who had wrought without ever having a weekday for fifty years', the *Daily News* correspondent reported, 'found themselves free to spend their time as they chose. Men got frightened by the novel sensation. . . . They stole into each other's houses, and droned stolid talk about the matter one unto the other, puzzling dimly into the future with sluggish wits. . . .' Among a hundred labourers there was not a pound's worth of silver. While still unreported in the press, the revolt of the peasantry spread from South Warwickshire through eight counties. By the end of March the meetings were obtaining full publicity and public subscriptions to the Agricultural Labourers' Union were under way. A Finance Committee was formed at the beginning of April on which Chamberlain's friend, Jesse Collings, secretary of the Education League, was prominent.* The Birmingham Radicals eagerly took up Arch's cause, Chamberlain somewhat ostentatiously announcing his own subscription of five pounds a week to the fund. The sympathies of Nonconformists were generally in favour of the Union, those of the clergy of the established Church usually against.

The means of rescuing the agricultural labourers had to be the political force of Radicalism in the large towns. Yet the most attractive features of the Radical programme applied to the counties—the plans to cheapen land and make smallholdings easily obtainable, and to give the agricultural labourer the vote. To the urban classes Chamberlain had relatively little to offer, and he tried hard to hammer out some means of appealing to them. The approach which most readily occurred to him was that of linking Church disestablishment to free education. On the platforms of the Liberation Society and at Disestablishment Conferences he produced the old argument that the Church was morally responsible for the education of the poor. One report describes how 'his estimates that the revenues of the Church applied to education would give a free and noble education to every poor man's child was applauded to the echo'. At a meeting of the Liberation Society a little later he elaborated on the same theme:

Chamberlain at Bradford, 10 October 1872: The simple fact was of course that tithes at all events were a national tax imposed in the first instance for the support of a religion which was a religion of the whole nation, and also for the relief of the poor. How was it that this last object had

---

* Letter of Arch to editor of *Morning News* of 5 April. Typical labourers' budgets printed in the newspapers showed as much as 8s 6d paid for bread out of a weekly wage of 10s.

dropped altogether out of the calculations and the recollections of 'their friend the enemy'? . . .

But . . . the wrong which had been done to the poor . . . might be tardily and partially repaired by the creation of a great system of national, free, and unsectarian education . . . the Church as a body, the Church as an establishment, had always been opposed to popular progress and reform.

One may detect in the tone of this speech the suggestion that the speedy concession of free schools might forestall the agitation for disestablishment, and indeed Chamberlain, though personally a convinced advocate of the latter policy, fully realized that it did not lie within the range of practical politics. Edward Miall's annual parliamentary resolution had dwindled to a mere demand for information concerning Church endowments, and there the question had got bogged down. 'So many men', wrote Chamberlain privately, 'are bound up in charities and endowments, and would fight for them to the death, that it is hopeless to go to the root of the matter at present.'7

As an orthodox Radical and a disciple of Cobden and Mill, he was unable to advocate anything which involved the direct transfer of wealth from one class to another. He believed in 'the magic of property, which turns sand into gold': in the enlightened self-interest of individuals as the driving force behind all exertion. Any redistribution of wealth, any artificial system which tampered with the inequalities resulting from human competitiveness and acquisitiveness, could not long survive. When he advocated state interference, therefore, it was to correct the self-acting and self-sufficient economic and social processes of *laissez-faire*, not to replace them. Speaking at an election dinner in his own ward of Birmingham he fulminated against the increasing class of millionaires, 'which did, he was sorry to say, very little for the happiness and welfare of the country', and he deplored the tendency of wealth 'like minerals in certain mines, to run into "pockets" ' while at the other extreme there were two million persons who resorted to poor relief. What was his remedy? Not the taxation of the rich for social welfare, but the opposite course. He called for 'such a revision of taxation as to relieve trade and commerce from the burdens which now unduly pressed upon them', and 'such an economical administration of the revenues as would at all events secure a "free breakfast table" '.* The mountains were to groan and give birth to this derisory mouse of free trade and the abolition of duties on tea, coffee and sugar.

Such was the part of his programme which Chamberlain offered particularly to the urban working class, and which he rather quaintly referred to as 'free labour'. The full-blooded version of the policy was delivered to a public gathering in Paradise Square, Sheffield, when Chamberlain was appearing as a parliamentary candidate for that ultra-Radical constituency on New Year's Day, 1874:

I am in favour of a great reduction of taxation in this country. I believe that if the government would only fully accept the principle of non-intervention . . . we might greatly reduce our present bloated armaments, and might secure a large remission of the taxation which presses upon the shoulders of the people.

I am in favour of a 'free breakfast table'. I support this great change —greater for this reason than for any other, because it tends towards the absolute abolition of all indirect taxation, which is a species of taxation which presses more hardly than any other upon the shoulders of the working classes. . . .

I am in favour also of the abolition of the income tax; that being a direct tax which is obnoxious in its character, unfair in its incidence, and which I think ought to be repealed. But I will not vote for the repeal of any taxation which presses principally upon the rich until I see my way to a corresponding reduction of the taxation which presses upon the poor.

This was pure Cobdenism, neither an inspiring nor an original policy, and indeed less inspiring than ever with the income tax at 3*d* in the pound and indirect taxation almost abolished by Gladstone's free trade budgets. The solution of the social problem was to come from making the necessaries of life as cheap as possible. In the same speech Chamberlain pointed to two cases where wealth was diverted out of the hands of those who created it. One was familiar—the question of the tenant farmer's right to a property in the improvements he made. To give full tenant right to every farmer regardless of the conditions in his lease would,

---

* Speech of 6 December 1872. The 'free breakfast table' was Bright's slogan for the abolition of the tea, sugar and coffee duties (at Edinburgh, 5 November 1868).

he believed, bring about the investment of more capital in the land with a consequent expansion of employment and wages, and a reduction in food prices. The other case was less familiar to the public, though it had been discussed in the writings of John Stuart Mill—the rise in urban land values. The landed proprietors, Chamberlain declared, 'have succeeded in shifting the burden of taxation from their own shoulders to the shoulders of the artisans and dwellers in the towns, and that is the more indefensible because many of these gentlemen owe their wealth, their prosperity and their influence to the proximity of their estates to great communities of thrift and industry as yours, and not to any exertions of their own. They are like the "lilies of the field, they toil not neither do they spin. . . ." ' The unearned increment of urban land values ought to be taxed, presumably by a revised method of assessing the local rates.

'Free labour' also embraced the matter of trade unions, but, like all good Liberals, Chamberlain was not at this time in favour of the right of picketing. There had, however, been gross unfairness in the treatment of the Agricultural Union. At Chipping Norton two clerical magistrates had sentenced sixteen women, the wives of labourers on strike, to prison with hard labour for 'intimidating' men brought in to replace the strikers, though their menaces were purely verbal and included an invitation to a free drink. Arch had to fight hard for the simple right to hold meetings in market towns. When therefore Chamberlain in April 1874 moved resolutions in the Birmingham Liberal Association in support of Arch's Union they simply called for general support and a subscription. 'They must bear in mind', he said, 'that the labourers were not only ignorant in the ordinary sense of the word, but they were absolutely without political education; and this great movement which they were called upon to support was similar to the great movement which before the Reform Bill obtained for the people of Birmingham their political education. . . .'

The programme of the 'four F's' which Chamberlain thus elaborated went far beyond the original objectives of the League, and he had begun to think of reforming the network of League branches into a Radical party organization. The League's intervention in by-elections had already turned it into something more than a pressure group. In the session of 1873 Mr Dixon had been asked to postpone the League's amending education bill to give place to a government measure. When the terms of this were known, the League felt it had been cheated once again. Nothing was done to encourage the formation of more school boards or children's attendance, and the payment of fees under clause 25 was transferred to the poor law boards and made obligatory. The obnoxious subvention to denominational schools was thus to be maximized while the parents concerned were to incur the stigma of pauperism. This challenge sent the League into headlong opposition. At a by-election in Bath the Liberal candidate refused to divulge his educational views, whereupon the League executive put up one of its members, Mr J. C. Cox, to split the Liberal vote. This forced the official candidate, Captain Hayter, to declare for Dixon's bill, and Cox withdrew. The episode fluttered the official dovecots and caused much controversy.

For Chamberlain this was the moment of decision, and he did not hesitate to force a party schism. To his friend Captain F. A. Maxse he wrote in June 1873 asking: 'Is it not possible to form a band of "irreconcilables" to smash up this gigantic sham called a Liberal party, and to secure re-organization on a new basis? . . . We should have to agree to take our turns . . . to fight every Ministerialist brought forward, and publish a manifesto to that effect.'[8] At a conference of the League and Nonconformist Committee held in London in July, Bright broke his long public silence to damn the Education Act as 'the worst Act passed by a Liberal government since 1832'. With Bright's full support the League's influence, already predominant in most boroughs, would have been overwhelming. Without Bright's support, while it would still have been relatively easy to break the party, it would have been very difficult to justify the action, such was the authority of the great tribune in all popular questions.

Bright in fact was working the other way, trying to heal the schism. This was made very apparent when on 6 August he consented to resume office to enable Gladstone to reconstruct his cabinet. Interviewed by J. S. Wright, the Chairman of the Liberal Association, Bright said he was joining the ministry 'most reluctantly, at [the] earnest request of Gladstone'. He shrank from facing a meeting of his constituents, and even threatened to retire from Birmingham if there was serious opposition to his acceptance of office. He was 'decidedly against [the] obstructive policy of [the] League'. A deputation of Chamberlain and others he might consent to receive, but, Wright cautioned, 'we shall have need of discretion both to avoid [a] split, and not to complete [the] ruin of [the] party in [the] country which would assuredly follow our falling out with Bright'.[9] A deputation was immediately sent, but got no satisfaction. Chamberlain expressed his view thus: 'We care nothing about the House, but want to know what the Ministry are going to the country with, and certainly they will not get the support of the Dissenters by pleading impotence.'[10] It was no good, and with Bright opposed, Chamberlain had to 'suspend operations' and await the government's new plans for the autumn.

The decision to revert to an armed neutrality was conditioned chiefly by the consideration that defeat in the coming general election was virtually a certainty. The Tory reaction seemed evidence that the League's appeal had been too narrow, and was in danger of degenerating into 'a sectarian contest, fed and kept alive by religious jealousies and rivalries'. In confessing this fear to John Morley, a passionate supporter of the aims of the League and now one of his closest associates, Chamberlain pleaded for the formal adoption by the League of his own Radical programme. 'I cannot think that much support will be lost by indicating the whole country to be won. The men who are with us on the Non-conformist question are perfectly ripe for the discussion and settlement of the others, while the assistance of the working class is not to be looked for without such extension of the argument. At the next election we shall be beaten, as you say, but we must not look to immediate results.'[11] Morley cared almost exclusively for education and disestablishment, and demurred at the suggestion that the League could embrace other extraneous objects. Chamberlain's response marks a new departure:

Chamberlain–Morley, 23 August 1873: Of course it is not feasible to alter the name or objects of the Education League, but I look forward to the possibility of a new organization on a wider basis. If we get any compromise from the government which we can possibly accept, it will probably be well to dissolve the League, leaving its still un-accomplished work to be taken up as part of the larger question. . . .

I do not expect, nor do I care, to have Gladstone entirely with us, and I am quite satisfied if he will not let his private prejudices stand in the way of our claims. . . . We are not going to attack Bright, because he says that he is on our side, and will do all in his power to bring the ministry to our views. . . .[12]

The situation was about to change more rapidly than anticipated. Within five months Gladstone had plunged the country into an unexpected January dissolution and an election which on the Liberal side was unmotivated and without a programme. Where the League, in one or two cases, ran candidates against official Liberals, it was demonstrated that the Liberal electors were against the official policy. But the working classes were not enthusiastic, and the party suffered from a malaise which Chamberlain diagnosed as leaders without principles and a party without discipline. In the autumn before the election he had published the first of his *Fortnightly Review* articles on the 'Liberal Party and its Leaders', damning Gladstone's leadership as hypocritical and his party as 'selfishness without organization'. In November Chamberlain had been elected mayor of Birmingham, entering upon a term of two and a half years' intensive municipal work which diverted him from national politics but imprinted an abiding image of his dynamic personality on the national consciousness. Newly installed as mayor, he contested Sheffield in February 1874 and was defeated in one of the most riotous contests of the time. The experience, which included being hit in the face by a dead cat and a police rescue from the mob, did not deter him from continuing to cultivate the constituency, and there he delivered an important speech winding up this phase of his career:

Chamberlain at soirée, Temperance Hall, Sheffield. 19 March 1874: The only difference I can see between the position of the advanced Liberals now and a year ago is this—that whereas from the last government we expected little and got nothing, from the present government we expect nothing and may get a good deal. You will see from what I have said that I do not desire, and I do not expect, the reconstruction of the Liberal party upon the old basis, upon the old premises. I look for the formation of a new Liberal—a new Radical party—knowing what it means, expressing its objects with definiteness, and appealing to the people from the privileged class if it is found necessary to do so.

I believe that we may employ the next few years with advantage in educating and organizing the working classes throughout the country; and if we succeed in this, we shall be able to do without the Whigs— they can join the Tories if they like. . . .

I hold that the first condition of success is a more cordial and thorough union between the Nonconformists as a body and the working classes. . . .

One final event completed the impression that a new era of Liberalism was about to open. Gladstone's long-expected retirement arrived when he laid down the leadership of the opposition at the beginning of 1875.

Like Palmerston before him, Gladstone was from the Radical point of view an ambivalent figure. In matters of constitutional reform he was quite advanced, while in questions of social and class legislation he was in Radical eyes a reactionary. He did not believe that there could be any legislative remedy for poverty, class inequality or the degrading conditions of urban slums. '. . . they are not your friends, but in fact . . . your enemies', he told a working class audience in 1871, 'who teach you to look to the legislature, or the government, for the radical removal of the evils which afflict human life'. Instancing 'the ravages of strong drink', the inequality of women, the growth of wealth, luxury and selfishness, and the problem of how 'to secure to labour its due honour', he characterized these as 'questions which it depends upon ourselves individually in the main to answer'. '. . . beneath the political questions', he concluded, 'lie deeper questions that . . . strike home to the conscience and the mind of every man; and it is upon the solution of these questions that the well-being of England must depend.' For Gladstone state interference in these matters was not only futile but pernicious, sapping the springs of self-esteem and self-help, thrift and charity. With this approach the older Radicals like Bright were in general concurrence. Nor must it be assumed that Chamberlain was wholly out of sympathy with it. Intellectually he believed in individualism and *laissez-faire*. His objections were illogical and emotional. He felt that the political system was dominated by a class bias, and that a popular movement needed legislative remedies to 'force the gates of privilege'. While he had been prepared to concede many points to Gladstone's earnestness and sincerity, he would not be so amenable to a leader drawn from the Whigs, whom he regarded as blatantly prejudiced and class-biased.

As mayor of Birmingham from the end of 1873 until his election to Parliament in June 1876, Chamberlain was able to implement the kind of municipal socialism he believed in. It would be unfair to dismiss it as merely 'gas and water' socialism, for this would rob him of the credit of raising the whole tone, competence and public estimation of municipal service. Unlike the Webbs and others who followed in his path, however, Chamberlain hated bureaucracy and central direction, believing in the necessity of basing political responsibility as much as possible on compact communities which had meaning to ordinary people. Later he was to regard the London County Council, a municipality of millions, as a monstrosity.

In his task of raising living conditions and encouraging 'a sense of the importance and dignity of municipal life' he enjoyed two advantages: an almost complete Liberal ascendancy on the town council and school board (of which he was chairman), and the opportunity of certain Acts of Parliament. He compared the council with the Duke of Wellington's army, which would 'go anywhere and do anything'. Behind him was the Liberal Association, originally designed to organize the double vote at parliamentary elections, but now employed to great effect in municipal contests. In 1876 for example the Liberals won every seat on the Board of Guardians, whom Chamberlain promptly invited to a luncheon to see what a board of one colour looked like. 'This', he commented, 'is Liberal tyranny with a vengeance, and completes the thing beautifully.'

His municipal reforms exploited the Act of 1871 setting up the Local Government Board, and the Public Health Acts of 1872 and 1875 enabling corporations to acquire gas and water concerns. The purchase of Birmingham's gas undertakings yielded profits—arising chiefly from the ability of the corporation to raise loans on very favourable terms—which could pay for parks, paving, museums and civic improvements. The municipalization of water was principally a matter of health, the object being to cheapen the supply in a town for the most part without tapped water.

In his second term of office Chamberlain launched an ambitious improvement scheme which in due time gave the town the ownership of a large central district, where rookeries of slum properties had been demolished. He was prominent among the municipal representatives consulted by Cross in the shaping of the Artisans' Dwellings Act of 1875, and helped to secure the provision by which local authorities could submit development plans for areas cleared of slums. This enabled him to appoint an improvement committee in July 1875 with the intention of rehousing thousands of slum dwellers. He found, however, that it was uneconomical to provide municipally built houses, and the land was let out as business property on 75-year leases. Two million pounds' worth of property was taken over, and the loss after re-letting was £300,000 or the value of a 3d rate: 'but', he wrote at the time, 'as I look ultimately to getting a 1s rate out of gas, I do not fear the cost.' By the spring of 1876 the scheme was nearly complete:

Chamberlain–Collings, 10 April 1876: The improvement scheme is I hope safe. The Commissioner on the second day's inquiry said something I did not like about not giving us compulsory powers between New St. and Bull St., so I talked of throwing up the scheme and mightily frightened some of the great property owners, who were standing out for exorbitant profits. . . . But today I have been to London and had a private interview with Sclater Booth, who has promised to throw over the Commissioner and give me all I want! Hurray for the Tories![13]

At this opportune time a parliamentary seat became available on George Dixon's retirement, and Chamberlain's election in June was unopposed. Just short of forty years of age, he took the seat he was to hold without a break until 1914.

After the familiar intimacy and acclaim of Birmingham, Chamberlain felt the atmosphere of the House of Commons 'strangely unsympathetic, almost hostile'. He also found that the Radicals were ill-organized and too self-willed for common action, and generally a 'poor lot'. Their Irish confederates below the gangway he thought a 'scurvy lot'. Entering at once into close relations with his friend, Sir Charles Dilke, he decided to disregard the opposition whip and form a splinter group. He writes describing the compact:

Chamberlain–Collings, 27 July 1876: I am getting into the work of the

House and making the acquaintance of members. You will agree that I have lost no time, when I tell you that I have already organized a 'party' of six members on the principle of the officers' committee of the League, i.e. perfect loyalty one to another, and ... each to do whatever the others think best. On Thursday we shall give a string of notices for bills and resolutions next session, and my impression is that the thing will go, and that we shall make a devil of a row.[14]

The true cause of Radical impotence lay in a cult of independence and an excessive reverence for the rights of private members. This was in harmony with the spirit of libertarian individualism usually associated with John Stuart Mill, whose brief career as member for Westminster had lent point and publicity to his support of the plan of proportional representation. Self-sufficient and doctrinaire, Mill had been the very prototype of the Radical 'private member', but had not strengthened the case for the return of more philosophical parliamentarians. Yet his cause was by no means dead, finding an able champion in Morley's friend, Leonard Courtney, who came out with a strong plea in the *Fortnightly* of 1876 for minority representation and a Parliament of talented debaters. For Courtney the 'Chamber of Mediocrity' (Morley's phrase) resulted from the adoption of party discipline and party programmes. He almost converted Morley, the ardent disciple and friend of Mill, and indeed the Westminster wirepullers were now casting Morley in the role of Mill's successor in the constituency. But Chamberlain succeeded in winning him back to the side of party and majority rule. Between Chamberlain and Courtney there was to remain a lifelong dislike bred of incompatible values.

In the formulation of the objectives of the new 'third' party Morley was invaluable, lending the columns of the *Fortnightly* to the movement which was to pioneer the way 'from sentimental Radicalism to Scientific Liberalism'.[15] In collaboration with Chamberlain he brought out a monthly commentary on 'Home and Foreign Affairs' which combined the punch and drive of Chamberlain's practical mind with his own widely informed European outlook. Morley was himself beginning to think of leaving his editorial chair for a seat in the Commons and was serving his apprenticeship in everyday politics: while for Chamberlain, whose 'genius for friendship' had quickly cemented an association between the two described by Morley as 'brotherly', Morley was an ideal mentor in intellectual Liberalism. The two were complementary types. Chamberlain had the hardness, confidence and strength of purpose of the man of affairs. Morley was diffident, self-conscious and erratic. He had no political judgment; was blind to the practical motives of men and the psychological forces of politics. Chamberlain was a master in this field but rarely saw far beyond it. In the long run Morley, conscious of his intellectual superiority but never able to score over Chamberlain in the wisdom of the world, was bound to feel slighted in the partnership.

While Morley remained out of Parliament and the Liberals were in opposition, these differences of personality had no ill consequences. Both men were admirers of Mill and seemed agreed upon the same creed. They were both non-believers who nevertheless regarded the religious question as the supreme issue of politics. They were both imbued with Mill's sense of the need for positive humanistic values and high secular ideals as antidotes for the prevailing evils of religious dogmatism on the one hand and cynical materialism on the other. They both read their age in terms of a spiritual crisis. Morley came near to being a follower of Comte, but a 'religion of humanity' pursued in the spirit of eighteenth-century Rationalism and a pre-Darwinian sociology did not satisfy him. Hence he was driven to the paradoxical position of resorting to Christianity for the spiritual inspiration which his kind of humanism required. An entry in one of his notebooks written about 1874 illustrates this:

Positivism: The present condition of English society offers all the signs that precede a strong moral and spiritual reaction against luxury, materialism, and secularity. The spiritual and devout element in humanity will inevitably raise its voice, as it did in the Florence of Savonarola.

Will this inevitable uprising be kindled by Positivism or the Religion of Humanity, even supposing that doctrine one day to produce a man of apostolic genius?

No; it will spring from the old source, this time and perhaps the next and the next. Positivism has no *book*, rich, noble and eloquent with the spiritual outpourings of Eastern fervour and imagination. It has no history of martyrs and high examples. Above all it is not ascetic. We want a new measure of life, as well as a new teaching and preaching. Comtism is not ascetic, but indulgent, casuistic, and politic. It does not strike the imagination enough to catch any of the vast mass of indifferents who can only be seized by the external.[16]

Morley is in fact the great exemplar of an important transition in Victorian thought. He was a rationalist who could almost share Mill's appreciation of Condorcet and the dream of human perfectibility. Yet at the same time he belonged to the younger generation which was assimilating the lessons of evolutionary biology and using for its time-scale of human progress the immensity of the ages. Like many progressives of his time, Morley retained the optimism and fervour of Rationalism while rejecting its scientific and philosophical foundations. The next generation would reject the optimism as well, and find the writings of Mill, so well known to the young Oxford of Morley's day, strangely uncongenial.

What distinguished the 'scientific' Radicals from the older rationalists and secularists was their acceptance of the idea of race and national characteristics in an accentuated form. In this respect Morley, Chamberlain and Dilke were in accord. Dilke's book, *Greater Britain*, looked forward to a twentieth century when the Anglo-Saxon race would inherit the earth, having conquered by the arts of peace and displaced peoples of inferior moral qualities and social organization. Morley came as near to a racial view of history as Dilke did. When Frederick Harrison proposed to contribute an article to the *Fortnightly* on the Paris Commune, Morley rebutted the suggestion that the proletarian communists could be said to share Positivist values, and prophesied their failure with the remark: 'The new society will have to be perfected, my dear Harrison, not by Celts, but by Teutons, who can take deeper draught.' Foreseeing a future Franco-Russian alliance, and condemning 'the Slav peoples' as 'the most instinctively and phrenetically communistic in their aspirations', Morley supported Bismarck in the Franco-Prussian war and looked upon Germany as England's natural ally—a remarkable choice for a popular literary exponent of French eighteenth-century thought.[17] In like manner Morley took a racial view of Balkan nationalism, believing that nothing could stand in the way of the ultimate triumph of the Christian peoples in their struggle for liberation from Turkish rule. 'The races', he main-

tained, 'which, for one reason or another, are unable completely
to assimilate our civilization, disappear on coming into contact
with it.'[18] So it must be with the Turks. It is uncertain whether for
Dilke or Morley 'race' was anything more than the accumulation
via long geographical and social conditioning of deeply ingrained
institutional and cultural traditions. But certainly their view reflected the introduction into Liberalism of a new and revolutionary
conception of 'scientific' nationality.

The importance of this new biological approach to nationality,
common to the younger Liberals, was about to be dramatically
demonstrated in the great agitation of 1876-8 over the Bulgarian
atrocities and the question of British intervention in support of
Turkey. Liberalism failed to hold fast to the policy of non-
intervention. Indeed, the most important and influential currents
of intellectual Liberalism ran counter to Mr Gladstone and the
policy of non-alignment in the Turco-Russian war. The ideological assumptions of the Gladstonian platform appeared to
many of the Liberal intelligentsia to be intellectually unsound and
'provincial' in spirit; and the cause of Liberal imperialism was
born, although the name was not yet acknowledged.

With the publication of his pamphlet on the Bulgarian Horrors,
Gladstone effectively came out of retirement and placed himself
at the head of the anti-Turkish agitation which had gathered
force in the late summer of 1876. By this self-identification with
the militant Nonconformists he found a ready way back into
their confidence. From this time until the summer of 1878 the
country seemed poised on the brink of war—a war on behalf of
the abominable Turk and the 'oriental' foreign policy of Disraeli.
Public opinion seemed to divide on lines of class interest. The
Court, the military, the bondholders, the bishops, and London
society and clubs on the one hand, allied with the dregs of the
public houses and music halls whose swaggering 'jingoism'
became a by-word: against which were arrayed the provincial
press and platform, the chapel, and the respectable though
perhaps somewhat philistine middle classes.*

In the eyes of the popular Radicals, Disraeli's policy and
methods were bound to appear iniquitous. His cynical and

---

* For an analysis of the rifts of opinion in the atrocities agitation, see R. T. Shannon,
Gladstone and the Bulgarian Agitation, 1876.

amoral support of a barbarous government, his contempt for public opinion and his circumvention of Parliament, his studied secrecy and diplomatic falsifications, and his appeal to the 'lowest instincts' of the masses were taken for the diabolical methods of an anti-christ bent on subverting the democratic church. For these reasons Bright and Chamberlain took the field with alacrity in full support of Gladstone. Morley was in even closer sympathy with Gladstone, and from the outset viewed with equanimity the prospect of Russian unilateral action against the Porte, and the occupation of Constantinople.

While most imperialists of the coming age emphasized the authoritarian aspect of the national polity, and slighted the individual's claims beside those of the mass, Morley emphasized the liberating effects of nationhood, which he saw as superseding less 'civilized' modes of power and coercion. 'The principle of nationalities', he writes in the *Fortnightly* at this time, 'is an immense and incalculable force, which the politician of the old school vainly persists in ignoring. Like all ideas that have their root in the heart of masses, this force is indestructible, and grows and spreads in the midst of reverses.'[19] There was therefore in his opinion no limit to the dismantling of centralized authority; which was rendered unnecessary and undesirable in proportion as truly national institutions were evolved. Any group, however small, which came to regard itself as a nation, *ipso facto* became a nation. Like Herbert Spencer, Morley imbibed the evolutionary lesson of differentiation and specialized development without going on to glorify the collective state or draw morals from the organization of ants or bees. He saw no hard laws of human existence or national survival, only benign forces and opportunities for spontaneous development. He was a passionate champion of minorities who wanted freedom or local autonomy. The grandeur of empire, which touched the imagination of his fellow-Radicals Dilke and Chamberlain, left him cold. He could wholeheartedly oppose every aspect of Disraeli's Near Eastern policy, and privately express himself with real vehemence on the subject, while Chamberlain remained silent, caring little for the moral issues of the question and opposing Disraeli mainly because of the Prime Minister's high-handed ways and seeming intention to drag the country into war.

In the eyes of the public the anti-Turkish agitation effected a *rapprochement* between Gladstone and the Radical ex-mayor of Birmingham who had attacked his leadership so savagely. Gladstone stood almost alone when he tabled his resolutions early in May 1877 condemning any moral support of Turkey and tacitly condoning the recent Russian declaration of war. Hartington, even Granville, shrank from giving any countenance to a Russian invasion of the Balkans, while Bright and the 'peace at any price' party stood aloof. Chamberlain was the only prominent Liberal to second Gladstone in the debate and to go the whole hog of trusting Russia. There was, however, no identity of policy or sympathy between the two. To the 'Anglo-Saxon' imperialism of Dilke and Chamberlain the Near Eastern question was irrelevant and they never argued it in the emotional, histrionic or conscience-stricken vein of the religious platform. Above all, Chamberlain resented the total eclipse of all domestic questions by this 'sentimental' controversy in the idiom of the past. In the mode of patriarchal leadership, grand manner and abstraction Gladstone revelled, and his speeches in these years before huge open-air assemblies culminating in his Midlothian triumph are assuredly the finest of his career. The remoteness of Bulgaria, the problematical nature of British interests in the Balkans, and the relative impotence of England in European affairs only served to heighten the tone of his crusade by eliminating practical motives to an extent not possible in his later and inevitably less glorious campaign for Irish Home Rule. His 'six points' laying down in the spirit of Palmerston the principles which should govern England's relations with Europe—the promotion of peace, concert, equality and freedom between nations—was in the altered condition of Europe a superb anachronism.

The compensating feature of the agitation for Chamberlain was that it got the Radical ship out of the doldrums. The enthusiastic public meetings and revived interest in Parliament suggested that the time had arrived when a democratic federation of the popular Liberal Associations (those founded on the Birmingham model) could be floated. To this end Gladstone might serve as a tame elephant, if he could be persuaded to speak in Birmingham to an assembly of delegates. The purpose of federation would be to secure 'something like unity of action': agreement might be achieved concerning 'the order which we desire that future reforms should take' and the acceptance of 'some fixed principles'.[20]

Gladstone seemed to aid and abet this new departure. At the end of April the tabling of his pro-Russian resolutions produced a rare opportunity to isolate him from the Whigs. When he was induced to 'cave in' early in May it was a deep disappointment for Chamberlain, who supported the resolutions in full to the end. 'Gladstone', he complains to Collings, 'has lost a splendid opportunity which unfortunately was ours as well as his. We must accept what we cannot avoid and wait quietly for our next chance.'[21] The Birmingham meeting of Liberal delegates was fixed for the end of May, but there could be no thunderbolts from Mr Gladstone. Still, he was invited to attend, and accepted. Amid scenes of massive but orderly demonstrations Gladstone was brought in somewhat ambiguously as godparent to the National Liberal Federation. He might well have approved some of the arguments which his Radical host put forward to justify a popular organization—the 'increased intelligence of the people', the 'greater interest in political affairs', and the extension of the franchise. But he could hardly have accepted the innuendo in Chamberlain's description of the Caucus as 'a really Liberal Parliament outside the imperial legislature and, unlike it, elected by universal suffrage'.

Within a decade, time would produce a strange and ironical sequel to this episode: for Gladstone was destined to wrest the control of the Federation from Chamberlain in the cause of Home Rule. In a longer context, the federated constituency organizations of both Liberal and Conservative parties were doomed to subservience under the tutelage of the central offices. This was certainly not Chamberlain's conception of the function of the Caucus. Yet, in spite of the fact that effective democratic organization in the constituencies was never to become an actuality, there was one sense in which the Birmingham model won a lasting success. At the heart of Chamberlain's objection to the existing system was a repudiation of the politics of 'drift', of the disorganization which rendered Liberal policy the sport of 'emergent affairs'. The traditional system only brought public opinion into play in the form of large agitations in periods of

crisis. It could only handle one great matter at a time. The remedy
of a preconceived party programme with the sanction of popular
organization (albeit centralized and 'guided') proved itself to be
the mainstay of the democratic system as it finally emerged. This
line of development was not at all obvious at the time the Liberal
Federation was launched, both Gladstone and Bright, for instance,
remaining opposed in principle to popular control over the
measures of the parliamentary party.

The force of residual anti-democratic feeling was attested by
the immediate response of the reviews to the Birmingham organization, dubbed the 'Caucus' by Disraeli with a slight twist of
the American usage. The recent experience of Tammany Hall
provided critics with a fertile language of allusion to machine
politicians, wirepullers, and the system of spoils. For the remainder of his career Chamberlain was suspected of a design to
'Americanize' British politics and bribe the working classes with
illicit rewards in exchange for their votes—a suspicion which
told powerfully against him as late as the tariff reform campaign.
In vain he pleaded that the U.S.A. was not such a bad country
after all. Had it not achieved the happy state of having no land
problem, no church problem, and no foreign policy?*

The chief aim of the Caucus was not to make governments
but to make opinion. The election of 1874 had in Chamberlain's
view returned individual Liberals 'without a leader and without
any policy . . . pledged to no measure, with no programme, for
every man to do what seemed to him right in his own eyes'.[22]
The apathy of the Liberal supporters in the country was the cause
and also the result of such a spineless party. The remedy was to
form a programme of interlocking policies serving the needs of
the various sections of Liberalism and carried by the combined
force of all. Only in this way, Chamberlain contended, could the
party make head against the concerted forces of 'organized
selfishness' which combined instinctively without formal organization. The forces of reaction also had the advantage of the
distracting effects of each major crisis in a political system which
seemed able to respond with animation only to the emergency of

---

* See especially Chamberlain's article on the Caucus, *Fortnightly Review*, November
1878.

the hour. The Near Eastern crisis was from this point of view a major setback to the interests of reform, a gigantic red herring. And before this damnable storm centre had faded from the scene, another appeared from the west in the shape of Irish agrarian discontent and the emergence of a determined Nationalist party under Charles Stuart Parnell.

As early as 1877 it was apparent that a prolonged and fierce struggle with the Irish nationalists was in the offing. The gentlemanly Isaac Butt, under whom the Home Rule movement had been initiated, had declared against parliamentary obstruction—he for one, he said, would never make war on the House of Commons. Not so Parnell, who with Biggar and others made the problem of obstruction a major concern in the session of 1877. Meeting in Dublin in January 1878, the Home Rule Conference Committee resolved to form a separate and disciplined party which could show by its actions that the Irish people had 'no community of interest with England' so long as they were denied their 'national right to self-government'. Parnell aimed unambiguously at complete legislative independence, and in 1879 (after the unobtrusive repeal of the Irish Convention Act of 1793) placed himself at the head of a 'sovereign assembly' in which 300 delegates imitated the old Dublin Parliament, claiming 'power to consider and advise upon all political questions'.[23] More ominous was the renewal of the land war in worsening agricultural conditions, which Parnell readily took up with a frank declaration that his object in fomenting the agrarian troubles was to pave the way to Home Rule. The full import of his strategy of anarchy in Ireland and obstruction at Westminster was not yet clear to the public, however, and Ireland did not play a major part in the elections of 1880.

CHAPTER TWO

Separatists and Socialists

An English Radical may be occasionally unreasonable . . . but he is never irreconcilable. The Anarchists of France, the Nihilists of Russia, and the Fenians of Ireland have very few sympathizers in this country.

Chamberlain, speech at Swansea, 1 February 1883

A N unwonted calm preceded the general election of April 1880, and the receding rumblings and· reverberations of Gladstone's Midlothian campaign did not awaken any livelier feelings than a languid revulsion from the Tories. Unexpectedly the Liberals gained a clear majority of forty-six seats over the Tories and Home Rulers. 'A solid meal must be provided for the Liberal lions', Chamberlain wrote to Harcourt, 'if they are to be kept from rending one another.' Yet the Gladstone ministry of 1880–5 is a dismal tale of cabinet schisms, vacillation and almost continuous unpopularity. It was quite usual even for Liberal ministries to have no programme, and the procedural powers of the ministerial bench in the Commons to combat obstruction and force progress were still minimal. But the root cause of the ministry's *malaise* lay in ideological divisions, exacerbated by Gladstone's growing reluctance to hold planning cabinets or settle ministerial feuds by strong leadership. Hartington could not understand Gladstone's meaning in conversation, and pursued an aloof course with his Whig adherents. Chamberlain, owing his cabinet seat as President of the Board of Trade to the extraneous pressure of the Liberal Federation,* frankly took to unilateral action to maintain Radical influence over colleagues who regarded him as a presumptuous intruder.

At first Chamberlain imagined that the Caucus would be able to dictate the strategy of the ministry. 'For programme of

---

* Of the success of the 'Caucus', Chamberlain informed Harcourt (10 April 1880): 'In 67 contested boroughs it was victorious in 60. In 10 counties it won in every case—in most against the advice of the old so-called leaders, who were opposed to a fight.'

legislation,' he wrote to Morley, 'county suffrage—but separate from redistribution of seats, which must be postponed—county boards, really representative, on the model of town councils, and some considerable measure of land reform. For Ireland . . . extension of franchise both parliamentary and municipal, and arrangements for transferring local business, including local acts of Parliament, to Dublin.'[24] The idea was to force through the enfranchisement of the rural masses, together with the popular aspects of land reform, and then gain a really sweeping Radical majority by appealing to the country either with the new electorate, or on the popular franchise question if the Lords threw out the franchise bill. The Parnellite menace was to be countered by setting up democratic local and regional councils in Ireland which would steal the thunder of the nationalist 'patriots' at Westminster.

Not even the Radicals, however, were solidly behind this or any alternative programme. They were neither strongly in favour of land reform nor decidedly against Home Rule (which was still a very nebulous policy). As had been revealed by the Turkish crisis, the Radicals were split into anti-imperialists of the persuasion of Gladstone or Bright distrusting all coercive imperial ties; and 'scientific' Radicals whose philosophy of nationality led them as easily to espouse the cause of national self-determination as that of maintaining the imperial connection. These latter Radicals would tend to stress the value of the imperial tie in the case of 'backward' peoples (in which category Morley for instance placed India) while sympathizing with the Irish demand for independence. Dilke, who like Morley became a Home Ruler, likewise slighted the value of the imperial tie with Ireland or Canada, as of little value beside the bond of cultural and racial affinity that existed in his opinion between Britain and the U.S.A. Chamberlain indeed was somewhat unusual as a Liberal imperialist who believed firmly in the legal bonds of empire.

To complicate matters, almost all Radicals were anti-imperialist when it came to invading Egypt, reacting to the idea that Tories and Suez bondholders were behind the adventure. The Disraelian conception of empire over Asiatics or foreign peoples clashed with that of a self-governing empire of Anglo-Saxons. 'Money bags' imperialism was becoming a bogy to Radicals, and in the case of Ireland the clamour for sterner coercion from Whig and Tory absentee landlords struck many Radicals as proof that the Union was an unnatural tie of the same sort. This feeling was encouraged when in 1881 the intensification of the land war in Ireland attracted the support of socialists such as H. M. Hyndman, who linked it with London Radicalism. The sensible political division seemed to be between, on the one hand, Whig-Liberal *laissez-faire*, landlordism and Unionism of the Hartington-Goschen type, and on the other hand socialist land reform and Irish Home Rule.

The main cleavage in post-1880 Liberal cabinets followed this pattern. Chamberlain's Radical associate, Sir George Otto Trevelyan, for instance, who latterly became Irish Secretary, opposed what he considered the reactionary land policy of his chief, Lord Spencer, and took objection to Gladstone's Land Purchase Bill of 1886: but he was prepared to accept Home Rule. The course of Chamberlain's own action during the 1880-5 ministry was individual and distinct from that of most Radicals. While to public appearance he was courting Parnell and promulgating a Radical Programme of socialist tendencies, he was in reality reacting decidedly against socialism and preparing his position for a struggle against the Irish separatists.

The worsening of the Irish situation was brought about by a combination of new forces of agitation operating against a background of agricultural depression. The wheat of the American prairies had started to undercut the home production, cheapened by the use of harvesting machines and screw-driven steamers. The golden age of farming was at an end, and the same forces which impoverished the rural vicarages of England drove the Irish peasantry to demand 'fair' rents. The Irish Land League, founded in the late seventies, demanded the 'three F's' (fair rents, fixity of tenure, and free sale) for the smallholders of southern Ireland, and this became the platform of Parnell's party. New elements also were entering the situation. The subsidies of the American Irish—a mysterious and uncertain factor—and the Fenian spirit appeared to be behind the dynamite outrages in England and the agrarian crimes in Ireland, seemingly with the intention of making a reconcilation between the two countries impossible on any other basis than complete separation. Parnell and his party were playing a perilous game, in attempting to embrace in their movement the extreme nationalists and paid terrorists for whom the success of the Land League's programme would mean simply a weakening of the springs of agitation. Moreover, in another respect the extremists were at odds with the Parnellites. Marxist socialists had begun to inject into the agrarian struggle the ideology of class war. Out of the Radical Clubs and Irish committees of London Hyndman created his Democratic Federation in 1881 to take up the cause of the Irish Land League and its English equivalent (the Land League of Great Britain).[25] Landlordism and the whole agrarian system became the target of an irreconcilable anarchism. The Liberal government was provoked into a policy of coercion which their opponents represented as an attempt to stifle the legitimate protests of a suffering and oppressed peasantry, but which the ministers themselves saw as a war between the opposed forces of order and chaos.

In the struggle over coercion Chamberlain played an important and a very significant role—indicative alike of the movement of English opinion in these years, and of his own personal re-orientation in the face of the new Irish nationalist spirit. At first he and Bright stood out as opponents of Forster's coercive policy, even after a wave of agrarian crime and the introduction of the more deadly device of 'boycotting' followed the failure of the government's remedial measures of 1880. The members for Birmingham were prepared to agree to coercion only if and when a Land Bill had been passed and proved ineffective. Forster's policy was playing into Parnell's hands. Of the latter's motives, Chamberlain writes (27 October 1880): 'He fears that the settlement of the land question would be the death-blow to his Home Rule agitation, and he wants to make all proposals impossible beforehand.'[26] By threatening to resign, Chamberlain was instrumental in preventing the cabinet from taking a line of 'coercion first'. He explained the upshot in a letter to Bunce:

30 December 1880: The Government will have to propose some restriction on personal liberty in Ireland *at the same time* as they bring forward their Land Bill.

What was not necessary two months ago seems to have become so recently. The agitation is getting out of the hands of the Land League, and is more or less used to serve personal ends and purposes of general disaffection. The grounds of legitimate agitation will, we hope, be removed by the Land Bill. What remains will be of a kind no Government can tolerate. . . . Bright and I believe that the necessity for coercion has not even yet clearly arisen—that measures of the kind might be postponed till *after* the effect of the Land Bill is seen.[27]

He wanted to draw a distinction between legitimate agitation and terrorism. So long as most of the outrages and intimidation arose directly out of evictions for non-payment of rent, the issues were clouded, and it was his policy to stress the legitimate claims of the agrarian movement.

In the session of 1881 he had the dual task of opposing the Chief Secretary—he tried to get Forster's Arms Bill withdrawn —and keeping Gladstone up to the mark to ensure a generous Land Bill. Gladstone's acceptance of the three 'F's', which had been recommended by the Bessborough Commission, was abrupt and unaccountable, like many other departures in his career. He was scarcely the real parent of the great Land Act of 1881, with its revolutionary principle of judicial rents, which contemporaries regarded as a stride in the direction of socialism. The Act was thus much more generous than the abortive Land Bill of the year before, and in Chamberlain's eyes it constituted a satisfactory solution, at least for the time being, of the Irish land problem. It was certainly a crucial test of the position of the Parnellite party—whether inside or outside the law. Did they really want to remove the causes of discontent?

Instead, they chose to move towards a repudiation of rent as well as of landlordism. Parnell began to advocate that rents should be settled not upon the statutory valuation but upon the mere 'prairie value' of land, its value 'when the Flood left it'. At the Land League Convention of September 1881 the newly passed Land Act was denounced as a 'sham', and Parnell declared that he proposed only to test the Act, not to make use of it. 'The effect of these speeches', Chamberlain comments, '. . . was unmistakable. . . . Rents were everywhere withheld, threats multiplied and acts of violence also. There was no longer the excuse of bad times. The harvest had been plentiful, and in many cases tenants actually boasted that they had the money for rent in their pockets.'[28] The government agreed, on Forster's application, to arrest Parnell, Dillon, Sexton and O'Kelly, who were lodged in Kilmainham gaol on 13 October.

Chamberlain's approval of the imprisonment of the Irish leaders was not shared by Morley, who denounced the latest action of the government in the *Pall Mall Gazette*, of which he had become the editor. Was Morley being consistent, and had Chamberlain changed his coat? At this point Chamberlain saw that he had to explain his position to the country, and not just defensively. He had in fact undergone one of the important reorientations of his career. He had always understood that force was no remedy—he compared coercion with a strait-waistcoat, which saved but did not cure the patient. He now saw that the importation of communistic notions of class war into the Irish question would give the Home Rulers an indefinite lease for agitation and terrorism, whether they sincerely believed in these notions or not. The lack of precision about the agrarian aims of the Parnellites was no disadvantage to them. They floated on a tide of sentiment rather than of tangible policy.

Perhaps the most influential theories were those of Henry George's *Progress and Poverty*, which appeared early in 1881. Henry George condemned landlordism, and advocated the appropriation of rent by a state tax. Actually he was an anti-socialist, and Marx denounced his book as 'the Capitalist's last ditch'. More directly slanted towards the Irish problem was H. M. Hyndman's *England for All,* written in the heat of the Irish controversy and distributed to the delegates at the conference that launched the Democratic Federation in June 1881. This, the first socialist work, Hyndman claimed, to appear in English, led to an estrangement between him and Marx. It was notable in linking the land and imperial problems together, advocating free, federated communities in place of the old colonial dependencies. Hyndman, in short, provided a ready-made ideology for the Irish extremists, with whom he was in fairly close communication.*

---

* Hyndman opened a 'fair rent' drive in London, enlisted the old Chartist leaders, and did all he could to link the Irish and London agitations together. He writes to Helen Taylor (2 October 1881): 'The fight has begun. The Liberal wirepullers, specially paid for that purpose, are at work taking the Clubs from us. . . .

'If only our executive can . . . keep our principles and our programme—virtually including therein free education and free justice—before the metropolis and the

It was against Hyndman's doctrines in particular that Chamberlain reacted. Justifying the imprisonment of Parnell, he reminded Morley of an important decision (18 October 1881): 'We might have taken the line of the Democratic Federation, and ranged ourselves with Miss Helen Taylor and Mr Hyndman. We deliberately adopted the other alternative.' The premises, he went on, were that the objects of the Irish party had changed since the first formation of the Land League. Now the object was 'to create sentimental grievances and to inflame national hatred in order to promote the success of a revolutionary programme, which has for its avowed objective the separation of the two countries.' Since national independence could not be given to Ireland, it was therefore 'war to the knife between a despotism created to re-establish constitutional law, and a despotism not less complete, elaborated to subvert law and produce anarchy as a precedent to revolutionary changes'.[29]

The same day as this was written, Parnell issued from his imprisonment the No-Rent Manifesto wrung from him by the necessity of restraining the extremists from acting independently. The government responded by suppressing the Land League by proclamation. These developments presented an opportunity to put the cause of the Union boldly before the country. In this, Chamberlain led the way. More prescient than some colleagues, he had never lost sight of the fact that the real matter at stake was not coercion or the land, but Home Rule. Speaking at Liverpool on 25 October 1881, he nailed his colours to the mast: 'I say to Ireland what the Liberals or Republicans of the North said to the Southern States of America, "The Union must be preserved". Within these limits there is nothing which you may not ask and hope to obtain.'[30] After this, there could be no yielding on Chamberlain's part to any future Home Rule measure that meant anything like separation. And Gladstone, speaking two days later, seemed to take the same course when he accused the

---

country, we shall win, forming indeed a definite and uncompromising party of the people. . . .

'Charles Murray and all the old '48 men are heartily with us. The Irish too we can fully rely upon if only they could shake off their religionism a little. . . . The very bitterness of the Liberals—the ministerial Liberals—and capitalist Radicals proves to me that they feel the ground tremble beneath them.' (Helen Taylor PP.)

Parnellites of marching 'through rapine to the disintegration and dismemberment of the Empire'.[31]

Two sessions had been spent on Ireland. In the session of 1882 a determined effort was made by Gladstone and the Radicals to reach an understanding with Parnell. Gladstone told Forster he could not expect the cabinet to accept a new Crimes Bill, and in April Parnell while on temporary release set off a negotiation between Captain O'Shea and Chamberlain with a view to obtaining an Arrears of Rent Bill. The so-called 'Kilmainham treaty' was supposed to include an understanding that Parnell would withdraw all countenance from the No-Rent Manifesto and co-operate in making the Land Act workable. The experiment was not destined to be made. Forster, while acknowledging that his powers of holding hundreds of suspects during pleasure had availed nothing, still chose to resign rather than accept the release of Parnell. Hence a new Chief Secretary, Lord Frederick Cavendish, accompanied the Viceroy (Earl Spencer) to implement the latest policy of conciliation. He was murdered in Phoenix Park, Dublin, on the day of his arrival. This was the terrorists' reply to the amenable line Parnell had taken. The result was that, instead of a respite to enable Parliament to turn to other affairs, the remainder of the session, and an additional autumn sitting, had to be devoted to a further Crimes Bill and a drastic reform of the procedure of the House of Commons. Chamberlain's first impulse in reaction to the adverse turn of events was to resign. He wrote to Spencer protesting against the new Crimes Bill:

20 May 1882: If we do not make some concessions to the Irish party we shall fall back to the position we occupied last session. All business in the House of Commons will be blocked, the House of Lords will be able to force a dissolution, and the general election will turn out the Government. Then you will see that the Tories will at once come to terms with the Irish. . . .

I do not believe in the efficacy of our bill to repress crime, though some bill was made necessary by the state of public opinion. . . . It will only further embitter the relations of the two countries, and Home Rule with all its possible dangers and consequence will be within measurable distance.[32]

One thing, however, did much to reconcile Chamberlain to the new régime at Dublin Castle. Cavendish was succeeded by Sir

George Otto Trevelyan, with whom Chamberlain was on very cordial terms. 'He is doing his work admirably,' Chamberlain admitted, 'with great firmness and with a manner which conciliates the most hostile critics.'[33] Parnell, also, was striving to save the situation. He still retained his influence, and Chamberlain was given to understand that instructions had been sent to the local offices of the Land League advising tenants to settle with their landlords and not to act on the No-Rent instruction.[34] Before many months had passed, the reports from Trevelyan suggested a hopeful trend in Ireland, bringing the establishment of Irish county councils within reach:

Trevelyan–Chamberlain, 31 December 1882: The fact is that the reaction from the system pursued by Forster is over. Ireland is assuming a new aspect. . . .

7 January 1883: My view of the situation is that the farmers are tired of agitation of the dangerous sort, and that the game is kept going by scoundrels of more or less deep—sometimes fearfully deep—dye, who have to live by it. Where the National League really means a gang of cut-throats who are trying to recommence the work of blackmail and intimidation, we stop the meetings for the protection of the farmers; and they are grateful for it. Where there is no immediate fear of outrages and conspiracies, we let the meetings take place, and they fall flat. . . .

I agree with you in your views about local government in Ireland. There is no use doing anything unless it is very big.[35]

In this optimistic atmosphere Chamberlain was perfecting his scheme for handing over to the Irish the control of all their local affairs and administration; not only on the level of county or parish, but on a provincial level superseding the various separate government boards at Dublin. The scheme for such a 'provincial council' was also applicable to Scotland, and did not imply a separate Parliament. Chamberlain assumed that Trevelyan would support the project: but at the last moment he backed out and went against it with Spencer; while Spencer, the chief opponent of the scheme, strained at the gnat of provincial councils in 1885, but swallowed the camel of Gladstonian Home Rule a year later. Gladstone himself approved of the provincial councils. When challenged to state his views on Home Rule in 1882, he answered that Irish control over purely Irish affairs should not be refused consideration, though he was 'not prepared to give to Ireland anything which . . . it would be wrong to give to Scotland.'* The failure of his project to revive the parliamentary grand committees to deal with the local affairs of Scotland and Ireland, as part of his procedural reforms, made devolution to local bodies the only practicable alternative.

The Phoenix Park murders had destroyed a bargain which the government had made with the Tories, as well as their understanding with Parnell. Gladstone had deferred to feelings on all sides of the House against closure by bare majority, and accepted the opposition proposal of a closure by two-thirds majority instead. This was to be the basis of his procedural reforms: enabling the two major parties to apply closure to the Parnellites while saving the opposition from a government tyranny. The Tories feared that the closure might be used to force through general legislation—Radical measures—as well as measures for the public safety. The Liberals believed, mistakenly, that the Tories had insuperable prejudices against any drastic strengthening of the powers of the majority. Hence Gladstone was willing to accept the two-thirds majority if he was given the rest of the procedural reforms practically without discussion. The offer had not been formally accepted, however, when the murder of Cavendish made it necessary to drop procedure and go at once to Irish measures. In Chamberlain's opinion, the bargain had thus lapsed, and he wished to revert to a demand for closure by bare majority.† He resolved to throw the whole force of the Caucus

---

* *Hansard*, 3rd ser., CCLXVI (16 February 1882), p.866. Cf. A. Ramm, *Correspondence of Gladstone and Granville*, I, p.341 & n. Gladstone's identification of Home Rule with local administration is best exemplified by part of his Guildhall speech of 13 October 1881. After alluding to 'what is popularly known . . . as Home Rule . . . which may be understood in any one of a hundred senses, some . . . perfectly acceptable . . . others . . . mischievous and revolutionary', he went on: '. . . after what I have said of local government in general and its immeasurable benefits, and of the manner in which Parliament is at present overcharged by too great a centralization of duties . . . I for one will hail with satisfaction . . . any measure of local government for Ireland or for any portion of the country, provided that it . . . shall not break down or impair the supremacy of the Imperial Parliament.' (*Manchester Guardian*, 14 October.)

† For these negotiations see Chamb. PP., Chamberlain–William Kenrick, 4 July 1882 (quoted below).

into an agitation for a plan he knew to be unpopular with the older Radicals as well as with other parties:

Chamberlain–William Kenrick, 4 July 1882: But if the autumn sitting is to be held, it ought to be held for something worth having. . . . There is no doubt that a number of Liberals object to the bare majority, and nothing but the pressure of the Caucus and of the constituencies will keep them straight. If there is a tremendous agitation . . . and if the most positive injunctions are given from the constituencies to their members, then we shall carry our proposals.[36]

Once again, however, external affairs, this time in the form of an Egyptian entanglement, swept all plans for domestic reforms into abeyance. Most serious for Chamberlain was the resignation of Bright, tendered on the arrival of news that the fortifications of Alexandria had been bombarded by the British fleet on 11 July. Bright could have split the Radicals into two sections— those, on the one hand, who condemned the occupation of Egypt as a major apostasy from the rule of non-intervention which Gladstone was supposed to uphold, a weak concession to the 'cotton jingoes' and Suez bondholders: and those who accepted Gladstone's characterization of Sir Garnet Wolseley's brilliant campaign as a police action to restore the Khedive. The machinery of the Caucus was set in motion to forestall an attack on the government. Bright, who was 'a little hurt that his resignation has been taken everywhere as a matter of course', wrote a 'savage' letter to the Birmingham Eight Hundred 'denouncing the government, and boiling over with moral indignation'. Chamberlain was at pains to silence the outburst. 'Up to the present time', he informs Harcourt, 'Schnadhorst and Co. have succeeded in suppressing this manifesto; but my pacific colleague may go on the rampage yet.'[37] The speed and efficiency of the British action disarmed the government's critics. The occupation of Egypt was supposedly a temporary one, and Chamberlain summed up his own view of it as the securing of a 'fair chance of tranquillity, and then clear out'.

The Egyptian imbroglio and the consequent unpopularity it brought Gladstone in some Radical quarters had the effect of rousing the 'Grand Old Man' (as he had been dubbed that year) into a resolve to take up the franchise question as a matter of urgency. By the end of the year his procedural reforms, with the closure by two-thirds majority, had been carried and the time was propitious for advance on the domestic front. Chamberlain drew a facetious caricature of the situation for the well-known Conservative hostess, Lady Dorothy Nevill:

28 December 1882: Political affairs are very quiet, as they ought to be during the holiday. We shall have to invent something before long which will 'stir the masses', something in the way of destruction and confiscation. The Whigs as a party are played out, and the next great fight will be between the Tory democrats and the democratic Radicals. It will never do for the latter to be outbidden, so you must prepare for something very drastic.[38]

Yet the session of 1883 was to be an interlude of relative calm and inactivity, of bits and pieces of legislation. The reason for this lay in the electoral strategy of the advanced Liberals, abetted by Gladstone. It was felt that even to carry the franchise bill alone would require a great agitation to lay siege to the Upper House, and to prepare the ground for this the bill was delayed until the session of 1884. 'I do not look to get more good out of the present House of Commons,' Chamberlain wrote to Dixon in July 1883, shortly after the cabinet had accepted the plan. 'Next year we must bring in county franchise, and dissolve.'[39]

For Chamberlain, therefore, the year 1883 was one of intense activity and preparation. In addition to his task of persuading the cabinet and the country to demand a full measure of reform—which should include Ireland—he had to prepare a Radical pro-gramme to put before the new electorate. This began to appear in the latter part of the year as a series of anonymous articles in the *Fortnightly Review*, written mostly by the new editor, T. H. S. Escott, in close collaboration with Chamberlain, and also by Morley, Collings, Francis Adams and Frank Harris. Under his own name Chamberlain promulgated the essential part of his programme in an article on 'Labourers' and Artisans' Dwellings', upholding the principle that the cost of making towns habitable should fall upon the unearned increment of urban land values. Local authorities, he argued, should have powers of compulsory purchase to promote slum clearance and general improvements, paying only the market price for their acquisitions. As elaborated in his speeches of 1884-5, the Radical Programme consisted of the following main points:

1. Free primary education.

2. Land reform to secure 'the multiplication of landowers', by a variety of means, viz: 'free trade in land' by the removal of primogeniture and entail and the cheapening of transfers: the taxation of sporting, uncultivated, and unoccupied lands: the restitution of common land illegally appropriated; the provision of allotments and smallholdings by local authorities armed with compulsory powers; the enfranchisement of leaseholds upon just and equitable terms; and in general by higher rating of large landed estates, and perhaps also by 'a progressive income-tax on the number of acres held'.

3. Financial reform to close the gulf between excessive wealth and extreme poverty, again by various means, viz: (*a*) The transfer of the burden of taxation from indirect to direct taxes, so that the former might be entirely dispensed with except for special objects such as the discouragement of alcoholic consumption; the yield of direct taxes to be increased by a graduated income tax up to 10%, with perhaps a distinction made between earned and unearned incomes, and by efficient death duties on landed estates. (*b*) The financing of local projects for the welfare of the poor (such as decent dwellings at fair rents, or mortgages for small-holdings) out of the rates, implying an increased importance of local as distinct from state expenditure. The yield of local rates therefore to be increased by the taxation of personal as well as real property (as in the U.S.A.) and also of ground rents and unoccupied sites. An 'allowance for the necessaries of existence' to be made, and only surplus earnings and accumulations to be taxed. In country districts the realistic re-rating of land would increase revenues for the projected county councils.

4. The consolidation of local government by the establishment of county councils, and the creation of 'national councils' in Dublin and Edinburgh to manage purely Irish or Scottish affairs and to assume responsibility for private bill legislation.

5. Some long-term objectives, such as Disestablishment, manhood suffrage, and payment of M.P.s.

Such was the 'Radical Programme', blazoned across the country in a succession of great speeches, and set forth in book form in

July, 1885—the first 'campaign handbook' of British politics. It raised Chamberlain to a commanding position in the Liberal party, the heir apparent to Gladstone's position. Chamberlain called it 'socialism', and the book pronounced itself 'the death-knell of the *laissez-faire* system'. But one can see now that it was the last fling, rather than the death-knell, of the established social order.

By 1883 Chamberlain was in conscious reaction against Marxist socialism, which he dimly perceived as a somewhat hysterical impulse (Morley called it 'shrieking Liberalism') to preach class war and advocate 'confiscation'. It had assumed menacing proportions through the link between the Democratic Federation and the Land League. The demand for land national-ization was being successfully popularized by Hyndman, Henry George, and Alfred Russel Wallace.* The policy gained a sudden vogue among the working men of London against the back-ground of the Irish land struggle. The new brand of socialism was exemplified by Hyndman and his paper, *Justice*, the ideals of which were in conflict with those of John Stuart Mill and earlier English socialists. Significantly enough, Mill's step-daughter, Helen Taylor, soon quarrelled with Hyndman. She had the delicate conscience of the communitarian socialists, whose creed was an ethic of personal truthfulness and courageous acceptance of all rational duties and obligations to the community. Hyndman had a trenchant masculine cynicism about politics and was not too scrupulous about methods or associates. Miss Taylor began to object to the 'anonymous and irresponsible defamation' in the columns of *Justice*. On being told that she had a 'duty' to work for the movement, she drafted the following indignant replies:

Helen Taylor–Hyndman, c. July 1884 [not sent]: Your letter is so hope-lessly arrogant that I feel it useless to argue with the man who could write it. . . .

---

* Wallace, who some years earlier had been persuaded by Mill to join the Land Tenure Reform Association, published in 1880 *How to Nationalize the Land: a Radical Solution of the Irish Land Problem*, and became president of the Land Nationalization Society set up in 1881. In 1882 his book *Land Nationalization* appeared. Henry George's *Progress and Poverty* upheld private property and capitalism (as also did Wallace) and argued that the 'land monopoly' could be remedied by a simple panacea, a tax to appropriate the whole value of rent.

Having had much longer as well as much wider experience of public affairs, literature and journalism, and been longer a socialist, I can judge you from a higher standpoint, and tell you that you are bringing the mean and cowardly element of secrecy into the work, which has always broken it up and always will. . . .

[sent]: [after repeating a milder version of the above] I advocated socialism publicly and alone, taking the whole open responsibility and sacrificing position to do it, years before you were a convert to it. . . . Secret methods do not train men for social life.[40]

It may safely be assumed that Chamberlain's attitude to Hyndman was much the same. To the agitation in favour of land nationalization he responded promptly with arguments culled from Mill's writings:

Chamberlain–Morley, 26 December 1882: Note that nationalization of land as . . . contemplated by Wallace means merely increased taxation on real as compared with personal property. But if land is a necessity and in the possession of a few monopolists, they can add the increased taxation to the price they ask in rent, and the charge falls back again on others. . . . Note also that if nationalization means ownership by the nation, it is antagonistic to personal proprietorship and all the schemes for uniting ownership and cultivation, and in either case how does nationalization assist the London workman, living in two rooms, or prevent the competition of the agricultural labourers?[41]

He wrote for Morley a long refutation of Wallace and George, which Morley published in the *Pall Mall Gazette*. He denied that the poor were becoming poorer, or that the monopoly of land enabled its owners to absorb all the surplus profits of both labour and capital, as Wallace contended. He showed that while the national income had increased by £600,000,000 or £700,000,000 per annum in the previous twenty years, the annual value of land had increased by only £9½ millions, and of houses and mines by only £56 millions. Thus the community had little to gain financially from land nationalization, and the abuses of landlordism could be best reformed by regulating private ownership. Wallace's scheme he summed up as 'veiled confiscation'. Against George's scheme to appropriate landed rents Chamberlain argued that 'a similar result would accrue if the state were to repudiate the national debt, or to revert to medieval precedents and torture the Jews until they gave up their property. . . . The pecuniary advantage would have to be set against the general insecurity which would follow, and which would affect all enterprise and limit the stimulus to exertion.'[42]

The pressure from the proponents of land nationalization did, however, force Chamberlain to pursue as vigorous a land policy as practicable in view of the agricultural depression and the patent inability of landed property to pay any considerable enhancement of taxation above the level imposed on other forms of property, or indeed above the existing rates. He shared the notion of Wallace and George, that the land system was at the roots of pauperism, believing for instance that the low wages paid to urban labour resulted from the constant influx of penniless labourers from the land. His basic position remained the same— that 'luxury' had increased too fast, and 'comfort' too slowly. He writes to Dilke in December 1882 asking him to introduce 'some distinctly *Radical* point' into his speeches, as, for instance, that 'the enormous increase in general wealth has not been accompanied by proportionate improvement in condition of the poor, nor by very considerable decrease in pauperism', adding that there would have to be before long a searching enquiry into the effects of the aggregation of great estates.[43] It was this juxtaposition of pauperism and the land that led to his scheme for urban improvements. His line of reasoning appears in a letter to Sir Edward Russell, editor of the *Liverpool Daily Post*, of 22 January 1883:

Education is the first step. . . . But it must be followed by changes intended to assist the more equal distribution of wealth.

Probably the most pressing need is . . . the provision of better dwellings, but this cannot be secured without a bold attack on the so-called 'rights of property'. We must find some way of throwing upon the land according to the value and length of the different interests which may exist in it the burden of making our towns habitable by the poor whose labour creates the increased value of the land. It is grossly unfair that the few improvements which are now made should be paid for by the occupiers and leaseholders, while the owners of the soil benefit not only by the results of the industry of others, but also especially by the improvements to which they do not contribute a farthing. We must also find some way of increasing largely the number of occupying owners in agricultural districts.

Where Chamberlain differed from the land nationalizers, socialist or otherwise, was in his scrupulous adherence to the canons of private enterprise. He sought to remedy, not replace, the *laissez-faire* system. He wished, for instance, to encourage landlords to improve town properties rather than to impose this responsibility on the municipalities except as a last resort. His ultimate objective was the limited one of rescuing the 'submerged tenth' of the population, in the interests of social stability and the morale of the whole community. He was at pains to show that he sought to introduce no new principle into legislation, that there was nothing revolutionary, nothing new, in the Radical Programme. The *Fortnightly Review*, in an anonymous article of December 1884, even went so far as to hail him as 'really one who makes for Conservatism'. It argued that the Poor Law had long been 'the price we pay for social tranquillity', and an 'insurance which the state levies against misery and distress'. Free libraries, museums, parks and gardens were other gratuitous benefits conferred upon the very poor. Why not then free education, or the compulsory purchase of property on equitable terms, or the establishment of minimum standards of decency in housing? The article claimed that there could be no danger of 'confiscation' if the principle of state interference were extended, for 'in proportion as the sense of citizenship is quickened, instead of class being pitted against class, there will be a fresh consolidation of classes, a growing cohesion and compactness of the various sections of the whole community'.[44]

There were two features of the Radical Programme which smacked of 'confiscation', the powers of compulsory purchase, and the doctrine of 'ransom' which Chamberlain proclaimed in a controversial speech of 5 January 1885. Powers of compulsory purchase were already wielded by school boards, and powers of persuasive purchase by local authorities under the Artisans' Dwellings Act: but the price paid included what amounted to compensation for disturbance. Chamberlain stood out for paying simply the current value. When a private member put down a resolution to extend the existing type of compulsory powers, Chamberlain intervened with the authority of President of the Board of Trade:

Chamberlain–Broadhurst, 28 August 1883: Under these powers School

Boards have been fleeced in the most shameful way, and property bought on such conditions will cost at least 50% more than its actual value. If under these circumstances you compel Corporations to provide workmen's dwellings, you will impose upon them in the large towns rates so enormous that trades people and the poor generally will find it absolutely impossible to live.[45]

He showed that the Birmingham Town Council had paid half a million pounds in excess of the value of the land it had acquired, in spite of special arrangements and the clauses of the Artisans' Dwellings Act which provided for conditions of arbitration. What was wanted, he concluded, was an alteration of the clauses of this Act so that local authorities could buy land compulsorily at the price at which 'a willing seller would sell to a willing purchaser'. Such powers would be largely held *in terrorem*, for he held that 'the duty of properly housing the poor is primarily a duty to be imposed upon the owners of property'.[46]

It had been a saying of Disraeli, in his 'Young England' days, that property had its duties as well as its rights—just as labour had its rights as well as its duties. Both of these truths had tended to be obliterated by the Manchester School's economic doctrines and the substitution of the 'cash nexus' for the social ties of the earlier society. The approach of the Radical Programme towards property had something of the backward-looking characteristics of the Young England movement. It observed, for instance, that under the feudal system land tenure was linked with the provision of armies, and that this obligation had been shuffled on to other forms of property, which now bore the brunt of taxation. It was in this connection that Chamberlain formulated his doctrine of 'ransom'. After asserting that private ownership, having taken the place of 'common rights of ownership' in land, had become too inextricably mingled with the whole social system to be abolished, he went on:

But then I ask, what ransom will property pay for the security which it enjoys? What substitute will it find for the natural rights which have ceased to be recognized? Society is banded together in order to protect itself against the instincts of those of its members who would make very short work of private ownership if they were left alone. That is all very well, but I maintain that society owes these men something more than mere toleration in return for the restrictions which it places upon their liberty of action.[47]

This was the language of the eighteenth century—and of the Whigs rather than the Jacobins. *The Times* attacked him on the obvious point of supposed 'natural' rights, but he stuck to his guns, quoting the newspaper's own leader of 6 February 1844 which had pleaded against the abuse of property and in favour of 'some regard to the right of the poor man under God's charter to live and breathe in this the Almighty's world'.[48] In the more intimate setting of the Eighty Club he defined what he had meant:

I hold that every man who comes into the world has a natural right to a fair enjoyment of life. By a natural right I mean a right not to have to live in immorality; and I say that that is a right which you ought to secure by law. If you think that is Utopian, then you ought to carry your principles out and adopt the Chinese practice—poison children when they come into the world. . . .

Mr Raleigh wants to know, too, what I mean by 'ransom'. I dare say he knows his Bible, and I think you will agree with me that the word is used in scriptural phraseology again and again as the compensation which a man has to pay for wrongdoing before he can be received into the congregation; and I tell you that society owes a compensation to the poorer classes of this country, that it ought to recognize that claim and pay it.[49]

The whole spirit of his advocacy was in favour of the institution of property. 'I am putting the rights of property on the only firm and defensible basis', he explained. 'I believe that the danger to property lies in its abuse.'[50] He was attempting to prevent, and not to inaugurate, a social revolution. As he remarked to his witty and Disraelian correspondent, Lady Dorothy Nevill, 'I am sorry to see that your friends are so angry with what I say. I laugh at them and they abuse me. Some day they will discover what a good friend I have been to them, and how I have saved them from the "wrath to come".'[51]

What was startling and novel about the Radical Programme was that it was propounded by a responsible minister while in office, and developed in parallel with a huge agitation which carried the most drastic parliamentary reforms of the century. Chamberlain was no thinker, no innovator in the intellectual sense. But he was a master in the art of the possible, and his programme was eminently well contrived for the situation as it existed. When he was pressed to make more extreme proposals by the Radical M.P. and journalist, Henry Labouchere—for instance an income tax of 50% on the highest incomes—he rejected such impracticable counsel. 'You must remember,' he retorted, 'that the only chance for the sheep is getting the wolves to attack the foxes, and vice versa. If you set all the *ferae naturae* against you at one time, they will make common cause, and the sheep will have a good deal to suffer. Therefore I am for step by step reform, and for not showing more of your hand than is necessary to gain the confidence of those whom we want to serve.'[52] With similar restraint he disclaimed in public any suggestion that the programme should be made a party orthodoxy. Labouchere pressed him to insist on 'unity upon specific tests, on some particular measures that are to form the programme of a Parliament'. The constituencies were Radical, he argued, while the parliamentary Radicals were ' a contemptible set of weak humbugs', clinging to Gladstone as their sheet anchor. 'When we lose him,' he adds, 'they ought to realize the fact that the sheet anchor ought to be you.'[53] But Chamberlain avoided a clash with Gladstone, which might have come of pushing his pretensions prematurely. He was content with the accession of influence and authority he had gained in the reform struggle of 1884, and even after the government resigned in June 1885 he did not attempt to commit the Caucus to his programme.

Much of the outcry against the Radical Programme came from Whig journals, and the 'ransom' speech offered a vulnerable point of attack to Chamberlain's opponents, with whom he had already become embroiled in his reform agitation—most notably Hartington and Goschen, and lesser figures such as W. T. Marriott and Foljambe. The Programme was indeed an inseparable part of the reform movement: and on this ground Chamberlain justified his vigorous platform campaigns against the criticisms of his Whig colleagues. By appealing to the country on issues still controversial within the cabinet he was breaking a constitutional convention—as he well knew. But he argued that the establishment of a democratic electorate rendered the traditional reticence of cabinet ministers no longer appropriate. He fully realized that he was straining constitutional usage to the limit. 'I have a difficult part to play,' he writes to Labouchere in December 1883, 'and my only wonder is that I have been allowed to perform it at all. I expect I shall get the sack sooner or later, and my object is to get the whole machine as far forward as possible before the smash comes.'[54] By his speeches in the country he had 'lifted the franchise into the first place, and now people will think of nothing else'.[55] The government and country Liberals were committed to introduce a franchise bill, separate from redistribution, and applying to Ireland as to the rest of the United Kingdom.

Whig opposition to the reform bills of 1884–5 was thwarted by Gladstone's own resolution to carry them through. The franchise bill was opposed by Goschen almost single-handed on the Liberal side. And the determination of Trevelyan, the acknowledged leader of the county franchise movement, to apply the bill to Ireland disarmed any serious revolt on the 'Irish point'. The bill passed by large majorities, and on reaching the House of Lords, it was held up *sine die* by a slight stretch of procedure. In approving of this move, Lord Salisbury robbed Chamberlain of the double-barrelled pistol he had hoped to level at the peers. The Conservative leader claimed that the franchise bill on its own was a measure to the party advantage of the Liberals to the extent of 47 seats, and that consequently it should not be passed until a fair redistribution bill should accompany it; and that in opposing a measure for which the government had no mandate the Lords were exercising a legitimate right of appeal to the people. In 1911 Chamberlain was to lend his name and authority to this doctrine. Yet now, in 1884, he denounced it. 'The constitutional privileges of the House of Lords were being strained to the uttermost,' he said, 'arrogant and monstrous pretensions are being put forward on its behalf, which if accepted would degrade the House of Commons to a secondary and subordinate position.'[56] He would gladly have seen the power of veto of the Lords curtailed by a device similar to the Parliament Act of 1911, which he was destined so strenuously to oppose. At the earlier time he had not discovered a use for a second chamber. It is not enough simply to admit his inconsistency, as he himself did some years after 1884 when he confessed in public that he had changed his mind. His guiding principle remained the same. He claimed a right of direct popular decision on major issues, and would never have burked a plebiscite. He felt in 1911 that the Commons were cheating the people out of a chance to reject Home Rule, which he judged the nation did not really want: just as in 1884 he felt the Lords were bent on emasculating a franchise measure which the nation enthusiastically supported, by claiming to determine what sort of redistribution bill should accompany it. The whole weight of the Caucus was thrown into the struggle against the peers, to uphold the policy of the government. Dismissing Goschen's Whiggish plea for 'serene composure' in the crisis, he compared it with the admonition which a newspaper had given at the end of its account of a fatality, advising 'any lady who should find herself enveloped in flames to keep herself as cool as possible'. [57]*

Meanwhile a committee of the cabinet composed of Hartington, Kimberley, Childers, Chamberlain, and Dilke, with Lefevre as draftsman, were formulating a redistribution scheme which Dilke considered one of 'extreme timidity'. The preservation of constituencies of 10,000 voters showed 'an altogether indefensible tenderness to vested interests', and two-member constituencies were retained. Then, quite unaccountably, Lord Salisbury declared publicly for single-member constitutencies, and Dilke began to wonder whether the Liberal scheme would stand up to Salisbury's 'revolutionary criticism'. It was modified to include some single-member districts in the densely populated parts of Lancashire and Yorkshire. The prospects of an agreement with Salisbury were much improved, and in a speech of 4 October Hartington used the word 'compromise' and suggested, purely on his own account, that an agreement might be reached if the Lords waited until the redistribution bill was introduced into the Commons, and then passed the franchise bill, 'relying on the good faith of ministers and the good sense of Parliament'. Against any such concession Chamberlain spoke at Hanley on 7 October in his most intransigent manner:

What if the two millions of men should object to have their rights

---

* He writes to Morley on 16 August of two schemes, one for 'a new political union *ad hoc*, to carry the franchise bill, and "mend or end" the House of Lords', the other for a march of Durham miners on London.

measured out and their liberties parcelled by fifty-nine almost unknown individuals? . . .

We grudge the Lords nothing that rightly belongs to them . . . but when they claim to dictate the laws which we shall make, the way in which we shall govern ourselves—to spoil, delay, even reject measures demanded by the popular voice, passed after due discussion by a majority of the people's House, and receiving the sanction and confirmation of popular assemblies such as this—it is a claim contrary to reason, opposed to justice, and which we shall resist to the death.

Both Chamberlain and Dilke feared that Gladstone would give way to the pressure from all sides, from the Queen, the Whigs, and the Conservatives. He could easily do a deal with Salisbury, and secure an overwhelming majority in both Houses for a scheme which involved devices for minority representation. A section of the party, represented by Mr Courtney in the government and supported by Goschen, condemned single-member districts and advocated proportional representation.

The Radical Programme itself had canvassed the claims of *scrutin de liste*, which Gambetta was said to have favoured over *scrutin d'arrondissement* as possibly applicable to England.* It was supposed to have the merit of preventing local and petty interests from dominating in a way that was thought inevitable in small, watertight voting districts. Chamberlain was himself very apprehensive of single-member districts, because they would remove a main *raison d'être* of the Caucus—the need to strive for both seats to obtain 100% representation from 70% or so of the votes—and would necessitate a major upheaval and decentralization in each Liberal association. Dilke on the other hand was ready to clinch enthusiastically Salisbury's stipulation that single-member districts should be created in both counties and boroughs. Since among the Liberals Dilke, as President of the Local Government Board, alone had a complete mastery of the intricacies of the subject, he got his way in the end. Chamberlain could reconcile himself to the system of 'electoral districts' by reflecting that at

---

* *Radical Programme*, p.26: 'Take a town with a population of 400,000. That would entitle it to eight members. The method of *scrutin de liste* would make each one of its representatives a member not for a section of the constituency, but for the whole constituency. *Scrutin d'arrondissement* would assign a representative apiece to the eight wards into which the whole constituency would be divided.'

least it put paid to even more repugnant alternatives, such as *scrutin de liste* combined with proportional representation or other minority devices. At one stage he appears to have had a real fear of a Whig–Tory *démarche* in this direction, for in his Hanley speech he pleaded against it:

What is the object of a representative system? Surely it is to secure that the majority shall rule. . . .
. . . Minority voting in every form . . . secures an over-representation of crotchets, which misrepresents great principles, which tempts the exhibition of personal ambition and personal vanity, which confuses the great issues we are called upon to decide, which divides the point of progress, and by all these means plays into the hands of the party of privilege. . . . The majority has the right to enjoy the fruits of victory.[58]

When later Courtney resigned office to launch a campaign for proportional representation, Chamberlain opposed him; and when Morley showed signs of sympathy he wrote: 'What is the effect of this system on the voters? They will give their preferential votes as men give used postage stamps to the first asker. They will be tempted and stimulated to range themselves in sections, and the result will surely be that even if the little rills of political thought are represented, the main current will be broken up and effaced.'[59] The major redistribution of seats forced a choice of two alternatives, multi-member constituencies, which in the parliamentary situation would probably have involved something like Courtney's scheme, or single-member constituencies. The Conservatives liked the latter for the reason that Courtney criticized them—that they would accentuate the politics of the vestry and the ratepayer, and enhance the representation of suburbia, especially in London.

Once Lord Salisbury had committed his party to the single-member system, and Dilke's amended scheme (published without authority by the *Standard* on 8 October) was seen to have accepted the principle, the issue had been decided. Chamberlain, who did not appreciate that Salisbury was prepared to give way on all other points, continued the battle. He played only an indirect role in the November negotiations leading up to the 'Arlington Street Compact', which was a triumph for Dilke over the views of both Gladstone and the Whigs. At Gladstone's instance some two-member constituencies, not involved in the rearrangement, were retained. The enfranchisement of the rural labourers and the transformation of the great majority of constituencies into 'one horse' seats was the most revolutionary parliamentary reform of the century, greatly increasing the 'swing of the pendulum' at elections. *The Times* and the moderate journals did not like it, and by contrast the Radicals became convinced that it would play powerfully into their hands. They assumed that the increased number of seats for large urban centres—London was to have an increase from 22 to 59 members, and the seven largest provincial towns an increase from 19 to 43 members—would mean a huge increase in Radical representation. These places were the 'source and centre of English political opinion', the mainstays of Radicalism. Yet they falsified all Radical predictions when they went Tory in the elections of 1885.

The successful accomplishment of the Radical design of parliamentary reform forced into the open the disagreements in the Liberal party. From Chamberlain's point of view an open breach with the Whigs would have been welcome to clear the stage before the coming appeal to the electors. His 'ransom' speech was a counter-irritant applied to the Whigs, and it drew forth Goschen into open opposition. Goschen took his stand behind Gladstone —vindicating Gladstonian finance on this occasion, just as he was to support Gladstone's tepid election manifesto against Chamberlain's 'unauthorized' programme later in the year. And while Gladstone became a stalking-horse behind which the Whigs attempted to rally a body of moderate opinion, the Whigs were binding themselves in support of Gladstone's leadership, all unsuspecting that they were helping him to gain a position of vantage from which to launch Home Rule.

Speaking at Edinburgh on 31 January 1885, Goschen protested against Chamberlain's language bidding 'the new democracy celebrate its advent to power by the dethronement of Gladstonian finance'. Were the new electors to storm the constitution 'on the principle of an enemy storming a town, who demands a ransom for abstaining from plunder'? Goschen pleaded for the unity of classes, 'union, freedom, justice, and common sense', and the 'old Radical doctrine, try freedom first before you attempt to interfere by the state'. The appeal was a distortion of Chamberlain's intentions, and a declaration of war. It was taken up by *The Times* and produced a sympathetic response in the sections of the press and the Liberal party which vaguely and mistakenly equated Chamberlain's programme with socialism. Chamberlain felt he was the victim of a 'plot' to eject him from the government, and responded with characteristic belligerence:

Chamberlain–Morley, 2 February 1885: *The Times* indicates a dead set, and I have special reasons for thinking that there is something like a concerted revolt of a section of the Whigs.

If you can do so conscientiously, pray warn or threaten the Whigs as to consequences. I have consulted Schnadhorst. He thinks every Liberal Association in the country would support me. . . . I hope and believe that you, Dilke and I stand together in this. If we do, we will utterly destroy the Whigs, and have a Radical government before many years are out. . . .

Goschen's speech is much what I expected. . . . He talks of upsetting and perverting Gladstone's finance. This is nonsense. I only proposed to complete it. Gladstone never said that it was finally settled on an equitable basis, and he has distinctly contemplated a free breakfast table and alterations of death duties. The only point of difference, which is a detail, is the graduated income tax.[60]

The objection to the Whigs was not so much ideological as practical. They were an aristocratic caste who presumed that the control of the Liberal party belonged to them by virtue of their social standing or by prescription. Surely they could not hope to survive into the democratic era?

But here the Radicals were mistaken. The middle classes were losing confidence in their ability to dominate and control the forces of the time. They were being driven over to the political right by fear of socialism, imperial uncertainties, European militarism, industrial recession, and a whole variety of social trends which seemed to menace their position. Instead of confidently demanding change, they were beginning to dig in their heels and resist it. The moderates or 'floating balance' of voters would cleave to such men as Hartington and Goschen as a guarantee of stability or as an alternative to a transfer of their political allegiance to the Conservatives. The bulk of the Unionist Liberals were to look to Hartington, not to Chamberlain.

Meanwhile, throughout 1885 the Whigs were able to preserve a state of deadlock. The final showdown which Chamberlain was planning never took place. In the first part of the year he was seeking constantly for an excuse to resign and carry the struggle into the constituencies. The Sudanese crisis stood in the way, damping domestic politics and leaving the Radicals high and dry as the case for vigorous action became stronger. Then on 5 February news of the fall of Khartoum reached London. The dispute over Chamberlain's indiscreet public utterances was shelved, but he did not receive his reprieve gladly:

Chamberlain–Sir Edward Russell, 6 February 1885: The bad news from Egypt will for the time throw all else into the shade, but we must return sooner or later to domestic questions. The Whigs of the Foljambe stamp have got into a state of hysterical fury and would if they could exclude Dilke and myself from the government. Personally I should be obliged to them. If I were free to attend to elections I think it would be possible to give every constituency a choice of a Radical, and the result would be the extinction of this intolerant faction, which is not satisfied with its great and disproportionate share of influence and office, but claims to silence every opinion which it does not approve or understand.[61]

He was bound to support Gladstone through the crisis, partly from prudence, and partly because he was counting on Gladstone's support against Spencer and Hartington for his scheme of an Irish National Council. This state of things remained up to the government's resignation in June, for the Khartoum disaster was followed by news early in April that the Russians had attacked the Afghans and taken Penjdeh. War with Russia seemed imminent, and the ministry seemed to assume a new lease of life after Gladstone's *tour de force* of a gigantic vote of credit. It was not until after the Whitsun recess and the abandonment of the National Councils Scheme, that the Radicals felt able to put matters to the push and overturn the ministry, Morley (now a member of parliament) tabling a resolution against the modified Crimes Bill which the cabinet had approved, and Chamberlain and Dilke taking the same line. By this time the Irish problem had come once more into first place, demanding settlement in one way or another before any proposals for English reforms could take on any reality.

CHAPTER THREE

Hawarden is Willin'

'When a man says he's willin',' said Mr Barkis . . . 'it's as much as to say, that a man's waiting for a answer.'

EVERYONE could see that the Franchise and Redistribution Bills would give Parnell at least eighty Home Rule members. Chamberlain had faced this issue long before. Speaking at Bristol on 23 November 1883, he had calculated that the extended franchise would make a difference of twenty seats for Parnell, giving him eighty instead of sixty followers. It was, he admitted, a matter of some importance, and twenty votes might turn out a government. But, he argued, 'If you extend the franchise in Ireland you will bring a new class into the electorate; and it may be . . . that there will arise a division in the popular party, and that so far from strengthening you might even weaken Mr Parnell's hands.' He did not feel that it was imperative to reach an understanding with Parnell. He wished, in Trevelyan's words, 'without quarrelling with the Home Rule members, to get at the masses who are behind them'. [62] He had no illusions about Parnell's intentions, realizing that Parnell would take nothing short of the restoration of Grattan's Parliament. Nevertheless he allowed Captain O'Shea to promote a long negotiation with Parnell over the questions of Local Government in Ireland and the renewal of the Crimes Act. Convinced that Parnell could not refuse a generous measure of local government, he wished to disarm any ostensible objection he might make by consulting his views beforehand. He thought that his scheme of a National Council was identical to one which Parnell had transmitted through O'Shea, though in fact Parnell's views had been somewhat misrepresented. Chamberlain's intentions are plainly stated in a letter to Morley of 21 January 1885:

The establishment of such a Board would at once find work for the most active men in the National Party. It would be a good education and political training for them, while the questions which would infallibly arise in regard to the incidence of taxation, the character of education, the nature and extent of public works, etc. etc., would occupy and divide Irish parties, and give them plenty to do in discussion among themselves, without involving any conflict with the external British authority. The newspapers must report its discussions and would have no space for the harangues of Irish patriots in the British House of Commons. [63]

On his side, Parnell was quite aware of the anti-separatist intention behind Chamberlain's advocacy of the scheme, and gave dilatory and evasive replies. His adherents were forced to extricate themselves by suggestions that Chamberlain was trying to buy their support, and finally, in an attempt to prevent Chamberlain and Dilke from appealing directly to the Irish people, Parnell's newspaper *United Ireland* was obliged to come into the open with a venomous personal attack.*

Gladstone was on the brink of a final retirement, as everyone thought, and Chamberlain wished to enlist his authority for the scheme and commit the party to it before he departed. He therefore made a determined effort to use the discussions over Lord Spencer's new Crimes Bill as the occasion, and to make the adhesion of the Radicals to Spencer's policy conditional upon the acceptance of National Councils. The Radicals liked Spencer as Viceroy no more than they had liked Forster, although some serious dynamite outrages in London had made the coercion of terrorism at least as justifiable as the coercion of boycotting had been. Spencer set out his case for renewed powers in a cabinet paper of 25 March 1885:

Fenianism is completely organized, and, although not active at this moment, would seize any opportunity when England is at war to create serious difficulty. About a year ago its members were calculated to be 36,000 in Ireland, and 11,500 in Great Britain. But the organization which is probably the strongest in Ireland is the National League, with its central office in Dublin and branches in nearly every county. In its avowed object it is constitutional and legal, but among its members are not only Fenians but men of desperate character who are either ready to commit crimes themselves, or belong to secret societies

---

* See Garvin, *op. cit.*, II, pp.19–23, for an account of the relations between Chamberlain and Parnell at this time.

organized for murder and outrage. These men use the League to cover their meetings and proceedings. The League through some of its branches and very generally at its meetings has declared open war against landlordism, and its efforts are strenuously directed to prevent the taking of farms from which tenants have been evicted. . . .

These elements, now kept in check by the Crimes Act, it would not be difficult to stimulate into dangerous activity. . . .[64]

The argument gained force from the imminent danger of a war with Russia in April, and Spencer, who had appeared at first favourably disposed to a Central Board at Dublin—which Chamberlain had represented to him as a '*sine qua non* of success in dealing with the Irish difficulty'—swung round to oppose the removal of the 'Castle' régime. Writing to Chamberlain on 25 April, he turned down what he called 'Parnell's proposals' in the same letter in which he insisted on the renewal of the Crimes Act.

The scheme he rejected was more limited than the one for a fully fledged 'National Council' which Chamberlain envisaged. Spencer conceived of the 'Central Land Board' or 'Central Local Government Board' as merely the apex of Irish local government, excluding police and justice, and all legislation, even upon purely Irish concerns. His objections arose from a general distrust of democracy:

It takes from government all patronage connected with the departments which it absorbs. . . .

I see further grave danger in constituting a representative body which may assume to itself the right of speaking for the Irish nation. . . .

I fear that the experiment will be very great to grant these large powers of administration to an untried body. It is very probable that we should find the present Irish Parliamentary Party, the Healys and O'Briens and T. P. O'Connors managing and leading this assembly. The idea of this will create well nigh a panic among the well-affected people of Ireland, and I doubt whether Ulster will agree to it. Many people think that it will be very rash to popularize local government for the same reason, that we shall hand over the control of local affairs to men who have shown themselves unfit for government.[65]

And yet Spencer and the new Irish Secretary, Campbell-Bannerman, were soon to support Gladstone in an attempt to hand over legislative as well as administrative functions to men they considered 'unfit for government'.* This is the measure of the Whig distrust of Chamberlain, who in the terms of the Spanish proverb could not look over a hedge with impunity, while Gladstone could steal horses with general acclaim.

Chamberlain's scheme drew the line firmly between 'national' and 'imperial' affairs. A separate Parliament, he affirmed, 'could never be granted by any patriotic statesman'. But an Irish National Council could supersede the Castle administration, and legislate for purely Irish matters. It would have powers of rating but not of taxation: and it need not be entirely elective—it could consist partly or wholly of delegates from the county councils whose establishment was regarded as an integral part of the whole plan. Gladstone approved of Chamberlain's scheme generally, but had no frank explanations with him, noting in a memorandum of 6 May: 'Chamberlain perhaps does not know that in regard to Police I go farther than he has gone—and that if he were to acquiesce in Spencer's present views I probably could not.' Gladstone also noted that 'nothing, unless Spencer were to be in decided concurrence with Chamberlain, could carry through the Cabinet the plan of a Central Local Board, essentially elective, though by double election and with a distinct property represen- tation'.[66] He could have forced the resignations of Spencer and Hartington, which in view of the known determination of Chamberlain, Dilke, Trevelyan, Childers and Lefevre to resign if the scheme were rejected, would not have been of much con- sequence to a ministry in all ways moribund.

Against this course, however, Gladstone pleaded privately to himself the consideration that he was about to retire. 'My

---

* For characteristic attitudes two of Trevelyan's letters to Chamberlain may be quoted:

[7 Jan 1883]: 'They are certainly a people of a singularly low type, and appear to regard public questions entirely from the amount of material for agitation that exists in them.'

[4 Feb. 1883]: [In the Irish newspapers] '. . . I have *never* found (1) A single ex- pression implying disapprobation of any sort or degree of crime which had the remotest relation to agrianism: or indeed of any crime at all. . . .

'(2) Any syllable of recognition of the services or desire to do service to Ireland of any English statesman whatsoever. This is I think unique in the relation of any two countries. Nothing is more marked in the history of a *great* people struggling for freedom than their eager gratitude to those of a dominant party who were their friends.'

engagements to my colleagues are fulfilled', and consequently 'the very last thing I should contemplate is opening the Irish difficulty in connection with my resignation should I resign.'[67] He preferred to let the government break up, and in opposition regain his own freedom of initiative, in the struggle over Ireland which he clearly saw to be impending. Had he forced things to a conclusion, he would have alienated Spencer and Hartington and disclosed his own hand to the country. He was resolved that cabinet solutions to the 'Irish difficulty' should not come 'antecedently to any Parliamentary treatment of that problem'.[68]

In other words, he had already reached the position which was only gradually and dimly revealed to his colleagues in the latter part of the year, namely that he would consent to an official part in 'saving Crown and State from an ignominious surrender in the next Parliament' only in a great crisis and on his own terms. He admitted (to himself) that the National Councils scheme might avert the crisis. But the real inwardness of his position was that he was already tracing in his imagination a different course of events. Presiding over a divided cabinet which was straining at the gnat of a Central Board, and in any case unlikely to survive another session, he believed that an Irish crisis would develop, and that only such a 'great imperial occasion' could set the stage and condition the public for the heroic role which he foresaw for himself.

Through the tense controversy of early May, therefore, Gladstone was concerned only to emphasize his independence of any obligations or commitments to his colleagues. He wrote especially to Chamberlain to explain, in case 'he supposes me in any way bound to act with any section of men or opinions on the impending Irish questions', that this was not so. When the Central Board scheme was finally rejected on 9 May, Gladstone remarked to Dilke that those responsible would within six months be repenting in sackcloth and ashes. From that moment he began to move towards an Irish settlement *de novo* on lines of his own.

The Radical ministers were committed to resign rather than countenance coercion or any mere 'tinkering' with Ireland. Chamberlain describes his view of the new situation in a letter of 17 May:

Chamberlain–Sir Edward Russell: We have arrived at a very critical time. A few months—possibly a few days—may decide whether the present combination of Whigs and Radicals can any longer continue. Mr Gladstone alone holds us together, and Mr Gladstone is almost certainly about to retire from active politics. The questions is, will the Whigs buy the titular leadership of the Liberal party at the cost of adopting the Radical policy? I have a scheme for the settlement of the Irish question—on Mr Gladstone's principle that we ought to give up to Irishmen *everything* that does not touch the integrity of the empire. A great opportunity for dealing with the matter has been lost owing to the pedantry and timidity of the Whigs, and for the moment we seem thrown back on the old worn-out policy of coercion.

I doubt if this can hold, and in any case I will not enter any new government nor meet a new Parliament except as the advocate and exponent of a system of local government which will relieve Parliament of much of its present work, and shall give to Irishmen effective control of their domestic affairs. Such a system would be suitable also to the case of Scotland and possibly of Wales. Dilke is heartily with me, and if it were not for the critical state of foreign affairs we should ere this have separated from colleagues who are persisting in the old lines. . . .[69]

Like Gladstone, the Radicals were planning to take independent action in the Irish question, but, unlike him, they committed themselves to a definite scheme which they made public in the final chapter of *The Radical Programme* as it appeared in July. They were the more free to do this, since they were counteracting and not co-operating with Parnell. Any overtures they made to him were intended to force him into the open. The salient features of Chamberlain's scheme were directly antagonistic to Parnell's Home Rule demands, as Chamberlain was anxious to stress. 'Please recollect', he writes to Harris 'that it is not Home Rule, nor a separate Parliament. The national council or board which is to take the place of the alien and non-representative boards now in Dublin will be only the Metropolitan Board of Works on a larger and more important scale. Above all, it will have no power of initiating special taxation, but will be confined to rating. . . .'[70] These were the features which made the scheme objectionable to the Parnellites and forced them to attack it.

After the Liberal government's resignation early in June 1885, a dramatic turn of events played into Gladstone's hands and modified his plans of retirement. The Conservatives set their faces against coercion and appeared to envisage something like Home Rule, and in the atmosphere of expectancy thus created the milder schemes of the spring seemed ancient history. As Gladstone put it, 'It is now said that a central board will not suffice, and that there must be a parliament.' Whether it would be Grattan's parliament, or an independent body meaning that 'Ireland is to be like a great colony such as Canada', Gladstone regarded the discussion as constituting 'an entirely new point of departure' raising questions 'of an order totally different to any that are involved in a central board appointed for local purposes'.[71] He was staking his claims to the new territory. Sounding Derby and Granville, he found that they were not more hostile to a large plan than to the rejected plan for a National Council.

The inescapable inference was that full Home Rule, on something like the Canadian model, was the only feasible scheme. No one liked the idea of Grattan's parliament, which had proved unworkable in the late eighteenth century because of legislative divergence from the line of the imperial Parliament at Westminster, and which would confer on the Irish separatists the power to keep Ireland in disorder while screening their responsibility under a nominal imperial connection. Outright separation would be preferable, as not a few official Liberals observed to Gladstone, not dreaming for an instant that he would take them at their word. When Parnell spoke of legislative independence at the end of August, the leading Liberal journals rejected the idea. Since there was no half-way house between any legislative body in Dublin and complete separation, Parnell should be met with an uncompromising resistance. The Liberal press called for a united front against him. There was no section of English opinion which 'would not unhesitatingly condemn or punish any party or any public man who attempted to walk in the path traced by Mr Parnell'.* Small wonder, then, that while their chief kept his counsel, the official Liberals allowed their attention to be engrossed by the Hartington–Chamberlain dispute over the Radical Programme, which seemed the only great matter at issue within the party. Thereby, incidentally, they afforded Gladstone

---

* This was the *Manchester Guardian*'s response to Parnell's Dublin speech of 24 August. For other press views see A. Thorold, *Labouchere*, p.233. Staunch Liberal papers such as the *Daily News* and *Leeds Mercury* followed *The Times* and *Telegraph* in roundly condemning Parnell's demands.

an excuse to remain at their head and compose for them an 'umbrella' manifesto for the general election.

Returning at the beginning of September from a Norwegian cruise intended to recover his voice and health, Gladstone was easily persuaded by Granville that his 'retaining the lead at all events for a time' was the only hope for the party. He composed a tepid and noncommital election manifesto, not avowedly as 'the programme of a Liberal government', but merely as 'a footing for the party at the election', his object being to keep the party together in order to 'cope with the great Irish question which may arise three months hence'. He did not show his manifesto to Hartington, and sent only a bit of it on request to Chamberlain, before it was published in mid-September. Hartington was suspicious, and wrote to Granville that if Gladstone 'now favoured a separate Irish parliament, he wished seriously to qualify the view that Liberals would unite only under Gladstone's leadership'. He asked for a party meeting, and a declaration on Irish policy.

Gladstone refused to put his address before the party leaders, but he urged them to adopt a waiting attitude, assuring Chamberlain that he was 'extremely unsanguine as to a legislative settlement' of the Irish question. Thus he deprived both his chief lieutenants of their opportunity of opposing him before the election. Even Granville was deceived by a categorical assurance from Gladstone that if his 'darkest estimate' of the Irish difficulty came true, 'and if the party and I are at variance as to the means of meeting it, I am fixed in my determination not on that account to enter into a schism, or aggravate the difficulties of others'. Believing that his chief was the only hope for unity, Granville aided and abetted his high-handed autocracy, and reinforced it by his own special prejudices.

The publication of the Midlothian address was accompanied by a declaration to the effect, as paraphrased by *The Times*, that Gladstone 'may at any time delegate to some other, or abandon to be scrambled for by several others, the power confided to himself personally' by the electors. *The Times* interpreted this to mean that 'a Parliament elected on Mr Gladstone's programme cannot be represented as having a mandate to plunge into any wild enterprises'.[72] His whole election strategy was as transparent as it was unconstitutional. On a personal plane, he was holding his ex-cabinet colleagues to a compact of silence on Ireland which they naturally assumed to imply consultation and common action in the future. It was therefore the non-Irish aspects of the address which struck Chamberlain as particularly unsatisfactory. 'I think his manifesto a poor affair', he observes, 'and I now feel that he rather stole a march upon me. It was not necessary to express his objections to free education—which by the way are very weak and irrelevant—and he might have referred to the question of increased powers to local authorities a little more favourably than he did. He was aware when he issued his address that Dilke and I considered these two points essential.'[73] For a moment Chamberlain entertained the idea of a break with Gladstone. 'If we chose to go into direct opposition we might smash him,' he confides to Dilke, 'but the game is not worth the candle, I think'.[74] Instead, he was content to write to Hawarden frankly observing that the official manifesto appeared to be a complete acceptance of Hartington's programme, and that he could not join a government formed on such a narrow basis.

The upshot of this divergence was that Gladstone invited Chamberlain to confer with him at Hawarden on 7 and 8 October. The exchanges were marked by outspoken frankness on Chamberlain's part, and on Gladstone's by a lack of candour and the withholding of the vital points bearing on the discussions. In short, Chamberlain was pumped of all his intentions, and given nothing in return. 'He is a good man to talk to,' Gladstone reported to Granville, 'not only from his force and clearness, but because he speaks with reflection, does not misapprehend, or (I think) suspect, or make unnecessary difficulties, or endeavour to maintain pedantically the uniformity and consistency of his argument throughout.'[75] On the first day they discussed Ireland, when Gladstone listened to Chamberlain's familiar policy as they walked through the woods of the estate. Land reform and local government, neither of which Parnell could resist: but nothing more than the National Councils scheme. Against this the old man threw out inconclusive remarks, as to the difficulties of carrying on a government against Parnell's opposition, or the possibility that the Conservatives might accept Home Rule. 'He did not say a word', Chamberlain notes 'about the negotiations which were then going on between him and members of the Irish party.' Ten days later Chamberlain was informed of these by Labouchere, who was the intermediary between Herbert Gladstone, on behalf of his father, and the Irish. The second day's conference turned on the Radical programme and Gladstone's manifesto, and in the discussions Chamberlain reduced his demands to an absolute minimum, 'he apparently assuming (wrongly),' as Gladstone characteristically noted, 'that I was ready for another three or four years' engagement.' Only after they had sat for some hours in the Hawarden library, and the Radical leader had put all his cards on the table, was he informed of Gladstone's intention to hand over the leadership to Hartington as soon as the party was 'fairly started in the new Parliament'. At this Chamberlain objected that he could not concede as much to Hartington, and spoke of friendly support while remaining outside the goverment. 'I did not think at the time that he was likely to maintain his expressed intention to resign,' Chamberlain commented years later, 'but it seemed to me indirectly a proof that he did not seriously contemplate a Home Rule programme with which, of course, any suggestion of resignation would have been entirely inconsistent.'

Writing just after the interviews to Morley and Harcourt, Chamberlain revealed no particular suspicion that Gladstone was contemplating a Home Rule departure.

Chamberlain–Morley, 9 October 1885: I had a pleasant visit to Hawarden, but with no special result. Mr Gladstone was anxious to understand exactly what our position was in reference to the formation of a government. I do not think he feels that our terms are impossible, although of course he would like to minimize them. He spoke very strongly of his intention to give up the lead very soon after Parliament meets, and I think he is quite sincere. But probably circumstances will be once more too many for him, and he will go on to the end.

Chamberlain–Harcourt, same day: The exact position in which we stand is this. We place three things in the forefront. First, revision of taxation in the interest of the working classes. As to this, we are satisfied with Mr Gladstone's declaration, and are content to leave the 'methods' to his judgment.

2ly. Free schools. On this we require absolute freedom to speak and vote as we please. We say it must be an open question in the fullest sense. . . .

3ly. Compulsory powers to local authorities to buy land. This we say must come up as the first business undertaken by any Liberal government, i.e. on the Local Government Bill, and as to this we must insist that clauses are inserted giving these powers. We are quite willing to discuss details, as to valuation, forms of arbitration, quantity of land to be taken, conditions of letting, etc., etc., but the principle must be admitted. This is a *sine qua non*. . . .

I explained the exact nature of our conditions as above. Mr Gladstone tried, naturally, to reduce them, but he did not appear to think them impossible. He urged the weakening effect of 'open questions' in a government. . . .

He suggested that the Irish question might delay local government, and that London government might be taken first. But I told him I thought this was unlikely, and I pointed out that if county government were taken first, the questions we had raised would have to be settled within a few weeks of our taking office. It was therefore absolutely necessary to come to a decision upon it before any government was formed.

He spoke of his intention to retire very soon after Parliament met. I protested strongly, and told him that if he did we should alter our terms, as we were prepared to take much less from him than from anyone else. . . . He is very full of the Irish question, but I do not gather that he has any plan of dealing with it. He deeply regretted the failure of our scheme for National Councils, and appears to think that more will now have to be conceded at no distant date.

The emphasis of the discussions had been upon the theme of unity, to achieve which both Chamberlain and Hartington sank their differences. They both assumed, with perfect justification, that by consulting with Gladstone upon the formation of a Liberal government, and accepting his Midlothian manifesto for the purposes of the election, they were upholding an understanding that (to use an expression of Bright's which Gladstone quoted to Chamberlain at this time) 'the average opinion of the party ought to be the rule of immediate action'. This was particularly applicable to the Home Rule question, concerning which Gladstone repeatedly admonished the official leaders that freedom of action—the absence of embarrassing pledges—was the great desideratum. Having been encouraged, indeed pleaded with, to hold their hands and avoid any overt opposition to Parnell, the

Liberal leaders were lulled into a supine attitude to Home Rule, which they might otherwise have defeated at the polls by seeing to it that every Liberal member was pledged against it. They were deceived into letting the enemy enter the citadel: and the enemy was Gladstone.

On the day after Chamberlain's departure from Hawarden, Gladstone's son received a card from Labouchere reporting the results of his attempt to make contact with the Irish nationalist leaders. Parnell himself had stood aloof. None of his lieutenants, according to Healy, knew his address, and his mail was collected only sporadically from the House of Commons. It was left to a small clique composed of Healy, McCarthy, Harrington, Dillon, T. P. O'Connor, and Sexton, to represent the Irish party. Healy told Labouchere, for consumption at Hawarden, that his group 'settle everything almost always, and he [Parnell] accepts it'. It was further explained that Parnell in any case could not afford to jeopardize his leadership of a party containing many extremists by accepting any compact: and that he was 'half-mad' to boot. The suggestion, therefore, was that Healy himself should be the Irish plenipotentiary. His letter to Labouchere of 7 October, forwarded to Hawarden, asked: 'Could we not learn exactly what Gladstone would give us?' Healy would favour an alliance with the Liberals 'if they could give us a guarantee about muzzling the Lords and would not mend the New Rules in the Commons till we were done with it'. To this Labouchere added his own suggestion for some agreement: 'Would not the connection between the Dominion of Canada and its provinces do for one?'[76]

Herbert Gladstone replied giving what he called 'my own impressions as to my Father's view' to the effect that the Nationalists should apply first to the Tories, but adding that he would be glad to hear again 'if you think I can throw any light on points of difficulty'.[77] Labouchere replied that he would tell Healy to 'take the United States, or the Dominion, or Austro-Hungary as a basis, and then let us have clearly your plan'. 'The fact is', he confided to Herbert Gladstone, 'that I never knew anyone with less constructive skill than Parnell, and his utter ignorance is perfectly astounding. He never reads a book, and seldom a newspaper, unless the former treats of geology, his favourite subject.'[78]

In Dublin on 10 October Parnell had a long conference with his lieutenants, and asked Healy and Sexton to draw up a Home Rule constitution. However, he appeared to be quite indifferent as to which party came to power, believing that his own ends would be assured either way, and personally hoping that the Tories might offer Ireland a protective tariff system.[79] When reported to Hawarden, these proceedings looked unpromising enough to drive Herbert Gladstone, himself a convinced Home Ruler, into the open:

Herbert Gladstone–Labouchere, 18 October 1885 [draft]: There is very little time to lose. I hope the leaders of the Irish party will act speedily —unless as I said in my last letter they think it advisable to sink or swim with the Tories—and that they will especially take into consideration the position of the landlords. This difficulty appears to be at the root of the whole matter.

. . . If we are to attempt to settle the question at the beginning of the next Parliament, it is certain that it must be with the frank cooperation of the Irish members. And it is desirable to know as speedily as possible exactly how we stand in order to carry the party with us. . . . For as you know the bulk of the party require a very substantial lead on [the] 'advanced' Irish question.[80]

Labouchere undertook to urge this view on the Irish, but gave it as his own opinion that 'Parnell is a natural trickster, and is afraid of losing his position if he agrees to any compromise'. He would compensate the landlords, but only at a reduced scale of value.[81]

Things had reached a deadlock. Parnell would not commit himself, and Hawarden could not. Gladstone knew that to announce a Home Rule scheme before the general election would mean the loss of the Whigs and a new House of Commons pledged against him. There were ostensible reasons for reticence, such as the undesirability of bidding against the Conservatives, who were supposed to be contemplating an official measure, and the recent enfranchisement of the Irish peasantry whose electoral verdict was awaited. But the real reason which prevented an open espousal of Home Rule, even for many weeks after the uncertainties both of Lord Salisbury's intentions and of the election results had been removed, was Gladstone's knowledge that his own party was not ready to follow him. To sweeten the pill for the Whigs he was planning to secure full compensation for the landlords.

A candid explanation of his full intentions would have lost Gladstone the support of both Hartington and Chamberlain, who would undoubtedly have composed their feud and joined in defence of the Union. In Chamberlain's opinion it was 'sharp practice' for the Liberal ex-premier to mask his plans from his ex-cabinet colleagues by silence and a pretence of intended retirement, and certainly there was no reason why a Liberal shadow cabinet should not have been summoned to discuss Irish policy in secret. This Gladstone refused, even after the election. But through Labouchere himself news of the negotiations with the Irish was purveyed to Chamberlain, who was informed in a letter of 18 October 'what the little game of our revered G[rand] O[ld] M[an] has been' (as Labouchere put it). The decided refusal by Chamberlain to go one iota beyond the National Council's scheme was probably transmitted by Labouchere back to Hawarden: 'My proposal is the maximum that English Radicals will stand and a great deal more than the Whigs will accept.' Gladstone himself now thought fit to intimate to Chamberlain that 'an instinct' blindly impressed him with 'the likelihood that Ireland may shoulder aside everything else'. There followed an appeal for restraint in the interests of party unity: 'I would beg you to resolve much in your own mind the policy and duty, without me as well as with me, of keeping together the Liberal party till its list of agreed subjects is exhausted.' In reply to this, Chamberlain left no doubt of his uncompromising hostility to Home Rule. 'For myself', he writes, 'I would rather let Ireland go altogether than accept the responsibility of a nominal Union.'[82] A war of mine and counter-mine had commenced.

On the very eve of the general election another attempt was made by Hawarden to offer the basis of an agreement to Parnell. The Irish leader had suggested that Home Rule might be achieved by retaining the Irish M.P.s at Westminster only for Imperial affairs, on which alone they would be enabled to vote. Here was a means of setting up a Dublin Parliament while maintaining the integrity of the Empire. Writing from Edinburgh, Gladstone drafted five points of such a Home Rule scheme in a letter to his son. Herbert Gladstone added a sixth point at the head of the list —the familiar caveat to which his father was committed—and transmitted the plan substantially unaltered to Labouchere for communication to the Irish:

Herbert Gladstone–Labouchere, 16 November 1885: If, however, we win it seems to me that the right course would be to summon a kind of Conference between the Irish representatives and the Liberal party to discuss the question of the Irish Government, and on the basis, which of course would be arranged previously, of:
  1. The maintenance of the unity and integrity of the Empire.
  2. An Irish Chamber for Irish affairs.
  3. Irish representatives to sit at Westminster for Imperial affairs.
  4. The equitable division of Imperial charges by fixed proportions.
  5. Protection of the minority in Ireland.
  6. Suspension of the Imperial authority for all civil purposes in Ireland. . . .
  I am confident that if (*a*) Ireland at the Poll declares for Home Rule, and (*b*) the Liberal Party are put by the election into the position to take up the question, my Father would be for entering into early communication with those who would represent the Irish nation. It is my belief that in view of the gravity of the position, and the inherent right of the Irish nation to make a constitutional demand to manage their own affairs in their own way, he is prepared to stand or fall by the satisfactory settlement of the question.[83]

Thus assured of the support of the Liberal leader for Home Rule, Parnell cynically ordered his followers in England to cast their votes for the Conservatives.

The first polls opened on 23 November, and in England the elections were not fought on the Irish question. Generally the results were a disappointment for the Liberals. The manager of the Liberal Caucus, Schnadhorst, had forecast a total of 366 Liberal seats, but only 335 were won, giving a majority of 86 over the Tories. This was exactly counterbalanced by the 86 Home Rulers returned under Parnell's banner. The Nationalists had won a commanding position, holding the balance of parties.

In other respects also the general election was a severe disappointment for the Radicals. The main cause of Liberal failure was the effectiveness of the Tory 'fair trade' cry in the boroughs, against which the Radical Programme had little to offer—no 'urban cow' as attractive as the offer of smallholdings to countrymen. Chamberlain's impression of things at the close of the election is recorded in a flippant letter to Lady Dorothy Nevill:

4 December 1885: The elections have been most interesting. They have not gone as I expected, but they are not on the whole bad for us, i.e. the Radicals. Six weeks ago I thought we were sure of a great majority, but the latest information before the polling gave me doubt.

The 'Cow' has been very well, and would have done much better if the Whigs had not been such asses, and had not done their best to discredit this admirable cry.

London is an awful disappointment to me. It deserves the fate of the cities of the plain. However, I am looking for a second Schnadhorst to organize the Metropolis properly before the next election. . . . The revolution is postponed, *voilà tout.* . . .[84]

Hard on the election results came a report that Lord Salisbury had decided to 'give a *non possumus* to all proposals for Home Rule' and was prepared if necessary to form a coalition with Hartington to oppose Gladstone. Lord Randolph Churchill (whose account of these decisions was retailed to Hawarden) discussed the contingencies at length with Labouchere on 3 December. He estimated that 200 Liberals would follow Hartington, while 60 would follow Chamberlain, if Gladstone retired: whereas he was confident of an anti-Home Rule majority if Gladstone remained.[85] To the last suggestion Herbert Gladstone reacted with pique and over-confidence:

Herbert Gladstone–Labouchere, 7 December 1885: Randolph Churchill's speculations as to the comparative number of the followers of Chamberlain and Hartington seem to me futile. There are probably not a score of men in the new House who have as yet made up their minds to follow either. But however this may be, I don't believe for a moment that Hartington would join Lord Salisbury.

As to the break-up of the Liberals on Home Rule, it is possible. But I have sounded many M.P.s who are fire-eaters on the question in public, and have found that their minds are singularly plastic when the solid facts and logical issues are presented to them. Will Parnell move a Home Rule amendment on the Address?[86]

Rumours of negotiations between Gladstone and the Irish were now circulating in the clubs, and Labouchere pressed for a more definite scheme to offer Parnell. An interview with Parnell was arranged, or rather requested, for the letter was not received by the elusive Irishman in time. At Lord Rosebery's suggestion it was decided, as Labouchere put it to Herbert Gladstone, 'thoroughly to stick to *your* views being *your* views, and to feel the way step by step'.[87] The Hawarden view was 'that any project conceived . . . even a short time ago would scarcely hold water now. . . . I believe the Liberals will hold together to carry a big measure through.'[88] This broad hint was wasted. Parnell failed to turn up.

Things looked black at Hawarden when this was known. Letters were arriving which told how the Radicals were planning to keep the Tories in office. This had been the upshot of a post-election conference called by Chamberlain. 'I should like', he wrote to Harcourt, 'to keep the Tories with their noses to the grindstone for a year at least, and then I think the Irish question would be in a much better position for settlement.'[89] Dilke agreed with this formula, and was bold enough to declare it to his Chelsea constituents. Morley dissented, and thenceforward gravitated towards closer relations and sympathy with Gladstone. For the plan was aimed as much against Gladstone as Parnell. To take office, Gladstone would require Parnell's support, and no one expected the Grand Old Man to contemplate anything less than a full term of office founded on a cordial understanding with the Irish. The Radical challenge focused attention on this point. This was the juncture at which Herbert Gladstone, stung by Dilke's speech,[90] went up to London and gave the press interviews summarized in the newspapers of 17 December and known to political legend as the 'Hawarden Kite'. Mr Gladstone was stated to be ready to take office to carry Home Rule on the lines indicated to Healy (whose negotiation was of course not disclosed). Doubts about possible dangers from party disagreements, hesitations about the chances of future protectionist or separatist movements taking hold of the Dublin Parliament, were confidently dismissed.

Labouchere happened to be staying with Chamberlain on 17th, when his host 'came in with the *Standard* in great excitement', saying, ' "This must be the scheme. Some of the Irish must have told it. There must be negotiations going on." '[91] Labouchere couldn't believe that his own communications with Healy had been leaked, and conjectured that Churchill had let out some Gladstonian scheme supposed to have been communicated to the Queen. He wrote for the benefit of Hawarden a Boswellian account of the conversation he had with Chamberlain that day:

Labouchere–Herbert Gladstone, 17 December 1885:

Labouchere: I doubt this being the scheme, for Mr Gladstone must know that he never could obtain the assent of the Irish to any Irish assembly being under the control of the Imperial Parliament in local matters.

Chamberlain: Mr Gladstone may do what he likes. I distinctly say that I won't vote for any such scheme. He would get nobody to support him. Not one Whig will be in favour of it.

Labouchere: But Mr Gladstone has great personal influence with them, and possibly you may be wrong.

Chamberlain: I do not believe it possible. He may have talked generally with one or two, and they may have replied civilly. This is more than separation. I prefer separation.

Labourchere: What do you object to in it?

Chamberlain: If the Irish were only to be in the Imperial Parliament when Imperial measures were under discussion, they would use their votes there to exact fresh concessions. The scheme is unworkable. It would ruin the Radicals for years to be allied with such a proposal.

Labouchere: Supposing Mr Gladstone were to take office and to bring in such a scheme, what would be the result?

Chamberlain: He would be beaten in the House of Commons.

Labouchere: Supposing he were not.

Chamberlain: This would be worse. There would be an appeal to the country, and the Conservatives would carry everything before them. . . . Why not leave the Conservatives alone?

Labouchere: Because they do not intend to be left alone.

Chamberlain: I suppose that they will be turned out in a few weeks. Then the Liberals would be turned out in a month or two, then we would have a dissolution, and we would pass stringent rules against obstruction if we got the majority which we should.

Labouchere: Possibly. . . . What then?

Chamberlain: We might give them some little sop, but they would gradually learn that they must take what we give.

Labouchere: And how long would this go on? . . .

Chamberlain: Until they are tired out—six, ten years if necessary.

Labouchere: You can hardly expect that Mr Gladstone would come in, utterly powerless, merely to be turned out in order to carry this curious programme.

Chamberlain: I don't suppose that he would.

Labouchere: Who then would?

Chamberlain: Well, I don't exactly know. The question of the moment is, what am I going to say in speaking tonight?[92]

Labouchere was beginning to be caught in the coils of his own duplicity. He could not tell Hawarden that he had indirectly divulged the Healy negotiation to Chamberlain. But he now belittled Chamberlain, casting doubt on his ability to carry as many as ten followers with him in any revolt. 'His Caucus is a piece of humbug. Besides, he can be worked through John Morley.'[93] While thus encouraging Gladstone to proceed with Home Rule, Labouchere was describing him to Chamberlain as insanely desirous of power, and suggesting that the Home Rule question should be used to 'shunt' both Gladstone and the Whigs.

The Whigs were proving hardly less amenable to persuasion than the Radicals, confirming Gladstone in the view Granville had put to him before the election, that an agreement on Home Rule among Liberals would be 'very difficult . . . before the pressure of necessity arises'.[94] Lord Granville, the party leader in the upper House, could be relied on. Spencer and Rosebery were pessimistic but compliant. But Derby was 'full of perplexities' and had reacted to the *Standard* disclosures by protesting that the plan would split the party, which he thought should not be committed to it without previous discussion. Hartington's opposition was a fair certainty, and with slow and courteous deliberation this sage and influential figure rejected Gladstone's attempt to beg the question of the necessity for action.

The assumption that the problem of Irish government would imperatively call for immediate solution was the basis of Gladstone's whole moral position. But the assumption was proving false. A letter from Labouchere of 17 December informed Hawarden that the Conservative rejection of Home Rule was final—Lord Carnarvon himself had admitted it to McCarthy on 13th, and the next day the cabinet decided to 'angle for the moderate Liberals' on an anti-Home Rule policy.[95] In vain Gladstone, writing to Balfour on the 20th, intimated that he would support a Conservative measure. His overture was scouted in Conservative circles with the utmost contempt. In these circumstances it was becoming apparent that the most potent factor by far making for an Irish crisis was Mr Gladstone himself. His view of the crisis was not shared by anyone else, and almost all his ex-cabinet colleagues were working against him. When Harcourt sent a request to Granville for a meeting of leaders 'to discuss the present state of affairs', Granville turned it down on his own initiative, informing Gladstone but also saying: 'Please consider that you know nothing of this.'[96] Spencer thought the Conservatives should be kept in, thus far agreeing with Chamberlain and Dilke, who with Harcourt and Hartington met at the New Year to call their evasive chief to account. But Gladstone would not consult with his colleagues or deliver his plan.

The truth was that Gladstone was waiting for the Nationalists to make up their minds. On 16 December he had sent through Mrs O'Shea an elaborate request that Parnell should communicate his wishes.[97] Parnell would not be drawn. But from Healy came clear intimations that the Irish demands would be high. Asked if he would accept any power of veto to be retained by the Imperial parliament over the measures of a Dublin assembly, Healy curtly replied: 'Absolutely impossible.' His idea of imperial control was a veto exercised by the Queen on the advice of an Irish Privy Council, which could be overcome if the Dublin parliament repassed the vetoed measure by a two-thirds majority in a subsequent session. Healy's views were developed in great detail in the screeds that Labouchere sent on to Hawarden.[98] Some features were reassuring, such as the readiness to compensate landlords and to admit a nominated proportion of the membership of the Dublin assembly (which Healy thought would strengthen the hands of the Parnellites against Orangemen and Fenians). But fundamental points remained in suspense, most notably the question of the removal or retention of the Irish members at Westminster. Granville was pressing for removal, declaring that 'the bribe necessary to satisfy Great Britain whether logical or not, would be to get rid of the Irish Members, the dry rot in the House of Commons'.[99] Ultimately he had his way, and the provision which tended most to brand the Home Rule Bill as separatist in tendency was written in for party reasons and not at the demand of the Nationalists.

Meanwhile the lack of any public utterance by Gladstone completely disarmed the opposition of those Liberals who supported the Union. 'It is really monstrous', Chamberlain comments, 'that our leader should throw every obstacle in the way of counsel and should be taking his own course under the pretence that he is standing still.'[100] After arriving in London in 11 January 1886 Gladstone interviewed his colleagues singl' and it was not until the 21st that the Liberal ex-cabinet assembled at Granville's house. By that date the parliamentary session with its tactical problems was upon them and the main issue was easily avoided. Ironically it was a Chamberlainite amendment, moved by Jesse Collings, which the shadow cabinet chose for turning the Conservatives out of office. Lord Salisbury had reverted to a policy of coercion, and there was in Chamberlain's opinion a danger that a sentimental revulsion of feeling might betray the Liberal following into supporting a Home Rule amendment. To scotch this he preferred to see Salisbury defeated on some neutral ground: while the Liberal leaders as a whole accepted this solution without hesitation or discussion 'as a way out of all their difficulties and differences'. In this manner Gladstone duly defeated his opponents on 26 January, and took office with no mandate beyond his thin election manifesto, and no obligations to his colleagues or followers beyond those moral ones implied by his appeals for reticence and his promises not to split the party. By this time, however, all the world realized that he was about to stake everything to carry forward his Home Rule policy, single-handed if necessary, against all odds.

CHAPTER FOUR

Gladstonian Home Rule

What vexes me is when differences disclose baseness, which sometimes happens.
Gladstone–R. H. Hutton, 2 July 1886

[Chamberlain] *has a following of 6 in the House personally and nothing to speak of in the Country. . . . Therefore he may be expected to give in, but he is vain and obstinate.*
Herbert Gladstone to his mother, 7 May 1886

ONE of the most extraordinary features of the Home Rule struggle of 1886 was that it should have been John Morley, Chamberlain's bosom companion and closest political ally after Dilke, who of all men proved to be Gladstone's indispensable adjutant. Some have seen in Gladstone's preferment of Morley to the post of Irish Secretary, while Chamberlain was given the Local Government Board, a piece of political craft intended to widen the rift between them.[101] But in fact Morley was uniquely qualified for his meteoric ascent to high cabinet office. He was perhaps the one statesman available who really believed in the Gladstonian form of Home Rule. He was more of a 'little Englander' than Gladstone himself, quite content to see England become a 'magnified Putney' divested of all influence over the territories beyond her coastline.[102] For most other English politicians Home Rule was more or less a counsel of expediency, with the object of satisfying Parnell and getting rid of the Irish from Westminster. Harcourt, for instance, made the last condition a *sine qua non* of his support. For many, such as Spencer or Granville, Home Rule was an unpleasant alternative to continued coercion, which had however the incidental advantage of covering the failure of their unimaginative Irish policies by its tacit implication that government on the former lines had become impossible. For Morley, on the other hand, a willingness to consult Parnell and to comply with his wishes, and to confer on Ireland a generous land settlement and a Parliament without cast-iron safeguards, was an adventure in statecraft, an exhilarating experiment in the force of just concession, trust and gratitude to overcome political difficulties. He did not entertain the idea of risk or failure. Indeed for him there could be no failure, for he regarded the Irish as a separate nation, and separation had no terrors for him. By contrast, Chamberlain could never lose sight of the overriding imperial consideration. 'My Radicalism', he told Balfour at this time, 'desires to see established a strong government and an Imperial government.' The rift between him and Morley was therefore fundamental, and it was already apparent to Gladstone before he made his appointment. Morley had distinguished himself before the country as the one man who supported openly and with conviction the policy which everyone knew Gladstone was contemplating.

The rupture between the two Radicals occurred quite suddenly and unexpectedly at the end of 1885. Chamberlain, writing to Morley after the 'Hawarden Kite', shows no awareness that Morley had already 'found salvation' in the new creed and its patriarch:

17 December 1885: What do you think about the Irish business? I hope you agreed with my speech the other day. I do not think there is the least chance of carrying a separate Parliament, in the House or in the country. But expectations have been raised which will make the situation very difficult.

I should like to know how it is proposed to deal with the House of Lords. Also how about all the functions of the Crown? And what is to happen if a British ministry with a large majority in the British House is beaten by the Irish vote in the Imperial chamber? Is it to resign or not?[103]

Four days later Morley, speaking at Newcastle, declared boldly for turning out the Conservatives and settling Ireland on Gladstone's lines. Such a course, he admitted, might 'rouse deep passions', and 'perhaps destroy a great party': but the difficulties and dangers had to be faced on behalf of the 'integrity of the Empire' and the 'interests of Parliament'. Chamberlain, on reading these phrases, was incensed by the looseness with which they were used, and stung by a vindication of Gladstone's line more open than Gladstone himself dared to put forth. After some hesitation, he sent off a sharp remonstrance to bring Morley to his senses:

Chamberlain–Morley, 24 December 1885: I disapprove of your speech, as much at least as you did of Dilke's. . . . Unless you have a plan of your own, which is not separation, and which will not directly lead up to it, and which at the same time satisfies the Irish, it seems to me most mischievous and inexpedient to raise false hopes by vague generalities, and to talk of maintaining the Unity of the Empire while granting Home Rule. . . .

Possibly you have a scheme which answers the necessary condition, but if so, you have not given me any indication of it. Do you know what the Irish plan (Healy's) is? This is it:

A governor, to be a member of royal family; a House of Commons, one third to be nominated by Crown for the first five years, afterwards all elected; a Privy Council nominated by Crown; a veto on acts of House of Commons by Governor, acting with advice of Privy Council; full control of the police force; full representation at Westminster for imperial business.

How long would such an arrangement last, I wonder? I should infinitely prefer separation myself.

Separation, however, means:

1. A conscription in Ireland, followed by conscription in Great Britain.
2. An increase in the fleet.
3. Expenditure on fortifications in Scotland and England, west coast, and finally, war, in which Ireland would secure the support of America or France. It is not a pleasant prospect, and we are playing with terrible weapons in discussing without the clearest practical ideas the question of an independent Parliament.

I know that I cannot convince you in this matter, or change your course. I have foreseen for a long time that we were drifting apart. . . .[104]

The letter was intended as a warning that Chamberlain might feel obliged to reply to Morley's arguments in public, though he undertook to 'lie low' and not commit himself. Yet he could see that the divergence was fundamental, and mentioned his bitter disappointment 'that we are not destined, as I once thought, to tread the same path in political life'.

Morley, not seeing the essential opposition of his own approach to that of his friend, was wounded by what he chose to view as an excommunication. Before he replied, however, Chamberlain wrote again in terms which should have informed him that nothing so drastic was intended. The occasion was the publication in *The Times* of an article by Labouchere on 'What the Parnellites would accept' much to the same effect as Healy's plan which Chamberlain had already criticized. Writing casually and informally, he tried to indicate that what he objected to was not the drastic nature of Home Rule as proposed, but its lack of precision and completeness and the ambiguity of its purpose:

Chamberlain–Morley, 28 December 1885: Labouchere's scheme in *Times* has been under discussion at Hawarden. It is ridiculous, and separation at once is infinitely preferable. There is only one feasible scheme of federation, viz. the United States constitution. But if you look into it, it means abolition of Monarchy and House of Lords, neither of which could survive the creation of five or six semi-independent but federalized states. I have no objection to such a revolution, but is it conceivable that the country is prepared for such a change?

There are stormy times ahead of us, and I do not see the end. Sooner than consent to what I fear Mr Gladstone is contemplating, I would go out of politics altogether. I do not think he can carry his party with him, though he may do much to break it up. He appears to be sulking in his tent just now, and will not reply to Hartington, Rosebery or myself.[105]

Morley did not answer any of these arguments. Instead he wrote, unfortunately before receiving the second of Chamberlain's letters, a petulant reply repudiating the idea that he could be treated as a powder-monkey in the partnership. What he was doing, as Chamberlain well knew, was much more than fetching powder. He had provided Gladstone with an Irish Secretary. The ill-feelings were removed in further correspondence, but Morley made it clear that he stood for the removal of the Irish from Westminster, and that he meant to go with Gladstone. 'John Morley seems to have shown wisdom,' comments Gladstone to Granville in the new year: 'I am told Chamberlain has dissolved the alliance.'[106]

Gladstone's Home Rule ministry was formed on the basis of an 'inquiry' into the Irish question, not upon any scheme or even principles of Irish self-government. Chamberlain knew that Gladstone was 'determined to go on *coûte que coûte* and to pay not the slightest attention to the claims or the wishes of his late colleagues'.[107] It suited Gladstone to neutralize Chamberlain's opposition by offering him the cabinet on terms which he could not refuse, and to make his inevitable resignation appear to be the origin and cause of the split in the party. Chamberlain suspected that he was walking into a man-trap, but he had been given no manifest excuse for refusal. He had to play the game on Gladstone's terms. His letter of acceptance, therefore, written on 30 January, was a carefully-guarded compact, in which he set down the extraordinary circumstances in which office had been pressed on him. He had said categorically that he was 'entirely opposed to the idea of an Irish Parliament', and preferred to deal with the Irish problem through local government and land reform. He understood that he accepted office with 'unlimited liberty of judgment and rejection' (Gladstone's phrase), on 'any scheme that may ultimately be proposed', and that 'full consideration' of his own schemes 'as an alternative to any larger arrangement' would not be excluded.[108]

Gladstone broke this compact. He settled the basic principles of his Home Rule scheme secretly, collecting information as to Parnell's demands from Morley,* and finally presented the essential principles of an Irish Parliament to his cabinet as a *fait accompli*. He was enabled to do this by taking advantage of Morley's total inexperience of cabinet procedure—Morley had never held office of any kind, and had not been three years in Parliament. Morley himself was misled by two assumptions which begged the whole question: that Parnell's agreement with the general shape of the Home Rule plan was necessary from its inception; and that the cabinet could only discuss Irish government on the basis of a plan whose essentials were laid down in advance.† He fell completely under the sway of Gladstone's subtly egocentric and domineering personality, and thought that ministers who did not essentially agree with him had no business to be in the government. Years after, when writing his *Life of Gladstone*,

---

* Morley, *Gladstone*, III p.304: 'From the first the Irish leader was in free and constant communication with the Chief Secretary.'

† *Ibid.*, p.295: 'Such was Mr Chamberlain's excuse for joining. It is hardly so intelligible as Lord Hartington's excuse for not joining. For the new government could only subsist by Irish support. That support notoriously depended on the concession of more than a limited scheme of local government.'

he was still unaware of this subconscious bias, and justifies Gladstone's failure to make any effort to conciliate or retain Chamberlain and Trevelyan on the curious ground that since they were fundamentally opposed to him, discussion or argument would have been futile.* For Morley a cabinet was not a council for hammering out state policy, but a pliant orchestra with a masterful conductor.

In spite of the absence of any reliable co-adjutor in the cabinet, such as Dilke would have been, Chamberlain retained for some weeks the hope that the cabinet might evolve a scheme of which he could approve. Morley notes, on the day after he had been offered the post of Irish Chief Secretary, that Chamberlain was 'anxious for continued alliance; thinks it could be done'.[109] Three days later he received a final appeal setting out an alternative to the Gladstonian policy:

Chamberlain–Morley, 4 February 1886: Thanks for your letter. I cannot help thinking that your difficulty in conciliating various statements of mine arises from the vague and indefinite way in which almost all those who have spoken or written on the Irish question have used such terms as 'home rule', 'autonomy', 'control of domestic affairs', and 'local government'. . . .

I say now, as I have always said, that some great extension of local government is necessary and urgent. It must be associated with any proposal for dealing either with the land or with the education question. . . .

I still stand by the expressions of my speech of June 7th, and am in favour of the concession to Ireland of the right to govern itself in the matter of its purely domestic business. I am willing immediately to reform the anachronism known as Dublin Castle. But one and all of these statements must be taken in conjunction with my determination to maintain unimpaired all necessary guarantees for the integrity of the Empire and the supremacy of Parliament, and I do not believe that these can be maintained in connection with a legislative body sitting in Dublin, or in connection with your proposal to put Ireland in the position of Canada.

It is the larger question only that I am anxious to postpone, and even as to this I only ask for postponement, as I admit that the circumstances

---

* *Ibid.*, p.303: 'Mr Gladstone knew the great burden that he had taken up and . . . his mind was no doubt fixed that success . . . would be hopeless in face of personal antagonisms and bitterly divided counsels.'

may be altered when the primary causes of social war and national hatred have been removed. . . .

You have a difficult task, and I heartily wish you success, but am not sanguine. You have spoken strongly in favour of dealing with the land first. Also strongly against separation, and in favour of maintaining the integrity of the Empire. If either Mr Gladstone or yourself can produce a scheme which fulfils these conditions, I shall not be placed in the painful position of opposing it.[110]

For some days after his appointment, Morley writes in his *Recollections*, 'I nursed the idea that I might be useful as a buffer between Chamberlain and the Prime Minister. . . . A few days were enough to dispel the illusion. No individual was to blame. The governing forces of the situation were intractable.'[111] Chief among these forces was the inexorable figure of Parnell. A ministry formed on the ground of 'inquiry' became a ministry based on the axiom that Parnell must be satisfied.

Morley's adhesion to the latter policy turned the scale. By 13 March, when the first cabinet discussion on Ireland was held, the die had been cast. Gladstone outlined a scheme of land purchase involving the advance of £120,000,000 to the new Irish authority. After 'considerable discussion and some hesitation', he stated also 'his intention to propose a separate Parliament for Ireland with full powers to deal with all Irish affairs'. On getting no assurance of alteration in any important particular, Chamberlain announced his intention to resign. Gladstone did not allow him to go at once, but kept him till the next cabinet of 26 March, the minimum of time, he said 'to make ready my proposals'. In the meantime Chamberlain regarded his resignation as final, having no desire to be entrapped (as Gladstone attempted to entrap him later by suddenly and unaccountably denying his right to refer in the Commons to the land proposals) into the appearance of objecting to the Irish Parliament pure and simple. News of his resignation was leaked by the Press Association, whereupon he sent a memorandum on the position to the editor of the *Birmingham Daily Post*:

To J. T. Bunce, 17 March 1886: My resignation has been tendered to Mr Gladstone, and at his request postponed. I do not think that either he or I have any hope that the difficulty will be bridged over. . . .

From statements made to me I am convinced the land purchase

scheme is so unpopular with Radicals as well as others, that it has no chance whatever of being carried, and if Mr Gladstone sticks to it he will be beaten. What I fear is that, as he has done on so many previous occasions, he may at once withdraw the weakest part of his proposals, give up the idea of paying out the landlords, and proceed with the Home Rule scheme. I am afraid that the majority of Radical members are inclined to accept almost anything under this name. The time has come to point out clearly the enormous dangers of the course proposed, and above all to prove that no solution adopted in a spirit of impatience with Irish obstruction, or of blind confidence in Mr Gladstone, will really be a final one. . . .

. . . It is certain that any scheme of the kind attributed to Mr Gladstone will lead in the long run to the absolute national independence of Ireland, and that this cannot be conceded without serious danger and the heaviest sacrifices on the part of Great Britain. This country would sink to the rank of a third rate power, and its foreign policy, already sufficiently embarrassing and absorbing, would be complicated by perpetual reference to the state of feeling in Ireland. . . .[112]

In the days following Chamberlain was already planning the strategy by which the Home Rule Bill which he rightly saw as imminent might be defeated in the Commons. Speaking in his most candid manner at a small dinner party on 22 March, he conveyed to Arthur Balfour the impression that he meant to be as active in opposition as Hartington: and Balfour felt that the Conservatives would find in him a more reliable and persevering ally than 'the lukewarm and slippery Whig'. By the time the next cabinet was due, he had crystallized his objections to Gladstone's measure into four points which he intended to make the fighting issues: whether the Irish representation was to cease at Westminster; whether the Dublin Parliament was to control taxation, appoint judges and magistrates and legislate on all subjects not specifically reserved rather than on delegated subjects only. All four points were answered in an unfavourable sense, and Chamberlain, accompanied by Trevelyan, walked out of the room. The Unionist cause had been born.

The Unionist front was consolidated under the 'flag' of Irish representation at Westminster. If this were retained, the essential safeguards of the Union could be preserved by the legislative and fiscal supremacy of Westminster: and there could be a separate assembly for Ulster. The Home Rule arrangement would then be transposed from Morley's principle of 'Colonial independence' to Chamberlain's principle of 'federal' government or 'home rule all round'. Gladstone though leaning to Morley's principle had not yet made up his mind on exclusion or retention, and, curiously enough, Morley and others believed that Parnell preferred the retention of the Irish members and regarded his agreeing to their exclusion as a concession.[113] It was not until 4 May that the cabinet considered the matter. Meanwhile Gladstone had been confirmed in the idea of exclusion by the arguments of Harcourt, Granville, Spencer and Kimberley, whose reasons, unlike those of Morley, were tactical and, in the gravity of the issues involved, frivolous. 'If we retained the Irish members', writes Granville, 'there would be a howl, and I believe no one excepting Chamberlain for obvious reasons, is anxious to retain them.'[114] 'Quite as many people', said Harcourt, 'support the Bill because it gets rid of the Irish M.P.s as those who oppose it on that ground.'[115] By 8 May, two days before the long-protracted debate on the second reading of the Home Rule Bill began, the cabinet had decided to stand by the exclusion of the Irish members.[116]*

Meanwhile Chamberlain had lost no time in establishing co-operative relations with Hartington and, via Lord Randolph Churchill, with Lord Salisbury. His position was very difficult, for while he was convinced that Gladstone would not make any concession and that therefore he must take every action to defeat the Bill, he knew that any overt collaboration with the other side would be exploited to damage his position in the country. He had been manipulated, slighted, and humbugged by 'the old Parliamentary hand' (as Gladstone had recently styled himself) in a manner which left no doubt of a rooted and implacable hostility, but the long background of manœuvre and scheming was not known or understood by the public. Equally little appreciated was the bearing of parliamentary procedure on the fate of the Bill. The Gladstonians wished, in Granville's phrase, to 'squeeze into committee', after which they could either defeat the Liberal dissentients in detail, or throw up the Bill and go to the country

---

* Morley (*Gladstone*, III, p.307) gives as a reason why the majority of the cabinet favoured exclusion that 'Mr Bright was known to regard it as large compensation for what otherwise he viewed as pure mischief, and it was expected to win support in other quarters generally hostile.'

with the advantage of having pledged the dissentients to the principle by virtue of their votes for the second reading. For the dissentients to oppose the second reading would appear factious and prejudiced, especially in the light of Gladstone's protestations that the difficulty of the Bill was such 'that nothing can place it fully before the world except a comprehensive and dispassionate debate upon it', and that, 'The determining condition will I think be found to be the temper in which men approach the question'.[117]

Chamberlain decided at the outset that he must at all costs defeat the second reading. He wrote to Hartington on 3 April, expressing a hope that Hartington would lead the opposition to the Bill and move its rejection at the second reading stage. At the same time he resolved to stand aloof from the public meetings held by Whig and Conservative Unionists. The situation was made more delicate by the defection of Schnadhorst and a threat that the issue might be represented before the National Liberal Federation as a personal one between idol and iconoclast. Chamberlain had to defend his citadel, and was pleased with the response of the Birmingham 'Two Thousand' to his judicious plea for the retention of the Irish. Writing to Harcourt in the ensuing week, he delivered some home truths and prognostications designed for consumption in higher quarters:

Chamberlain–Harcourt, 22 April 1886: I do not expect any compromise or concession. I imagine we shall fight the matter out to the bitter end, and break up the Liberal party in the process. . . .

Nothing will induce me to support the second reading of the Home Rule Bill, without a pledge that the Irish representation will be retained at Westminster. I quite understand that Mr Gladstone does not mean to yield this, and I am not going to fall into the trap of postponing my objections to the committee stage. I wish the matter could have been squared, but it is hopeless, and we shall have to take the gloves off very soon.

Chamberlain–Harcourt, 26 April 1886: I have no misgiving in consequence of the defection of Morley and Schnadhorst, although the former has pained me and the latter is inconvenient. But Morley is timid, and the basis of all his policy is simple 'funk' of the Irish. He has not said one word in favour of the Bills, which he hardly seems to understand. His argument is one for total surrender to Mr Parnell. . . .

I doubt if you are right as to the future. I think the tide is rising against both Bills, and after a time I think the secessionists will be forgiven and even approved. But no doubt the Tories will be the chief gainers. The caucusses will go for Gladstone—but many of them will demand modifications. The rank and file are more evenly divided.[118]

By the beginning of May the exact numbers of Liberals prepared to vote with Chamberlain and Hartington had been given to the Gladstonians via Harcourt and Labouchere. There were 119 Liberals who had promised to vote against the second reading, of whom 70 were publicly committed to this course, and a further 23 were regarded by Chamberlain as 'absolutely certain' in their promises. The Home Rule Bill was doomed unless the concession asked for were granted. This was simply a declaration of the government's intention to retain the Irish representation unchanged, upon which the second reading would be assured by the vote of Chamberlain's personal following of some 55 out of the total number of dissentient Liberals.* On this information, Labouchere embarked on a strenuous negotiation which failed only at the last moment, when, in moving the second reading on 10 May, Gladstone unexpectedly and unaccountably omitted the concession. Labouchere declared that Harcourt, who was 'playing for the succession', was behind the failure. But in Chamberlain's opinion the real opponent of all concession had been Morley:

Chamberlain–Labouchere, 2 May 1886: The fact is, he is much more concerned for his own personal position than for Mr Gladstone's. Mr Gladstone has expressed a readiness to consider the subject, and nothing could be easier than for him to say that he was personally in favour of the retention, and in view of the evident desire of many Liberals the government would consent, etc. . . . It is only Morley who is pledged against this. From a talk I had with Harcourt, I gather that he would not make any serious difficulty.[119]

Morley had just angered Chamberlain by writing to Labouchere:

---

* Chamb. PP., Chamberlain–Labouchere, 2 May 1886: 'Of the 119', he comments, 'I reckon that 55 would vote with me for second reading if I said the amendments were satisfactory. . . . If I considered my personal interests alone, I should be inclined to say that the best thing would be for the bills to be defeated, and for the Tories to come in either after or before a dissolution. . . . I consider that Mr Gladstone's action has in any case destroyed the Liberal party as a controlling force in politics for a considerable time.'

'I don't think there is a pin of difference between you and me as to the desirableness of passing the second reading at almost any cost. But Chamberlain wants us to go down on our knees, and this cannot be done for the money.'[120] Chamberlain penned a contemptuous rejoinder, which was read before the whole cabinet. Morley, he wrote, had recently told him he did not want to be admiral of the fleet, but would not consent to be a powder-monkey. 'He had now changed his ship and his captain, but he has to recognize that his position in the service is much the same as before.'[121] He was alluding to Morley's deep commitments to Parnell and Spencer, rather than to Gladstone. With the idealist's eager and imaginative sympathy with the spirit of the Irish movement, Morley cared little and knew virtually nothing about the practical tendency and working of political machinery. What he knew he got from books, and he had recommended his principle of Colonial self-government to Chamberlain by asking him to read a constitutional theorist, Alpheus Todd.[122] Chamberlain could see how he would not have held his position as a constitution-maker for a week on his own merits and subject to parliamentary criticism. But he served as a screen for men more sophisticated in practical politics.

The negotiation was complicated by the existence of the Land Purchase Bill. If Irish members were retained, it would no longer be necessary to buy out the Irish landlords. The Whigs, and indeed a wide circle of English opinion, had begun to regard the Land Bill as one of the redeeming features of the Home Rule scheme, and Spencer, with whom Morley was in the closest relations, warmly backed it. Trevelyan elaborates the position:

Trevelyan–Chamberlain, 3 May 1886: My real objection is to the Land Purchase Bill . . . if the ministry alters the Govt. of Ireland Bill in such a way as to justify them in dropping the Land Purchase Bill, I should be prepared to support the second reading. . . .

[second letter of same day]: Spencer, who has a strong family feeling, is guardian to Lord Clifton, who has very large Irish estates which Spencer has managed for the last twenty years. He would never what he would call 'throw over' Clifton and a very great number of other Irish landlords with whom he is very closely connected, who used to worship him, and who now regard him with suspicion tempered by a desire for the Purchase Bill.

I feel certain, from those people I have seen of late, that not only would Hartington and the Whigs go for the Purchase Bill, but a great number of moderate middle-class Liberals, who will resist the Home Rule Bill, would do so too.[123]

The abandonment of clause 24, which excluded the Irish from Westminster, would entail the dropping of the Land Purchase Bill. Even the postponement of the decision upon the clause would be fatal to the Land Bill. For this reason, if for no other, Morley could not give way. But he did not reason. He simply declared that Chamberlain was irreconcilable, and that it would be a humiliation to surrender to him.

Strangely enough, it was left to Dr Dale of Birmingham, who had not been in political communication with Chamberlain for several months, to draw up a paper stating in lucid terms the case for the retention of Irish members.[124] Gladstone replied evasively, and Dale renewed his appeal, writing to Morley on 6 May. He suggested that for clause 24 there should be substituted a provision that the question of Irish representation should be referred to a joint committee of both Houses and the new Irish legislature. The pliable Morley took up the idea, but side-stepped its main point:

Morley–Dale, 8 May 1886: I have weighed your suggestion pretty carefully, and have sent it on to Mr Gladstone with my opinion that we ought to look in this direction, and that he will perhaps be able to throw it into shape by this afternoon.

But we must, I fear, give up the hope of conciliation with Chamberlain. His letter today is—and is designed to be—fatal. It is meant to wreck the Bill, to expel Mr Gladstone, and to break up the party, already divided in two, into three mutually antagonistic sections. So much for Samson and the Halls of Gaza.

[telegram, 6 P.M.]: Suggestion discussed in proper quarter has been most favourably received. Pray ventilate it among your friends.

[Second letter]: I have just sent you a telegram. . . . Of course the excluding clause—24—would remain in the Bill, and your clause would be attached as a proviso to it.

I repeat my apprehension that it will fail to meet the objections of Chamberlain, but I think it is good on its merits, and we owe you a debt for propounding it.[125]

Dale repudiated Morley's plan of retaining clause 24 with the proviso, which would be to 'ask men to vote for exclusion on condition that the question of exclusion should be reconsidered'.[126] He wrote to both Morley and Gladstone on Sunday 9 May, so that his letters would have been received on 10th, and may well have been responsible for the unaccountable way in which Gladstone moved the second reading without reference to any concession. Gladstone and his son went about telling people that they were not going to give way. Clause 24 with Dale's clause as proviso had got the best of two worlds, and might have detached sufficient of Chamberlain's supporters. But when Dale denounced his own suggestion, it had to be dropped.

Meanwhile Chamberlain on his side had remained sceptical about the frequent hopeful bulletins he received from Labouchere about the dropping of clause 24. On the Sunday he cautioned Labouchere against being 'bamboozled by the old Parliamentary hand', but on receipt of a final communiqué written on 10 May recounting how Gladstone's Chief Whip, who had been with Labouchere till 1 A.M. that morning, had assured him that 'having given up the principle they asked for nothing better than to make it full', Chamberlain believed the concession was real. His response is significant. He wrote to Hartington saying that 'if this should prove to be the case, your line will be to comment on magnitude of change and suddenness of conversion, and ask that the new Bill should be produced before any opinion is called for'.[127] He suspected, rightly, that it was a case of Greeks bearing gifts, and his political instinct, always leaning towards personal confidence and fidelity, kept him on Hartington's steady course. He had nothing but distaste for the idea of collaborating with the Gladstonian crew, as he had recently told one of them:

Chamberlain–Harcourt, 5 May 1886: I do not know what Morley means by his 'five barrelled ultimatum'. It is one of his phrases, inaccurate as such things usually are. . . .

I do not like the idea of trying to work an arrangement that *I* am convinced will fail, and I cannot contemplate the reconquest of an independent Ireland or the coercion of Ulster with a light heart. I think there are evil times in store for the country, and I am not much inclined to accept responsibility for a policy that I loathe and detest.

You will, if you succeed, drive away from the Liberal party all the 'classes' so graphically described by Mr Gladstone in his manifesto. The remnant will be 'kittle cattle' to drive, especially as the G.O.M. will no doubt be employed in making his peace with his maker, and will leave to Mundella and Morley and you the task of resisting irreconcilable demands. No doubt you will have the invaluable assistance of Bradlaugh and Labouchere, while I should hope that Granville and Kimberley will be always with you. All this I shall watch without envy from my Capua at Highbury.[128]

It was therefore with something like relief that he witnessed the non-fulfilment of the Gladstonian part of the bargain, and the end of the Labouchere negotiation.

With the commencement of the second reading debate, which was destined to last up to the final division in the morning of 8 June, the Unionist defensive alliance began to take regular shape. On 12 May fifty-two of Chamberlain's followers met at Princes Gardens, and expressed 'a unanimous determination to vote against the Bill unless it was recast to meet their views', and the 'feeling of the meeting was that in the event of the Bill being defeated a Hartington–Chamberlain Government should be formed'.[129] Two days later Hartington summoned a gathering at Devonshire House, which Chamberlain and thirty-two of his men attended. Thus began the Liberal Unionist partnership which was supposedly *ad hoc* and temporary but which lasted eighteen years, until Chamberlain supplanted Devonshire and became chairman of the Liberal Unionist Association in 1904. Chamberlain explained his reasons for open collaboration with Hartington to his brother:

Chamberlain–Arthur Chamberlain, 15 May: I went to Hartington's yesterday, first to show that we were a united party of opponents, and not heterogeneous atoms,

2ly, because Hartington has frankly adopted my policy of Federal Local Government as an alternative to separation,

3ly, because it strengthens our party in the House to know that we are solid, and that one section is not likely at the last moment to leave the other in the lurch, and

4ly, because Mr Gladstone has burned his boats on the question of the retention of Irish members, and does not intend to make any further attempts to conciliate me, though he may try to draw off my opposition.[130]

The danger of the 'drawing off' of Chamberlain's supporters was very real. The game that the Gladstonians were now playing was a purely tactical one. Early in May the National Liberal Federation had gone over to Gladstone, and in their more hopeful moments the Gladstonians believed they would sweep the board in a general election. They construed their opponents' insistence upon the modification of clause 24 to avoid being driven to a hostile vote as a conscious admission of weakness. 'It is not unnatural that they should prefer our being rendered impotent', comments Granville, 'rather than that they should have a dissolution, which frightens them out of their wits.'[131] Moreover, an uncompromising attitude and a forced dissolution would retain Parnell and the Irish vote, worth 25 seats either way. And so the Gladstonian policy was to use the vote on second reading as a means of committing as many Liberals as possible to Home Rule.

With this intention, Gladstone called a meeting of Liberals at the Foreign Office on 27 May, and proposed that after the second reading the Bill should be withdrawn, and a new Home Rule Bill introduced in the autumn, with the contentious clause 24 remodelled. The members of Chamberlain's group who were afraid for their seats and anxious to find an excuse to vote for the Bill were shrewdly shaken by this manœuvre. William Sproston Caine, who acted as Whip for Chamberlain's group, was himself converted, and explained the position on the next day:

Caine–Chamberlain, 28 May 1886: I was at the House all last night. Quite 30 of our men are shaky, and I think will eventually vote for the Bill. The question is, will you lead them?

As far as I can make out from the bewildering deliverance of yesterday, the Prime Minister surrenders the fort and the armaments, but asks for a cotton pocket handkerchief and some old muskets, that he may please the women and children as he marches out. . . .

Winterbotham, Kenrick, Powell Williams, R. Chamberlain, Dixon and myself will go whither you lead, but with the exception of Winterbotham . . . all think we shall have to come in. . . . Already the Whips have got 10 or 12 of our men pretty well pledged, and they will get more every hour tonight.

If we are to come in, you ought to lead the way, and at once.[132]

But that same evening occurred the memorable scene in which

Gladstone was drawn into a most inopportune confession that, in Randolph Churchill's expression, 'the new Bill would be the old Bill'. Taunted by Hicks Beach about a procedure which made the Bill tantamount to a 'Continuance-in-Office' Bill (which was truer than Beach knew, for Parnell had just threatened to vote against any second reading which was merely *pro forma*), Gladstone denied that he intended to remodel the Bill. 'Never, never . . .' he exclaimed; only clause 24, and that in an undisclosed way. Once more there was nothing definite to be got from the old Parliamentary hand. Even Labouchere, patient and pertinacious as he was, gave up in disgust. 'Is it not terrible', he writes to Chamberlain, 'to have to deal with a lunatic at large, whose intelligence seems to be now limited to a sort of low cunning. . . . The public do not know the object of their adoration as we do.'[133] From Churchill came a similar comment:

Churchill–Chamberlain, 29 May 1886: I learned last night from Labouchere that the G.O.M. had properly and finally 'put his foot in it' by his speech in answer to Beach. Several other Liberals also expressed to me their disgust for his shiftiness. . . .

I do not believe in the G.O.M.'s threat of dissolution . . . and your men are probably being frightened by a shadow. . . .

All the G.O.M.'s difficulties arise from his shilly-shallying, not only on this occasion; but this has been the case as you know for a long time past.[134]

In the circumstances, Chamberlain leaned towards recommending that his followers abstain from voting in the division, which would allow the Bill to pass and avoid a dissolution while keeping his men uncommitted. He summoned a meeting of his group for 31 May, resolved to abide by their decision. Meanwhile he answered in a conciliatory spirit an eleventh hour appeal from Harcourt:

Chamberlain–Harcourt, 30 May 1886: I will most carefully weigh all that you say with a full sense of the responsibility of the decision to be taken. The position is a very difficult one for me, and the pressure from many quarters very strong, but I am sincerely anxious to save the Government from defeat, if I can help to do this without weakening the chance of future opposition to a measure that I honestly believe to be fatal to the best interests of the country.

Mr Gladstone's positive declaration that he will re-introduce this same Bill—that he considers himself pledged to the main lines of the measure,—etc, etc,—seems to make it certain that five months hence we shall all be in the same position.

I have already allowed it to be known that I lean to abstention as the proper course.[135]

The latest calculations which Chamberlain received from Caine suggested that the second reading could not be defeated. The fixed quantities in the coming division were:

For the Bill:	Gladstonians	220
	Parnellites	86
		306
Against:	Tories	244
	Hartingtonians	45
		289

Thus abstention would allow the Bill to pass by 17 votes, while producing the maximum moral effect in the form of a 'really big walk-out' by about 60 Chamberlainites. A walk-out would attract, in addition to the 24 Chamberlainite 'stalwarts', a further 25 of the 31 members listed by Caine as 'doubtful', and about 11 Gladstonian waverers. On the other hand, a hostile vote would drive pretty nearly all the 31 'doubtfuls' into the Gladstonian lobby and lose the Gladstonian waverers: while at the same time bringing into the other scale the 24 Chamberlainite 'stalwarts'. That is, making a net loss of up to 18 votes, and increasing the majority for the Bill to about 35.[136]

The outlook was dispiriting. Only one chance remained, that of inducing John Bright to rally the waverers. Bright had been asked to cover with the shield of 'his great name and unquestioned honour' the independent action of the seceders—in other words, to fortify them against their constituents—and had been reported as inclined to vote against the Bill. If he spoke and voted, Caine thought, he might rally all the 'doubtfuls' and raise the Chamberlainites to 55 voting against the Bill while inducing others to walk out. It was thus possible that the Bill might be defeated by some 38 votes. But Caine could not view these possibilities with any certainty:

Caine–Chamberlain, Sunday, 30 May 1886: It rests with you to save or kill the Bill. All my desire is for blood, but I now feel sure our policy is, if we can really make sure of a big walk-out, to spare the victim for six months.

I am not sure that even with a strong rally from Bright we could beat the Bill. The most popular course with our men would be to walk out. By this means we grant the truce that is asked for, and give up nothing.[137]

There was no option but to throw the decision on the party meeting.

Bright was not present at the meeting in committee room 15 at the House of Commons on 31 May. Chamberlain had, however, received from him that day a letter intended to recommend abstention, but in fact having a very different effect. Bright declared his intention to vote against the Bill, which, as he pointed out in another letter to the press, would not have the support of twenty Liberals, outside the Irish party, if Mr Gladstone's great authority were withdrawn from it. This was enough. Although Chamberlain put the pros and cons before the meeting with every appearance of impartiality, the reading of Bright's letter was conclusive. Two votes were taken, the first for abstention, which was defeated by 38 votes against 12, the second for voting against the second reading, which was approved by 46 votes while only 4 still stood out for abstention. News of this decision spread quickly in the Lobby, and the immediate reaction was a feeling that the defeat of the Bill was assured.*

That evening Caine walked into the office of the *Pall Mall Gazette* and gave an interview 'strictly for publication'. In order to defeat the Bill, he said, it was necessary to detach 79 Liberals from the ministerial ranks. He had on his list the names of 88 'stalwarts', followers of either Hartington or Chamberlain, 'who cannot be induced to vote for the Bill on any pretence whatever'. That gave him a 'minimum majority of 9' against the Bill. In

---

* There are slight discrepancies in the numbers given by the various contemporary reports. These are based on the reports in the *Birmingham Daily Post* of 1 June 1886, p.5 (versions by a special correspondent and by the Press Association).

addition there were 12 'waiters upon providence' vacillating between the two camps. The Bill was doomed, and a dissolution was in prospect. Many of the dissentient Liberals, he thought, would lose their seats 'if a dissolution comes upon us now', but nevertheless they were determined to make a stand against the blandishments or terror of the Caucus. They were prepared to quit political life rather than become 'the animated funnels of the executives of their associations'. The ministerialists were threatening to run candidates against every one of them, while Hartington threatened counter measures. The Liberal party would go down in fratricidal strife. To avoid this, the ministerialists had only to substitute a Home Rule resolution for their Bill, and they would obtain a majority of over 100, and a reunited party.[138]

There was every reason to anticipate that Gladstone would hesitate to appeal to the electorate after a defeat in the Commons. For one thing, it was against the Peelite canon. For another (though less reliable) reason, Gladstone had said categorically that he would not do so. For a third, it meant ruining the party. At the outset Morley had said publicly that this might be necessary, but Gladstone had written, 'I for one will have nothing to do with ruining the party if I can avoid it'. One must not, however (as Disraeli said of Peel), compare too closely the hours of courtship with the years of possession. The Gladstonians now thought that they were masters of the constituencies. The Council of the National Liberal Federation, consisting of 'strong Gladstonians', met on 2 June and showed no desire for conciliation, receiving the names of Chamberlain and his friends with marked hostility.

Above all, Schnadhorst remained absurdly optimistic about the electoral prospects of the Gladstonians. On 7 June, just before the final division, an interview he had given to the *Pall Mall Gazette* appeared. He dismissed the expulsion of Chamberlain and his supporters as of little consequence: 'The only change, therefore, that we know of in the Caucus is that we have lost three or four officers, and gained 24 associations . . . . I think,' he said, 'that the feeling of the local associations is as Gladstonian as the Federation, and that the local associations accurately represent the feelings of the Liberal electorate.' He discounted the importance of any turn-over of Liberal voters: 'No doubt there will be a considerable number of the better-to-do class, who have hitherto voted Liberal, who will vote Conservative, but they are not sufficient in number to exercise any appreciable influence upon the decision of the mass of the electorate.' An appeal to the country, therefore, had no terrors for him:

Schnadhorst: Certainly I think that Mr Gladstone will be able to secure the return of a sufficient majority if he were to appeal to the country now. There has been a certain shedding of influential persons here and there, but the majority which he will obtain will be much more compact. He will be returned on a clear and unmistakable issue, and there can be no doubt as to the enthusiasm which prevails among the masses.

Interviewer: Enthusiasm, Mr Schnadhorst? What for?

Schnadhorst: For the Grand Old Man and the grand new cause. . . . There is no doubt—Mr Chamberlain has admitted it in the frankest possible terms—that the enthusiasm of the British democracy for Mr Gladstone is unabated . . . and at the same time the recognition on the part of the rank and file of the party of the principle of allowing the Irish to manage Irish affairs without our intermeddling.

With such views, the Gladstonians calculated upon the deterrent effect of a dissolution. They thought that the Unionist Liberals believed they would be smashed, and would come to heel at the last moment. Further support for this hope was afforded by a scrutiny of the numbers that had attended Chamberlain's meeting. Labouchere contended that 22 of the 46 who were for opposing the Bill were 'decoy ducks' from Hartington's contingent, and that the feeling of Chamberlain's own men was equally divided.[139] This put a very different complexion on matters. And hence the probable result of the division remained very uncertain in the opinion of the Gladstonian leaders.

Gladstone, therefore, did not give way to the urgent appeal to proceed by resolution, although the second reading of a Bill that is forthwith to be dropped is hardly distinguishable in parliamentary terms from a resolution. The old man's pride forbade a climb-down, and his gambling instinct blinded him to the absurd disproportion between the punctilio he was insisting on and the enormous uncertainties and dangers of attempting to achieve it. Instead, he cast one final fly on the water. He replied to a letter from J. Fletcher Moulton, M.P., both letters appearing in *The Times* of 4 June. Fletcher Moulton asked if he was correct in assuming:

First, that in voting for the second reading . . . one is affirming only the principle of the establishment in Ireland of a legislative body for the conduct of Irish as distinguished from imperial affairs.

Second, that the government will consider and hold themselves free to accept any proposals made to them prior to the introduction of the autumn Bill, consistent with the five main conditions laid down by them as essential principles . . . and their assurances as to the representation of Ireland at Westminster upon imperial subjects.

Gladstone's reply was laconic but by no means free from ambiguity. Answering the two queries in turn, he said of the first 'I hold this to be indisputable, indeed elementary'; of the second, 'My assent is again unequivocal, and I may add that the government would not only be at liberty, but would be in duty bound to consider any such amendments.'

Here was another Delphic utterance, which might mean much or little. Could he have conceded anything, if he was in duty bound to grant it? Or if the proposition was 'elementary'? Most probably the correspondence was designed as a bridge to allow some of the waverers to return to the fold. On 5 June Mr Gladstone was reported to be 'still sanguine that he will be able to carry the second reading',* and on the eve of the final debate two days later things looked much more favourable to him. The objections of at least four waverers had been removed, and Caine's total of 'stalwarts' had declined from 88 to 80—Labouchere put it at 70. The votes of some 20 members remained uncertain, and if they could be induced to support the government, a majority was assured.†

The general feeling in the Lobby, however, was that while

---

* *Birmingham Daily Post*, 5 June 1886, citing Press Association report, which adds that the followers of Mr Gladstone 'believe that on Monday night he will make an announcement in winding up the debate which, if it does not convert Mr Chamberlain himself, will at any rate have the effect of detaching a considerable proportion of his following.'

† *Ibid.*, 7 June 1886. Caine admitted that the twenty waverers were the masters of the situation, and that if they were won by the government the Bill would pass by a majority of four votes.

members would give a 'tolerably united support to a resolution' if the Bill were withdrawn, the government would be defeated if the division were pressed. Many of the Gladstonian Liberals thought that it would be wiser to make the concession than to risk a division, and, said the Press Association, 'privately express themselves strongly opposed to a dissolution'. But, said the same account, 'A section of Mr Gladstone's supporters are confident of the results of a general election, and equal hopefulness is expressed by the majority of the Unionist Liberals'.[140] In spite of this confidence, most Liberals appeared to prefer somehow to avert the defeat of the government, and rumours circulated conjecturing on all kinds of means by which a compromise might be reached. It was thought that the Premier might make some announcement, in winding up the debate, which would detach a sufficient number of Chamberlain's following.

Yet, paradoxically, the general desire for compromise did not dispose the ministerialists to concession. On the contrary, it was upon 'this evident desire for a reconciliation that the friends of the government place their chief reliance'.[141] Over the last weekend not a stone was left unturned 'to detach from Mr Chamberlain a portion of his following', and 'much diplomacy' was used 'to bring about the desired interviews'.[142] The last reports from the House of Commons, made at 9.30 P.M. when the final debate had begun, showed that the issue still hung in the balance, and it rested in the hands of Gladstone alone to determine the result:

Everything depends on the course taken by the Prime Minister. It is believed that if he were to assert definitely that he will count the second reading as affirming the principle of an Irish executive body, and would formally absolve everyone voting for the Bill from assent either express or implied to anything else which the Bill contained, the requisite number of absentees would be made up forthwith, and the Bill would be saved. He is not unlikely to take this course, and on the likelihood of his doing so efforts have been made, with a favourable result, to get together the necessary number of abstainers. The complete success or otherwise of these efforts can only be known after the division is called, but the whips are decidedly sanguine.[143]

Gladstone's great speech in the last debate did not, however, stoop to practicalities, except for a most unfair attack on Chamberlain as a trimmer.* The speech was intended as a rousing appeal on higher issues. For Gladstone had decided to appeal to the enthusiasm of the electorate, and no longer cared for what could only have been a small and useless majority. When the division was taken, the second reading was defeated by 30 votes, the Liberal party being split up as follows:

	For 2nd Reading	Against	Absent
England & Wales	190	70	9
Scotland	38	23	1[144]

This was just after 1 A.M. on 8 June. That very day Gladstone summoned a cabinet, and although three ministers strongly favoured resignation, he settled the matter without discussion by producing a list of twelve reasons for dissolution, seemingly drawn up by Schnadhorst.†[145] No decision in nineteenth-century politics was of more diverse and far-reaching importance than this. Arrived at without due deliberation, it has the strongest claims to be ranked as the most foolish and irresponsible gamble of the century.

For Gladstone himself, for whom the Home Rule crusade was of such paramount and critical importance, there was some excuse for not heeding the risks or counting the cost. As he wrote forthwith to the Queen, in his letter requesting a dissolution, 'Mr Gladstone himself has no skill in these matters, and dare not lay an opinion before your Majesty on the probable general result.'[146] To continue the struggle by every means in their

---

* This needs stressing in view of Morley's insistence that 'the speech was a masterpiece, the temper of it unbroken, its freedom from taunt and bitterness and small personality incomparable'. Morley then proceeds to quote this attack on Chamberlain in the speech: 'I do not see how a dissolution can have any terrors for him. He has trimmed his vessel, and he has touched his rudder in such a masterly way, that in whichever direction the winds of heaven may blow they must fill his sails.' Chamberlain's provincial councils and federal schemes are then described as 'creations of a vivid imagination, born of the hour and perishing with the hour'. (Morley, *Gladstone*, III, pp.341–2)

† Morley tells how Gladstone 'at once opened the case with a list of twelve reasons for recommending dissolution, and the reasons were so cogent that his opening of the case was also its closing. . . . His conclusion was accepted without comment.' (*Gladstone*, III, pp.341–2)

power was natural and understandable in men like Gladstone and Morley. But in the case of the Harcourts and Laboucheres, who had no great faith in Home Rule, the forcing of a party split looked like the worst kind of political opportunism. And, whatever the motives of the Gladstonian leaders, they came to represent in practice the spirit of petty faction trading on the great name of their leader.

A revelation of the debased form of Gladstonian partisanship appeared in an article by 'A sanguine Radical' in the *Pall Mall Gazette* of 11 June outlining the Gladstonian strategy. 'We shall attack these Unionist gentlemen without mercy', it declared, 'and we shall manage to replace one-half, or at least one-third, of the 90 by Radicals who can be relied upon to vote straight without any nonsense.' The transfer of the Irish vote to the Gladstonians was expected to restore twenty-five seats, a net gain of fifty votes. Even if they were to lose, 'We have made up our minds to obstruct. . . . If they attempt to govern by coercion, they will find that before they have to coerce Ireland they will have to dragoon the House of Commons.'

Before the fatal division was taken, arrangements were being concluded which ought to have made the Gladstonians more cautious. Not only had a 'Unionist Committee' been formed, and liberally subscribed to, so that it could meet on equal terms any attempt to run candidates in opposition to Unionist Liberals: but also 'a tacit agreement' with the Conservatives was announced, 'as to an interchange of support where seats now held by Conservative or Unionist members are threatened by Home Rule candidates.'[147] 'In every constituency', another article announced, 'so far as the leaders of the party can manage it, no Unionist Liberal will be opposed by a Conservative candidate. Just reflect for a moment what that means.'[148] This was the origin of the 'Compact' which preserved the Liberal Unionists in a state of symbiosis with the Conservatives for decades.

But at first it was not at all certain how the arrangement would work in practice. The Liberal Unionists had lost the Caucus, and were dependent for any retaliation that might be necessary upon the subscriptions that flowed in to Hartington, and upon the 'eloquent young men' of the Eighty Club. Chamberlain, however, could not envisage political life without a local machine, and he set about forming a Unionist organization of his own:

Chamberlain–Arthur Chamberlain, 4 June 1886: Up to the present time
I have not been able to join the Unionist Committee. I propose to do
so as soon as the division takes place on the second reading.

I am not at all indisposed to the idea of forming a separate committee
with headquarters at Birmingham, but I have been too busy to decide
on this. Will you talk it over with a few friends? Would you take the
Chairmanship with half a dozen men to help you? The object of course
would be partly electoral—that is, the usual Caucus work—partly
educational, to promote the federal plan which I have been advocating.[149]

The object he defined in another letter as 'To secure the extension
of local government on similar principles to all parts of the
United Kingdom under the supreme authority of the imperial
Parliament.' Writing again after the government defeat, he hit
on the name 'National Radical Union'.[150] He had sent a paragraph to all the papers, and decided to subscribe £1,000 and
invite all his forty-six Radical M.P.s in the Home Rule Bill division
to be vice-presidents. A tricky point was the relations of the
new Union with the Liberal Federation. 'We cannot of course
influence the Tories,' he writes, 'but we ought not to be the first
to attack Liberal seats. What I am told is that the Home Rulers
will attack us if the Tories attack Broadhurst or Cook. In this
case we must take off the gloves, but if they let us alone we must
stand aside.'[151] A further question at Birmingham was whether
Bright would associate himself with the new organization. 'You
can ask Bright,' Chamberlain wrote to his brother, 'but he will
decline.' Bright's refusal is full of the misgivings of a man who
did not see his way in the new era that was opening:

Bright–Arthur Chamberlain, 15 June 1886: I think we have now a large
control over our own domestic business, and that little more is
required. Something of municipalities for the country districts, or
county divisions, seems all that is wanting, and this question is scarcely
so important as we have sometimes imagined it to be. . . .

Will not your proposed association have the appearance, and will it
not be in fact, a rival to the existing Liberal Association or Federation;
and will it not add to the confusion into which Mr Gladstone has so
unfortunately plunged us?

I have never had much faith in the Federation movement, and now that it has cast off its founders or devoured its leaders, and prostrated itself and the Liberal party before a minister who in our view has been guilty of a great error, I have not courage or faith to enter upon a new crusade. Will you have another Mr Schnadnorst, and shall we have a continual war between the two Secretaries and the two Presidents? . . .

Perhaps I am lost or blinded in the fog which surrounds us.[152]

Bright's general foreboding was to prove all too true. Chamberlain imagined that Gladstone would retire soon after being defeated at the polls, and that the schism would then heal. For a year he was destined to cherish this hope and work for such a solution. His attitude to the election was defensive. But the government's defeat unleashed against him a storm of virulent calumny. Gladstone himself openly bore a grudge, seemingly from some fixed idea that his 'federal' scheme was not genuine nor consistent with his earlier scheme, and that he was pursuing an opportunist policy. Thus, although Hartington was equally involved in advising the electors to vote Tory rather than Gladstonian, it was for Chamberlain that special condemnation was reserved. 'There is this difference between Hartington and Chamberlain,' Gladstone confided to Granville, 'that the first behaves like and is a thorough gentleman. Of the other it is better not to speak.'[153] This prejudice, translated into the vernacular of the Gladstonian journals, brought down on Chamberlain years of malignant abuse from which his reputation still suffers.

The election campaign of the Gladstonians took the form of an attack on the dissentient Liberals rather than a positive exposition of the principles of Home Rule, about which they did not commit themselves:

Chamberlain–Bunce, 21 June 1886: I fear you are too sanguine as to any possible reconciliation.

Mr Gladstone has never really given the least intimation of any willingness to meet his Liberal opponents. On the contrary he has exhausted himself in sneers at the folly of our objections, and the impracticability of our alternative.

He has allowed intermediaries without responsibility to suggest concessions or modifications which he has adopted without any reference to us, and his object has evidently been to detach our followers and not to meet the difficulties of the leaders.

If he would say clearly what are the principal provisions of the legislation he intends to propose in the autumn, we should know where we are. What about the Land Bill, for instance? What about the case of Ulster? About the judges, and the provisions for maintaining the criminal law? About the financial arrangements, and the two Houses and minority representation?

These are the points of difference, and it is unfair to go to the country with no definite policy in respect to them.[154]

When the first election results were out, and appeared unfavourable, Gladstone for the first time seriously entertained the idea that he might find himself in a slight minority.[155] The full returns disclosed a Unionist majority of 118 over the Gladstonians and Nationalists.

Gladstone's action had recreated a multi-party system. No party commanded a majority in the Commons, and it was not at all certain whether Salisbury, Hartington, or Gladstone could form an administration. Gladstone could have had a fair majority if he reconciled the Unionist Liberals. Kimberley hoped they would keep Gladstone in office, and Granville mentioned 'the possibility that the Seceders (who are by no means deficient in hatred to the Tories!) may, alarmed at the Tory strength, prefer our remaining in Government utterly crippled to letting in Salisbury'.[156] But, for Gladstone, 'The idea of dealing with Chamberlain or his fluctuating schemes is surely out of the question'.[157] He meant to stick to his own scheme. That would of course mean a parliamentary defeat if he went on. Harcourt nevertheless advocated continuance in office: so that as he told Gladstone, 'the seceders should be compelled to *vote you out*'. Gladstone, however, demurred at the idea that 'the new Parliament should begin by solemnly committing itself against Home Rule'.[158] On 20 July he persuaded the cabinet to resign without meeting Parliament.

Chamberlain maintained that there could be no *rapprochement* between himself and Gladstone while the latter clung at all costs to his Home Rule scheme. He put his views quite openly before Harcourt:

Chamberlain–Harcourt, 19 July 1886: I assume that the government will resign, and that Lord Salisbury will come in. . . .

It may be that the differences between us were too great to be bridged over, but certainly I do not think that any effort was made to test this point. At the general election I think you were also deceived by Schnadhorst and others. The armchair politicians defeated you this time, and if there had been no Unionist Liberals in the field the result would have been much the same. Your policy was thoroughly unpopular. Hardly anyone defended it, and your only cards were the popularity of the old man and the strength of party feeling. . . .

The situation is a curious one. There is a majority for the Liberal party, and an immense majority against the policy of its leader. Mr Gladstone's view appears to be to widen the split, and to drive all his former supporters either out of politics or over to the Tories. The result would be to secure to the Tories a long lease of power. I am sanguine that the common sense of the majority will make this impossible. But time is needed to heal the wounds which recent events have made. Personally I look forward to an easy time for the next two years, during which my natural modesty and love for retirement will have full opportunity of exhibiting themselves.[159]

In his reply Harcourt mentioned the possibility of renewed obstruction and the likely expulsion of the Irish members. 'That of course would only be the beginning of the end, for I fancy even you are hardly ripe for *Crown Colony* policy.' He still clung to the axiom that to propose any Irish legislation which the Parnellite party would not accept 'was, and always will be, futile'.[160] Here was the real touchstone of difference, and Chamberlain wrote a harsh but unequivocal observation on the future. He had never identified the Parnellites with the Irish people, and now he said of the former, '. . . if they yield to the temptation to commit either Parliamentary or personal outrages, they must be crushed, and I for one will not be deterred from advocating the strongest coercion by any fear of the unpopularity of the word'.[161]

Unknown to the Gladstonians, Chamberlain had already, before the general election, reached a kind of agreement with the Conservatives. In an informal conversation with Balfour on 13 June, he had avowed that 'Our great object must be to get rid of Gladstone'. If the Conservatives came in, he said, Gladstone would probably go, while if a Liberal Unionist government were formed he would be tempted to stay and make mischief. Chamberlain at this time rightly foretold that Hartington would not want to take office in a coalition government, but believed that the Liberal Unionists might keep Salisbury in office by informal support. 'My idea is that you should form a Government with a definite and complete understanding with Hartington, and an adequate though less complete understanding with me.'[162] And so it transpired. This was to be roughly the basis of things up to 1895, when at last Chamberlain and Hartington (or Devonshire as he had become) took office under Salisbury. The essence of the Liberal Unionist–Conservative alliance was the electoral 'compact' concerning seats. Otherwise, the two parties maintained separate organizations.

The history of the Liberal Unionist organization illustrates the maxim that nothing is more permanent than the provisional. Hartington's Committee for the Maintenance of the Union was formed *pro tempore* and might have been disbanded if he had taken office. But Hartington, though offered the premiership in a coalition government, decided that his following would be best preserved if he remained in an independent position and avoided a separation from Chamberlain. He took this decision on 24 July, when his Committee assumed the name of the Liberal Unionist Association and embarked on the task of forming local organizations. Hartington had decided like Chamberlain to have his own Caucus. Close relations were established between his body and Chamberlain's National Radical Union, and the two became in time inextricably merged. Their purpose was to maximize the electoral support of different classes of voters, from the respectable supporters of the Whigs to the artisans who could never vote Tory. The more diverse the 'catchment areas' the better. Moreover, Hartington expected to resume the Liberal inheritance with Chamberlain on Gladstone's retirement, and then to recreate the Whig–Radical dichotomy. Meanwhile it was clear that the Liberal Unionists could bring most strength to Salisbury's government by preserving the appearance of being a separate party, willing to save Salisbury from resignation but prepared to vote against him on some questions.

The arrangement was particularly difficult for Chamberlain to operate, even on a temporary basis. Hartington could easily support Salisbury, sharing the belief that Ireland needed twenty years of resolute government. But Chamberlain was pledged to a constructive solution in Ireland, and he became the particular target of both Parnell and the Gladstonians. He wished to avoid getting involved in disputes with the latter, which would destroy the chances of re-union. What he wanted was to weather out the situation until Gladstone retired, as he explains at this time:

Chamberlain–Collings, 29 July 1886. [The situation] is dominated by the question of Mr Gladstone's action. If he retired, all would come right pretty quickly. If he remains, it is no use issuing manifestoes or anything else. All action intensifies differences which it is our object to remove, and I believe we must 'lie low' till the inevitable disappearance of the G.O.M. from the scene.[163]

It was of course very difficult to imagine that Gladstone might continue to wield the menace of Home Rule, as he did, until 1894. Nor could Chamberlain foresee that the Gladstonians would do everything they could to make it impossible for him to rejoin them.

CHAPTER FIVE

Chamberlain and Beatrice Webb

In his relation to me there has been a strange lack of chivalry and honour. In mine to him, of womanly dignity.

Beatrice Webb's diary, 9 June 1889

AMONG Chamberlain's letters to his closest friends—Morley, Collings, Dilke, and others—and even to his relations, the biographer does not find 'personal' passages, or indeed anything that throws light upon his 'private' life. There was no less introspective a politician, and all his writings are of one piece, practical, sometimes humorous, but always decisive, objective, devoid of inner uncertainty or debate. The apparent Chamberlain was the real Chamberlain, and all the energies and interests of the private man went into his public life. He had no time for a purely domestic life, and the common characteristic of his wives was that they were women devoted to his political activities. When in 1883 Chamberlain—then twice a widower, his second wife having died eight years before—met the vivacious and witty Miss Beatrice Potter (later Mrs Sidney Webb), the clash of two dominant personalities produced a most unfortunate incompatability. Although he was looking for a wife, and very nearly became engaged to Miss Potter, Chamberlain could find little time to pursue the courtship, and he made not the slightest concession to Beatrice Potter's very different intellectual background, or to her demands for freedom to discuss critically his cherished opinions. On her side, it must be said, there was a total ignorance of Chamberlain's previous career, and a gulf that separated the cabinet minister of forty-seven from the cloistered and bookish young woman of twenty-five. Miss Potter, friend and devotee of Herbert Spencer, had also something of the priggish arrogance of the doctrinaire feminist of those days. Her descriptions of Chamberlain and their encounters need to be taken with caution. Nevertheless, they afford some of the most revealing impressions of him that have been recorded: and if any moral is to be drawn from them, it is that Chamberlain lacked the elasticity to modify his habitual manner and preoccupations even for a courtship.

Her first impression of him was characteristic. In June 1883 she dined with Chamberlain on one hand and a Whig peer on the other. 'The Whig peer talked of his own possessions, Chamberlain *passionately* of getting hold of other peoples' for the masses. Curious and interesting character, dominated by "intellectual passions", with little self-control but with any amount of *purpose.*'[164] Two months later Beatrice spent a whole week with Chamberlain's eldest daughter, also Beatrice, 'a quiet, genuine woman'. Recording the episode in her diary, Miss Potter soliloquizes on the question of whether Chamberlain is an honest politician or the demagogue for which he tends to be taken in polite circles:

26 September 1883: Coming from such honest surroundings, he surely *must* be straight in intention. . . . Much might be learnt in studying the life and thought of such a man, discovering how *representative* he was, how much his convictions were the result of individual characteristics, and how much they were the effect of surrounding circumstances. They *are convictions passionately held*, his whole energy is thrown into the attempt to realize them. Is the basis of those convictions honest experience and thought, or were they originally the tools of ambition, now become inextricably woven into love of power, and to his own mind no longer distinguishable from it? What is his principle?[165]

So speculates the politically jejune mind of the raw Spencerian: no happy augury for the success of the critical encounter that took place in January 1884, when Chamberlain appeared at the Potter's house at Standish. But it was Chamberlain who, by her account, was most curiously deficient in the manner appropriate *à la recherche d'une femme*:

January 1884: After six weeks of feverish indecision, the day comes. House full of young people, and the three last days passed in dancing and games: I feel all the while as if I were dancing in a dream towards some precipice.

[Saturday 5th]: remainder of the ball party chatting round the afternoon tea table, the great man's son and daughter amongst them. The door opens, 'Mr Chamberlain', general uprising.

I advance from amongst them, and in my nervousness almost press six pounds, just received, into his hand. General feeling of discomfort;

no one quite understanding the reason of Mr Chamberlain's advent. . . .

At dinner, after some shyness, we plunge into essentials, and he begins to delicately hint his requirements. That evening and the next morning till lunch, we are on 'susceptible terms'.

A dispute over state education breaks the charm. 'It is a question of authority with women, if you believe in Herbert Spencer you won't believe in me.' This opens the battle. By silent arrangement we find ourselves in the garden.

'It pains me to hear any of my views controverted', and with this preface he begins with stern exactitude to lay down the articles of his political creed. I remain modestly silent; but noticing my silence, he remarks that he requires 'intelligent sympathy' from women.

'Servility, Mr Chamberlain,' think I; not sympathy, but intelligent servility: what many women give men, but the difficulty lies in changing one's master, in jumping from one *tone* of thought to the exact opposite—*with intelligence*. And then I advance as boldly as I dare my feeble objections to his general proposition, feeling that in this case, I owe it to the man to show myself and be absolutely sincere. He refutes my objections by re-asserting his convictions passionately, his expression becoming every minute more gloomy and determined. He tells me the history of his political career, how his creed grew up on a basis of experience and sympathy; how his desire to benefit 'the many' had become gradually a passion absorbing within itself his whole nature.[166]

As they wandered up and down the paths of the garden, Chamberlain showed 'not a suspicion of feeling' towards his nervous and politically unsophisticated partner. But one can see that there was misunderstanding on both sides. 'If I remained silent', Miss Potter notes, 'he watched my expression narrowly, I felt his curious scrutinizing eyes noting each movement, as if he were anxious to ascertain whether I yielded to his absolute supremacy.' He 'smashed objection and qualification by an absolute denial'. This was not Chamberlain's usual manner, and one senses an extreme anxiety on his part to find a common ground, and dispel the false atmosphere created by the young woman's lack of understanding and sympathy. As they came in he remarked that he felt as if he had been making a speech, while Beatrice felt 'utterly exhausted'.

The next morning the scene was repeated, but this time Chamberlain ended it on a note of peremptory irritation. The credulity of the young feminist was too much, as—appears in the brief dialogue she recalls:

Chamberlain: I have only one domestic trouble, my sister and daughter are bitten with the women's rights mania. I don't allow any action on the subject.
Beatrice: You don't allow division of opinion in your household, Mr Chamberlain?
Chamberlain: I can't help people *thinking* differently from me.
Beatrice: But you don't allow the expression of the difference?
Chamberlain: No.
And that little word ended our intercourse.[167]

It was an artificial relationship, not improved by Chamberlain's wooden manner: and so it was to remain, through their infrequent encounters during the next three years. There is a dimension missing from Beatrice Potter's perception of her 'great man'. He appears in her descriptions as a zealot governed by self-centred and power-loving impulses. And although she came to confess herself as desperately in love with him, there was no friendship or understanding between them. She worshipped, and suffered, at the feet of an idol, a daemonic personality, which was largely the figment of her own imagination. She knew, and regretted, that 'absorption in the peculiar nature of our relationship left me so little capable of taking the opportunities he gave me of knowing him'.[168] But if she failed to discover the genuine idiom and purpose of Chamberlain's career, she possessed a penetrating vision for the external traits and apparent or real weaknesses of the man whose political personality had such a fascination for her. Her vignettes of Chamberlain and his household are caricatures, with the truth and distortion of the bold and brilliantly overdrawn descriptive style she develops in her diary.

The impression which Beatrice set down immediately after Chamberlain's stay at Standish was of an 'enthusiast and a despot', someone who transposed everything into black and white and would crush all opposition to his will. 'The political creed is the whole man: the outcome of his peculiar physical and mental temperament, played upon by the experiences of his life.' He was no thinker, reasoning from an impartial survey of evidence or from set principles. His power rested 'on his intuitive knowledge of the wishes of a certain class' and his faculty of 're-impressing those wishes forcibly on a mass of indifferent-minded men'.[169] He hated the idea of moderation or empiricism in politics, preferring to believe that he was right and his adversaries wrong:

January 1884: In this belief he, as a man with a vigorous reason, occasionally feels shaken. If it were to fall the rationale of the whole tenor of his thought and action would be destroyed. Therefore he hates the moderate man, the man who refuses to allow that political principles are a question of morality, and asserts that they should be the result of exercising your reason on certain disputable facts. He prefers the adversary who regards him as the incarnation of the evil one and answers his cold sneers with virulent abuse.

Enthusiasm and self-will are the dominant forces in Chamberlain's mind. A keen, calculating intellect, admirable in manipulating practical detail and in adapting the means to the end, considerable diplomatic power and personal influence over men, are the instruments whereby he effects his objects.[170]

Chamberlain was, in fact, the complete antithesis to Beatrice Potter's ideal of the dispassionate social investigator, which her later career was to realize, though not without evidence of an authoritarian streak in her own character.

Before the month was out, Beatrice ventured on a visit to Highbury to see 'Democracy at home'. 'Receiving a pressing letter from Miss Chamberlain, and feeling convinced that the negotiation was off,' she 'saw no harm' in going to Birmingham for two days 'to watch the great man at home'.[171] Highbury, built elaborately of red brick with numberless bay windows and long glass orchid houses, did not at first strike Beatrice as a very attractive place:

January–February 1884: Inside there is very *much taste*, and all very bad. At first you admire the bright softness of the colouring, and the general luxurious comfort of the rooms and furniture, but after four and twenty hours the whole palls on you, and you long for a bare floor and a plain deal table.

The two Miss Chamberlains sit ill-at-ease in the midst of the luxury. They are dressed with the dowdiness of the middle class, and are both of them simple and genuine, naturally inclined for hard work and simple fare, and loving the easy intercourse of family life and intimate friendships. From the great man they get conversation but little sympathy, possibly they don't give it. He comes and goes, asks his friends and entertains them, and sees little of his womenkind. In Birmingham they make kindly homely hostesses, and are useful to him; in London they are glum, and sit silently between the distinguished men who dine with the future 'Prime Minister', and try in vain to interest and be interested in the fashionable worldly-wise wives who stay the correct time in their drawing room. . . .

. . . a gloom overhangs the 'Home'. The drawing room with its elaborately carved marble arches, its satin paper, rich hangings and choice water colours, has a forlornly grand appearance.[172]

Here, on a Tuesday afternoon,* Beatrice found the whole family, except its head, assembled to receive her. Chamberlain has to make a speech in the town that evening, along with Bright. 'Presently', Beatrice recounts, 'the great man himself emerges from his glass houses and gives me a constrainedly polite welcome. Are we about to take part in a funeral procession, think I, and sink oppressed into a perfectly constructed armchair.' John Bright appears, and seems to know of the young woman who is introduced to him: he is reminded that he knew her grandfather. 'The old man is too miserable and restless with the prospect of the evening to sink quietly into his favourite topic—reminiscences of the past—and presently he leaves the room. "There is one consolation for me", remarks Mr Chamberlain as he gets up to follow him. "Bright's in a terrible fidget, he is a good deal worse than I. Miss Potter, I shall reserve the orchid house for tomorrow, and then I shall do the honours myself. I don't want my sister to take you there"—and he forthwith retired to his library.'[173]

At dinner all are subdued. A guest from Liverpool 'fawns upon and flatters Chamberlain till I feel inclined to shriek with nervous irritation'. Austen Chamberlain, 'a big fair-haired youth of handsome feature and open countenance, and sunny, sympathetic temperament', is deputed by his father to escort the womenkind to the town hall. Arriving there, Chamberlain's guests are placed in the front seats of the balcony overlooking the platform:

A long row of Chamberlains and Kenricks continue our line. The men

---

* Other sources indicate that this is 29 January 1884.

look earnest and honest, the great man's brothers perhaps have a bit
of the cad in dress and manner; the women are plain and un-pretentious,
essentially ungraceful, might be labelled 'for use and not for ornament',
and are treated accordingly. Arthur Chamberlain, by whom I sit,
instructs me concerning the Liberal Association, describes to me the
theory of the organization, and points out proudly as proving [its]
representative character . . . strong-featured artisans and mechanics
scattered amongst the sheepish-looking individuals who compose the
majority.[174]

The representatives of the Caucus are arrayed behind the platform.
In front, below the balcony, some thousands of men stand,
packed close together and fenced by strong barriers. Faint cheers
greet a favourite member of the Nine Hundred as he seats himself.
The band strikes up, and the three members for the town come
on to the platform, Bright first, then the rabbit-like Muntz,
'comically out of place as a materialized vacuum' between Bright
and Chamberlain, who is received with deafening shouts.

As Chamberlain rose to speak, the crowd became wild with
enthusiasm, and hats, handkerchiefs, even coats, were waved
frantically, in an uproar of applause, until, 'exhausted and
expectant', the cheering subsided into fitful and murmuring
cries. 'At the first sound of his voice they became as one man.
Into the tones of his voice he threw the warmth and feeling which
was lacking in his words, and every thought, every feeling, the
slightest intonation of irony and contempt was reflected in the
face of the crowd.'[175] Such was the Chamberlain style, which
could make even his pronunciation of the names of his opponents
iridescent with feeling.

After the speeches, Chamberlain entertained twenty members
of the Caucus at supper. He sat silent, 'in a state of suppressed
exaltation, acutely sensitive to sympathy or indifference even
from an outsider'. From the talk of the guests, Beatrice gathered
that his authority over the organization was absolute. The
Chamberlain–Kenrick household 'stand far above the town in
social functions, wealth and culture, and yet they spend their
lives as quiet citizens taking an active and leading part in the
municipal, political and educational life of their town. . . .' Their
eternal refrain was that Birmingham society was 'superior in
earnestness, sincerity and natural intelligence' to any other, and

Beatrice conceded that 'earnestness and simplicity of nature' were strikingly present in the family. One could make a religion out of politics in Birmingham, in a way that would not have been possible amid the 'somewhat cynical or at any rate indefinitely varied and qualified political opinions of London society'. Chamberlain made a virtue out of provincialism. But what could account for his ascendancy over the whole town?

... the submission then of the whole town to his autocratic rule arises from his power of dealing with different types of men: of enforcing submission by high-handed arbitrariness, attracting devotion by the mesmeric quality of his passion, and manipulating the remainder through a wise presentation of their interests, and consideration for their petty weaknesses. ...
It is to this power that Chamberlain owes all the happiness of his life, and it is the reaction of this power which intensified his sympathies and also his egotism.[176]

The only sphere in which Chamberlain failed to manifest a talent for diplomacy was in his quest of a wife. But in this connection the diarist mentions a small incident which shows that the lack of diplomacy was conspicuous on both sides.

On the day following her arrival, Chamberlain conducted Beatrice Potter, as promised, round the orchid houses, his chief hobby in which his interest was well known. 'We wandered amongst his orchids, and he seemed curiously piqued, because I said that the only flowers I loved were wild flowers, and at dinner apologized to me for my own want of tact!' Little wonder that Beatrice, who was handing out remarks of this kind, got the impression that Chamberlain was unduly concerned about finding points on which she agreed with him. 'That evening', she continues, 'I felt that susceptibility was increasing. It did not show itself in any desire to *please me*, but in an intense desire that I should *think and feel like him* (even in small details of taste), by a jealousy of other influences, especially that of the old philosopher Herbert Spencer, and in his serious attempts to drag me into his interests.'[177] After this occasion, they did not meet for some time. 'Of the simple spontaneous love', she recorded, 'there was nought between us. He has it not to give, and my feeling for him was gradually created within me by mixed motives.'[178]

In spite of the disheartening experience of her visit to High-bury, Beatrice Potter remained absorbed in her passion for Chamberlain. 'The commonplaces of love', she notes, 'have always bored me. But Joseph Chamberlain, with his gloom and serious-ness, with absence of any gallantry or faculty for saying pretty nothings, the simple way in which he assumes, almost asserts, that you stand on a level far beneath him, and that all that concerns you is trivial; that you yourself are without importance in the world except in so far as you might be related to him; this sort of courtship (if it is to be called courtship) fascinates, at least, my imagination.'[179] A little later she records: 'His temperament and his character are intensely attractive to me. I feel I could relieve the gloom, could understand the mixed motive and the difficulties of a nature in which genuine enthusiasm and personal ambition are so curiously interwoven.'[180] Her proud and independent nature had been challenged by the masterful and dominating personality of a man old enough to be her father. But he required 'subordination and absolute dependence', and after pointing out the hardships of the life of a politician's wife, he had said that 'only devotion to my aims would justify you in accepting it'.[181] She felt no such devotion, did not believe in the usefulness of his career, and indeed had to twist her reasoning even to tolerate what he stood for. She was still far removed from the knowledge of politics and social problems she was to achieve in her Fabian years. At this time her viewpoint was naïve and detached. Chamberlain stood for despotism. While, she affirmed, 'I hate every form of despotism. My admiration first for Goethe, then for Herbert Spencer, rested on their great faith in natural development.'[182]

Chamberlain the despot remained true to the role he had been cast in when they met again in July 1885. Leonard Courtney, an old acquaintance of Chamberlain's and a fellow Radical, was married to Beatrice's sister. Beatrice could not understand why Chamberlain should have to oppose with such determination Courtney's scheme for proportional representation. At a dinner party to which Chamberlain had been invited, she records how he declared, 'looking at me intently to see how I took it, "Your brother-in-law is an ass. Proportional representation lost him his chance of distinction in political life, *this* [voting against a medical relief Bill] has lost him his seat." ' The Courtneys arranged a picnic for a day the following week, 'on purpose we should meet'. The result was another bitter disappointment:

That day will always remain engraved on my memory as the most painful one of my life. The scene under the Burnham beeches, forcing me to tell his fortune, afterwards behaving with marked rudeness and indifference. The great reception given to him at the station, we all running after him like so many little dogs, his mysterious hint that he would consider it his duty to prevent the return of men like Leonard Courtney.[183]

On their return home, the Courtneys, 'pained at my evident misery, having spent time and also money they could ill spare on this meaningless party', opened their letters and found their attention drawn to a public appeal from 'Chamberlain's henchman' Jesse Collings, begging all true Liberals to vote against Courtney as a renegade.

After this incident, Beatrice attempted in vain to extricate herself from the emotional entanglement she had got into. Part of the trouble was her friendships with Clara Ryland, Chamberlain's sister, and Beatrice Chamberlain, his eldest daughter, so that she received constant invitations to Highbury. She contrived to go there when Chamberlain was absent, but even so, the family were aware of her plight. One evening, in the winter of 1885, she recounts, 'when I was sobbing so bitterly, I heard Clara talking to him [Mr Ryland] in a low voice below—and at the time I little doubted that he was told all. I don't think I resented it—what is pride beside true, deep feeling. True, deep feeling, that never leaves one's mind in placid rest, but keeps the depths stirred, and tinges all one's thoughts with deep emotion. Will the pain of it ever cease?'[184]

It was at this time that Beatrice Potter began to cut herself off from the fashionable world, and, pursuing her philosophic interests into the social sciences, began also to take a part in the researches into poverty and slum conditions which were claiming an increasing share of public attention. She took employment in an East End sweat shop in order to study the ways and mentality of the 'depressed tenth', and achieved a sudden but anonymous notoriety when in February 1886 her experiences were published in the *Pall Mall Gazette* as 'A Lady's view of the Unemployed at the East End'. This brought upon her another poignant encounter with her 'evil genius'. Chamberlain, now in office for a brief interim at the Board of Trade, was confronted with the problem of acute unemployment in the East End. He was concerned to find a means of helping the unemployed who refused to have recourse to the Poor Law. Noticing her publication, he wrote briefly:

25 February 1886: Dear Miss Potter,
    Will you be at home on Sunday afternoon, and if so may I come and talk to you about the distress at the East End? I read your letter with great interest and agreement, and should very much like to know your experiences. I hope Mr Potter is stronger again.
    I am, Yours very truly, J. Chamberlain.[185]

To this request Beatrice replied from Bournemouth, protesting that her knowledge of the East End was 'superficial', evidently sceptical of Chamberlain's wish to consult her seriously. She did, however, make a suggestion that foreshadowed the future labour exchanges. 'We practical workers', she wrote, 'have one great desire, perhaps because we are too ignorant to appreciate the difficulties of the undertaking, a wish that there should be some systematic investigation of unemployment on the one hand, and of labour on the other.' She deplored the indiscriminate charity of the Mansion House fund, which did 'an incalculable amount of mischief'.[186] Brought up in the most rigorous school of Malthus and Herbert Spencer, she had no short-term remedy for distress.* Chamberlain had hardly any better idea of how to deal with unemployment, and answered her letter with an argument very significant of his position with regard to socialism:

Chamberlain–Beatrice Potter, 28 February 1886: Pray do not think that I can have too much information on the subject on which I consulted

---

* Her extreme position may be seen in her rejection of all state intervention implied in the following comment (*My Apprenticeship*, p.166) of July 1884: 'I object to these gigantic experiments, state education and state intervention in other matters, which are now being inaugurated . . . they seem to me . . . the crude prescriptions of social quacks seeking to relieve vague feelings of pain and discomfort experienced by the masses.'

you. I know that you have much experience, and that you are not 'crotchety', and you will find me ready to profit by your suggestions. . . .

My department knows all about paupers and pauperism, but has no official cognisance of distress above the pauper line. Yet this is surely the serious part of the problem . . . the suffering of the industrious non-pauper class is very great and is increasing. . . .

I cannot think that any registration of labour would be more than a trifling convenience. Whenever there is work wanted, workers will find it out very quickly for themselves. If the distress becomes greater, something *must* be done to make work. The rich must pay to keep the poor alive.

My idea is that the workhouse is for the old, infirm, and the chronic paupers. . . . The test must be maintained for these classes.

But for the workman who has been in ordinary constant employment, and who . . . finds himself on the verge of starvation, it will be necessary in each district to find some poorly remunerated employment which:

a. will not tempt him in any way to remain in it longer than is absolutely necessary.

b. will not be degrading in its character,

c. will not enter into competitition with workers at present in employment, and

d. is of such a kind that every workman . . . can turn his hand to it.

There is only one kind of work which answers these conditions, and that is spade labour . . . works of sewage, extra street cleaning, laying out recreation grounds, etc.

. . . I wish you would tell me when you have time what you think of these rather crude suggestions.[187]

Beatrice found even this guarded admission of state responsibility for preserving the lives of the unemployed who were too proud to accept poor relief more than she could concede. Her reply shows that her doubts as to the usefulness of Chamberlain's policies arose from suppositions altogether different from those with which she became associated in her later career. She was still an exponent of the starkest social Darwinism and *laissez-faire*. And her letter was couched in terms of self-conscious deference tinged with a slightly facetious but nevertheless genuine diffidence on the sore point of women's political views:

Beatrice Potter–Chamberlain, 4 March 1886: You take me out of my depth! . . . As I read your letter a suspicion flashed across me that you wished for some further proof of the incapacity of a woman's intellect to deal with such large matters. . . .

I agree that 'the rich *must* keep the poor alive'; always supposing that the continued existence of that section of the poor with liberty to increase is *not* injurious to the community at large. And this depends primarily on facts of which *I* have no knowledge. . . . If the depression be due to a permanent relapse from the abnormal activity produced by the extension of railways, etc., depopulation is to some extent a necessity? . . .

I fail to grasp the principle 'something must be done'. It is terribly sad that 100 men should die in semi-starvation—should prefer that slow death to the almost penal servitude offered them by the work-house—but quite apart from the community's point of view, if by relieving these 100 men you practically create 500 more, surely the unsatisfactory nature of these men's lives outweighs in misery the death of the smaller number? . . . Death after all is a slight evil compared to life under many conditions. We hear the death groans of the 100, we do not hear the life groans of the 500 until it is too late! If I am wrong, it is not from shallow-heartedness, but because I have not sufficient intelligence to see how the measures you propose would work. . . .

I have no proposal to make, except sternness from the state, and love and self-devotion from individuals—a very sad and self-evident remedy.

But is it not rather unkind of you to ask me to tell you what I think? I have tried to be perfectly truthful. Still, it is a ludicrous idea that an ordinary woman should be called upon to review the suggestions of Her Majesty's ablest minister, especially when I know that he has a slight opinion of even a superior woman's intelligence in these matters—I agree with him—and a dislike of any independence of thought. . . .[188]

Chamberlain might have read this missive with equanimity, even conplacency, for its artificial deference ill-concealed an undertone of real lack of confidence and of submission. But instead, it drew from him a stiff and wounding rejoinder. One can think of many excuses for him. He was in the throes of the greatest crisis of his career, overworked and harassed. He doubtless also was hurt by the revival of the argument that he was intolerant of freedom of thought, and of the suggestion that he was after a wife who should be a mental cypher. One does not know how deep his disappointment was after the failure of this courtship. But for all that, he responded with the stoicism but also with the wooden formality and inflexibility characteristic of his personal relations in general:

Chamberlain–Beatrice Potter, 5 March 1886: I thought we understood each other pretty well. I fear I was mistaken. In the hurry of this life it is not easy to get a clear conception of any other person's principles and opinions.

But you are quite wrong in supposing that I under-value the opinions of an intelligent woman. There are many questions on which I would follow it blindly, although I dislike the flippant self-sufficiency of some female politicians.

Neither do I dislike independence of thought. On the contrary, the only men with whom I have cordially worked are men of striking originality of ideas—a very rare but a most reliable quality in man or woman.

Of course eccentricity is not true originality, and fertility of resource is a very different quality to the ignorant self-confidence which assumes that virtue.

I hardly know why I defend myself, for I admit that it does not matter what I think or feel on those subjects.

On the main question, your letter is discouraging, but I fear it is true. I shall go on, however, as if it were not true, for if we once admit the impossibility of remedying the evils of society, we shall all sink below the level of the brutes. Such a creed is the justification of absolute unadulterated selfishness; and so we must go on rolling the stone up the hill, even though it is almost certain that it will roll down again, and perhaps crush us.

I do not think your practical objections to public work . . . are conclusive . . . If men will starve rather than dig for 2/- a day, I cannot help them, and I cannot greatly pity them.

It will remove one great danger, viz. that public sentiment should go wholly over to the unemployed, and render impossible that state sternness to which you and I equally attach importance. By offering reasonable work at the lowest wage to the really industrious, we may secure the power of being very strict with the loafer and the confirmed pauper.

I thank you for writing so fully, and do not expect any further answer. . . .[189]

Wounded by the laconic style of this letter, and seeing personal innuendoes in it which possibly were not intended, Beatrice sent back an agonized note in these terms:

Now I see I was right not to deceive you. I could not lie to the man I

loved. But why have worded it so cruelly, why give unnecessary pain?
Surely we suffer sufficiently. Thank God! that when our own happiness
is destroyed, there are others to live for. Do not think that I do not
consider your decision as *final*, and destroy this.[190]

Finality, however, had not yet arrived. Neither Chamberlain
nor Miss Potter wished to break off the relationship entirely. In
September 1886, Beatrice notes: 'Spent two days castle building
about the great man at Highbury, and re-read that episode of
six months ago. He either has a courteous wish to show that he
has forgotten, or he does not wish to lose all hold on me; for he
half asked through Beatrice [Chamberlain] for an invitation here
(which he did not get), and sent for my opinion about an East
End charity.' A month later she has another Highbury visit to
record, again without meeting her 'hero'. By the end of the year
she had 'six or seven times . . . refused his overtures, made
directly or through his family', and she decided to cut herself
off entirely from the Chamberlain family, although admitting
that 'in a strangely blundering fashion they have tried to treat me
well—to smooth down my hurt feelings by respect and admiration'. But the resolution did not last, and in June 1887, after
attending a Birmingham meeting at which Chamberlain spoke,
she met him and his daughter at Arthur Chamberlain's house.
'Result—invited him to come and see father, and enjoy bracing
air and beautiful scenery. In six weeks the great man comes!'

At the end of July, Chamberlain spent a day at The Argoed, the
Potters' house on the Welsh coast. What exactly happened to cause
another misunderstanding is not recorded, but very likely things
followed the pattern of previous encounters, only complicated by
Beatrice's feeling that he ought not to cultivate her friendship,
now that she had declared herself, unless he intended to marry
her. She had already resented his behaviour towards her when they
met in June:

If he had treated me with simple respect when we met at his brother's
house, there would have been a reason in his advances. He could well
have said—'You told me to forget, and I thought you wished me to
mark my continued respect for you.' But he behaved towards me as the
triumphant lover—as a man who is sure of his conquest.[191]

Immediately after their meeting at The Argoed in July, she sent him another desperate note, reproving him for insisting on meeting 'a woman who had told you she loved you, in order to humiliate her further', telling him she cared for him 'passionately', and suggesting they should not meet again.[192] Chamberlain's reply, though guarded and somewhat stilted, at least made the concession of acknowledging some dependence on his part:

Chamberlain–Beatrice Potter, 3 August 1887: I thank you sincerely for your kind letter. I cannot help feeling depressed and discouraged at times, and I value greatly the sympathy which you have shown me.

The concluding part of your letter has given me much pain. Did I indeed do wrong in accepting your invitation? If so, forgive me, and allow me to tell you frankly what I feel. At your request I destroyed your letter of March 1886. There was one passage in it on which I did not presume to put a definite interpretation, and which I thought at the time was rather the outcome of a sensitive mind, overstrained by suffering and work, than the expression of settled feelings. I thought you had forgotten it, and wished me to forget it also.

So much for the past—now as to the future. Why are we never to see each other again? Why cannot we be friends—'camarades'—to use your own expression? I like you very much, I respect and esteem you, I enjoy your conversation and society, and I have often wished that fate had thrown us more together. If you share this feeling to any extent, why should we surrender a friendship which ought to be good for both of us?

I have so much confidence in your generosity as well as in your common sense, that I am encouraged to make this appeal to you in what I feel to be a very delicate matter.

The circumstances of my past life have made me solitary and reserved, but it is hard that I should lose one of the few friends whose just opinions I value, and the sense of whose regard and sympathy would be a strength and support to me.

I cannot say more. You must decide, and if it is for your happiness that we should henceforth be strangers, I will make no complaint.

I return your letter, as you wish it, but there is surely no reason why you should be ashamed of feelings which are purely womanly, and for which I have nothing but gratitude and respect.[193]

To this appeal Beatrice responded favourably: 'Of course I was weak and gave way again—weak and romantic. But he did not like the tone of my letter. Perhaps that has saved me from more entanglement.' Two months after this, Chamberlain sailed for the

United States on a diplomatic mission, where he met his third wife, a woman who believed in, and lived for, his political work.*

The portrait, or mosaic, of the private Chamberlain which may be pieced together from the diary of Beatrice Potter, is that of a man with 'one idea', his political monomania, to which everything else is subordinated. He had 'no faith in science, no understanding of its methods . . . no interest in philosophy or metaphysics, no care for music or poetic prose, no inkling of religion'.[194] To his political aims, Beatrice Potter did less than justice. Later she revised her opinion concerning his ambition and the vulgarity of his aims, and, looking back in 1901, she confesses that 'bound up in the pedantry of dogmatic individualism, I was then incapable of appreciating Chamberlain's intense desire to remedy the grosser forms of social misery'.[195] Her perceptions of Chamberlain's personal traits are more reliable. The positive qualities were 'energy and personal magnetism, in a word masculine force to an almost superlative degree',[196] organizing ability and diplomatic skill.

But associated with these was an 'intense egotism, showing

---

* Of the last of Chamberlain's visits Beatrice Webb comments in her diary under 1 January 1901: '. . . he saw a woman, no longer young, living without the surroundings of wealth and social position, badly dressed and without any apparent distinction. And in spite of knowing that I loved him desperately, he turned away and left me.'

It would perhaps be as well to observe that the diary is coloured by her feelings for Chamberlain long after 1887 and after she met Sidney Webb, in January 1890, although 'from the first', she notes, 'I realized that he would fall in love with me'. She cautioned him that 'the chances are 100 to 1 that nothing follows but friendship', and privately comments: 'His tiny tadpole body, unhealthy skin, lack of manner, cockney pronunciation, poverty, are all against him. . . . This self-complacent egotism, this disproportionate view of his own position, is at once repulsive and ludicrous.' Later that year she commemorates 'The Day' (of Chamberlain's wedding) and congratulates herself that 'even the scar is well-nigh imperceptible'. But she rejected Sidney Webb's first proposals of marriage with the reasoning: 'I cannot bring myself to face an act of *felo de se* for a speculation in personal happiness. . . . Personal passion has burnt itself out, and what little exists still haunts the memory of that other man. Why did I watch for hours at the entrance of the South Kensington Museum for two days last summer, unless in the hope of seeing him—a deplorable weakness for which I despised myself too much to repeat [it] the third time?' She became engaged to Sidney at the Co-operative Congress of May 1891, but observes a month later: 'On the face of it it seems an extraordinary end for the once brilliant Beatrice Potter . . . to marry an ugly little man with no social position and less means. . . . And I am not "in love", not as I was. . . .'

itself on one side by a strong desire for personal power, on the other by a love of ease, luxury and splendour'. He was 'bitterly resentful of personal slight or personal injury', yet his 'intense sensitiveness to his own wrongs was not tempered by a corresponding sensitiveness to the feelings and the rights of others' [197]* This last impression, however, was largely the product of Beatrice Potter's almost total ignorance of the politics of the 1880's, which appears very strikingly in certain passages of her diary, making Chamberlain's opposition to men like Courtney appear like personal vendettas. She did not appreciate that during the years of their personal acquaintance he was engaged in some of the largest political struggles of the century, and that very much more turned on the details than she realized. But, all the same, the prolonged relationship disclosed a very real personal deficiency on Chamberlain's part. He could not see things from any viewpoint but his own, and he lacked imagination and elasticity to adapt his manner to the psychology of others. He preferred to antagonize and defeat his opponents rather than to win them over by conciliation.

---

* 'Epitaph' on Chamberlain entered at the end of 1888. Here the loss of Chamberlain's first wife is said to have been 'a death warrant to his faith in a Personal God'.

CHAPTER SIX

The Making of Unionism

I do not doubt that we may in the end succeed in raising, out of the clash of parties which has been brought about by the unfortunate action of Mr Gladstone, a party which is greater than all other parties—a party of the nation, a party which shall have national interests, national security and national faith as the only watchwords to which it owes its existence.

Chamberlain at Bradford, 20 September 1888

THE terms on which the general election of 1886 was fought did a great deal to ensure that the Home Rule split should be perpetuated. The majority of moderate Liberals—who did not believe that war to the knife between the two sections was justified in the circumstances—were frustrated in their attempts to heal the feud by the bitterness engendered by rivalry over seats. No Liberal was more genuinely conciliatory than Dr Dale, whose only intervention in the election was to support a Gladstonian candidate. Yet Dale was driven to the conclusion that Gladstone's method of appealing to the country was unconstitutional, and would have been 'a political disaster' if successful. 'We are asked to believe that the Bills of last Session are dead; what the Bills of next Session are to be we are not told. The Liberal party has been asked to give Mr Gladstone a majority in favour of his Irish policy, though his Irish policy is undisclosed.' It was a 'personal plebiscite', the country being asked to give Gladstone a 'blank cheque'.[198] In practice those Liberals who had opposed Gladstone's Home Rule Bill found themselves attacked in their constituencies. Gladstonians coalesced for electoral purposes with the Irish Nationalists against Liberals, while Unionist Liberals coalesced with Tories against Gladstonians, creating deep and lasting divisions.

Among the Gladstonians only Harcourt had any hope that agreement could be reached with Chamberlain. He invited Chamberlain to stay at Malwood, and got a bantering reply agreeing to come in the new year, when Chamberlain expected to have plenty of leisure and Harcourt could snatch a weekend by devolving the cares of leadership 'on Osborne Morgan or Labouchere or whoever else may be heir apparent'. Doubtless Chamberlain's intention was to discuss Liberal reunion informally, but he only confessed a wish 'to join you in historical researches, and inquire into the morality of the Norman Conquest, or the "blaggardly" treatment of Boadicea'. Then, on 23 December, Chamberlain read with astonishment in *The Times* that Randolph Churchill, his only confidant in the Salisbury government, had suddenly resigned.* Promptly he recast the speech he was to make that evening to include an appeal for a conference of Liberals to reach a minimum agreement on Ireland. He did not intend to break with Hartington or Salisbury, though these allies initially had misgivings. His real motive was to protect himself against any Tory backsliding into illiberal Irish policies, which Churchill's resignation might have presaged.

The Round Table Conference, which met sporadically in January and February of 1887, was made up of Harcourt, Morley and Herschell on the Gladstonian side, Trevelyan and Chamberlain on the other. Herschell and Trevelyan were virtual cyphers, though the latter—in spite of his reversion to the Gladstonian side shortly afterwards—was convinced at first that the talks had to succeed. 'The Gladstonians', he told Chamberlain, 'must see that it is their only chance of retreating from their terribly false position to come to terms with you. . . . The great bulk of the respectable Gladstonians and of those who would be glad to come back to office some day must recognize that it is the only way out of the business. . . .'[199] But the addition of Morley to the conference was fatal to its success. Even Harcourt had to reprimand him for being over-suspicious of Chamberlain's motives. He had an idea that Chamberlain was 'foxing', and, like Gladstone himself, believed that 'Coriolanus' was being driven back to their side. 'I am as anxious as you to make things easy for J. Chamberlain,' he wrote to Harcourt, 'but the chances

---

* Lord Salisbury gave as a reason for Churchill's resignation 'his friendship for Chamberlain, which made him insist that we should accept that statesman as our guide in internal affairs'. Of Churchill, he went on: 'His character moreover is quite untamed. Both in impulsiveness and variability, and in a tendency which can only be described by the scholastic word "vulgaris", he presents the characteristics of extreme youth. . . .' (Fitzjames Stephen PP., Salisbury–Stephen, 30 December, 1886)

are ten to one against *modus vivendi.*' Again, 'I am utterly and incorrigibly incredulous. He has found out that his egotism, irascibility and perversity have landed him in a vile mess. . . . He has proved himself to have no wisdom and no temper. Never more let me be asked to believe in his statesmanship. *C'est fini.* . . .'* Such was the view of the ideologue who took his practical politics from Gladstone.

Gladstone himself likewise saw the affair as a capitulation by Chamberlain. 'In your conversation', he reminds Harcourt, 'you *three* will represent in one sense 280, and in a fuller sense 195 votes. They *two* will represent six, or eight? The 195 with firm ground under their feet; the six or eight (if they be so many) floating in the air. . . . Chamberlain is under a great necessity of moving. We are not! All our necessity is to avoid a reasonably founded charge of overlooking a pacific overture which might have been accepted without compromise of our policy.'[200] Granville shared, as might be expected, the same over-confidence. He understood from Harcourt that the Gladstonian representatives would act under their chief's 'auspices and superintendence', and observed that while he did not see 'the bridge over which even the Prince of Opportunists can pass', it would be a mistake to 'barricade it against his passage'.[201] Only Harcourt was capable of a fair estimate of the importance of Chamberlain and the position he represented—for Chamberlain was the spokesman of a viewpoint shared by a very large section, perhaps a majority, of the entire Liberal party, especially when the issues were transposed into terms of policies rather than of persons.

The strength of Chamberlain's position in entering the Conference lay in the self-evident fact that unless Home Rule became a matter of early realization, adherence to the full rigour of the Gladstonian measure would perpetuate the deadlock between parties and render the attainment of other important Liberal measures impossible. But who among the leading Gladstonians desired important reforms? The most prominent demand from the ranks was that for disestablishment, strongly advocated by Scots and Welsh Nonconformists: and in addition, there was a

---

* See letters between Morley and Harcourt in A. G. Gardiner, *Harcourt*, II, pp.20, 21, 24 and 29. To the last diatribe Harcourt replies: '. . . the least happy part of our business consists in your incurable inveteracy against J. C.'

growing sentiment in favour of 'safe' socialistic reforms, tempered by a fear of 'continental', insurrectionary or doctrinaire socialism. Gladstone and Morley had no sympathy with either of these aspirations, Harcourt very little. It was left to the minor figures to propound the programme for the party, Labouchere, Lawson, Conybeare, Illingworth, Osborne Morgan, Ellis, and other representatives of Nonconformity, the temperance movement, the National Liberal Federation, and the Liberation Society. At this juncture Labouchere assumed the initiative, and did much to keep up the alliance between the London Radicals and the Irish Nationalists. Yet, unlike Hyndman who had done the same thing, Labouchere was no socialist, but a militant champion of *laissez-faire* capitalism. He also regarded the Irish question as paramount, and was not unduly concerned that it had put a stop on other reforms. Although he had a year before urged Chamberlain to go with Gladstone in order to 'shunt' the Nationalists, he now threw himself into the Nationalist cause, and did his best to use Gladstone to 'shunt' Chamberlain. The promotion of the Round Table Conference only intensified Labouchere's attacks, which were founded on the assumptions of the Nationalists that any retreat from the Gladstonian Bills would be a betrayal, and that Chamberlain's public appeal for 'imperial' unity was an affront to their cause.

These views found expression at the Leeds conference of the National Liberal Federation in January, just when the Round Table discussions had made considerable progress on the principles of Irish land reform. There had been no truce during the discussions—Morley for instance had dissuaded Harcourt from putting his foot down on Labouchere, arguing: 'Personally he carries no weight, but what he says on this business is what all our staunchest friends are thinking . . . the chances are ten to one against *modus vivendi*, and then we shall want all our friends: don't let us damp their ardour in the meanwhile.'[202] The suspicions of the Gladstonian leaders as to Chamberlain's motives were magnified and published in the Gladstonian press, and drove him to defend himself. He writes to Bunce on the eve of a speech he was due to make at Birmingham:

Chamberlain–Bunce, 25 January 1887: It is most difficult to speak usefully at such a time, and perhaps it is almost too much to hope for such a patriotic combination as I have suggested.

You see how the matter is treated by Labouchere and *hoc genus omne*. They want confusion and anarchy, but unless the moderate men on both sides speak out boldly and clearly we shall be condemned to a long period of Tory reaction, and I think I shall retire altogether from public life. I have no pleasure in supporting Tories, but I am not going to sacrifice the true interests of the country even to re-unite the Liberal party.[203]

But the moderates did not speak up. And Bright, who described the attempt of five Liberals to settle a policy for the party as 'a piece of impudence', stood aloof. 'I am entirely against Mr Gladstone', he wrote, 'and yet I cannot get up any enthusiasm for schemes based on systems of federation or on the example of the Canadian constitution.'[204] Chamberlain was obliged to vindicate his own actions and views. Attacked on all sides from Gladstonian platforms, he had no one to represent his opposed point of view, while in representing it himself he was bound to prejudice his position as a negotiator. His Birmingham speech of 29 January gave offence to the other side. Gladstone told Harcourt that no good could come of an alliance with Chamberlain 'at this moment'. And Morley on 9 February publicly condemned Chamberlain's lack of taste and good feeling in canvassing before the public the affairs of a private conference.

Even so, the Conference still continued to make progress, in its meetings in mid-February. A Land Scheme was agreed in principle, and Harcourt undertook to prepare a Home Rule scheme on the Canadian basis, reserving points of disagreement. Tevelyan called upon Hartington, and was convinced that he 'would come in to an agreement. His view of the situation is essentially the same as ours and Harcourt's.'[205] Morley, who felt that he was too deeply committed against the retention of the Irish at Westminster, contemplated retirement from public life if the point were carried against him. The situation was critical, especially in view of the attacks on Chamberlain in the press:

Trevelyan–Chamberlain, 17 February 1887: There is great danger in delay. Just read the clever amusing letter, full of theatrical and literary gossip, which the correspondent of the *Northern Echo* writes daily.

I notice how under the guise of an English Radical the author is running down the Conference. I am told that he is T. P. O'Connor, and that he corresponds for all the North Country Liberal papers. This is only a specimen of what the enemies of the Union are doing in every corner of the country, and as long as our efforts are in secret they have the field to themselves. What is done ought to be done as soon as Mr Gladstone gets to London.[206]

But it was a false hope. About this date Chamberlain received an invitation from the editor of the *Baptist* newspaper to reply to a public letter by Gladstone which laid the blame for the postponement of all Liberal legislation and especially Welsh Disestablishment on the Liberal Unionists. He sent off a reply in his usual trenchant style stating the opposing point of view: but it amounted in the circumstances to an anti-Gladstone manifesto. If the Welsh constituencies, he argued, wished to support 'Mr Gladstone's Irish policy' and his contention that no other legislation could be contemplated until the Irish question 'had been settled on his lines', then they had no right to complain of delay, but must wait patiently until the country changed its mind and was 'prepared to hand over the minority in Ireland to the tender mercies of Mr Parnell and the Irish League'. He asked for the support of all Liberals interested in remedial legislation. 'The issue of the Round Table Conference will decide much more than the Irish question. It will decide the immediate future of the Liberal party, and whether or no all Liberal reform is to be indefinitely adjourned.' The letter was couched in terms highly offensive both to Gladstone and the Nationalists, the latter being described as 'representing the policy and receiving the pay of the Chicago Convention'. It afforded a perfect excuse for Gladstone to intervene and suspend the proceedings which had otherwise been so promising.

Chamberlain certainly did not wish to break up the Conference. Rather he had been provoked into a trial of strength with Gladstone, after a further proof that the latter was still completely inflexible. His attitude is elaborated in letters to Harcourt, after Harcourt took strong exception to his *Baptist* letter:

Chamberlain–Harcourt, 27 February 1887: You appear to have thought it possible for me to remain absolutely silent and passive for months, while the Gladstonians high and low were doing everything—by organization, by speeches, by letters, by articles in the newspapers and by proceedings in the House of Commons—to strengthen their position. This would have been a very one-sided armistice, and if the Conference failed, it would have left me in an entirely defenceless position.

My view was that until an agreement was arrived at, each side was at liberty to fortify itself against the possibilities of the future. . . .

This morning I have two letters from Wales both speaking of the great effect produced by the misrepresentations of the Gladstonian Liberals, who throw on the Unionists all the blame for the delay in Welsh Disestablishment. I am bound to counteract these misrepresentations as far as I am able, and if the Conference is held to close my lips while leaving your friends and Mr Gladstone himself perfectly free, then the sooner the Conference is openly abandoned the better.[207]

Harcourt's position was extremely awkward. He had throughout acted on the principle that nothing should be done which might give personal offence to Gladstone. Now he knew that Gladstone wished for the suspension of proceedings while shrinking from the responsibility of terminating the negotiation. He does not appear to have explained this new development to Chamberlain, but instead he seems to have taken the responsibility for the change of front upon himself.

In *The Times* of 3 March, Harcourt commented that Chamberlain's leading principle, as one 'who calls himself a Unionist', was to disregard the opinion of the representatives of Ireland, and to regard exclusively the interests of the Irish landlords. 'If this is peace', Chamberlain observed to him, 'frankly I prefer war.'[208] Four days later Chamberlain was obliged to dispute the contention, which had crept into the discussion, that the Conference was based on acceptance of the Bills of 1886. He was pressing for a resumption of the negotiations, and especially for the communication of a memorandum which Gladstone had drawn up on the discussions. Met with repeated evasions, the cause of which he did not know, he was mystified by the unaccountable behaviour of Harcourt, and wrote to Trevelyan abandoning any further part in the proceedings:

Chamberlain–Trevelyan, 9 March 1887: The Round Table Conference has come to an end so far as I am concerned. This has resulted from a long correspondence with Harcourt. . . .

I have met with a series of excuses, the validity of which I entirely contest, and I am forced to the conclusion that having ascertained our views, Harcourt and his friends now shrink from committing themselves to any opinion on them.

The reasons given for further delay were, first, the desirability of ascertaining Hartington's views on the subject. To meet this, Hartington has written me a letter. . . .

Secondly, Harcourt alleges my letter to the *Baptist*. . . . I have replied that I do and always shall condemn the *policy* of the Bills of 1886, although I have never objected to the principle as stated by Mr Gladstone himself. I have pointed out that this condemnation was the basis of the Conference, and that it was our business to find an alternative policy.

Lastly (and I think this is the true reason for their conduct) Harcourt says that time is working on their side, as is proved by your recent declarations, by Hartington's more conciliatory attitude, and by the general weakness of the government. He therefore declines to fix any time for the resumption of our discussion, and seems to think that he can keep us waiting in the ante-chamber until his present mood of exultancy gives place to the next fit of depression. I do not think his conduct loyal or wise, and I shall now act independently and without further reference to the Conference.[209]

So ended the last serious attempt to promote the reunion of the Liberals. It could only have succeeded if Gladstone had been prepared to abandon the Nationalist alliance, or if Harcourt had been prepared to promote an anti-Gladstone schism. There was never the remotest chance of either of these courses being taken. On the contrary, everything disposed the Gladstonians to anticipate the success of their policy. The 'Plan of Campaign' in Ireland, the unpopularity of the government's resort to coercion and the problem of governing Ireland or maintaining order in Parliament in the face of Nationalist defiance, seemed likely to give an early and conclusive demonstration that there was no alternative to Home Rule.

The next five years, culminating in the formation of Gladstone's final ministry of 1892-4, were years of extraordinary difficulty for Chamberlain. But in fact time was on his side. The 'Gladstonian' party was something of an anachronism at its inception. It was an amalgamation of groups, with the aims of which Gladstone had had but little sympathy in his earlier career. One axis of the party might be properly considered to represent his real predilections—the Home Rule-cum-Little England section, best personified by Morley. But the strength of the party in the 'Celtic fringe' of Great Britain lay in the Nonconformists, who demanded Disestablishment, temperance legislation, and state control of denominational schools. While these causes were at the height of their sway over the electorate, Gladstone had done little to advance them. Now, in the late 'eighties, together with 'Little England' cries for things such as the abandonment of Egypt, they were passing their zenith. The dominant trends were making towards collectivism or state socialism and imperialism, not only among the electorate at large but also among the younger Liberals, most notably Rosebery, Asquith, Haldane and Grey, who were to lead the Liberal imperialists; and also in the case of Lloyd George and the popular Labour movement, which was still largely contained within the umbrella of the Liberal party.

Both state socialism, in any of its diverse forms, and imperialism, were anathema to Gladstone. Yet he addressed his appeal to the 'masses' and was content to see the exodus of property, wealth and education over to the Unionist side. A long-standing theme with him was that the hearts of the ordinary people were uncorrupted where often those of the better-to-do had become hardened. The 'New Radicals' now obtained his benediction. But the Radical element of the Gladstonian party was perhaps the most anachronistic of all. The cry of 'retrenchment' had become a hopeless shibboleth in the face of the huge increases in public expenditure and the extension of state commitments. Also the programme of constitutional reforms—such things as the curtailment of the powers of the House of Lords, or 'one man one vote' —would not satisfy the Labour movement or the working classes now beginning to think in terms of wages, employment, housing, and conditions of work. Indeed, the priority which Labouchere and his group insisted on giving to Home Rule and its concomitant, Lords' reform, meant the relegation of social reform to an indefinite future. Many Gladstonian followers were content that this should be so, as well as many Unionists. Home Rule, in short, became a glorious red herring, treasured by all the anti-socialist elements in British politics who knew that its removal from the scene would bring to the fore an even graver menace.

The essence of Gladstonianism in these years (1887–92) was an uncompromising adherence to certain broad principles of political right and conscience. Gladstonians had a 'conscientious' objection to Balfour's methods of Irish coercion, to the liquor traffic, to the privileges of the parson and the bishop, to the state church and state-aided denominational schools. Chamberlain, as has been seen, was prepared to enlist the Nonconformist conscience in his causes, and he genuinely believed in and always supported Disestablishment. But his approach had always been practical and secular, and the abstract principle was for him always of secondary importance. It was for this reason that, as the enemy within their gates, the Nonconformists attacked him after 1886. Gladstone and Morley, the reasoning went, adhered to principle at all costs, but Chamberlain compromised. To uphold the Union he was prepared to support Tory coercion and landlordism in Ireland, or at least to give a general support to the iniquitous methods of Balfour.

For this, he became the special target of the Nonconformist press, and his motives and morality were impugned with all the suggestions and suspicions that self-righteous priggery could invent. He was forced to abandon his advocacy of the cause of Disestablishment, though he continued to support it by his vote. As he complained to Sir Henry James in 1889, '. . . ever since I have been in Parliament I have advocated without the least regard to consequences to myself the Nonconformist cause. I have publicly championed the Disestablishment movement, and never failed to identify myself with my fellow Nonconformists on all questions in which they are specially interested... yet . . . the bulk of the Nonconformist party have not only ignored all this, but have been among the most violent of our assailants since we were compelled to differ from Mr Gladstone.'[210] He had one inadequacy, however. For while the Nonconformists demanded Disestablishment as a matter of right and an end in itself, Chamberlain wanted it because, as he explained to Dale in 1891, 'I believed that the established church was an obstacle to progress in educational and other social reforms.' But he found that Nonconformity presented the same kind of obstacle to legislative progress as the Church had done. 'Now', he went on, 'I find the active section of Nonconformists more fanatical, more bitter, more selfish, and more unscrupulous than I have ever known the champions of the Church to be.'[211]

Before Gladstone took office in 1892, his party had begun to go to pieces, and Harcourt did not expect to remain in office more than six weeks. There was no efficacy in the old cries, and when the House of Lords rejected the Home Rule Bill of 1893, thus bringing together the Home Rule and anti-Lords causes, not a dog barked. The independent course taken both by the Labour movement, in its various forms, and by the Liberal imperialists, had produced internal schisms in the party. And it was the relatively new and intruding forces of socialism and imperialism, rather than his sporadic warfare with the orthodox Gladstonians, which were driving Chamberlain into an entirely new alignment of his political policies.

What was variously called 'socialism' or 'collectivism' was at this time still very ill-defined and confused. Chamberlain, still deeming himself a socialist in the older sense, called Marxism 'collectivism': whereas the Webbs and others more meaningfully used the word to denote the 'collective' or 'organic' society in contradistinction to the libertarian individualism of Bentham and the Mills. England in the 'eighties and early 'nineties had, through the influence of post-Darwinian thinkers and sociologists of diverse schools but similar anti-individualist tendency, come to think of society in terms of collectivism instead of in terms of *laissez-faire*.* When the Gladstonian, Harcourt, said 'We are all socialists now', he might better have said 'We are all collectivists'.

'Collectivism' understood in this sense was by no means a progression towards socialism. It had much closer affinities with imperialism. The nation state was its natural unit or community. It had no place for the idea of class war, the materialism or the suppression of individuality which, rightly or wrongly, were associated with socialism. Collectivists like the Webbs and the Fabians, or the younger generation of Liberals, tended to be and often to call themselves 'imperialists', and to make a stand against

---

* In this connection one might instance Sir Henry Maine, Sir E. B. Tylor, T. H. Green, F. H. Bradley, David Ritchie and Leslie Stephen. The prevailing direction of the studies of sociology, anthropology, ethics and philosophy was towards an intense appreciation, one might almost say a rediscovery, of the collective entity, political and social.

the social doctrines of Marx. Other collectivists, who might, like Labouchere, be also Gladstonians, reacted against Marxism and the idea of class war which began to pervade the Labour movement by calling themselves supporters of 'individualism': which does not mean that they are to be equated with the Cobdenites of the mid-nineteenth century.* Amid the confusion of terminology, a new political dichotomy was emerging, between Marxist socialism on the one hand, and 'collectivism' or 'imperialism' or 'individualism' on the other. In the practical world, as distinct from the realm of speculation and intellectual debate, England had become aware of a Labour problem, now reinforced by a menacing and challenging ideology known as socialism. Although spread in debased, distorted and popularized forms, at many removes from the fountain-head, and indeed acting (as for instance in the case of Keir Hardie's socialism) more as an agency to harden and sharpen older creeds than as a new and self-contained doctrine, none the less socialism was recognized at the time as something which one had to be for or against, and which would alter the division of parties. For those who were against it, imperialism, evolving into a philosophy of society as well as of empire, offered the readiest alternative. It countered what was considered to be the false ethic of socialism—its appeal to feelings of discontent, greed, satisfaction with material values, and class hatred—by stressing the importance of social loyalties, bonds and traditions, and the ideal of service to the community, the Empire, and the English-speaking peoples overseas.†

---

* For Labouchere's defence of private capitalism, see his disputation with Hyndman of 8 February 1894 (reprinted in Thorold's *Life*). In an earlier debate, Bradlaugh made this very characteristic declaration: 'Instead of making the state all-powerful, I would make the individual so strong for good that the state would have little left to do. Every state interference with liberty is only defensible today because of the corrupt social state which we have got to remedy'—*Will Socialism benefit the English People?* (1884), p.32. See also Auberon Herbert's antithesis in *A Politician in trouble about his Soul*, p.293: 'Are you a Socialist, a believer in the majority, a believer in force, or do you take your stand on the fixed and inalienable rights of the individual? The mixed and party systems . . . are mere halfway huts. . . .'

† When Chamberlain launched the reconstructed Radical Unionist party in 1889, it was to promote social unity at home and imperialism abroad. See e.g. his attack on the 'new Radicals' (speech in Commons, 29 July 1889), who represented 'the class jealousies, the petty spite, and the enmities which they do their utmost to stimulate': who were 'the Nihilists of English politics.' See also his Birmingham speech of 23 January 1889 attacking Morley's phrase 'an Empire of swagger' and the policy of 'universal disintegration'.

One need not stress too much the importance of the ideological conflict. The children of this generation were far from being all little 'socialists' or 'imperialists', and to a large extent these two creeds as popularly understood were merely the symbols or rationalization of practical conflicts, of a dilemma, kept in prominence by everyday events. What Chamberlain had always called the 'Labour problem' had become acute, and politics were manifestly becoming dominated and fashioned by the demands and the growing power of the Labour movement. Gone were the days when it was generally believed that the state could do nothing to create employment or raise the level of wages: although as yet there was little inkling of the enormous, logarithmic expansion of production and wealth which could be achieved by improved industrial techniques. Other countries were acquiring social welfare schemes, insurance against unemployment, sickness and destitution in old age, while Britain retained the punitive system of the Poor Law.

In Britain, two courses were open to the Labour movement. The most obvious, and, many believed, the only effective course was to organize a separate fighting movement and exacerbate industrial and political conflict on a Labour front, turning the Trades Union Congress into a kind of industrial equivalent of the former Irish Land League. But could the country afford a long and fierce internal conflict, when it was losing its industrial supremacy and was conscious of a dangerous isolation in a rearming Europe? Were not the welfare and livelihood of the British working class bound up with the maintenance of British naval power and the retention of her overseas possessions and markets? If the Empire was, as Rhodes insisted, a 'bread and butter question', was it not expedient for Labour to avoid a head-on collision with Capital and to demand instead the benefits of Empire tempered by the kind of state-socialist welfare schemes which Bismarckian Germany enjoyed? Such was the choice. And the British Labour movement, cumbrous, diversified, undecided even as to whether it wished for separate political representation or not, and, in the mass, of a complacent and conservative temper, was incapable of choosing. But the Labour leaders, and politicians of all parties, were driven one way or the other, towards supporting the idea of class war, or the idea of Empire.

Chamberlain was provoked into a public stand against socialism in the early 'nineties. Two letters which he received from the Conservative Poet Laureate, Alfred Austin, express views with which he was in complete accord, in asking him to strike a new note by writing an article appealing to the real wishes of the working classes in an anti-socialist sense:

Alfred Austin–Chamberlain, 14 February 1891: If bye-elections carry any practical lesson, it is that the great mass of voters are not influenced mainly, if indeed to any serious degree, by the question of Home Rule for Ireland, but are thinking of other matters . . . of work, wages, conditions of labour, leisure reform, recreation, personal dignity, family comfort and happiness, and increasing facilities for securing to themselves a larger and lovelier life.

These, to you . . . are, I am well aware, mere commonplaces. . . . Plainly, I want to urge you to write an article . . . striking the note of warning and expounding the policy as to the future which I know is yours. . . .

Alfred Austin–Chamberlain, 17 February 1891: At the date to which you refer, and when you say you were preaching the gospel of humanity, I for one was neither startled by your doctrines, nor repelled by your manner of advocating them. . . . With the exception of one phrase, viz. 'ransom'. . . I do not remember any passages in any of your speeches with which I felt disposed to quarrel, as I confess I frequently did with proposals in the speeches of the late Mr Bright, and . . . in the speeches of Mr Gladstone tending to set class against class. That seems to me a sin against good citizenship; the main object of a patriotic politician . . . being to secure the coherent and continuous march of the entire nation. . . .

I think anyone advocating a policy you indicate should not suffer himself to be entrapped into allowing that it is a 'socialistic' policy. That is a question-begging appellative. . . . As I understand socialism, it means and involves the destruction of the present organization of society by the suppression of individual liberty . . . the most precious thing on earth. [One] cannot too often and too emphatically repel the insinuation that a tender and intelligent concern for the weaker brethren is socialism.[212]

The upshot of this correspondence was an article by Chamberlain on 'The Labour Question' in the *Nineteenth Century* of November 1892. By that date the Gladstonians had committed themselves to the heterogeneous 'Newcastle programme', beside which

Chamberlain's proposals looked very moderate. But the important feature of the article was its attempt to refute the theory of Karl Marx, which Chamberlain characterized as 'essentially foreign and exotic'. His argument was the common one that genius, talent, even the qualities of prudence and industry would be lost to the country 'failing the stimulus of self-interest and personal advantage which is found to be all-powerful in ordinary human affairs'. He acknowledged that the remuneration of labour was often too low, and that the inequalities of wealth and poverty were 'a distressing and dangerous feature of our modern civilization'. His remedy contained the germs of a new departure. At home, thrift, self-reliance and unity, promoted by such things as loans for house purchase: abroad, the promotion of trade through Empire. For the future condition of labour was 'more dependent on the success of our all-pervading foreign enterprise than on any artificial attempt to stimulate production' by socialistic schemes to provide work for the unemployed.

It was in 1891 that Chamberlain, who up to that time had thought of forming some third or 'national' party, began to contemplate seriously the possibility of taking office under the Conservatives. Lord Salisbury had conceded much to his Liberal Unionist allies, particularly by the institution of democratic county councils in England, Wales and Scotland (1888-9), free education (extended to the whole country in 1891), and various measures for providing allotments and smallholdings. Of free education, Chamberlain commented to Dale: 'In 1885 I partly wrote, and wholly supervised, an article . . . suggesting this arrangement, yet the political partisans and turncoats of the Gladstonian party have accused me of inconsistency and treachery because I am now willing to accept gladly a concession which five years ago I could not get Mr Gladstone to look at.'[213] When Dale mildly demurred at his failure to stress his preference for board school education, Chamberlain explained:

Chamberlain–Dale, 1 May 1891: I was addressing myself to the opponents of free education on the Tory side. . . . It must be evident to you that in the present position of affairs I can only work through the Conservative party. They have been most loyal, and in this matter especially have undoubtedly given up old prejudices in order frankly to accept the views that I have pressed upon them.

I have in the last five years seen more progress made with the practical application of my political programme than in all my previous life. I owe this result entirely to my former opponents, and all the opposition has come from my former friends. I am bound to bear this in mind in my future speeches.[214]

In addition to feelings of gratitude, other considerations were disposing him to regard the alliance with the Conservatives as permanent. With the passing of time the 'compact' over seats, which had worked in the main with smooth efficiency, became almost necessary for the preservation of his dwindling following, who were approximating more and more to the Conservatives with whom they habitually associated. Chamberlain himself worked very well with Balfour, especially after inheriting the leadership of the Liberal Unionists in the Commons from Hartington, who went to the upper House in 1892. While the Unionists were in opposition between 1892 and 1895 the relations between the two sections of the party in the Commons were easy and intimate, owing to Balfour's open-minded approach to problems and the close partnership between him and Chamberlain in the struggle against the second Home Rule Bill. The friendship which thus grew up was of prime importance in forming Chamberlain's decision to throw in his lot with the Conservatives. It was also to lend a pathetic interest to the later relationship of the two men, which would provide a striking illustration of the saying that in politics there can be no trusting to friendship— a lesson which Chamberlain could never learn.

CHAPTER SEVEN

The New Radicalism

*Those men who were glorious . . . in the history of the Liberal party—
their object was to raise the individual man, to free him from tram-
mels and from fetters, and to give him opportunities to develop his
faculties. . . . And now comes the new Radical, and his object is to
merge the individual in the State, to reduce all to one dead level of
uniformity, in which the inefficient, and the thriftless, and the idle are
to be confounded and treated alike with the honest, and the industrious,
and the capable, and by which all of us, rich and poor alike, are to be
fenced in with limitations and parliamentary restrictions.*

Chamberlain at Leeds, 26 February 1894

IN the long parliamentary fight during the session of 1893 to
defeat Gladstone's second Home Rule Bill, Chamberlain played
the principal part. Two things especially damned the Bill in the
eyes of the public; first, the provision finally written into the Bill
that the Irish should have continuous and not intermittent
representation at Westminster—so that while they managed their
own affairs at Dublin they could still disrupt all the business of
the House of Commons: and second, the unprecedented use of
the closure to carry by small majorities a measure of fundamental
constitutional change. Whole sections of the Bill were never
discussed. Moreover, a majority of the members for Great
Britain were against the Bill, which was carried only by Nationalist votes. When the House of Lords rejected it, there were not
the materials with which to wage a campaign in the country.
Gladstone was in favour of an anti-Lords dissolution, but the
colleagues who had followed him thus far would go no
further. He was forced to retire amid disputes over the
choice of his successor. Harcourt was a 'single chamber' man,
and would gladly have seen the upper House completely
abolished. But, singularly enough, Morley worked against
Harcourt's succession to the party leadership—he had been
quarrelling with Harcourt for some time—and in favour of

Rosebery, whom the Queen called for when Gladstone resigned.*

Rosebery—imperialist, devotee of the turf, and associate of city financiers—was bound to pigeon-hole Gladstone's policies. He put Home Rule on the shelf, where it remained till 1910. As a premier in the House of Lords, he was the least suited of Liberal chiefs to lead a campaign against his own order. What Rosebery did was to launch a campaign to reform the Lords—a very different thing from abolishing them, as he carefully explained in his letters to the Queen. In such a course he could not hope for success, because the majority of Harcourt's following, who wanted to destroy the Lords, would not consent to buttress their House against the future by reforming it.

The whole episode, in Chamberlain's eyes, disclosed a menace which would recur in the future in spite of Gladstone's retirement. In the speeches he delivered in 1894 he was at pains to explain the danger. The Gladstonians, he argued, were bent on creating a single-chamber despotism with the aid of the Nationalist vote. They were bound in time to destroy the Lords, not simply to pass Home Rule, but because the socialist elements in their party demanded it, while the more moderate elements found it expedient to placate their demanding allies by allowing through the Commons all sorts of extravagant measures on the assurance that the Lords would reject them. This doubled-edged procedure was calculated to arouse popular indignation against the peers. To counter it, Chamberlain went back upon his erstwhile policy of curtailing the Lords' powers, and began to regard the Lords as a necessary defence against a 'despotic' Home Rule government.

This change of front might appear to contradict his former principles of popular government and majority rule. But it should be remembered that his advocacy of such things as the closure by bare majority in the Commons had been founded on the assumption that major acts of legislation, as for example the Education Act of 1870, should be shaped and amended in committee by direct pressure from the country through the Liberal Associations. What had happened, in his opinion, since the

---

* Gladstone disliked Rosebery's approach to foreign affairs and would have named Spencer as leader, but the Queen did not seek his advice. For the caballing before Gladstone's being 'put out' (his own words), see Gardiner, *Harcourt*, II, pp.261–5.

Gladstonians captured the Liberal Caucus and Schnadhorst moved to London, was that the power of the machine and the closure was used to consolidate Gladstone's personal autocracy, exercised through the central office. They had made a 'fetish' of their venerable leader.

The Home Rule Bill of 1893 had been amended in vital particulars in its course through committee, yet it had always been found perfect by Gladstone's followers. On the final night of committee, Chamberlain provoked an outbreak of fist-fighting on the floor at midnight by remarking on his opponents' subservience. 'The Prime Minister calls "black" and they say "it is good", the Prime Minister calls "white", and they say "it is better". . . . It is always the voice of a god. Never since the time of Herod has there been such slavish adulation.' Shouts of 'Judas' from the Irish, and an ill-considered move by a Mr Logan across the floor, produced the worst parliamentary 'scene' of the century.

Chamberlain had seen his closest associates—even the self-styled 'stalwart' Mr Caine—defeated by the party machine and driven back into the Gladstonian ranks. Only the strongest could withstand it.* And he had seen the closure used against the members of Great Britain at the dictation of members 'nominated by priests, elected by illiterates, and subsidized by the enemies of this country'. He believed that Mr Gladstone had 'demoralized' his party.† His resentment was more than the result of party feeling, however. He was witnessing the destruction of the principles of party organization which he had done so much to establish. In building up the Caucus he had struggled to create the means of making the Commons amenable to the country,

---

* 'I feel rather lonely in politics sometimes,' Chamberlain complained to Dale (21 May 1891), 'deserted as I am by so many of my old friends, who have left my side not because they really disagree with me, but solely because they have been too weak to resist the party machine and the party leader.'

To Caine he wrote (26 March 1892): 'I have been grieved and wounded by your defection from the Unionist ranks. I cannot explain it, and I cannot justify it', alluding to the time when Caine 'invented the description of "stalwarts" '. Caine pleaded the temperance question as his reason for changing sides.

† Chamb. PP., Chamberlain–Dale, 10 December 1890: 'Mr Gladstone has not only divided his party. He has demoralized his section of it, and it is no longer Home Rule alone which separates us.'

and now these means were being used to keep it amenable to a Minister. In advocating closure, he had sought to give decisive power to the parliamentary party, not to the whips' office.

Although Chamberlain had still supported the closure in 1890, in an article entitled 'Shall we Americanize our Institutions?' he had become aware of its disadvantages. By putting a time limit on discussion, the closure also put a premium upon 'talking out' opponents and denying them the chance of making their points before Parliament and the country. The United States legislature had, he considered, taken the closure too far; as he observes, writing from Washington:

Chamberlain–Collings, 28 October 1890: Another subject of interest to me has been the rules of Procedure in the House of Representatives. My eyes! wouldn't they make the Parnellites sit up! They have absolutely destroyed the possibility of obstruction, but they have destroyed free discussion also. Fancy carrying a big contested bill through all its stages in seven hours![215]

At Westminster things were moving in the same direction. The process by which ministers gained control over the procedure and time of the House of Commons was however obscure, complicated, and determined by broader and more long-term causes than the changing tactics of political parties. And the Unionists, certainly Balfour, were to prove among the most ruthless exponents of the closure. But the 'railway time-table' procedure that Balfour introduced after 1900 was a very different thing from the simple notion of enforcing progress which Chamberlain had been advocating. At this time (1894), while prepared to acquiesce in the tightening of ministerial control as an inevitable process, he saw that it rendered necessary a second chamber capable of enforcing some kind of reference to the people. He criticized the Gladstonians, because he felt that they were denying the need for any check on the novel kind of disciplined House of Commons that had emerged:

Chamberlain at Leeds, 25 February 1894: When I first went into the House of Commons, when we spoke of the opinion of the House . . . we meant 'the common sense of most', but now we mean the decision of the majority, the party majority of the day. We meant then that in the process of free discussion, and as a result of mutual concession, legislation assumed a form which, if indeed it were not universally accepted, at all events met the strongest objections of its opponents. Now everything of the sort . . . is in the course of disappearance, and the very men who urge on you that a second chamber should be abolished . . . desire to make the government of the day . . . absolute masters of the time of the House.

Convinced, then, by the trends that party organization and parliamentary procedure were taking, and taught by the lesson of the House of Commons defying, as he believed, the will of the nation in 1893 in the same manner as the Lords had defied it in 1884, Chamberlain became a supporter of the second chamber and its right to force a dissolution. He tried to vindicate this principle by advising the House of Lords in 1893 to pass the Home Rule Bill, but with a conditional clause that the Bill be put to and accepted by a referendum. The idea had been put forward by one of his following, Parker Smith, and supported by Professor Dicey, who replied to a query from Chamberlain: 'I am much interested in Parker Smith's suggestion as to the referendum. Whether it ought to be made at this stage or not I don't know, but that to the referendum we shall come at last I am certain. It is the only scheme for giving the constitution any permanence, which is at once effectual and unmistakably democratic.'[216] To support the authority of the second chamber, Chamberlain was prepared to agree to explore a plan of Leonard Courtney's for an elective assembly of 'life' peers, chosen in three equal sections by the hereditary peers, by county councils and similar bodies, and by the government of the day. Lord Salisbury, however, was not prepared to go beyond accepting a few life peers, and Chamberlain, unwilling to 'stir the waters for so small a result', was ready to defend the House of Lords as it was, in default of a better.[217]

Commenting on the 'utter and egregious failure' of Rosebery's attempt to get up a popular movement against the House of Lords, he made the following observations in a private memorandum to be sent to Devonshire:

13 November 1894: I never remember anything so ridiculous in the history of political agitation, and it is evident that the Gladstonian organization has fallen to pieces. In the old time we should have at least managed to follow up such a declaration by the leaders of the

party with public meetings and resolutions. There would have been the appearance of energy, even if there were no popular enthusiasm.

Personally, the House of Lords seems to me to fulfil excellently the necessary duties of a second chamber. It is able to secure delay and reconsideration where there is no strong popular feeling, while it is powerless to oppose permanently the clearly expressed will of the nation. The only question is whether it ... could resist, even for a time, the decision of a large majority of the House of Commons. ...

If the House of Lords has great courage and initiative they might take the present opportunity to create a strong second chamber, but I doubt whether the majority are prepared for any great change.[218]

When the Unionists took the matter of the referendum and Lords reform up seriously at the eleventh hour, in 1910, it was too late.

In the confused situation following the defeat of the second Home Rule Bill and Gladstone's retirement, new features seemed to be emerging on the political scene. The enthusiasm for constitutional reform was declining, giving place to greater curiosity about social questions and the socialist preachings of the Labour movement. The Trade Union Congress passed Marxist resolutions in 1893 and 1894, while the Fabian 'Progressives' dominated the London County Council. In municipal elections, as Chamberlain noted, the Independent Labour Party directed their attacks upon the Gladstonians, avowing 'that they will treat them as enemies until they have accepted the Socialist Programme'. 'It seems to me obvious that this will be their ultimate fate', he concludes, but in accepting socialism the Liberals would risk 'a further secession of all that remains to them of wealth, intelligence, and moderation'.[219]

The aspect of things most disturbing to Chamberlain's mind was the danger of a realignment of parties on a division of classes. Even in his most Radical days when he had appeared as a 'Jack Cade' leading a proletarian attack on the propertied classes, he had in reality been inspired by a vision of justice and harmony between classes. He attacked the rich for shirking their social duties and avoiding their fair share of taxation: but like almost all statesmen of his time he equated 'fairness' or social justice with a properly-regulated system of *laissez-faire*. He had always disapproved of the direct redistribution of wealth between classes or the taxation of the rich because they were rich. The idea of a party of 'have-nots' formed to expropriate the rich by act of parliament—a peculiarly British compromise between capitalism and socialism—did not, indeed, achieve any wide acceptance until the Edwardian era. But it was clear at least a decade earlier which way things were tending. Doctrines of class hatred and attacks on wealth and property such as had never disturbed the earlier Victorian scene now became the standard weapons of contestants in every working-class constituency, while the flight of the propertied classes from the Liberal side undermined the party's moral resistance to socialism:

Memo. by Chamberlain, 13 November 1894: . . . the electors are much more interested at the present time in social questions and the problems connected with the agitation of the Labour Party than they are with either the House of Lords or any other constitutional subject. There is much searching of heart among the more moderate, and above all the wealthier, Gladstonians. The men who have anything to lose are getting uneasy now that they see that Gladstonianism is not likely to be confined to an attack upon Irish landlords or British millionaires, but will probably result in an onslaught on capital generally.

. . . The resolutions of the Trades Union Congress . . . amount to universal confiscation in order to create a Collectivist State . . . and there is grave reason to anticipate that [the Gladstonian leaders] will yield to the demands of the New Unionism just as they have previously yielded to the claims of the Irish Nationalists, the Local Veto fanatics, and the Radical opponents of the House of Lords. The Independent Labour Party are proceeding on this assumption. . . .[220]

The threat of social war and crippling internal disunity transformed Chamberlain the aggressive Radical into Chamberlain the defensive Unionist.

One of the most alarming spheres of socialist progress was the London County Council, founded with Lord Rosebery as its first chairman in the pious hope that party politics might be excluded, but soon captured by the enterprising 'Progressive' party led by the Webbs. County Hall under the tutelage of the Webbs bade fair to become the seat of a socialist republic, menacing the other assembly across the river. 'It is the place where Collectivist and Socialistic experiments are tried', Lord Salisbury declared. '. . . Where a new revolutionary spirit finds

Joseph Chamberlain as a young man

John Morley *c.* 1883

Sir Charles Wentworth Dilke

Beatrice Potter *c.* 1885

Gladstone *c.* 1886

(*overleaf*)
Boer reinforcements leaving
Pretoria, November 1899

General Jan Christian Smuts,
1901

Lord Hartington, later eighth
Duke of Devonshire

The Chamberlains and Sir Alfred
Milner in South Africa, 1903

Arthur James Balfour *c*. 1906

Chamberlain as candidate in the general election of 1906

its instruments and collects its arms.'[221] The L.C.C. paid their employees a 'moral minimum wage'. It sought to gain the management of the gas and water concerns of the metropolis 'avowedly to give effect to certain political dreams'. It demanded control over the London police force. Finally in 1894 it proposed to take over the City of London. Lord Rosebery had foreseen that it would not be easy to 'sew the purple of the City and the linen of the Council together'. Now the report of a royal commission, from which after a dispute the City solicitor had withdrawn, presented the terrifying prospect of the Council migrating to the Guildhall, assuming the titles, dignities and ceremonies of the ancient corporation, and seizing its rich endowments: the City area itself becoming one more district under the Council.[222]

This was municipal socialism with a vengeance, and the Unionists threw all their resources into the L.C.C. elections of 1895 to counter it. An Electoral Council composed of delegates from the Central Conservative Association, the Municipal Society, and the Moderate party, sat daily receiving reports from the constituencies and deploying swarms of canvassers, drawing on a fund of £30,000.[223] This Unionist effort succeeded in gaining an equality of seats with the Progressives. 'Slim aristocrats', Beatrice Webb comments, 'and slightly dissipated frequenters of London drawing rooms and clubs' were at least from the 'scenic point of view' an improvement on the 'stunted figures of the labour representatives and the ungraceful corpulence of the "progressive" men of business.'[224] The 'gentlemen's' party were, however, loud and insolent in their ways after their victory. They had destroyed an illusion. The Progressives had in actuality been supported very largely by the middle-class vote, as Mrs Webb admitted, pointing to the paradoxical fact that electorally the party did best in 'good' times of employment. The party had also been supported by Liberal capitalists, and she feared that these would defect from the cause after it had been proved that a collectivist programme could fail in popular appeal, saying 'No more of your collectivism for us, it cannot even buy votes for our party.'* The L.C.C. had been dished, and the process was

---

* Beatrice Webb's diary, March 1895. 'We forget', she comments further, 'that it was not until the dark years of 1881–5 were well over that *constitutional socialism* as distinguished from revolutionary socialism began to grow.'

completed when under a Unionist scheme the metropolitan boroughs were set up in 1899, leading to a decentralization of much of the Council's functions.*

The socialist threat was potential rather than real, but none the less it was a bogy which frightened many capitalists over to the right. Perceptive politicians were concerned not so much with socialism *per se* as with the rapid changes in the social order which were taking place independently, and of which the new creeds and new manners were merely a reflection. The disturbing feature of these changes was that they were tending towards social and political anarchy. For at least three centuries the English polity had flourished, or been preserved from ruin, by standards of public conduct and a jealous regard for traditional values to which even revolutionaries paid tribute. The Irish nationalists were the first parliamentarians who openly sought to destroy Parliament. They had a good, or at least an intelligible, reason for their policy. But the new 'representative men' seemed willing to destroy the parliamentary institutions and traditions of the country merely from ignorance, demagogy, low ambition, or social climbing. They made a trade out of democratic politics. Whereas old corruption had meant selfishness and a high-handed contempt for the mob, the new demagogy could be practised only by men who lacked education, ability, integrity, honour, or common honesty. The ancient enemy of democracy, the demagogue, had arrived in English politics.

Such was Chamberlain's view at this time, however we appraise it. He wrote a play indifferent as drama but good as a piece of self-revelation, which he called *The Game of Politics*. It is well worth study as a work of transparent spiritual autobiography. In an esoteric way the play is quite witty and amusing, but it could never have held the attention of audiences freshly dieted on Shaw and Wilde—though its style is modelled on these

---

* Chamberlain had always thought that the establishment of borough councils in London ought to have preceded the creation of the L.C.C., believing that a population of 500,000 was the largest that could properly be administered by a local authority. He scoffed at the L.C.C.'s pretentious control of a population of 5 millions: 'Their idea is to leave the drudgery to the local authorities; but all the dignity and the honour to themselves. They favour one vast overreaching centralized despotism to which all London is to be subject.' (Speech at Stepney, 7 February 1895)

dramatists. Nevertheless Beerbohm Tree, to whom Chamberlain sent the manuscript for serious consideration, thought quite highly of it. His first comment was: 'The dialogue is stronger than the plot.' Having had the manuscript for six months, he delivered his verdict:

H. Beerbohm Tree–Chamberlain, 12 January 1896: I have come to the conclusion that though the dialogue is brilliant, the work is more of a satire than a stage play—that is to say, the plot is not (from the dramatic point of view) sufficiently progressive—the skeleton of the drama is not strong enough to bear the weight of the flesh and muscle of the dialogue.[225]

He thought the situations were not 'strong enough to ensure a prolonged success'. The main theme of the play is political—a satire on the Irish 'mercenary patriots' and the 'new Radicals' and demagogues making a trade out of collectivist doctrines. Although these characters are grotesquely overdrawn, an undertone of seriousness and occasionally of bitterness, and a directness of allusion to contemporary politics, are mingled with the comic structure of the work. Chamberlain was too much involved personally in the topics of the comedy to be able to get away from himself.

The central character, the Rt. Hon. Arthur Hartley, Home Secretary and 'future Prime Minister', is the mouthpiece of Chamberlain himself, and the main action consists of a plot by a 'cave' of demagogues in his own party to discredit Hartley by producing a disturbance at a socialist gathering in Trafalgar Square. Hartley, the only minister with a sincere concern for the hardships of the working classes in a time of unemployment, does not see fit to ban the demonstration. The 'cave', a heterogeneous group master-minded by Weston, a clever and cynical figure with a personal grudge against Hartley, plan to produce violence by an Irish contingent armed with shillelaghs: but they in turn are made the tools of continental anarchists, who produce a bomb explosion and turn the demonstration into a real convulsion, terrifying Weston's cowardly and pusillanimous creatures. Broadly, then, the play is a parable exposing the folly and danger of irresponsible demagogy.

In the first scene we are plunged straight into the medley of shabby M.P.s who make up Weston's group, on the terrace of the House of Commons. They are contemptuously described by an old and experienced member, the Rt. Hon. Hugh Sutton, for the benefit of the young and ingenuous Miss Myra from Chicago, who wants to see some 'representative men'. This is all that her aristocratic admirer, Lord Reginald, can do to satisfy her curiosity, for 'celebrities' are getting scarce. Sutton points out Brandon, 'who pretends to be a politician in order to be a peer', Biffin, 'a pushing tradesman who believes that the House of Commons will give him the entry to good society', and Spragge, a representative of Labour and a semi-literate with a prison record. A caricature Irish Nationalist, O'Halloran, and a fussy and harmless academic crotcheteer, Professor Potts, make up the rest of Weston's backbench group. But so far as Lord Reginald and Sutton are concerned, these are just representative types, 'products of the enlightened democracy, to which we owe so many of our blessings'. Sutton confesses to having been a Radical fifty years before, 'but', he says, 'the machine has ground all that nonsense out of me', and continues:

The House of Commons is not what it was when I entered it. There were giants in those days, Reggie. . . .
The new democracy resents pre-eminence of talent and everything else. The ideal is a dead level of commonplace and mediocrity. This is the age of small men and small things . . . now the men who are called leaders are only straws blown in front of every gust of popular opinion. . . .
Your orators mould themselves on the eloquence of the parish vestry or even the public house, and they gain the suffrages of the mob by barefaced appeals to their cupidity and their passions. . . .[226]

Having invited his specimens to tea at five, Lord Reginald goes off with Sutton and Miss Myra, leaving Weston to hold a quick consultation with his malcontents.

Weston first flatters and bribes O'Halloran in a ludicrous fashion with promises of political perquisites to be got out of Home Rule, while O'Halloran displays the sturdy conscience and mercenary opportunism of his supposed type. Having squared the Irish, Weston is ready to deal with the grasping but hesitant ruck of his followers, who are to pay for and wink at the revolution which is his ultimate objective, and then be discarded. They gather to hear the 'manifesto of the New Party'. What follows is a thinly disguised satire on the Gladstonian programme, which offers everything to everybody. 'It is only a programme, you know', declares Weston, 'and binds nobody. A programme nowadays is a list of measures which are not to be carried.' The preamble is an absurd farrago of nonsense:

. . . we demand the immediate abolition of the invidious distinctions and odious principles by which the toilers of the earth are dispossessed of their rights, and a luxurious oligarchy battens on their labour.

We regard the House of Lords as a nest of hereditary miscreants, and we require in the name of an outraged democracy its instant destruction. . . .

Wealth wrongfully acquired must be redistributed, and the unholy gains of the greedy capitalist must be utilized for the benefit of those whom he has worsted in the struggle for existence. . . .[227]

Brandon (who later becomes Lord St. Pancreas) demurs at the abolition of the House of Lords, but is assured: 'We will not put the House down, till you are safely inside it.' Biffin, who owns a store, is against an attack on property, and suggests instead the Church or the universities. Professor Potts objects at this, but Spragge insists that 'unless you attack some great interest or another you'll never arouse popular enthusiasm.' On the programme also are total prohibition, votes for women, and payment of members, and Spragge is made honorary secretary of the party —'with an honorarium'.

The tea party at five is an encounter between these men and the 'classes', who maintain an attitude of good-humoured incredulity. Miss Myra questions O'Halloran about the Irish practice of shooting landlords instead of partridges, and Sutton, impressed with her account of America, decides to emigrate, because, as he says, 'I like the laws under which I live to be as near the ten commandments as circumstances will permit.' Another member of the party, Lady Euphemia Vernon—very brisk and active at seventy—declares that things are so bad with the 'classes', she would be glad of the new system to enter politics herself and turn an honest penny. Her amusing reminiscences are cut short by the appearance of Hartley, coming directly from a special meeting of the cabinet on the troubled industrial situation, and the discussion becomes serious.

There is no burlesque about the characterization of Hartley—his speeches are perfectly straight and sincere. He is engrossed in his concern for the miners of the North, who have come out on strike rather than take a reduction in their wages, arising from the fact that the mines have been operating at a loss. The miners are starving and near to desperation. But they have been 'badly advised', and are afraid of returning to work individually for fear of 'being called blacklegs'. This, Miss Myra exclaims, is a regular tyranny, whereupon Sutton explains to her:

In this country, Miss Myra, no one can do as he likes. Everyone is occupied in compelling somebody else to do what he doesn't like, and that is modern progress and the new community.[228]

O'Halloran is glad to think that England is getting on so finely in copying the Irish pattern of democracy—grimly alluding to the fate of Irish jurors or tenants who collaborated with the English—but Sutton rounds on him:

... in your servile loyalty to party combinations, you have none of the courage to tell this new democracy the truth. It has achieved power, but it does not know rightly how to use it because none of its natural leaders dares to be frank with it. You all truckle to it and deceive it, and raise its expectations. Some day you will be found out.[229]

This warning is not heeded, and merely sets off another discussion between Biffin and Potts about their objectives—which Sutton characterizes as 'No rank, no religion, no property, no law, no anything'. Hartley, who has been silent and pensive, now begins to remonstrate with his backbenchers:

I do not blame them [the miners] if they complain loudly, and are dissatisfied with the conditions in which they live. But you are only mocking their wretchedness when you offer them political reforms which will not fill their stomachs, or social revolution which will plunge them into deeper misery than before.

Our business is to seek the real cause of their distress, and if possible to remedy that, not to use their condition for political ends, or to lead them into agitation which must be barren of practical results.[230]

His exposition is cut short by the division bell, upon which the party breaks up leaving Hartley alone with Lord Reginald's sister, Lady Mary Amesbury, whom he has asked to be his wife. At first their conversation is political. Lady Mary asks him why he does not, in the changed conditions of the times, draw nearer to the Conservative side:

I have to defend you now against my own friends. You are so terribly earnest. Sometimes you hit them so hard. They confuse you with that party, the Biffins, the Brandons, the O'Hallorans. They tell me you are just as bad, only more dangerous. . . . The place of a gentleman in times like these is surely with those who are defending the established order.[231]

This was a situation which Chamberlain himself knew only too well. And the reply he puts into Hartley's mouth exactly describes his own view of the dilemma involved in supporting the Tories:

They are so narrow, so apathetic, so indifferent to everything that does not touch themselves or their privileges or their fortunes. Am I to sit still in the presence of want and misery and ignorance . . . ?

Between reaction and revolution there should be a middle path, if only I could find it. . . .[232]

In the midst of his political preoccupations, Hartley is pressing Lady Mary for an answer to his proposal of marriage. She now produces an anonymous letter which accuses him of paying attentions to Lucy Hill, the daughter of a socialist intellectual John Hill, a former school-fellow of Hartley's. Hartley plausibly explains that he has only a paternal interest in the young girl, and on this uncertain note the curtain descends on act one.

In the next act the stage is set in John Hill's bookshop in the Strand. Hill is a dreamer who believes in 'the religion of humanity', and a socialist who believes that property is theft. He is the catspaw of the agitators and revolutionaries who hold their committee meetings in his upstairs room. On the day of the Trafalgar Square demonstration, Hartley comes to dissuade him from attending. At first Hill is distant with the school-mate who has 'risen so high above him', and Hartley finds himself defending his right to the fortune he has made by his own exertions, and condemning the communistic schemes of his friend:

But I cannot accept your dreams as a remedy, my poor John, or believe that the wild schemes you advocate would be otherwise than disastrous to those whom you seek to benefit.

Who are the poor for whom you plead? Many, I doubt not, deserving of every sympathy. But how many idle, drunken, and even vicious, who bear the penalties of their own faults.

You are an enthusiast. You think that by a stroke of legislation you can alter the character of men. You think that you can destroy all the motives which, since the beginning of the world, have stimulated men to exertion and to sacrifice, which have prompted invention and encouraged effort. And you believe that after you have done this, the world will be a better place to live in. I do not. . . .[233]

Hill is persuaded, however, to stay away from the Square, and Hartley leaves.

The good resolution is undone by the appearance of Weston and Spragge with a disreputable ruffian called Doggett. Weston succeeds in persuading the unobservant Hill that Hartley is trifling with his daughter while intending to marry Lady Mary, and incenses him so that he resolves to speak on the platform at the meeting. We are treated to some incidental sidelights on the motives of the agitators. Spragge, M.P., a 'representative of Independent Labour' who votes as he is told, aspires to be an Under-Secretary. His views on the political objectives of his party are absurdly simple:

First you take all the money in the world and put it in a heap—that's collectivism. Then you divide it share and share alike—that's socialism. Then we spends our whack and shares again—that's the religion of humanity.[234]

The demonstration is to be a factitious affair. When Doggett boasts of 300 banners, Spragge is incredulous: 'I didn't know the trade 'as got as many as that.' But Doggett explains how he has brought in all the Teetotal Lodges and Bands of Oak: 'A banner's a banner, and the chaps as 'ave 'em like to cart 'em about, so I wrote and said this was a general fraternization. . . .'

Weston is openly contemptuous of these ineffectual means of agitation. But we are in for real trouble, for a secretive continental anarchist, Von Strolski, comes to collect what is obviously a bomb under its paper wrappings. The demonstration has begun. But before the serious business starts, Hill comes back into his shop. His quixotic nature has got the better of him, and he has rescued two ladies from the grip of the crowd—one very elderly, the other

young and well dressed. They are none other than Lady
Euphemia and Lady Mary. There follows a dialogue which may
be quoted as a fair example of Chamberlain's dramatic style:

Lady Euphemia: My dear good man, you are a perfect angel. If it
hadn't been for you, there would have been nothing left of us but
a sensational paragraph in the evening papers.
Lady Mary: I shall never forget that awful crowd.
Lady Euphemia: They *did* smell. All the perfumes of Araby, my dear!
Hill: What brought you to this neighbourhood on such a day? Did
you not know there was a meeting—a demonstration?
Lady Euphemia: Certainly not! I came to buy a packet of needles, and
I was told they were cheaper in the Strand. In these bad times it's
only the poor that can afford to be extravagant. And Lady Mary came
with me. If you call that a demonstration, I should like to know what
you call a pandemonium.
Hill: The people mean well, but they are sometimes badly guided. If
only they could be brought to see what it is they want. . . .
Lady Euphemia: They seemed to know exactly what they wanted just
now. They grabbed my diamond brooch, and they were trying to
get hold of Mary's rings off her hands when you came up.
Hill: Have they stolen your jewels? (wringing his hands) Unhappy
men! They little know what they are doing.
Lady Euphemia: No. I suppose not. Otherwise they might know that
my brooch was only paste.
    Yes, my dear, it is true. The family diamonds are all false. I have
taken the real ones long ago. . . .[235]

Meanwhile outside in the Square the meeting is becoming a
serious riot. There is a bomb explosion, buildings are set ablaze,
and troops, called in to disperse the crowd, are obliged to open
fire. The agitators return in panic, and betray the cowardice and
mutual treachery that one has been led to expect of them. In
front of Hartley and his men, who have come to make arrests,
Spragge denounces Hill for his inflammatory ideas, while Biffin,
finding that it is his own store which has been set alight, accuses
the others and clamours for a dictatorship to protect property.
Hartley concludes the act by a fitting condemnation: 'And this
is a man who only yesterday was panting for a breath of revolution. So much for the New Radicalism.'
    Hartley has, however, rendered himself vulnerable by shielding

Hill and hiding him in his own house. Weston, who has escaped arrest and discovered from Lady Mary the place of Hill's concealment, is now in possession of the means to strike Hartley down. At a Foreign Office reception Biffin and Brandon are already driving nails into Hartley's coffin. They have become, complete renegades from the popular cause, and are prepared to charge Hartley in Parliament with a culpable laxity, in 'giving countenance to the party of disorder'. The sceptical Sutton, who is present, reminds Brandon that Hartley could not have banned the meeting, because 'you would have been the first to vote against him'. 'That's nothing to do with it,' rejoins Biffin. 'We are private members, and have no responsibility.' At this point Weston appears, and plans to blackmail Hartley into admitting Brandon and himself into the cabinet. His other associates he intends to leave to their fate and the law. At the gathering Weston confronts Hartley, who is well aware of the danger of shielding Hill (but 'A man must stand by his friends') and who has just been knocked sideways by the revelation that Lady Mary has betrayed him. But Hartley is stoically incorruptible, and defies Weston to do his worst. Things are bad enough for him, however, without any further scandal. A 'royal personage' comes by, and snubs him: 'Nice mess you've made of it, Sir!' The audience know that Lady Mary has repented her inadvertent disclosure to Weston, and has warned Hill to quit Hartley's house at once before he is discovered there.

The last act is set in Lady Euphemia's house, six months later. Hartley has had to resign, but without serious scandal. Spragge and Doggett have served a three months' imprisonment, and now appear in workmen's overalls to do a plumbing repair. Spragge's union has failed to pay his £300 maintenance allowance as an M.P., and he is glad to get back to an honest trade. The scene is a final grand ensemble, in which the courtship of Lord Reginald and Miss Myra leads to their engagement, and Lady Mary and Hartley dispel the misunderstanding which has separated them. The assembly of all the characters is also an occasion for a further commentary on the times. Hartley's qualities are beginning to be recognized, for reasons which are explained by Sutton:

And now they say that he is absolutely indispensable. In these times of

progress . . . what everybody said yesterday everybody denies today. . . .
He is the only strong man in the government. He knows his own
mind, and that is a great distinction nowadays . . . sooner or later he
will be prime minister. We have had worse ones. In the age of universal
flabbiness I begin to think that strength is the greatest of all virtues.[236]

The 'flabbiness' of the age is illustrated later by the appearance
of Weston and his henchmen Brandon and Biffin. The latter have
formed a new group called the 'Consistents', with 'principle
before party' as their motto. They declare their principles to be
sympathy with Labour and social movements, so long as they do
not go too far or interfere with the accumulation of capital or
the preservation of social distinctions. Weston himself keeps
cynically aloof. He has lost this round against Hartley, who cuts
him before the others, but this does not hurt him or destroy his
demagogic power. He is confident of ultimate success through
the new morality of deception:

Lady Euphemia: Do you believe the British public will approve of this
   new morality?
Weston: They will shut their eyes, so long as their prejudices are
   flattered and their wants supplied.
Lady Euphemia: But suppose you cannot give them what they want?
Weston: I can always promise it, and that satisfies them just as well.

Politics, Weston declares, is an amoral art. And in his argument
we discern Chamberlain's distaste for the new morality of the
House of Commons as well as of the hustings:

Weston: Ah, you shouldn't bear malice. I never do. You take things too
   seriously. Politics are only a game, you know.
Hartley: Even a game should be played fairly.
Weston: Ba! There are some games in which cheating makes all the
   fun, and one of them is politics. I like to have an ace or two up my
   sleeve, and the trick in my pocket, and I am honest enough to say
   so. If you want to beat your opponents you must score how you
   can. If you don't load the dice, they will. What you call cheating, I
   call skill. Parliamentary tactics are a form of high art, and it is only
   a philistine who would trammel art with rules of morality.
Lady Euphemia: You certainly practice what you preach, Mr Weston.
Hartley (to Lady Mary): Let us go, Mary. This man makes me sick.[237]

The other characters are more tolerant, or less perceptive, than Hartley, and there is no question of Weston being expelled from polite society. The ending of the comedy, though crowned with a double betrothal, is but an uncertain victory for morality.

Sufficient, perhaps, of the play has been recounted to reveal its autobiographical importance. Had it been staged anonymously, Chamberlain would certainly have been identified as the inspiration of Hartley if not as the author of the piece. Whether contemporaries would have recognized the power and truthfulness of his self-exposure, supposing the authorship to have been admitted, is more doubtful. For many it would have been the devil quoting scripture. Only those intimately acquainted with his private personality, and the inner history of his struggle to uphold against Gladstone and the New Radicals what he conceived to be the elementary principles of political morality, could have recognized its burning sincerity. And only those who understood his deep conviction of the mischief wrought by agitators promising what they could not practically fulfil, or spreading discontent in order to undermine the whole political system, could have appreciated the fundamental distinction between his early Radicalism and the latter-day socialism. In the last analysis, Chamberlain was for things as they were, the agitators against. He wished to eliminate faults, they wished to build anew. And, mistakenly or not, he interpreted the difference between himself and the new popular leaders in terms not of ideology but of character and motive. He had never seen politics as a struggle between the 'haves' and the 'have nots', and when Radicals with this approach seemed to exult in the destruction of the old standards and the old values, the hardworking and practical industrialist of Birmingham threw in his lot with the 'gentlemen of England'. He did not imagine that there could be working-class politics, with working-class leaders who needed, for their self-esteem as well as for other reasons, to create a new parliamentary style, a new ethos, a new set of values which were meaningful in working class lives.

Chamberlain had never seen his way very far in the kind of social reforms which the socialists were beginning to demand. But when he set himself to formulate an alternative programme, he now saw clearly that its basic principle should be the encouragement of thrift, providence and self-reliance. Henceforward he would have nothing to do with anything which looked like bribing the working classes. The first plank of his programme was old age pensions.* Here he was prepared to allow, as other countries were doing, the use of state taxes for the encouragement of private saving. Would not a voluntary old age pension scheme, promoted by the state, but operated through the Friendly Societies to obviate the host of officials who administered the German system, remove the disincentives to saving and cause private insurance to flourish as never before? A new spirit of self-reliance and foresight would be promoted among the working classes, and only the really improvident or incapable would end up in the hands of the Poor Law. Such was Chamberlain's reasoning. It was diametrically opposed to the arguments advanced by Mr Charles Booth† and later by the Labour advocates of old age pensions, who thought that they should be given to all persons in need out of state taxation. A non-contributory scheme, giving pensions to all old persons 'without reference to character' who were in need while withholding them from those who had saved for themselves a living competence, was anathema to Chamberlain. It was subsidizing improvidence at the expense of the provident. But this was to be the form that the Liberals adopted in 1908.

The other main item of his programme was the advancing of loans by local authorities to promote house purchase among the working classes. Lesser items included the amendment of the Artisans Dwellings Act to cover all street and public improvements, courts of arbitration to settle industrial disputes, compensation for industrial injuries and accidents, labour exchanges, the empowering of local authorities to arrange for cheap workers' trains, and the control of pauper immigration. He tried hard to persuade the Unionists to adopt an electoral programme along

---

* Chamberlain first publicly proposed old age pensions in 1891, and chaired an informal parliamentary committee to explore the subject.

† Charles Booth was married to a cousin of Beatrice Webb, who describes him as 'conservative in politics and strongly anti-socialist in temper and economic views' (*My Apprenticeship*, p.217). He was converted to the plan of universal state-provided old age pensions by Samuel Barnett, who had advocated them in the early 'eighties (*ibid.*, p. 179). Booth's scheme held the field on the Labour side till Asquith's premiership.

these lines in 1894, and recommended it to Salisbury as 'attractive as well as safe'. He even suggested to Salisbury that the House of Lords should send a batch of such measures down to the Commons, 'to show the ordinary elector that the kind of legislation he desires may be had more readily from the Unionist peers than from the Gladstonian House of Commons'.*

It was, however, on the development of the Empire that Chamberlain now began to place the main emphasis. 'We believe', he said in a public speech, 'in the expansion of the Empire, in its legitimate development . . . we desire . . . to develop that commerce and that enterprise upon which I am convinced the happiness of the population depends much more than it does upon any legislative action.'[238] His ideas for the political integration of the self-governing colonies were still beyond the range of practical politics. One thing was clear to him privately: the key to the realization of his social and imperial programme lay in his tenure of the Colonial Office in a Unionist government.

The acceptance of office under Lord Salisbury raised the delicate question of whether, and to what extent, the Liberal Unionists should give up their separate party organization. In the autumn of 1894 Chamberlain began to consult with Devonshire and other Liberal Unionists on the problem. He took it for granted that the central organization should remain distinct from the Conservatives, and that local mergers of the constituency associations should be permitted only where it would not entail the loss of voters who could not vote Tory. The power of this sentimental consideration he points out, in a letter to his son:

Chamberlain–Austen Chamberlain, 27 January 1895: We must maintain a separate organization, and our Tory friends must regard this without jealousy. . . .

From the first the Gladstonian tactics have been to minimize and if possible to destroy the Liberal Unionist party. They have been wise, and if they had succeeded it would have been almost impossible to

---

* Chamb. PP., Memo. on a programme of social reform, 29 October 1894, addressed to Lord Salisbury. His criticism against the Gladstonians was that 'measures affecting the moral and material wellbeing of the people are being put aside to gratify personal and sectarian prejudices and to promote party interests'. The Unionists, he thought, should 'ask the working classes to choose with their eyes open between political revolution and social reform'.

defeat Home Rule. No one who has not worked among the electors can be aware how strong are old prejudices in connection with party names and colours and badges. A man may be a good Unionist at heart, and yet nothing can persuade him to vote 'blue' or give support to a 'Tory' candidate.[239]

After the Unionist victory of the summer, and the acceptance of office by Chamberlain, Devonshire, Henry James, and other Liberal Unionists, the question of the fusion of the two parties was raised again. In general, the Liberal Unionist leaders were content to leave matters to the local associations, but in the Birmingham region, Chamberlain declared, his party would not accept fusion even if he pressed them. The solid group of Midland members was a visible token of his influence, and its stability—it remained relatively unshaken even during the 1906 landslide —was a testament to his electoral skill and energy. Naturally and instinctively he clung to his own organization, and events were to prove that he was prudent to do so. But for most people the distinction between Liberal Unionists and Conservatives was minimal. In 1895, for the first time, Chamberlain took his seat in the Commons on the same side as the Conservatives, when he sat on the government front bench as Colonial Secretary. And, Gladstone having retired, although he was in no hurry to drop the label of 'Gladstonians' for his opponents, he began to call them 'Radicals' as the Conservatives did. In his policies he was one of the most consistent of English statesmen, but his Radical days were over. 'It is you who have changed,' he said to his former associates, 'and not I.'

CHAPTER EIGHT

The Struggle for South Africa

South Africa is on the eve of a terrible blood bath, from which our people will emerge either as an exhausted remnant, wood-cutters and water-carriers for a hated race, or as victors, founders of a United South Africa, of one of the great empires of the world . . . an Afrikander republic . . . stretching from Table Bay to the Zambesi.

Jan Christian Smuts, 4 September 1899

THE Boer War is usually regarded as the high water mark of imperialism. It was also called 'Chamberlain's war'. From it J. A. Hobson drew the moral that imperialism was a necessary adjunct of advanced capitalistic states, providing Lenin with this congenial theme. The outcry raised by Liberals against 'Randlords' and 'Chinese slavery' matched well with the supposition that Chamberlain and the government were secretly in league with Cecil Rhodes and engineered the war under pressure from capitalist circles. To this day, in spite of the wealth of evidence bearing on policy formation now available in the Colonial Office and other archives, the old accusations against Chamberlain are still repeated. Afrikaner historians have continued to obscure the issues through their fascination with the guilt of Chamberlain, to the neglect of the general attitudes and motives behind the British position—shared with a fair consistency by a wide range of officials, politicians and public controversialists at the time.

The war arose directly from a political crisis, of which the degradation of the 'Uitlanders' of the Transvaal—mostly British subjects—was but a symptom. The Uitlander problem in British eyes was only the by-product of a struggle between 410,000 Dutch and 430,000 British for supremacy in the whole of South Africa. And whereas the British thought of themselves as secure in conditions of political tolerance and equality, the Kruger régime in the Transvaal refused these conditions, overawing the civilian population of Johannesburg with military forts while they rearmed to supply the militant Afrikaners in the whole of

South Africa with the leadership and weapons to drive the British into the sea.

The urgency of the situation arose from the high rate of Uitlander immigration into the Transvaal. Under the London Conventions of 1881 and 1884, Kruger could not prevent such an influx. When he tried to do so in 1897 he was forced to retract by the threat of war. Already the Uitlanders were calculated greatly to outnumber in adult males the Boer burghers, and lacked only political rights in order to take over the Transvaal state. Time was on the British side, providing the British Government resolutely upheld the Conventions. It was thus the Transvaal which forced the pace, starting to rearm even before the Jameson Raid of December 1895 provided a heaven-sent excuse for full militarization. Four years later the Transvaal's armaments were sufficient to equip both itself and the Dutch outside the Transvaal, who readily joined them.

The contest between Chamberlain and Kruger, therefore, was produced by the opposition of two totally incompatible ideals, brought into precipitate conflict by the rapid development of the gold-mining industry of the Witwatersrand. At the Bloemfontein Conference with Milner in June 1899, Kruger lamented that he was being asked to give up his country, and buried his face in his hands. The equality of the two white races, the freedom of immigration and the acquisition of burgher rights by immigrants, which had been promised in the discussions that had preceded the Convention, were not found to be compatible with the preservation of what Kruger, veteran of the Great Trek, stood for. It had suited the immigrants to decline service in the Boer commando and to forgo burgher rights and naturalization. In like manner it suited Kruger to treat the Uitlanders as birds of passage. With the vote and their own representatives, they would have commanded a majority of the Volksraad and reduced him and his people to a minority group in their own country. Even to have granted representative municipal government to Johannesburg would have been to set up a rival state, able, if it chose, to defy and overthrow the Pretoria régime whose revenues it supplied. And so Kruger was constrained to attempt to maintain a state of things which had no parallel in any other country: to confine an educated and wealthy European community by bonds of paper, and to keep without the elementary rights of citizenship the preponderance of numbers, wealth and intelligence within his state.

To do this, it was necessary for him to destroy the London Convention and the moral position of Britain as paramount power in South Africa. His government claimed that the Transvaal was a sovereign state, and did all it could to enlist the sympathy of foreign powers. It encouraged the militants of the Afrikaner movement, which aimed to create a Dutch United States of South Africa. It exploited the fact that a British intervention on behalf of the Uitlanders needed an unlikely combination of circumstances—a respite in British relations with the European powers, a resolute understanding between the High Commissioner and Colonial Secretary, and a practical and moral *casus belli* convincing enough to persuade the Liberal opposition and the British public to agree to the despatch of a large field force to South Africa.

On the British side, both Liberal and Unionist statesmen— even the 'pro-Boer' Campbell-Bannerman—upheld the doctrine that their country as the 'paramount power' in South Africa had the right and duty to maintain peace in the area. More specifically, it was held that the Convention of 1884 was not a treaty between two sovereign states, but a statement by the Queen of the conditions under which she consented to allow certain of her subjects to conduct their internal affairs. But even supposing that the Transvaal had been in reality a sovereign state, Britain would still not have tolerated the degradation of British nationals to second-class citizens, and the moral effects of this throughout the whole of South Africa—a country where gradations of racial inferiority had become a system. Men like Milner felt this keenly. Something of the arrogant and contemptuous treatment meted out to the natives by the Boers was retained in their treatment of the British, in their policing of Johannesburg and their dispersal of political meetings. It was this, at bottom, which hardened the British resolution to redress the situation by force if necessary. Added to this was a feeling, reflected in the correspondence and minutes of British officials both in South Africa and in the Colonial Office, that the Boers employed trickery in their official dealings with the British.

Britain had been twice on the verge of war with the Transvaal, —in 1894 over the attempted forcible enlistment of British subjects and in 1895 over the closing of the drifts—before the Jameson Raid ushered in a new phase in the diplomatic relations of the two countries. In December 1895, the British government knew that an uprising of the Uitlanders was likely, and there is no doubt that Chamberlain for one felt that a revolution would be both justifiable and welcome if it could be achieved without bloodshed.* But he had done nothing to create the situation, and what scant evidence there is of his attitude before the Raid seems to indicate that he was concerned with the dangers, not the opportunities, involved in a rising.† It was obvious that the British government could not allow a bloody suppression of an unarmed and defenceless city, and would have had to intervene if a rising had occurred. But there were no ready means of intervention. And there is not the slightest warrant for believing that Chamberlain, who was not a party to the intrigues of Rhodes and the Chartered Company, regarded the small Bechuanaland police force of the Company as adequate to cover even the immediate exigencies of a rising.‡ Only a thorough knowledge of the total situation in South Africa could have enabled a Colonial Secretary in London to judge and assume responsibility for the contingencies which would follow upon an Uitlander revolt, and this Chamberlain did not have. The High Commissioner at this time, Sir Hercules Robinson, was pro-Boer, and with Rhodes and his agents Chamberlain's liaison was distant and inefficient.

---

* See, e.g. Chamberlain's despatch to Transvaal of 4 February 1896 (*London Gazette*, 7 February) and his letter to Prime Minister, 26 December 1895: 'I have received private information that a rising in Johannesburg is imminent . . . and I have given secret instructions to Sir Hercules Robinson [High Commissioner] how to act in an emergency . . . we have, of course, our usual garrison at the Cape, and Rhodes has the Bechuanaland Police. There is nothing more to be done but to watch the event, which we have done nothing to provoke. . . .' (quoted Garvin, III, p.78)

† It was clear from the attitude of Germany that a Uitlander rising which coincided with an international crisis would present serious difficulties; for British intervention (planned since the time of the Liberal Colonial Secretary, Lord Ripon, and his High Commissioner, Loch) depended on large military reinforcements. When tension if not war was threatened by President Cleveland's message to Congress over British Guiana (17 December 1895) Chamberlain wrote of the rising: '. . . either it should come *at once* or be postponed for a year or two at least. Can we secure this ?'

‡ While the usefulness of the police in the event of a rising was obvious to all, their potential usefulness as filibusters could never have impressed anyone.

Chamberlain knew, as he put it, 'of the precautions, the preparations, if you like, in view of the expected trouble in Johannesburg'.* On 29 December 1895—the very day on which Jameson's
filibustering band of armed police invaded the Transvaal—
Chamberlain believed the danger of a rising was over and wrote
with relief to Salisbury: 'I think that the Transvaal business is
going to fizzle out. Rhodes has miscalculated the feeling of the
Johannesburg capitalists, and it is now quite possible that Kruger
will make some concessions, in which case the affair would be
terminated for the present at any rate.'† The momentous events
which followed—the miserable failure of Jameson's 'mad'
escapade, the Kaiser's telegram implying German diplomatic
support for the Transvaal as a sovereign state, and the public
incrimination of Rhodes seeming to portend the collapse of
British influence in South Africa—are well known.‡ They placed

* The best discussion of the antecedents of the Raid is in Garvin, III, pp.30–125,
and Elizabeth Pakenham, *Jameson's Raid*. The supposedly incriminating 'missing
telegrams' to Rhodes from his agent Harris in London, giving garbled and unauthorized accounts of Colonial Office views, were seen by Chamberlain and his
officials in June 1896. Chamberlain saw in them 'a deliberate plot to commit the
Colonial Office involuntarily and by a partial confidence to a general approval of
Rhodes's plans, and then use this afterwards as a screen for the whole conspiracy'
(Garvin, III, p.114). This is no doubt too strong, but the solicitor of the Chartered
Company was certainly prepared to exploit the ambiguities in the telegrams—phrases
which looked very sinister after Jameson's action—to blackmail the government into
sparing the Company's charter. To find an innocent explanation for the texts composed by the 'slim' and unscrupulous Harris was an exercise in ingenuity and
historical patience not expected from the enemies of England, and the missing
telegrams were not published at the time. '. . . if they put me with my back to the
wall they'll see some splinters' was Chamberlain's comment, but he was not given
the opportunity of defending his position publicly.
† The day before, Chamberlain was informed that the Chartered Company's solicitor,
Hawksley, had mentioned that Rhodes 'might be driven into an attitude of frenzy
and unreason, and order Dr Jameson to "go in". . . and manipulate a revolution';
but another Company agent, Maguire, had called this 'absurd'. Nevertheless
Chamberlain warned the High Commissioner on 29th that he would have to condemn any such invasion. On receiving the news the following evening that the Raid
had been launched, he told his family: 'If this succeeds, it will ruin me. I am going
up to London to crush it.'
‡ It is regrettable, however, that in their eagerness to implicate Chamberlain in
Rhodes's policies, South African historians have obscured an important divergence
of aim. When Rhodes, aided by Sir Hercules Robinson, Sir Graham Bower, and the
Boers, attempted to prevent the annexation of Bechuanaland (1884–5) and talked of
'eliminating the Imperial factor' (Pakenham, *op. cit.*, pp.22–3), Chamberlain took
the side of the native chiefs and sent this message to the 'Cape Afrikanders' via
James Anthony Froude: 'Tell them in my name that they will find the Radical

the Transvaal question in the forefront of British politics, and made the resolution of the Uitlander difficulty, which hitherto had not greatly concerned the Colonial Office, a matter of the first moment.

To deprive the Chartered Company of Rhodesia of all its powers of civil administration seemed to Chamberlain too drastic to contemplate. 'Rhodes', he told Harcourt, 'is the one man who combines energy, wealth, ability, and popularity. If he goes, the whole population will be in a state of ferment, and their attacks and demands upon the home government will be strenuous and persistent.'* The solution as he saw it was to draw the teeth of the Company by taking away its military forces while leaving intact the civil administration. To fill the gap left by the fallen colossus a new High Commissioner, Sir Alfred Milner, in whom complete confidence could be placed, was sent to the Cape.† Milner was classed along with Chamberlain and the

---

Party more sternly imperial than the most bigotted Tory' (Chamb. PP., Froude-Chamberlain, 1 December 1884). Robinson, reappointed High Commissioner in spite of Chamberlain's protest, explained in 1895 that 'nine out of ten Englishmen in the Transvaal . . . dislike the native policy of England—they dislike the meddling of the House of Commons and the philanthropic societies—and they dislike the attempt to force the Indian coolie into a position of political and commercial equality with the whites. They would therefore prefer to remain independent' (Garvin, III, p.60). His Secretary, Bower, who was guilty of complicity in Rhodes's conspiracy, shared Robinson's dislike of 'direct Imperial rule' as well as his racial views. He thought the Colonial Office was controlled by 'missionaries, philanthropists and Jews' and looked upon the Africans as 'black savages' (Pakenham, op. cit., p.155). Bower and his chief had the strangest notions about Chamberlain, and were as little concerned to discover his views as to obey his instructions.

* Chamb. PP., 19 November 1896. '. . . no Crown administration would do better', he adds, 'unless Parliament would place unlimited funds at its disposal.'
† Milner's view of Rhodes and of the imperial government's role vis-à-vis Rhodesia appears in a letter to Chamberlain of 22 March 1898 (Chamb. PP.): 'Rhodes and I have got on excellently so far. How long this will last I can't say, for he would no doubt be a ruthless adversary if I found it necessary to oppose his general policy. . . . At present his influence in the [Cape] Colony is entirely on our side, the breach between him and the Bond being, I believe, irrevocable. . . . His efforts to develop the North are gigantic and really admirable . . . I told him quite frankly that I thought the time was unfavourable for trying to enlist either the British government or the British public on the side of a new scheme of African "expansion", that we had already too much hay on our fork. . . . The danger is that our people will lose heart and cease putting capital into a country which has swallowed up so much capital without apparent result. . . . Of course the country will never pay, at least in our lifetime, without some gold. . . .'

Kaiser as a 'pattern jingo' by the 'little Englander' Harcourt when he showed himself at the outset to be solidly behind a tough policy toward Kruger. Chamberlain wrote privately a long discursive reply which contains the best statement of his South African policy in the lull before the final contest. Kruger, he said, had told a private meeting of the Transvaal Executive that England would bluster, but 'provided they did not openly defy her, they would be able to whittle away the Convention until there was nothing left'. Perhaps Britain could 'sit down tamely and submit to this', Chamberlain went on, if the Transvaal alone were in question: 'but the result would infallibly be that we should lose South Africa and probably much more besides'.*

The threat that the Transvaal presented to the whole global security of the British empire was not imaginary. These were the very worst years of British isolation. Against a hostile combination of powers Chamberlain and his associates in the Colonial Office were prone to take a belligerently defensive attitude. When, for instance, Germany and Russia seized Kiaochow and Port Arthur on the Chinese mainland and threatened thereby to prejudice Britain's influence and trading rights in China, Chamberlain took a very high line. An assurance from Germany that Kiaochow should become a treaty port was to be demanded, after which 'if Russia refuses these terms we should summon her fleet to leave Port Arthur and make her go if necessary. . . .'[240] The same kind of situation developed later in 1898 over the fate of Delagoa Bay, a Portuguese possession controlling the Transvaal's outlet to the sea. Portugal had made a definite offer to Britain, which, however, the cabinet treated without urgency, inviting Germany to participate in the discussions. Against this supposed abdication of British rights and interests Lord Selborne, Chamberlain's Under-Secretary, remonstrated with Balfour. To let another power gain practical control of Delagoa Bay would be regarded throughout South Africa as 'the sign of the abdication by us of our position of paramount power'; it would 'make a war between us and the Transvaal inevitable', and 'so weaken

---

* Chamb. PP., 4 September 1897. War with the Transvaal should be avoided, he argued, because 'such a war could bring us no particular glory or credit; and . . . because it is almost inevitable that before twenty years are passed the Transvaal will be part of a South African Federation and, I hope, under the British flag.'

the ties which still bind the British (as distinct from the Dutch) South Africans to us that our whole position in South Africa would be jeopardized'. Pressure from France and Russia, Selborne feared, might lead to international control of Delagoa Bay, in which the Transvaal itself might gain representation. 'I say with the utmost deliberation', he concluded, 'that sooner than permit this we ought to occupy Delagoa Bay and defy all these powers.'[241] The solution actually reached by Balfour was to conclude a package deal with Germany over Mozambique and Angola which included a resignation of German interest in Delagoa Bay and the Transvaal. Germany's supposed friendliness, said Balfour, had encouraged the Boers 'to adopt a policy towards this country which, now that they are shut out from all hope of European assistance, may perhaps be modified to our advantage'.[242]

At this juncture Chamberlain was contemplating a renewal of the diplomatic controversy with Kruger, which had got bogged down in the 'sovereignty' issue. His real objective was to educate the British public in the full significance of the dispute over the Uitlanders' rights. As a practitioner in the art of the 'new diplomacy',* he realized that the despatches between himself and Kruger were an appeal to public opinion, and must somehow dramatize and develop his case so that it could be grasped by a lay audience. In the dialectical contest the advantages lay with Kruger, who had only to defend the *status quo*, while Chamberlain had to overcome all the objections and suspicions involved in 'bullying' a small power into altering things. The British public had to be persuaded that the situation in South Africa—the complications and bearings of which it could never be expected to master—was becoming intolerable. It had also to be satisfied that every reasonable concession and opportunity to redress grievances had been given to the Boers.

Chamberlain's task was therefore to reduce his demands to the barest minimum to secure adequate reform, and formulate them in a way that would reveal the importance of the principles at

---

* Like 'New Radicalism', the term 'new diplomacy' meant different things at different periods of the century. At this time it signified open and popular methods and perhaps bluster, in contradistinction to secret negotiation absolved from popular control.

stake. These demands could not be presented suddenly and baldly, indeed they could not be presented at all until both the cabinet and the public were thoroughly alerted as to their importance, and were resolved to enforce them at the risk of war.

The efficacy of any reforms would in any case depend very largely upon the goodwill and co-operation of the Kruger régime. Here was the crux of the matter. If by diplomacy Chamberlain could test the goodwill or hostility of the Transvaal, he would ensure that any sterner demands that might have to follow would be supported. 'I am not prepared,' he noted on 2 August 1898, 'to put H[er] M[ajesty's] G[overnment] in a position in which the refusal of the S[outh] A[frican] R[epublic] to comply with their demands would place them under the necessity of going to war or retiring ignominiously, but it *may be* worth while considering . . . a despatch for publication setting forth more in sorrow than in anger and in moderate terms all our grievances against the govt. of the S.A.R., and expressing regret at their unfriendly attitude.'[243] He thought of enumerating all the points on which Kruger had failed to make good his promises, given at the time of the Jameson Raid, to effect reforms and to 'forgive and forget': the long-standing grievances of the witholding of the franchise, the refusal to allow English-speaking schools or the municipal self-government of Johannesburg, and newer grievances concerning the press, treatment of aliens, and the judiciary. Finally the general position of affairs in the Transvaal should be described as 'unworthy of a state professing to be civilized, and unparalleled'.

Such a despatch was discouraged by the Colonial Office secretaries, Graham and Wingfield.[244] The former thought it 'wouldn't do much good in the press in this country', while the latter thought it would 'infuriate the Dutch' and cause the jingoes to accuse Chamberlain of allowing the Boers to break the Convention with impunity. On this advice, Chamberlain agreed to await the visit of Sir Alfred Milner, the High Commissioner, to London. Re-written in successive drafts, it remained in the Colonial Office files until the revival of agitation on the Rand, when the presentation of the celebrated Uitlander petition of 1899 to the Queen produced the conditions favourable to its being unleashed.

This momentous despatch, which drew the two countries into a grapple which could only end in a climb-down by Kruger or war, took the form of a remonstrance upholding the substance of the Uitlanders' petition. But it would probably still have been sent had there been no petition. On 26 March 1899 Chamberlain took note of a speech by Kruger which 'challenged me to prove my charges against him'. Would not this, he minuted, 'make a splendid excuse for launching another despatch at him . . ."setting myself right" with the President' and then letting him have 'a full list of his iniquities'.[245] The long-pending despatch was refurbished along these lines in April, after news of the petition and its contents had arrived at the Colonial Office.*

In preparing a brief for a cabinet meeting on 2 May, Chamberlain drew up a paper stressing the need to send a despatch in answer to the petition which should be 'a protest and still more an appeal to public opinion', but not an ultimatum:

J.C. 28 April: Our relations with the Transvaal have again reached a critical stage. We have to send a reply to the petition . . . which is signed by 21,000 British subjects. The complaints made . . . are, I think, fully justified, and the secret despatches from Sir A. Milner . . . show the serious view which he takes of the situation.

If we ignore altogether the prayer of the petitioners it is certain that British influence in South Africa will be severely shaken. If we send an ultimatum to Kruger, it is possible and in my opinion probable that we shall get an offensive reply, and we shall then either have to go to war or accept a humiliating check.

We cannot expect any support from the present Cape government, which is a Bond government with strong leanings towards the Transvaal. I think the view of those best qualified to advise is that we must examine into and affirm the grievances of the Uitlanders, and indicate that the present state of things is a source of constant danger and cannot continue indefinitely.[246]

The famous telegram from Milner, comparing the Uitlanders to the downtrodden serfs of ancient Sparta, had not arrived by 2 May. It was solicited by Chamberlain at the end of April, who asked Milner to telegraph his views. 'What I fear', he minutes,

---

* The Uitlander petition was sent on 28 March and arrived in London on 14 April, but its contents had been telegraphed earlier and are recited in a draft of 'the despatch' of 6 April.

'is the charge that I have rushed off a despatch without waiting to know the views of Sir A. Milner. Of course I do know them from secret despatches, but I can't say this, and I think it will be considered too "pushful" if my despatch *seems* to be altogether independent of Sir A. Milner's views.'[247] Actually, as the Colonial Office staff had good reason to anticipate, Milner's views were stronger than Chamberlain's. By 9 May the cabinet had before it Milner's vitriolic text* and also a suggestion from Milner that the despatch should offer a conference to Kruger, which he could not refuse without losing the support of the Cape Dutch. Hard on this came news that Steyn, President of the Orange Free State, had offered Bloemfontein as a place for the conference. The cabinet grasped the idea of a Milner–Kruger meeting, and authorized the sending of the despatch, justifying its intervention on three grounds: its right to hear, and secure redress for, the grievances of British nationals in foreign states; the special rights secured by the Convention; and the serious effects on the peace and prosperity of the whole of South Africa produced by the discontent and unrest in the Transvaal.

The Bloemfontein Conference sat from 31 May to 5 June 1899. Before the first encounter of the two redoubtable opponents, it had become clear to the Colonial Office that they would not reach agreement. Milner's line was to insist on a minimum of franchise reform and representation, which he calculated might in favourable conditions enable the Uitlanders to work out their own salvation. His terms were 7 seats in the Volksraad for the Uitlander districts, thus increasing the assembly from 28 to 35 members: and the franchise to Uitlanders after 5 years residence, to be granted retrospectively to those who then qualified. At the Colonial Office, Mr H. Lambert considered Milner's demand for 7 seats 'very moderate', since 'the Rand has half the population and nearly all the wealth' of the country. At the same time he thought Milner's idea that the reforms should be passed forthwith in the current session was 'tying the Boer down tightly, and he may kick'.[248] Independently of Milner, Chamberlain set out his

---

* Chamberlain's comment on Milner's 'helots' despatch was: 'This is tremendously stiff, and if it is published will make either an ultimatum or Sir A. Milner's recall necessary.' (Quoted in R. H. Wilde, *Archives Year Book of South African History*, 1956, I, p.102)

own ideas for reform, which were very similar, and offered municipal reform for Johannesburg as an alternative to franchise reform. Lambert considered that the Boers were much too afraid of creating an *imperium in imperio* to grant municipal reform. Mr Graham observed that recent discussion in the Volksraad clearly indicated that Kruger would not grant a reasonable franchise reform unless he obtained a substantial *quid pro quo* to show his burghers, such as the abolition of article IV of the Convention, or some other condition which Britain could never accept. Graham continued:

The Conference therefore being probably foredoomed to failure, the utmost we can do is to make it quite clear that the unreasonable conditions are imposed by Kruger, not by us. . . .

So far as we can judge (I have been watching both the London and the provincial press) there is still a good deal of misapprehension on both sides as to the circumstances and as to the aims of H.M. Govt., Mr Chamberlain being accused in some quarters of conspiring with the 'Rhodesian gang' for an excuse to forcibly annex the S.A.R. . . . on the whole it does not seem possible that H.M. Govt. would be supported by public opinion in threatening forcible measures to secure redress of the Uitlander grievances.[249]

This last comment on public opinion was not endorsed by Chamberlain or Selborne. Selborne thought opinion was 'on the turn of the tide, to ebb or flow is not yet certainly apparent': while Chamberlain noted: 'I do not feel certain about public opinion here. If we could have got our despatch published first, its reception would probably have enlightened us.' Only after the failure of the Conference was the despatch of 10 May published in a blue book.*

Chamberlain's idea was to use the Bloemfontein Conference to secure publicity for the British point of view, and to ask the Cape premier, Schreiner, to attend in order to influence Kruger or witness his intransigence. Milner, on the other hand, regarded the Conference as a final presentation of British demands, to be

---

* Although the contents of the despatch of 10 May had been 'communicated' to the Transvaal and formed the basis of the Bloemfontein Conference, the despatch itself was not 'delivered' till after the failure of the Conference. The practice was to avoid formal delivery if possible, which involved publicity and the crystallization of the dispute into an overt disagreement.

followed, if necessary, by an ultimatum. Having reduced his demands to a minimum for the Uitlanders—'a great deal less than they may fairly claim'—he was not going to be fobbed off with anything 'clearly illusory'. Just before the Conference opened, he declined to follow Chamberlain's suggestion about admitting Schreiner with an alarmingly bellicose impatience:

Milner–Chamberlain, 27 May 1899: It is important, of course, owing to the accident of Bond being in power. . . . But after all, he only represents about half the [Cape] Colony. Taking white South Africa as a whole, those on our side are as numerous as those against us, though unfortunately they are not so well prepared for war, and there could be no greater error than to disappoint the half who are still cordially attached to Great Britain in the idle hope of conciliating the half who never can be so, at any rate so long as S.A.R. continues successfully to defy us.[250]

On receipt of this telegram, Chamberlain minuted: 'It seems to betray the existence of somewhat strained feelings—whereas coolness and sweet reasonableness are more than ever necessary at the present stage.' Graham imagined that Milner might be under an erroneous impression that H.M. Govt. 'have made up their minds to go on at any price'. Another official, Mr H. W. Just, summed up the difficulty when he commented that he could not see how 'public opinion could be expected to endorse war upon the S.A.R. in order to secure the franchise to a certain number of British subjects' who would *ipso facto* become aliens.

True to expectation, the talks reached a deadlock almost as soon as begun. Kruger would offer only a seven years' residential qualification for the franchise, not to be retrospective, and involving a period during which British citizenship would have to be renounced before the vote was obtained. He epitomized his argument in a brief observation:

Our enfranchised burghers are probably about 30,000, and the new-comers may be from 60,000 to 70,000; and if we give them the franchise tomorrow, we may as well give up the republic. I hope you will clearly see that I shall not get it through with my people.[251]

It was useless to argue that seven Rand seats would not swamp the Volksraad. On 3 June Milner telegraphed that Kruger's offers were 'quite inadequate', and spoke of breaking off the

Conference—which in fact he did, before Chamberlain's instruction not to do so could arrive. Too late, Chamberlain enjoined patience and haggling, after the Boer fashion, in order to commit Kruger to the principle of reform or place him 'clearly in the wrong'. The Conference broke up without affording much material for propaganda.

Britain had been worsted in the first round. The opportunity of remonstrating with the Transvaal which had been given by the Uitlander petition had been dissipated in an inconclusive parley. In consequence, the government had got seriously out of step with public opinion, which had hardly become aware of the gravity of the situation. By authorizing the despatch of 10 May, the government had committed itself to action. As Selborne put it, writing to Milner, 'We have entered a lane . . . where no turning back is possible without humiliation and disaster. We must eventually force the door at the other end, by peaceful pressure if possible, but if necessary by war.'[252] But after the refusal of adequate franchise reform, a basis for formal demands had yet to be found. Chamberlain sounded Milner on this point as follows:

Chamberlain–Milner, 7 June 1899 (tel.): If H.M. Govt. should decide to send an ultimatum, what should they ask for? It seems difficult to treat as *casus belli* refusal by state to which we have given complete internal independence to grant a particular form of franchise to aliens. Yet we must ask for something definite which will meet the existing situation.

What do you think of the following? 'The repeal of all legislation since the Convention of 1884 restrictive of the rights and privileges enjoyed by aliens when the Convention was arranged.'[253]

This was the true ground of the British position. The franchise demands—the 'Bloemfontein minimum' which Milner had put forward tentatively and conditionally—were adequate only for a co-operative settlement.

Kruger himself, however, kept the franchise question in the foreground by introducing legislation for a seven years' franchise scheme immediately after returning from Bloemfontein. The scheme was complicated, and it was only after some weeks that its insufficient and illusory nature became apparent. Just before its introduction on 12 June, Milner's observations on the general situation show that for him, at least, there could be no bargaining over his franchise proposals, which he was disposed to withdraw:

Milner–Governor of Natal, 9 June 1899: The position is rapidly defining itself. Dutch South Africa is evidently going back to Kruger, he having with his make-believe of reform given them just sufficient excuse for doing so. . . .

A most dangerous attempt is being made by the Bond press here to represent the crisis as over, Kruger having yielded so much. Remember British government has never demanded franchise, and probably never will. Their position is to urge franchise in order to deviate necessity of formal demands for protection of British subjects. . . .

Kruger's proposal is totally inadequate. He therefore must either enormously better it so as to come up to moderate scheme suggested by me at Conference . . . or be prepared for demands directly securing fair play to British subjects, which demands would very likely end in war.[254]

In London, the political temperature was much lower. Some steps were taken. In the Commons, Chamberlain spoke of a 'new situation' arising out of the failure of Bloemfontein, and announced that the despatch of 10 May would be presented— which meant that it could appear, with Milner's 'helots' despatch and other papers, in a blue book published on 14 June. The reception of the blue book by the press confirmed the cabinet in its opinion that 'another stage or stages must intervene' before an ultimatum.

Chamberlain observed that the public had been 'sensibly affected' by the blue book, but cautioned Milner that it was 'clear that we must be able to show that we have exhausted every form of diplomatic pressure and every suggestion for arrangement before we take active measures'.[255] Military preparations were being quietly proceeded with, but no spectacular move could be undertaken:

Chamberlain–Milner, 20 June 1899 (tel.): A demonstration in the shape of large reinforcements would be unmeaning unless it were to support an ultimatum, and public opinion seems to be entirely with you in thinking that time has not come for this yet. . . .

It would be mischievous and tend to confirm Kruger's obstinacy if we were to provoke a parliamentary division by premature action, and thus show him that the country is divided.[256]

Milner was not so moderate as Chamberlain thought, and two days later demanded an early show-down. He feared that if the crisis were protracted, Kruger would succeed in wearing down the business community of Uitlanders, for whom war would mean private deprivation, and who did not particularly want to be placed under the British flag. His telegram caused disquiet at the Colonial Office. Chamberlain minuted on 23 June:

Milner's policy is an ultimatum for a bill of rights. He must intend to include franchise, and indeed it is very difficult to see what other specific claim we can make. But if we do ask for franchise it must not be for franchise's sake, but as a means to an end—peace and tranquillity in South Africa. It is all very difficult at present.[257]

Graham commented that he thought Milner was in danger of being 'rushed' by the party 'which, while its sympathies with the Uitlanders is genuine, has for its chief aim the wiping out of Majuba and the speedy annexation of the Transvaal'. His minute with marginal comments by Chamberlain, continues:

Graham, 24 June 1899:

I do not think he has gone as far as this.
—J.C.

To give the Boers only two months from now to set their house in order or fight is quick work under the circumstances, and especially so for slow-thinking people like them; and yet this is what Sir A. Milner contemplates. If public opinion were emphatic and practically unanimous it would be different.

We shall pay no attention to to any demand going beyond Milner's.
—J.C.

We hear rumours that the Boers show signs of yielding to the influence of Fischer and Hofmeyr, and concurrently comes an ominous report that the Uitlanders are not content to start with Sir A. Milner's programme . . . but want a much larger measure of reform at once.

It is, however, evident that situation cannot long remain at present tension
—J.C.

The exodus from Johannesburg shows that there is a strong impression that we have made up our mind to fight *quand même*, and to fight soon. But . . . I very much doubt the accuracy of the report that business is at a standstill.[258]

The formal diplomatic position was that the British government awaited a reply to their despatch of 10 May. It was thus still premature for Chamberlain to utter any public criticism of the Transvaal government. But he nevertheless decided to make his speech to the Birmingham Liberal Unionist Association on 26 June the occasion for a broad review of the Transvaal situation. 'Probably it will be misrepresented,' he notes, 'but I will do my best to define the situation as I see it.'[259]

Both the Colonial Office officials and his Under-Secretary, Lord Selborne, were at this stage pressing for a bolder public lead from Chamberlain. Wingfield was 'much impressed with the importance of bringing home to President Kruger's mind the final determination of H.M. Govt. to have a satisfactory settlement'.[260] Selborne addressed a long appeal to Chamberlain, on the eve of his speech, pressing for a bold declaration. They were drifting towards war, while avoiding the task of alerting the public to the seriousness of the situation. To recede would spell absolute disaster. It would indicate that the rising star in South Africa was Dutch, not British, while in the eyes of Europe it would be seen as a reversion to 'pre-Fashoda' weakness. Milner would resign and the party would be jeopardized. The difficulty at which British diplomacy had stuck, was that whereas only putting a pistol at Kruger's head would effect anything, the public was not ready for this and did not appreciate how utterly untrustworthy he was. Consequently the government did not feel 'strong enough to apply that pressure which alone can fulfil their policy without war'. Chamberlain had already composed his speech with these considerations in mind, and left the public in no doubt that a settlement had to be reached.*

Selborne had been preparing successive drafts of a second despatch, taking note of the failure of the Bloemfontein Conference, and pressing for franchise reform or else full municipal rights for Johannesburg. The sending of this had to await the Boer reply to the earlier despatch. Meanwhile Milner had to be placated. 'Until it is quite clear that no substantial concession will be made', Chamberlain told him, 'it is difficult to formulate demands or to send troops.'[261] But if a satisfactory reply to the second despatch, when sent, was not given, an ultimatum would

---

* 'We will not be hurried . . . we will not be held back. . . . But having undertaken this business we will see it through.'

follow. This was very thin gruel for Milner, and worse was to follow. It gradually appeared, to his utter consternation, that Chamberlain was prepared to accept less than his Bloemfontein 'minimum'. The mediation of Hofmeyr and others secured a revised franchise scheme, which was submitted to the Raad on 8 July. Chamberlain received advance news of this on 6 July through Rothschild, to the effect that Kruger meant to grant at once a 'seven years' retrospective and retroactive franchise', and that this 'would be accepted with acclamation by the non-British Uitlanders who it is feared expect Lord Salisbury to go to war'.[262] A telegram was sent instructing Milner not to reject Kruger's proposals even if they were 'a compromise between your and his original suggestions'.[263]

Milner wanted to get away from the franchise question, with its baffling complications and scope for chicanery. But he was prevented from doing so:

Chamberlain–Milner, 12 July 1899 (tel.): My present view is that having put substantial and immediate representation of aliens in the front as tending to relieve tension and ultimately to secure a settlement of all differences—and also to approach to that equality of races which Convention was to secure—we had better stick to this line and not open a new issue. If Kruger agrees to negotiate, we must press for further amendments. . . .

If we could show conclusively that latest proposals are a sham, our cause would be much clearer. But if they involve substantial and prompt recognition of the claim to representation, the use of force cannot be justified.[264]

Shortly after, on 18 July, news reached London that the Volksraad had granted a seven years' retroactive franchise and five new seats to the Uitlanders. Chamberlain authorized *The Times* to report that, if these details were true, the crisis 'may be regarded as ended', and telegraphed to Milner congratulating him on having driven Kruger 'almost' to the Bloemfontein position. 'No one', he said, 'would dream of fighting over two years in qualification period.'[265] Further, he proposed to wind up the long-delayed second despatch with a proposal to Kruger for another conference to settle all other outstanding differences. Receiving this, with the ill-considered announcement in *The Times*, Milner, ill, tired, and near to despair, noted in his diary that

British public opinion 'is going to be befooled, and that is the long and short of it'.[266]

Selborne took Milner's side against Chamberlain, and worked strenuously to prevent the cabinet from accepting Kruger's franchise offer without guarantees. Sending a draft version of the despatch to Balfour, he pleaded that the moment of crisis in the negotiations had arrived, and that Milner, the loyal part of South Africa, and the Unionist press expected something more than a tame acceptance of Kruger's initiative. Without a British insistence upon a conference it was dangerous to accept the franchise scheme, for Kruger could work it so as to 'jockey the Uitlanders and us'. Jockeying was the invariable vice of the Boers, and 'trickery as natural to them as water to a duck'. Once cheated in this way, could 'we ever work up the steam again at leisure, and shall we ever again have on our side all our people in South Africa?' On receipt of Selborne's letter, Balfour raised with Chamberlain the further difficulty that it would be imprudent to 'commit ourselves to the proposal of a second conference between Kruger and Milner'. If Kruger refused, on the ground that the franchise scheme was a matter of internal administration, 'we should have received a diplomatic rebuff'.[267]

But what could be the alternative? As it happened, the Colonial Office received a telegram from Milner arguing against Chamberlain's general position and incidentally suggesting the substitution of a joint commission of inquiry for the conference:

Milner–Chamberlain, 21 July, No. 6: I hope despatch will make it clear that satisfactory agreement on all essential details is necessary if we are to recommend scheme as a whole to Uitlanders.

As regards arbitration, I am glad you favour project of tribunal without foreign element. Prospect of referring future disputes to arbitration should go far to make Govt. of S.A.R. ameliorate on outstanding questions. . . .

Supposing satisfactory scheme of enfranchisement can be agreed to, general reforms . . . may be left to time, but specific questions referred to [in my tel. of 1 July No. 2] cannot be allowed to remain where they are. British subjects will hesitate to become citizens of S.A.R. while there is danger of conflict between it and H.M. Govt. on other points, and unless they take it, franchise as remedy for grievances will prove fiasco.

As regards conference, I think that it is useless to discuss multitude of subjects involving complicated details with Kruger. Better leave to British Agent supported by good lawyer . . . to thrash out all points with State Attorney and State Secretary at Pretoria, and submit results to us and Govt. of S.A.R. as a whole. . . .[268]

From the time that this was received, it became the precise policy that Chamberlain was henceforth to pursue. On 22 July, Mr Just minuted with reference to the idea of a joint commission: 'If Kruger declines, could still go ahead. If accepts, appear like a climb-down.' On reading this the next day, Chamberlain agreed: 'I think despatch will have to be altered as to meeting between Kruger and Milner, and the combination above may be suggested. The moral effect of a new Commission would be as Mr Just suggests.'[269] In the idea Chamberlain saw a way out of the whole diplomatic entanglement. He would, if Kruger refused to co-operate, set up a unilateral commission, whose findings could be used to frame an ultimatum. The despatch was altered to allow for this, approved by the cabinet, and sent off on 27 July.*

While awaiting the Transvaal's reply to his telegrams of 31 July and 1 August pressing for a joint inquiry to settle the franchise and other questions, Chamberlain debated with Milner how to counter a possible refusal. He considered that an inquiry conducted unilaterally by the British Agent might suffice. Milner disagreed, feeling that the latter body could not elicit from the S.A.R. a 'binding statement of their intentions'.[270] Selborne agreed with Milner, with the additional argument that a unilateral inquiry could not obtain the necessary factual information, and could be shown by the Boers to be inaccurate in its findings. If a joint commission were refused, Selborne wanted a general ultimatum. But Chamberlain stuck to his point, arguing that although the report of a unilateral commission would be challenged by the Boers, it would be 'good enough for us', and

---

* This despatch of 27 July, containing a formal demand for another conference, was not delivered until after 23 August, and technically the South African Republic was presented with requests contained in two telegrams transmitted through Milner. The first, of 31 July, invited Kruger to appoint delegates to investigate whether his franchise reforms gave 'substantial' and 'immediate' representation to the Uitlanders: the second of 1 August suggested a conference after the delegates had reported, to settle the franchise and other questions, including arbitration of future disputes under the Conventions.

would strengthen the British case by agreeing upon far more: 'We shall base our ultimatum on their report. . . .'[271] What Chamberlain wanted was some clear and intelligible *casus belli* to present to the British electorate, if the despatch were evaded.

Further debate upon the effectiveness of the franchise as a means of ultimately securing reform was beginning to reveal many uncertainties. The Boers appeared to have insuperable objections to giving the Uitlanders the vote which elected directly the President and the Commandant General. Milner did not believe that even here the Uitlanders could hope to swamp the old burghers. He was pessimistic in his calculations of the numbers of Uitlanders who would opt to change their nationality, and thought they could not hope to carry an Uitlander President for many years to come.* To meet the case, Chamberlain suggested that the vote for President might be relinquished, if in exchange the Uitlanders on changing their nationality might be absolved from the duty of bearing arms against the country of their origin. This he thought would be an important inducement which would cause greater numbers to enfranchise themselves. Milner, on the other hand, insisted on the 'absolute equality of the old and new burghers', which appeared to him essential to secure the 'gradual fusion' of the two races.[272] But he acknowledged that there would probably be no spectacular alteration of the electoral forces in the Transvaal.

In mid-August, after Parliament had been prorogued and when the cabinet was dispersed on holidays, news of an extraordinary interview between Smuts, the Transvaal State Attorney, and the British Agent at Pretoria, Greene, was telegraphed to London. Isolated, overworked, and without secretarial assistance, Greene may have been thought by the Boers to have been invested with the powers of a plenipotentiary after the British proposal that he should superintend the joint inquiry into the franchise. But in fact he did not possess the complete confidence of Milner,

---

* The Colonial Office estimated that there were about 200,000 Uitlanders (mostly adult males) in the Transvaal as against 30,000 burghers. Milner reckoned that a three years' residential franchise would yield 44,000 possible Uitlander voters, a five years' franchise, 30,000 voters. But it was not thought that anywhere near such numbers would opt for the franchise at the cost of relinquishing British nationality. (C.O. 417/280. Minute by Mr Just of 13 August)

and he had been ostracized by the Kruger government. He had recently complained that his official relations with the régime were 'an absolute travesty of the ordinary acceptations of diplomatic intercourse . . . [and] as far as friendly official communications are concerned, I might just as well not be here at all'.[273] Greene was sounded by Smuts about a 'simplified draft franchise law', and asked if the British government would waive their demand for a joint inquiry. 'I suggested', Greene recounts, 'that I should have a personal interview with the State Attorney.' Smuts came to see him, and Greene explained that he had no idea whether H.M. Govt. would consent not to press their demand but that he thought the only choice for the S.A.R. Govt. was 'an immediate surrender to the Bloemfontein minima'. Smuts held out for a seven years' franchise, and went away. But later he returned with what appeared to be a complete acceptance of the Bloemfontein scheme, the details and conditions of which Greene collected verbally, promising to recommend them to Milner for acceptance by H.M. Govt. in return for the dropping of the demand for a joint inquiry.

Greene was assured by J. W. Wessels, the intermediary in these transactions, that the Boers would never grant an inquiry jointly with Britain into their internal affairs, 'preferring, little as the burghers themselves desire war, to fight sooner than admit it'. Greene continues:

They are, however, horribly frightened at our evident intention to settle trouble by force if need be, and are prepared to make great concessions above mentioned.

I have not committed H.M. Govt. in any way as to acceptance or refusal, but I have said I feel sure if the present is a bona fide attempt . . . to settle once for all the political rights of our people, that the govt. of S.A.R. need have no fear that we shall either wish or have cause to interfere in their internal affairs in future.[274]

Smuts' offer, as understood by Greene, was a five years' retrospective franchise, eight new seats for the Rand, making ten in all for the mining industry in a Volksraad of thirty-six, equal rights in the election of President and Commandant General, and new members of Volksraad to be allowed to use their own language. The details of the new franchise law, which was to be immensely simplified, were to be discussed with Greene and his legal adviser. In return, Smuts expected Britain to drop her demands for a joint inquiry and conference, and to concede arbitration 'as soon as the franchise scheme has become law'. He said his government 'will assume that H.M. Govt. will agree that a precedent shall not be formed by their present intervention for similar action in future', and that the suzerainty controversy should be 'tacitly allowed to lapse'.

There was considerable ambiguity in the Smuts proposal, which could be regarded either as a 'basis' for a broader settlement, or as a self-contained bargain designed to sidetrack the latest British demands. Thus it received a mixed reception. Greene enthusiastically hailed it as a 'huge surrender' in his telegraphic report to Milner, but Milner in transmitting the telegram to London condemned the whole negotiation. Greene in his opinion had 'gone too far'. 'Nothing but confusion can result from this irregular method of negotiation.' Milner wanted to insist on holding a joint inquiry into any franchise scheme before acceptance, and he declined to commit himself on other matters such as the necessity for a conference. In these objections, however, he was not supported by the Colonial Office. Selborne minuted: 'I think the final negotiations must be between Milner and Kruger; but I do not object to this method of paving the way.'

At Highbury, where Chamberlain was resolutely trying to take a holiday, the household was thrown into confusion after breakfast on 16 August when news of the latest developments arrived, and Chamberlain felt obliged to return to town immediately.[275] On studying the telegrams, however, he found that they were more satisfactory than he expected. He acted decisively against Milner's recommendations, directing that everything should be done to encourage the Boers to put their 'immense concession' on record. He told Milner to avoid provocative language and to suspend the unilateral inquiry just authorized in view of the 'altered situation'. His telegrams betray an optimistic mood:[276]

Chamberlain–Milner, 16 August No. 5: No change will be made in military preparations at present, but if present negotiations are successful it would be most desirable if we could come to some permanent arrangement as to armaments. If Boers would disarm Johannesburg fort, and give promise to cease importing arms and ammunition, we might reduce troops in South Africa by half.[277]

Feeling that Milner had been 'unnecessarily suspicious and pedantic', he wrote to Salisbury about this latest 'assurance of another climb-down on the part of Kruger',[278] and returned to Highbury by the night train. It was not until 4 September that Chamberlain returned in person to his Office, by which time, contrary to all his calculations, the diplomatic position had become hopeless.

For ten days the real intention of the Smuts offer was misunderstood in London. Greene had reported that the S.A.R. would embody their offer in a formal note if 'H.M. Govt. are willing not to press their demand for the proposed joint inquiry'. The three conditions or 'assumptions' stipulated by the Transvaal concerning future intervention, suzerainty, and arbitration were mentioned inconsequentially in the first of Greene's telegrams initialled by Smuts. No one at the Colonial Office took these assumptions seriously. 'There is plenty of time to talk about suzerainty and non-intervention in future', Graham minutes on 18 August, adding his opinion that unlike the stipulation about dropping the joint inquiry, these assumptions were not 'essential conditions of the S.A.R. offer'.[279] Under Chamberlain's instructions Graham therefore began to prepare an official reply to the note awaited from the Transvaal (which was informed on 17th that this note would be considered on its merits), waiving the joint inquiry and returning noncommittal answers on the other points.

The official offer of franchise reform was contained in a note of 19th to which the State Secretary, Reitz, telegraphed an explanatory rider on 21st. The note of 19th omitted some important details which had been included in Greene's report, but was substantially the same. The discrepancies were noted by Graham as follows:

Minute by Graham, 21 August: In the informal proposals the 'details of the franchise law' and 'any other points which may arise' were to be discussed with the British Agent. . . . In the formal note the S.A.R. merely express themselves 'ready to consider such friendly suggestions regarding details of franchise law as H.M. Govt. may wish to convey through the British Agent'. This difference is important and must be pointed out in a separate telegram as a reason for our insisting on an investigation of some sort. . . .[280]

The offer was to be guaranteed by exchange of notes, but, Graham insists, 'This must apply to the whole settlement and not be confined to the concessions now offered and those asked for in return.' Other omissions included the use of the English language in the Volksraad. These were bad omens, but worse was to follow. Reitz's telegraphic 'explanation' reached London early on 22nd. This extraordinary document can only, in the light of later events, be interpreted as an intentional retraction of the franchise offer, though it is just conceivable that Reitz thought he was stating the minimum which the Volksraad and burghers would accept. His rider declared that the franchise law already passed was 'both fair and liberal' and the Transvaal's new offer was a bid to avoid a racial war. The offer was declared to be 'expressly conditional' on the acceptance of the three conditions concerning suzerainty, non-intervention and arbitration; and the Transvaal government would only consult the Volksraad on the new franchise law after H.M. Govt. had given an affirmative reply.

Even Greene had told Smuts that H.M. Govt. 'will not and cannot' abandon their rights under the Convention, and at this juncture the Colonial Office could not imagine that Reitz's telegraphic afterthought, as it seemed, was the S.A.R.'s final word. Reitz had not made it clear that his offer was meant as a self-contained bargain and as his one and only proposal for a settlement. If he desired a peaceful settlement, his way of proceeding was foolish and irresponsible. If, as seems more likely, he was seeking a *casus belli*, his tactics were quite cleverly contrived. What is certain is that Chamberlain, not yet believing that the Boers were intent on war, did not take his rider seriously. 'I do not believe they will insist on assurance in this form,' he minutes on 22nd: 'The omission of this categorical demand from the formal note [i.e. of 19th] is I think significant. Note also that the wording of this last communication is different from the terms of State Attorney's conversation, which however were the same as formal note.'[281] Acting on this assumption, Chamberlain made no change of direction. He drew up a telegram listing the omissions from the formal note, and asking for a formal assurance from the

S.A.R. government that they 'adhere to State Attorney's proposals in all their points', on receipt of which 'a formal reply will be sent'. His official reply, already drafted by Graham, was approved with only slight alteration, and his incidental comments show no awareness of imminent breakdown in the negotiations:

Minute by Chamberlain, 22 August: I have altered Mr Graham's telegram as I should now propose to send it, subject however to two remarks.

1. I do not know Milner's opinion as to place of conference. I should prefer to name Cape Town. . . .

2. Nothing is said about military preparations on both sides. Probably this had better wait for the Conference or at least for a subsequent telegram. . . .

The following points have also to be considered.

1. I think Milner should at once instruct British Agent—assisted by Fiddes and (as I strongly hope) by Rose Innes—to report on the new [franchise] proposals.

2. If not already done, our despatch of July 27th should be at once delivered. Greene can explain that having been written before the last proposals it only deals with situation as it was when sent.[282]

Chamberlain did not even discuss the Transvaal's note as if it were meant to be a complete solution in itself.

To Selborne, as to Milner, their chief's reaction to Reitz's communications did not seem strong enough. Chamberlain had already seen a telegram from Milner protesting that the S.A.R. 'evidently wish to escape' from a Conference, and condemning the whole transaction: 'We cannot', he insisted, 'tacitly give the go-by to all outstanding questions and proceed as if political representation and the establishment of arbitration tribunal were the only questions to be considered. To obtain latter is great object of S.A.R., and once assured of it they will be intractable on outstanding differences.'[283] Some differences, Milner thought, which were not suitable for reference to arbitration, had to be settled before arbitration was conceded. Another telegram arrived on 23rd with the official text of the S.A.R.'s notes of 19th and 21st. Milner commented that Reitz's explanation 'appears to me to stiffen appreciably the terms of the note and make it more difficult for H.M. Govt. to agree to it without the strongest reservations'. He pleaded against 'tying our hands for the future' or 'being debarred from proceeding at once to the discussion of the other matters which it is impossible to drop'.[284]

Receiving these communications at Whitehall, Selborne took the opportunity to return the British note to Highbury instead of transmitting it. He explained in a note to Chamberlain '. . . we think no time will be lost thereby', adding: 'We thought we ought to give you the opportunity of noting from the full text of the answer of the S.A.R. now received . . . that their offer is categorically and beyond all doubt conditional on their receiving a satisfactory answer to the assumptions set forth in their rider. We do not, however, suggest any further changes in the draft on that account. We would send it as it is all the same. . . .'[285]

Thus Chamberlain received on 23rd both Selborne and Milner's views emphasizing the unacceptable nature of Reitz's conditions. In scorching weather he had been preoccupied with a small conference on West Indian affairs, holding informal discussions on the lawns. After a final conference on the morning of 23rd, he gave his mind to the problem which Reitz had posed. Graham's draft of the British note already contained a demand for a conference to settle 'other matters of difference' besides the franchise question. Concerning intervention, it mildly hoped that the just treatment of the Uitlanders would render future intervention unnecessary: and at this point Chamberlain now felt he had to make his own position absolutely explicit. 'In view of the State Secretary's note', he wrote, 'I would now add ". . . but H.M. Govt. cannot of course debar themselves from their rights under the Conventions nor divest themselves of the ordinary obligations of a civilized power to protect its subjects in a foreign country from injustice".'*[286] These terms were almost identical with those of the despatch of 27 July just being delivered. Moreover it is apparent that Chamberlain did not anticipate that his refusal of Reitz's demands would create a rupture. He thought that Reitz was merely being dilatory, as is seen in his train of thought:

Minute by Chamberlain, 24 August: If the principal despatch [i.e. of 27

---

* Graham's draft of the note waived the joint inquiry and made this reservation after expressing the hope that the just treatment of the Uitlanders would render any further intervention unnecessary. It asked that the other matters of dispute between the two countries be settled concurrently with the franchise question at a conference.

July] is delivered in its present form I think Greene should be instructed to accompany it with an unofficial or semi-official statement to the following effect:—

H.M. Govt. note the desire of the S.A.R. for an early settlement and fully share it, but must point out that the Govt. of the S.A.R. took 3 (?) weeks to reply to their last offer and in all cases have been very slow in replying. . . .

We hope therefore that on the present occasion we may have an immediate and categorical reply to present telegram.

Might not Greene further express his own opinion, *referring to his conversation with State Attorney*, that if the reply is not satisfactory and it becomes necessary to despatch further troops from England and India, H.M. Govt. will feel justified in demanding payment of the cost of all their preparations, and will probably formulate their own demands for settlement not only of Uitlander question but of the future relations between the two governments. It is clear that we cannot go on negotiating for ever and we must try to bring matters to a head.

The next step in military preparations is so important and so costly that I hesitate to incur the expense . . . so long as there seems a fair chance of a satisfactory settlement.

But I dread above all the continual whittling away of differences until we have no *casus belli* left, although the Boers may claim a partial diplomatic victory and be as disagreeable and intractable in the future as in the past.[287]

It did not therefore seem to Chamberlain that the note he was about to send off would effect much, without strong verbal representations.

On Saturday 26 August the British note was about to be telegraphed in the evening. To reinforce its effect Chamberlain had prepared a speech criticizing Kruger for procrastinating and dribbling out reluctant concessions like a squeezed sponge, which he delivered to an afternoon gathering of Liberal Unionists on the lawns at Highbury.* An hour or two later the Transvaal's reply to his query about the omissions of the note of 19th was received in London. Smuts was reported as having seen the State Secretary, Reitz, who stated that the Transvaal's official

---

* 'The present is not a convenient moment for him to speak', Mrs Chamberlain writes to her mother, 'and yet they are his friends and will be woefully disappointed if he doesn't.' (Chamb. PP., 25 August)

note had been very carefully considered and that he did not believe 'there is the slightest chance that those terms will be altered or amplified'.[288] On receipt of this communication, Wingfield kept back the British note, which was once more sent back to Highbury. Stripped at last of its ambiguity, the Reitz note was tantamount to a refusal to treat further, while the State Secretary's contemptuous tone and procedure evinced no desire to reach a compromise. 'The abrupt form of the answer of State Secretary to our enquiries is most significant', Chamberlain minutes: 'I fear the S.A.R. government mean trouble.'[289]

Technically the Transvaal's repudiation of the Smuts negotiation meant simply a reversion to the position created by the British despatch of 27 July. Milner desired this, but Chamberlain intended to hold the Transvaal government to the Smuts franchise offer and not allow it to be retracted. By strict conventional usage Graham was correct when he minuted that, 'We must consider the new proposals of the S.A.R. as if the conversations between Greene and Smuts had never taken place. We cannot even allude to it [sic] in our formal reply.' Chamberlain did not agree. 'I do not see this,' he retorts. 'Smuts withdraws or is repudiated. *Non constat* that he did not say the things that Greene reports. . . . I do not think the fear of their repudiation need affect us. It would be the word of an Englishman against that of a Boer. *I* should believe the former.'[290]* In this frame of mind he directed that Greene's unilateral inquiry into the latest franchise proposal made by Smuts should proceed as if it were still valid, ignoring Reitz's explanation that it could only stand if H.M. Govt. forthwith relinquished all other claims or indeed the means of enforcing the franchise offer itself. The British note held back on 26th he proposed to send with little alteration. One detail in it caught his eye—an approving phrase describing the Smuts offer as 'a better basis than any yet offered'. 'I omit these words', he directed: 'In the present

---

* Five points of discrepancy between Smuts' informal offer and the Transvaal's formal note were listed by Graham. They were: no complicated franchise conditions, permitted use of the English language in the Volksraad, Uitlanders to be allowed to vote in the election of the President and Commandant General, the franchise scheme to be discussed with the British Agent, and the whole settlement to be guaranteed by exchange of notes. All these points were omitted from the formal note.

circumstances I will make no admissions whatsoever.' The note was finally transmitted on 28 August accompanied by instructions that Greene should hint that further procrastination might lead to an ultimatum.

The net result of the diplomatic exchanges of August had been that a definite answer to the British despatch of 27 July and notes of 31 July and 1 August had been avoided. Delay, as Milner observed, was the Boer trump card, and the position of Johannesburg was becoming desperate. Now Milner wanted an immediate despatch of troops. 'I venture to differ', he telegraphed on 29 August after receiving Chamberlain's instructions to proceed with the unilateral inquiry: 'I think that we should render ourselves ridiculous by sending persons to Pretoria to examine proposals which may never be made.' But he was over-ruled, Chamberlain still feeling that a compromise was yet possible:

Minute by Chamberlain, 30 August: I do not understand Sir A. Milner at all. The Govt. of the S.A.R. have given more than an outline—they have made a definite proposal, viz. . . . 5 years' retrospective franchise and 8 new seats.

. . . this as a basis of negotiation is much more definite than anything proposed by Milner at Bloemfontein. . . .

If we do not appoint commission at once it means a further delay of a week or a fortnight before we can formulate our requests, if the answer of the S.A.R. to our last telegram is satisfactory, or our demands if it is unsatisfactory.

My desire is to quicken the rate of progress. . . . In other words the offer of 10 seats to the Uitlanders immediately ought to and will satisfy us . . . provided . . . the objectionable demands accompanying it are dropped and . . . we have some security that it will not be taken away as soon as the pressure is removed.[291]

It was still by no means obvious that Kruger would prefer to go to war rather than test further the British intentions with regard to suzerainty and non-intervention in the future.

Immersed in the tense and treacherous atmosphere of Cape politics, Milner took a very sceptical and probably a more accurate view of the intentions of the Boer government. Rumours of imminent invasion, military preparations and the ubiquitous collusion and deceptions on the part of the Afrikaners in the

British territories, added to the plight of Johannesburg, led him to ask for an immediate remedy for an intolerable situation. He became convinced that Kruger was being dilatory either to gain time to prepare an attack or in the hope of an Uitlander cave-in. He never for a moment lent any credence to the Smuts offer, and asserted his point of view in an official despatch to London sent on 23 August. 'A particular proposal,' he wrote, '. . . a mere outline . . . with regard to a single question . . . has been treated as if it were by itself not only a panacea for the grievances of the Uitlanders, but a settlement of all questions at issue. . . .'[292] Privately he played his last card for the cause he had passionately at heart, writing a letter to Chamberlain which would take about a fortnight to arrive by sea mail. He asked for an army to be brought to the borders of the Transvaal to enforce a satisfactory settlement:

Milner–Chamberlain, 23 August 1899: The after effects are to my mind not open to doubt. With the Transvaal under real popular government, either as a republic or a British colony, the scales in South Africa would definitely and for ever incline on the British side. If things remain as they are, the stronger cards remain to the Africanders. They will have had a shock, but the fighting power will still be theirs.

With a strong military power on our borders, which can only be coerced by an expedition such as England will always shrink to undertake, and with half our subjects sympathizing with that power, our 'paramountcy' will be an idle phrase. We shall keep for a long time our naval base in the Cape peninsula—the Africanders do not object to the protection of the fleet—but outside the coast towns the Englishman will be the 'underdog' unless he 'Africanderizes', or in other words becomes a virtual republican.

Writing as I do, *quite privately and frankly*, I should deplore the loss of this opportunity of consolidating our position here, especially as, with the artificial weight in the scale against us removed, the natural forces would make that position more and more impregnable every year, and as I do not believe that that opportunity will ever recur, I do not yet despair or give up the fight.[293]

Significantly enough Milner did not regard the British note sent on 28 August as a change of direction, any more than Chamberlain did, for he wrote to Selborne on 30 August asking for matters to be brought to a head. Further delay over franchise schemes seemed to him a dangerous waste of time, after the goodwill of the S.A.R. had been tried and found wanting:

Milner–Chamberlain, 1 September 1899; No. 4: I am doing my best to carry out your wishes. At the same time I doubt whether, if the Govt. of the S.A.R. refuse to meet us, course proposed will really expedite matters. Time will be spent on working out franchise scheme of our own . . . and at the end we shall be face to face with the old difficulty of basing ultimatum on differences of detail on franchise only.

Assuming their last communication to be unsatisfactory, I think time has come to take broad ground indicated by Prime Minister and yourself. Justification of change of attitude would be evident determination of Govt. of S.A.R. not to satisfy us as to *bona fides* of any of their numerous franchise proposals, and impossibility of allowing present state of tension to continue indefinitely. We should . . . no longer be bound by Bloemfontein proposals, success of which depended on their being accepted in the spirit in which they were made, and which by themselves are inadequate, if rammed down the throat of reluctant government able and evidently determined to prevent their working the gradual and peaceful revolution I contemplated.[294]

On reading this, Chamberlain signalled back that the franchise inquiry need only take a week, after which the cabinet could decide upon the terms of an ultimatum. 'I do not think we could send such an ultimatum until more troops are actually in South Africa', he minutes on 2 September.[295]

The Transvaal's reply to the British note of 28 August was received in London in a preliminary version on 3 September. It was in effect an 'answer answerless'. The Smuts offer was withdrawn, and objections were raised both to a joint and a unilateral inquiry, the latter being described as 'probably of little value'. On the question of a conference, the S.A.R. declared themselves to 'await further information from H.M. Govt.' 'This government', the note declared, 'could never have anticipated that the answer of H.M. Govt. to their proposal would be unfavourable.' Withdrawing the proposal, the S.A.R. made no effort to press any alternative or to appear at all anxious to work for an agreement.[296] Whitehall was left with no opportunity to suggest a compromise, even had it been willing to do so. Wingfield's reaction suggests that in other and more favourable circumstances the Colonial Office might have made concessions:

Minute by Wingfield, 3 September: Altogether it is a very shuffling and unsatisfactory reply. . . .

It seems to me that we must now not accept any franchise or representation scheme short of the proposals which the S.A.R. now desire to treat as lapsed—and we must insist on inquiry . . . the Conference must also be pressed as we cannot now leave any of the outstanding differences unsettled.

But it is of course a question whether in viewing the uncertain character of this answer, H.M. Govt. should not now formulate their own demands and put them forward as an ultimatum.[297]

The crisis had arrived. Selborne took the despatch to Lord Salisbury, who decided 'that everything should wait' for a cabinet called for 8 September. Chamberlain returned to London and began to work intensively on the problems presented by the new phase of diplomacy.

This now hinged on military considerations. To land reinforcements in South Africa might be (and in fact was) treated by the Transvaal as a provocation: yet as things stood the Transvaal was militarily superior. The nettle had to be grasped, and Chamberlain composed a cabinet paper asking for a large reinforcement. The responsibility was a heavy one, which ultimately devolved on Chamberlain alone.* The cabinet followed his advice, the gist of which is conveyed in his preliminary remarks to the long document he prepared on the position:

Cabinet paper by Chamberlain, 6 September 1899: The latest despatch of the Transvaal government in reply to my telegram No. 1 of the 28th August is clearly dilatory. It is possible—as some reports state—that they have determined on war, and desire a few weeks further preparation; but it is more probable that they seek delay in the hope either of division of counsels in this country or of a diversion on the part of the Uitlanders, who are being ruined by delay. . . .

If the reply now sent had come in the early stage of the negotiations I should have been inclined to treat it as the basis for further discussion.

---

* Mrs Chamberlain writes: '. . . he has no one to share it with him in one sense, for his colleagues cannot know the intricacies and details of the question, and it devolves on him to carry out all the negotiations and the decisions of the government.' (Chamb. PP., To her mother, 20 September 1899)

But it is the last of a series of communications extending altogether over a period of three months since the Bloemfontein Conference— all of them vague, inconclusive and unsatisfactory, by which illusory hopes of a satisfactory settlement have been kept alive while no real progress has been made. It is impossible that this state of things should be tolerated any longer. I doubt if public opinion in this country would stand it, but what is of much greater importance, I am certain that it cannot be prolonged without the most serious danger in South Africa. . . .[298]

The despatch which the cabinet sanctioned was written by Chamberlain and was an exact restatement of the familiar British standpoint and demands, ending with the threat of an ultimatum. It elicited one or two diplomatic exchanges which, however, lacked much reality since the British were now playing for time as well as offering last chances. The cabinet ordered the immediate embarkation of 5,700 troops from India for Natal, who might take five weeks to arrive in South Africa. Four battalions and some artillery batteries were sent from the United Kingdom, and plans for mobilizing an army corps were put into effect. A very critical month and more lay ahead, before the position could be stabilized.

At the beginning of October, before the reinforcements had arrived and after the diplomatic deadlock was complete, the problem for Chamberlain became that of discouraging any sudden *détente* or, equally, any provocation which might precipitate hostilities prematurely. A *détente* would have been highly embarrassing if exploited by the Liberal opposition, when Parliament met to sanction the calling out of the reserves, and might have frustrated the military movements which were the fruit of much preparation and expense. On the other hand, Chamberlain was very apprehensive lest a sudden offensive from the Transvaal should overrun the whole of South Africa except perhaps Natal and the coastline of the Cape. Thus his object was to maintain the diplomatic equilibrium for as long as possible and reserve further moves, whether threatening or conciliatory, until the reinforcements had arrived. The delicacy of his position appears in his final instructions to Milner:

Chamberlain–Milner, 2 October: Our despatch reviewing the situation and stating latest conditions of settlement can be sent by telegraph in a few days or delayed indefinitely as may be most expedient.

The advantage of delay is that we shall gain time for arrival of reinforcements; and also that we shall not have disclosed our hand. The disadvantage is that we may again be entangled in negotiations about five, six or seven years franchise or other details which will cause delay, alienate our friends, encourage opposition in this country, and after all lead to no permanent settlement. If Boers were to make new offer, before presentation of ultimatum, it would be almost impossible to refuse consideration, and I have now lost all hope of a real settlement on the lines of your Bloemfontein proposals.

If however presentation of new proposals were to precipitate a conflict and your military advisers think that there would be substantial risk . . . political considerations must give way to military exigencies.

The question is, can you hold your own till reinforcements arrive. If so, it is not our policy to do anything to encourage efforts of Free State or others to delay offensive proceedings on the part of the Boers.

All this is on the assumption that Kruger will certainly not make concessions sufficient to ensure a lasting peace and render unnecessary the permanent maintenance of a large force in South Africa. Otherwise of course I would still preach patience.

But if war is inevitable, it is best for us that the Boers should begin it, and if possible before our ultimatum is sent. If they think we are holding it back till reinforcements arrive they may be induced to anticipate.

Subject to your answer on the military question I am at present inclined to return curt replies to inquiries and to delay ultimatum for another ten days.[299]

Milner's report of the military position was alarming, to the effect that the British could not hold their own for more than ten days. Chamberlain had previously had a very low opinion of the efficiency of the War Office, and henceforward his comments were exasperated and scathing. Why, he asked Balfour, had the War Office not insisted on reinforcements before, when he had first proposed them? But still he did not alter his conviction that the Boers would not attack first: and that, even if they did, there would not be 'any serious risk of a reverse'. On 8 October, the eve of the Boer ultimatum, he noted privately that he distrusted Milner's procrastinating negotiations with President Steyn, which 'may lead us into an entanglement of negotiations which will make our position very difficult'. 'We *know*', he concludes, 'that the Boers do not mean to make any substantial concessions—and under these circumstances the sooner they begin the better.'[300]

The Boers had begun. On 2 October the Raad had approved the declaration of war and dispersed. Hitches in the mobilization of the burghers delayed the presentation of the Transvaal's ultimatum, which had been ready prepared for some weeks, until 9 October. It demanded the instant withdrawal of British troops from the borders of the republic, the removal from South Africa of all British reinforcements landed since 1 June, and that 'Her Majesty's troops which are now on the high seas shall not be landed in any port in South Africa'. Kruger had indeed played Chamberlain's cards for him.

The true measure of the success of Chamberlain and Milner's diplomacy is the extent to which it had succeeded between May and October in promoting an understanding on the part of the British public of the vital interests at stake in South Africa. That was the criterion which they themselves put forward. Critics of Chamberlain's policy condemned it on this very ground, that it was provocative by being made public in a series of blue books, aggravated by his few but bantering public speeches. Whether a secret and more conciliatory method would have cut any ice with the Transvaal is very doubtful. For Chamberlain such a method was unthinkable. His one trump card, at a game in which he felt that Kruger held most of the honours, was the backing of an aroused British public, and no one understood better than he that this favourable condition of opinion was attainable only with careful preparation, that it could not be long sustained, and that it was subject to many hazards of distraction. The parliamentary vacation was a favourable period in which to work up to a crisis, when the newspapers had space, the political stage was uncluttered, and the Commons was not assembled to scrutinize and impede. But it so happened that long newspaper accounts of the Dreyfus trial caught the attention of the public, and stole his thunder in August and September. In South Africa itself this problem of the phasing of diplomatic pressure was even more formidable, for a crisis produced desperate effects on Johannesburg and indeed over the whole area.

It was often suggested—and still is—that Chamberlain's

'pushful' diplomacy was resented and resisted by members of the Unionist cabinet. This criticism has little to support it. Those who dragged their feet, such as Hicks Beach or even Salisbury himself, usually did so in ignorance of diplomatic telegrams. Only Beach, who had been intensely suspicious of Milner, retained a permanent feeling that the diplomacy had been mismanaged. He reminded Salisbury in 1902 not to repeat the mistake by which the telegram of 28 August had been allowed to go off without a cabinet decision. 'I had regretted', Beach notes privately against this letter, 'that a cabinet was not summoned to consider the proposals from the Transvaal government forwarded by Mr Cunningham Greene. On Milner's advice they were only partly accepted. The war followed.' Salisbury, Beach found in 1902, had not lost much sleep over this omission: 'I had wholly forgotten it. It was a very grave mistake.'[301]

The critical point in the long train of exchanges with the Transvaal was, by general agreement, the fortnight after Greene's transmission of the Smuts offer. After the outbreak of war, the Colonial Office drew up a cabinet paper recounting the course of events, in the light of Smuts' later denial that he had ever intended his conversations with Greene to be conveyed to London. Not only, the paper argued, did the Transvaal's note of 19 August confirming Smuts' proposals omit a number of concessions, but it was followed by a note two days later in which the three 'assumptions' as put forward by Mr Smuts appeared as express *conditions*, thus bearing out Mr Greene's contention that the Transvaal had gone back on their first offers. Later, Greene was accused by the Transvaal of having misled them. Chamberlain's personal interpretation of this extraordinary switch of policy was given privately to Balfour as follows:

Chamberlain–Balfour, 7 January 1900: My own impression is that when the Smuts negotiations began with the conditional proposal of a 5 years franchise, it was meant to pave the way for at least a temporary settlement. But the younger Boers . . . protested, and Reitz was forced to withdraw it and substitute the ultimatum, which according to a statement of his published in the newspapers had been provisionally prepared some weeks before.

It is clear that war was inevitable *at some time or another*, unless we were prepared to give up all we were contending for; but I believe there were times during the negotiations when the Boers were ready to patch up a peace and wait for a more favourable opportunity.

I think this fairly represents Milner's opinion also.[302]

Behind the diplomatic game there was of course the broader, permanent antagonism. The Transvaal would not accept the gradual and peaceful fusion of races and cultures which Milner envisaged. In isolation, this aspect of the problem might not have found the cabinet unanimous. Balfour, for instance, in May 1899 expressed sympathy with the Boer viewpoint, and almost deprecated the 'transfer of nationality' involved in an Uitlander franchise. But Balfour, along with less philosophic observers, was converted to the Chamberlain-Milner analysis of the situation. His correspondence in September reveals more than a perfunctory sympathy with the official policy. 'I think, however, you are wrong', he writes to a Unionist M.P., 'in supposing that racial animosities would be more embittered and prolonged by a war than by a solution, however peaceful, which should give the Dutch-speaking population the impression that they were in future to be the paramount influence in South Africa.'[303] To James Bryce, who had sent him an appeal at the eleventh hour arguing from his knowledge of South Africa that war would engender permanent racial resentment, he replied:

Balfour–Bryce, 2 October 1899: The outcome of the present crisis can hardly, I fear, make the feeling between the English and Dutch-speaking population much worse than it is. My hope for the future lies in the expectation that when our supremacy—and as a consequence of our supremacy equal laws—are really established through South Africa, race jealousies may die down as they have died down under similar conditions in Canada.

. . . few of us, I should think, are sufficiently self-satisfied to be absolutely confident that the particular course we may happen to recommend is beyond all question the right one. Yet in this case I feel little doubt.[304]

It was indeed in its broadest aspects that the government's South African policy was most completely supported by the nation. The Liberal opposition supported the upholding of the Convention, suzerainty, and the doctrine that Britain was the paramount power in South Africa.[305] Even John Morley, who had quarrelled with the Liberal leaders over their 'imperialist' leanings, and for whom 'imperialism' meant only militarism, vast expenditure, and 'killing people because it is good for trade', was to be found in September supporting the government's demand for an immediate five year franchise: while on the same platform Leonard Courtney hailed Chamberlain's latest despatch with satisfaction. Where Morley and other critics of Chamberlain did differ was on the question of means, objecting fundamentally as they did to the use of war as an instrument of imperial policy. A large section of Nonconformist ministers found it in their conscience to regard a war against the Boers as 'sinful'. And the socialists who were howled down and pelted in Trafalgar Square on 24 September attributed the impending war to 'the spirit of unscrupulous imperialism, grasping capitalism, and aggressive militarism'. But the great mass of the nation, of all parties, had come to support the government before the Boer ultimatum and attack, in their policy of backing their demands by war if neces-sary. Milner's logical analysis of the South Africa position, tempered by Chamberlain's caution and skill in the intricate craft of manœuvre and persuasion, had carried the cabinet, the opposition and the nation. Looking back, at the end of the year and in the midst of military reverses, Chamberlain could unaffectedly congratulate himself and Milner on the successful outcome of a course whose difficulties and dangers very few men besides themselves were in any position to measure:

Chamberlain–Milner, 6 December 1899: Let me say at this stage that our policy of extreme patience coupled with full explanation of the issue has been thoroughly successful, and that the country now under-stand the South African question as they have never done before.

It was all very well for you and for me to know, as we did, what a tremendous issue was behind such questions as franchise and alien immigration; but the public did not. They could not see that the things that we were contending for were worth a big war, nor were they particularly pleased with the clients on whose behalf we appeared to be acting. There was too much 'money bags' about the whole business to be agreeable to any of us.

Fortunately, as the argument developed and especially owing to the diplomatic mistakes made by Kruger, the country became alive to the intolerable position into which we were settling. Even some of our strongest opponents were at last awake to the intentions of the

Transvaal government, and . . . see that if we had gone on in the old rut for a year or two longer, nothing could have saved South Africa to the British Crown.

The Liberal party as a whole have behaved extremely well. . . .[306]

At this stage Chamberlain was only getting round to some formulation of his requirements for a peace settlement. His officials had some strange and conflicting ideas on the subject, ranging from guaranteeing the future independence of the Transvaal, to annexation or including it in a federation of the South African states.[307] Chamberlain had no preconceived ideas, but like them he had not adjusted his mind to the wider horizon that lay beyond the outbreak of hostilities. 'Solvitur pugnando' was all the comment he could make.

CHAPTER NINE

State Education

It is often possible to get the Tories to pass good measures without knowing it, as Mr Webb and Mr Morant are supposed to have induced them to pass an Education Bill.
      Cecil Chesterton, *Gladstonian Ghosts* (1905), p.16

THE Education Act of 1902, the most constructive and lasting piece of legislation passed by the Unionist party, was politically disastrous to its authors. It presented the Liberals, who were riven by disagreement over imperial policy brought to a head by the Boer war, with a splendid opportunity to close their ranks, seize the initiative, and reanimate their supporters in the country. At the same time it split the Unionists along the line which separated Churchmen from Nonconformists, driving the latter, who were chiefly to be found among Chamberlain's section of the Liberal Unionists, into the arms of the Liberals. One might well ask how Balfour and Devonshire—the two chief architects of the Act in the cabinet—ever came to embark on this course of reform, when Lord Salisbury was lukewarm and apprehensive, and Chamberlain positively hostile to it: or, again, why Chamberlain was not more resolute in his protestations against it.

It is true enough that Chamberlain was at the time something like a captive—he could not resign until he had effected a peace settlement in South Africa without gravely damaging his reputation and throwing away the fruits of his long and costly policy. But this is not the real explanation either for Chamberlain's acquiescence or for the alacrity with which Balfour appeared to be satisfying the demands of Churchmen and Conservatives at his expense. The true state of things, fully recognized by Chamberlain, was that the education problem had to be tackled, and only the drastic solution to which the cabinet was forced by the inescapable logic of the situation was politically feasible. Chamberlain prophesied that: he Education Bill would send the party to destruction: but, as he admitted to Balfour: 'In saying this . . . I am not boasting my own sagacity. On the contrary I think many of my colleagues, including yourself, fully recognized the dangers ahead of us, but you thought, and very likely you were right, that any alternative course would lead us into still greater difficulties.'[308] How the Unionist party got itself into this impossible position is a question which calls for explanation.

The Unionist government returned in 1895 was committed to relieving, by some means or another, the plight of the church schools. The school boards, representing the rival interests of Nonconformity, successfully withstood the Unionists' onslaught of 1896; but it was disclosed that they had an Achilles' heel in the form of the questionable inroads they had made into the field of secondary education. After the establishment of county councils by the Act of 1888, the school boards had continued to develop their provision of secondary education in rivalry with the councils, and had been encouraged in this extension of their activities by the officials of the Education Department. Sir George Kekewich, the Permanent Secretary, and Arthur Acland, the Vice-President, went beyond the bounds of administrative impartiality in their dedication to the political cause of the school boards. The same, however, could be said of the bias, in the opposite direction, of Acland's successor, Sir John Gorst, and the official who became his private secretary, Sir Robert Morant. Morant in particular was an implacable opponent of the school boards. Entering the Education Department in 1895 after re-organizing the educational system of Siam with the powers of a pasha, he was an almost fanatical believer in centralized, uniform and authoritarian direction. At once he began to counteract the tendencies of the Kekewich régime. Delving into the archives, he soon discovered that the secondary provision of the school boards was *ultra vires*, and had in fact already been ruled as such by decisions of the Local Government Board even before the 1888 county councils act.

This discovery became very material in the dispute which arose in 1898 between the London School Board and the London County Council over a clause in the Science and Art Directory which permitted the Council to assume responsibility for these subjects. The London School Board regarded a proposal of the Council to avail itself of this clause and to set up in competition in these fields of secondary education as a 'hostile act', and appealed to the Science and Art branch of the Education Department. At the South Kensington inquiry, Gorst ruled that the Council's application should be granted, and asked that steps should be taken to test the legality of the London School Board's whole position. The result was the celebrated Cockerton case, a legal struggle which was frankly political, Asquith taking the brief for the School Board, and Lord Robert Cecil holding the brief for the Council. Judgment against the School Board was given in December 1900, and upheld on appeal in April 1901. It was a sweeping condemnation of all the Board's higher grade and evening school work. At once it was clear that the line of demarcation between elementary and secondary education and the appropriate local authorities for each needed to be defined by statute afresh.

Since taking office, the Unionist government had done much to consolidate the position of the county councils as the authorities for secondary education. The trend of development was towards a centralized system, and away from *ad hoc* authorities. Morant was doing all he could to promote this trend: and the favourable impression he made, in supplying Gorst with technical advice during the passage of an Act of 1899 consolidating the various central educational departments under one Board of Education, led to his appointment into a key position, as Gorst's private secretary. The peculiar personal relationships in the new Board of Education at this time were described by Morant to Beatrice Webb:

Beatrice Webb's diary, 4 May 1902: Sidney had Morant to stay here. Morant is the principal person at the Education Department. He has occupied the most anomalous position in the last six months. Taken into the office as a nondescript of humble capacity some years ago, Gorst picked him out for his private secretary. In that way he became acquainted with the politicians—cabinet ministers and Conservative private members. . . .

Presently these folk . . . found him a useful substitute for Kekewich (Permanent Head) who was deadly opposed to their policy, and to Gorst, with whom they were hardly on speaking terms, the situation being complicated by the fact that Gorst and Kekewich were complete 'incompatibles' having no communication with each other![309]

Gorst was an eccentric, whose brusque manner and cynical criticisms offended his fellow ministers, and it was Morant who was exclusively engaged to consult with the cabinet committee over the drafting of the great Education Bill of 1902. Kekewich and Gorst only saw this Bill after it had been printed, and when Morant sent it to Gorst for his signature, Gorst returned it with the comment: 'I have sold my name to the government; put it where they instruct you to put it.'[310]

The Cockerton judgment forced the government to undertake another educational voyage with every prospect of shipwreck. Balfour was afraid of a repetition of the fiasco of 1896, and it was not until late in 1901 that he fell under the spell of Morant's compelling personality. Devonshire, who was nominally in charge of educational affairs, had yet to be persuaded that a major scheme of revision was necessary, but was circumvented by Morant, who rashly and unwarrantably dismissed the Duke as an incompetent old bungler. The cabinet in general, and Devonshire in particular, could anticipate serious trouble with Chamberlain if they gave way to the demands of their partisans or the resolutions in favour of rate aid passed by the Convocation of the Church of England.

The cabinet of 5 November 1901, after several divisions, decisively rejected direct rate aid to voluntary schools. There followed a month of intense discussion, during which Devonshire became confirmed in favour of rate aid. No bill, he now felt, could be passed without it, and it was necessary to the establishment of an overall elementary system:

Devonshire–Chamberlain, 3 December 1901: Have you seen Macnamara's article on the Education Bill in the *Fortnightly Review*? It puts the case for doing something for the voluntary schools very strongly. . . .

We could make a logical demand if the new authorities, county or borough, could take cognisance of all the schools within their area which are providing education, but we meet with hopeless difficulties at every step if these authorities are compelled to ignore the schools which are educating more than half the children in England.[311]

Three days later the Duke had a long conversation with Chamberlain, to try to persuade him to accept some form of rate aid. Reporting the result to Balfour, he thought, but was 'not sure', that Chamberlain would accept a decision to confer the power permissively upon local authorities; but that he deemed it unwise and believed that the large towns would not avail themselves of it. In spite of Chamberlain's misgivings, the Duke went on to advocate a comprehensive plan, involving rate aid. The Bill before the cabinet, he argued, professed to establish local authorities for elementary education, but did not do so. 'There are no such authorities, because school boards are only authorities for the supply and management of schools where a deficiency of other schools exists. But we profess to establish an authority everywhere.' Rather than adopt any half measure, the Duke preferred to leave elementary education alone: which would be an 'immense disappointment, but perhaps not much more than the Bill in its present form'.[312]

Balfour also had decided that the scheme before the cabinet committee would please or conciliate no one. To prevent him from retreating, Morant pleaded with him in his best manner. Having gone through the main points of the Bill with the Duke in order to brief him for his talk with Chamberlain, Morant had found him 'quite fluid': Devonshire did not seem to have thought out any one of the various plans—and this, Morant believed, 'must mean a collapse in Parliament'. Clearly the cabinet committee needed to do some more home-work before they could be in a fit state to determine such momentous issues. Morant's suggestion, therefore, was that they should revert to a discussion of first principles—or, more accurately, that they should be coached by Balfour in the principles which Morant had concerted with him:

Morant–Balfour, 7 December 1901: May we on Monday try and get the Committee to put the Bill on one side, and to go step by step through the various points. . . . Thus:

Is the new County Borough authority to be the authority for all education in the borough? Yes.

Is it to set the standard of efficiency of the town schools? Yes; for if not, it is not *the* authority. But if it may not finance the non-board schools it cannot bring *them* up to proper efficiency. Obviously, and therefore it *must* be able to finance these schools where necessary.

But will there not be a turmoil at every town council election, as to whether or not the rates are to go to such and such a denominational school? Yes, if there be an option. . . . Then either you must forbid the giving of rates to voluntary schools, a course which is barred by our fiscal question above, or you must give no option. This means that where a denominational school exists, the town council *must* find out of the rates the funds requisite, over and above the government grant, to maintain it efficiently. . . . This means compulsory rate maintenance of all existing schools.

But that means that my rates may go to teaching Mariolatry! No: the religious instruction must be paid for by the managers, if it is denominational. . . . It is a fifth part of the school time: let it be a fifth part of the expenditure on school maintenance. . . .

But then the growth of (e.g.) Baptist population would start a new school and deplete the existing school. Would the latter cease to have a claim for maintenance? Yes, certainly, when its numbers are sufficiently near vanishing point. This is the only rational system: and it would work quasi-automatically without raising *any* election riots. It meets the nonconformist difficulty in Wales. . . . [313]

Morant wished to persuade the committee and then the cabinet that without rate aid the Bill would be neither workable nor welcomed, and that 'mere permissive rate aid will (as in 1870) mean a crash in the middle of the session'.

On receipt of Morant's cogent reasonings, Balfour drew up a cabinet paper more or less restating them, and coming down decisively on Morant's side of the fence. Devonshire also submitted a paper in the same vein, concurring with Balfour in the opinion that the cabinet's instruction to the committee to avoid rate aid could not be executed.* Chamberlain was not a member of the cabinet committee, but it was felt that his consent to the committee's change of direction was necessary, and Morant was deputed to see him and argue his case. The disputation between the two men—surviving in Morant's account—has been claimed as a dialectical victory for Morant. It certainly shows up some outdated prejudices, and some ignorance, on Chamberlain's part. The truth is that Chamberlain, having given up all interest in

---

* P.R.O. Cab. 1/2. Printed papers by Balfour and Devonshire, 11 and 12 December 1901. The school boards, Devonshire argued, were in no sense educational authorities, only authorities for supplementing education and enforcing attendance. If they were to be replaced by county councils as the authority over the whole country, the councils could not be given powers to inspect and render efficient all schools without universal rate aid.

educational reforms, had ceased to study the question. He argued without conviction, merely probing for a loophole through which he could avoid the political difficulty:

Conversation noted by Morant, 12 December 1901:

Chamberlain: This whole plan will mean *rate war* in every town as in 1870. . . .

Morant: But conditions are now very different from 1870. *Then* it seemed easy to kill the voluntary schools. Now it is seen to be almost impossible. . . . *Then* people cared far less about education. *Now* many people feel that the education of the nation is retarded by the low level of voluntary school work: and that to deny money to voluntary schools is retarding education. . . .

Chamberlain: Your Cowper-Temple veil is a very thin one: it is too disingenuous.

Morant: Granted: but we take their own words, their own 'sacred safeguard'. *We* know that it won't stop denominational colouring. . . . If it is so sacred a guard in board schools, we *extend* it into voluntary schools. . . .

Chamberlain: I could not possibly *compel* the local authority to give its rates.

Morant: We don't propose this. It is 'adoptive'. It is in this that we meet you, yet (we hope) without the evils of 'precarious existence' and 'ruined elections'.

Chamberlain: Yes, and they will always decide against it: and you will have gained nothing by all the row.

Morant: Not everywhere. The Liverpool School Board decided yesterday that rate aid ought to be given. The Town Council would say ditto. Moreover, it will be infectious.

Chamberlain: No: the voluntary buildings are so bad it won't mean saving any building expenditure from rates. . . .

Morant: Pardon me. We say the school is *not* to be maintained out of rates if it cannot be made really suitable in structure etc. . . . This will no doubt 'break' many managers. . . . [314]

Chamberlain's alternative plan was to encourage the 'transfer' of voluntary schools to the local authority, which should take charge of the secular teaching and the appointment of teachers. Morant appears to have convinced him that such conditions would deter all managers, since 'nowadays it is felt that they must have a religious man to do all the secular teaching'. Then, replied Chamberlain, confine the Bill to secondary education. But

Morant objected that even this course would not avoid the religious controversy and an undesirable dual authority, because school boards would have to be preserved and represented on the new secondary authority. Chamberlain admitted this, and suggested that only the board schools should be dealt with, and given over to the councils. Such a plan, said Morant, would mean barring the new authorities from half the field of elementary education:

Chamberlain: Oh, but the new authority *must* be able to string up the standard *everywhere*.

Morant: To insist without funds would *certainly* break us [the government].

Chamberlain: But would it break us? Who would vote against us on this point? Say 50 Tories, and 60 Irish. The regular opposition would *support* the prohibition of rate aid. . . .

Morant: Oh, no. Far more than 50 Tories. There are 'educationalists' too. It would be a *hot* struggle. . . .

Chamberlain: What then do you suggest?

Morant: We have tried to build you a bridge. . . .

Chamberlain: I can't see myself walking on it unless:

i. You insist on an option to the town council,

ii. You make the managers' contribution not ridiculously small,

iii. You make it plain that no bad buildings are to be foisted upon the ratepayers.

But even then I don't say we *can* do it. . . . I fear many Liberal Unionists will refuse to vote for your proposal.

Morant: But you admit, yourself, that it would necessarily be a vote of confidence, and we should have to go out on it?

Chamberlain: Yes.

Morant: Surely our Liberal Unionists, however much they might hate rate aid, would refrain from breaking us on it, while the war is still on?

Chamberlain: Then you mean that the war would be the means by which *our* nonconformists are to be bound into rate aid to sectarian education?

Morant: In a sense, yes. But by our retention and extension of Cowper-Temple we enable them to *save their face*: and to say that no sectarian education is allowed from the rates by the new clause.

Chamberlain: It is difficult everyhow.[315]

The interview terminated without the discussion of any alternative to Morant's plan. But it had not left Chamberlain with any confidence that the defeat of the government could be avoided by following it.

Chamberlain had already told Devonshire that he firmly believed his scheme would be 'fatal to the government', and now, after seeing Morant, he put his alternative on paper, feeling that 'it is not enough to be a destructive critic'. Writing to the Duke on 14 December, he first sympathized with the committee 'in your almost hopeless task', and then indicated the points of his own approach. He wished not to touch elementary education. Or, if that were unavoidable, he wished to hand over all initiative to the localities. The government should abolish school boards and set up the proposed municipal authorities, but then wash its hands of the matter and leave these authorities to make what bargains they would with the managers of voluntary schools. London should be decentralized by making the local borough councils rather than the London County Council the authorities. Finally, since it would have been impossible for the Board of Education to deal with the infinite variety of local conditions which must have emerged from such a plan, Chamberlain was prepared to accept the complete abdication of central responsibility for elementary education:

Chamberlain–Devonshire, 14 December 1901: . . . in future—and in view of local responsibility—the Board of Education should be charged only with the duty of estimating and controlling results—the Board would make its own tests, whether of the efficiency of the scholars separately or of the school as a whole, and the grant would be made according to a scale arranged by them; but they would no longer be responsible for the *means* by which the results were obtained.[316]

But the expectations of the Conservative party as the session approached were decidedly in favour of a full-blooded measure. And then Devonshire, who had been gradually coming round to an understanding and acceptance of Morant's comprehensive approach, came out early in February with a masterly cabinet paper in which he expounded the scheme for full rate aid with lucidity and conviction. Morant was to find that 'the slow digestion of the old Duke' was a more reliable help than the fertile but shifting expedients of Balfour. While Balfour was ready to yield his own convictions to placate Chamberlain,

Devonshire stood for what he came to believe was educationally best with unmovable firmness.

The basis of the Duke's case—which he unfolded so resolutely before the cabinet that Salisbury brought the proceedings to a close without a formal decision for fear of forcing his resignation —was the argument that 'free optional rate aid' would not work. Under it voluntary schools would play off the local authority against the voluntary schools association, and both against the Education Board. There would be no common standard of cost or efficiency—the expense per child already varied widely even in the board schools. The alternative principle of 'complete rate maintenance' would, Devonshire argued, place things on a totally different foundation. The local authority would control the voluntary schools absolutely even though it nominated only a third of the managers. Parents had a right to demand denominational education for their children, and since this could not be provided by public authorities, it must continue to be provided by denominational managers. 'The fact', however, 'that a school is partly maintained by endowments or voluntary subscriptions, ought not to exempt it from some supervision or control by the public local authority.'[317]

Although Devonshire's latest scheme was embodied in an entirely new draft of the Bill and presented to the cabinet in mid-February, substantially in the form in which the measure was later introduced into Parliament, it was not accepted until weeks later. In fact it was rejected by the cabinet committee. Deserted by Balfour, the Duke stood alone: while Morant and Chamberlain battled it out in discussion over the London Education Bill.[318] Early in March, when it became clear that no agreement could be reached on elementary education, the party whips were summoned by Sandars to a conference at which it was decided to recommend the deferment of the whole educational question. Quite apart from the contentious problem of education, the session of 1902 presented other formidable demands on parliamentary time—the prior claims of procedural reforms, the coronation, and questions arising from the South African war and coming peace settlement. The position was explained to Balfour thus:

Sandars–Balfour, 8 March 1902: As you know there will be a question raised at Cabinet in favour of the policy of dropping the Education

Bill. Chamberlain, in conversation with me on Thursday, told me plainly that was his view. The committee of cabinet which met on Tuesday last were of that opinion, the Duke dissenting.

The mere party aspect of this decision seemed to me so serious that I summoned the Skipper and Bob and Willie* to a conference last night.[319]

The obvious plan was to proceed with secondary education only. But Sandars' little conference decided that even a secondary Bill would necessarily raise all the difficulties. It would have to define the limits of elementary education, repeal the Cowper-Temple section of the Technical Instruction Act of 1889, and decide as between the London County Council and the London boroughs. In debate the intentions of the government with regard to school boards (which were being deprived of their secondary provision) would be bound to transpire. Would Chamberlain like 'to see the ground thus cut away'? 'In fine,' Sandars' report concludes, 'throughout the whole course of the debates we shall be fighting an undisclosed Elementary Bill, with all the difficulties of the attendant issues.' Better to abandon the whole question, postponing it by some interim provision. The party would be disappointed, but '*any* result is preferable to the failure to pass a Bill which has once been introduced'.

Everything remained still in suspense when on 14 March the cabinet had to finalize its plans for the session. To the alternatives of Devonshire and Sandars, Chamberlain added an entirely new plan of his own which was startling in its simplicity and presented no difficulty except that the whole Conservative party would be up in arms against it. He boldly advocated a reversion to '*ad hoc*' —the handing over of secondary education to the school boards. This would have solved the administrative problem posed by the Cockerton judgment, and, viewed as an interim measure, it would have required very little alteration of the educational system. But politically it meant the strengthening of the stranglehold of the school boards over the denominational schools, and the loss of what was regarded as in all likelihood the last opportunity to place the latter on a sound footing. How seriously Chamberlain's proposition was taken is not apparent, but it drew from Morant a strenuous memorandum stating twelve good reasons

---

* i.e. Capt. Middleton, Akers-Douglas, and Walrond, the party manager and whips.

in favour of local authority control. Did Chamberlain mean to reverse the consistent policy of the party during the last twelve years: to end the beneficent activity of 316 municipal authorities which were rating themselves for technical and secondary education? 'Is the great Birmingham Institute, and the new Manchester Institute—the largest in England—to be taken from the town council which built it, and given to the school board?'[320] These arguments of Morant's were superfluous. Chamberlain's intention was probably to mark his dissent from Devonshire, and not to raise his alternative seriously. By doing this, he demonstrated to his Conservative colleagues beyond mistake that what they were intending to do was not forced upon them by the necessities of education but, ultimately, by the demands of the Conservative party. How inexorable these demands were needed no proof beyond the fact that when it came to a decision, the cabinet accepted Devonshire's Bill with heavy hearts and an assurance from Balfour that it meant political destruction. 'The die is cast', notes Devonshire's official secretary after the cabinet of the 14 March: 'the Education Bill is to be introduced on 24 March. Devonshire and Balfour think the question will wreck the government. Balfour is to take charge of it, and go on if the second reading is taken.'[321]

The Education Bill's protracted passage through the House of Commons, and the agitations it aroused in the country, amply fulfilled the worst fears of the government. No measure had ever before been met by so many amendments when in December 1902 it received the royal assent. While its concessions to the Church party had barely prevented their secession, the same concessions had aroused the fighting Nonconformists in the country to a pitch of agitation recalling the days of Disraeli and the Bulgarian atrocities. In the debates of the summer and autumn Chamberlain played hardly any part at all, nor could he do much to stem the inundation in the country, as Liberals made common cause with Nonconformists and press and platform resounded with the old cries he knew so well. All he could hope to achieve was to minimize the defection of Liberal Unionists. Foreseeing the need for a clear line along which he could hold his men in order, he had supported the 'adoptive' clause of the Bill, so that it could be argued that no area need implement the section of the Bill dealing with elementary education and rate aid until a majority of the ratepayers willed it. All the brunt of the educational struggle would thus be transferred from national to local politics. It must be admitted that this would have been a most undesirable outcome. The adoptive clause was generally condemned by educationalists: and when the Commons reached the clause in July, Balfour allowed a free vote and it was excised by a large majority. Nevertheless this decision was the pretext for a great Nonconformist exertion in the cause of the Cowper-Temple principle, which was now to be demolished by statute.

Parliament was due to reassemble after the recess on 16 October, and Balfour was to outline his modified education proposals to the cabinet on 11 October and then make an important declaratory speech at Manchester on 14 October. The agitation against the Bill had reached a crescendo at the meeting at Woodhouse Moor, Leeds, on 20 September, whither multitudes of Liberal and Nonconformist supporters had been brought by excursion trains to be harangued from five platforms. In the intensification of the struggle in the last weeks of the recess, a meeting of Birmingham Liberal Unionists held at the end of September condemned the form of clause 7 of the Bill, and demanded a majority of local authority managers in control of rate-aided voluntary schools.* Some threatened to leave the party if concessions were not made, invoking against this management clause the principle of 'no taxation without representation'. Chamberlain set to work in earnest to prevent the liquidation of the party he had maintained for sixteen years. He called a meeting for 9 October when he could meet his challengers face to face: and, if need be, promise a minimum of concession. At once it became necessary for him to reach an understanding with Balfour.

Balfour wrote on 4 October to Chamberlain simply mentioning his recent consultations with his educational advisers and suggesting that Morant should inform Chamberlain verbally of the

---

* The local authority could supply only two out of the six statutory managers, the other four representing the denominational interest. Balfour considered this equitable 'considering how little the managers had to manage' under the Bill. Their chief concern would be religious teaching, which Balfour intended to take out of the sole charge of the parson.

results: 'I should like you to know the upshot before cabinet.'[322] In response to this suggestion Chamberlain invited Morant to dine at Highbury on 8 October and stay overnight. It suited him to be briefed by Morant just before he faced the Birmingham Liberal Unionists. But Morant went up to Birmingham thoroughly instructed to resist any suggestion that Balfour might give way:

Morant–Balfour, 7 October 1902: Mr Chamberlain has written me to dine and sleep tomorrow (Wednesday) as he wants (he says) a talk before he has his private conference. I have seen Sandars and talked everything out. I have had a good talk with the Duke; he is strong against altering clause 7, or the denominational majority: says that to try that *now* would not save a single seat. Go through with it, he says. . . .[323]

Morant of course had come to regard Chamberlain as the arch-enemy of his whole scheme, while Sandars added to Morant's prejudice a suspicious hostility to the Liberal Unionists. After Chamberlain's conspicuous loyalty and resolute self-effacement, Sandars' jealousy is not easily accounted for:

Sandars–Balfour, 8 October 1902: I despatched Morant off on his mission to Chamberlain today after a very prolonged interview when he rehearsed the kind of representation it was wise to make on your behalf.

The point upon which I begged him to dwell was that the important declarations you had in your mind *must* be put forward by you at Manchester, and that they must *not* be anticipated by any soothing words at Birmingham. . . .

. . . as a mere matter of party tactics *you* and not Chamberlain must be the expositor of policy on the Bill, and the Bill must not appear to be altered to suit the wavering legions of Birmingham.[324]

Morant and Sandars had in fact overreached themselves, with a curious sequel. Returning from Birmingham on 9 October, Morant reported to Sandars what he understood to be Chamberlain's demands, which Sandars wrote down that day and posted off to Balfour. They were first, that Balfour's Manchester speech should not be of a 'declaratory and rallying character'; and second, that 'the issue must be changed', which Sandars interpreted to mean that 'we must surrender on the present question of management as settled by clause 7 to the Nonconformists, and get our safeguards for denominational schools in some other way'. This was a complete misapprehension of Chamberlain's meaning, as soon transpired. But meanwhile Sandars had set in train a reaction among the Conservative whips which is most significant of the underlying tensions within the Unionist alliance:

Sandars–Balfour, 9 October 1902: I have had an interview with Douglas and Middleton on the party aspect of it. I think it is absolutely necessary you should see Alick Hood and the Skipper on Saturday morning *before* Cabinet. . . .

With Chamberlain in his present mood—of course we do not know how he will fare with his Liberal Unionist flock tonight—it seems plain that he will raise the Education question in its thorniest form at Cabinet on Saturday. Hence you clearly must know . . . how his proposals affect the general view of your more immediate friends and supporters *before* you go into Cabinet. After Cabinet Chamberlain has also designs on you, and thus we must seize our only opportunity. . . .

If the decision be forced upon you to make *any violent change* in the measure *to meet the Birmingham Liberal Unionists*, we think, on the whole, there is hardly any other alternative but to withdraw the Bill. That, of course, means an election and a rout.[325]

The next day Sandars received a letter from Chamberlain, written just before the Birmingham meeting, which supplied the correct version of his intentions. The letter was forthright enough, saying that if Balfour 'nails his flag to the mast on Tuesday at Manchester, I consider the Unionist cause is hopeless at the next election, and we shall certainly lose the majority of the Liberal Unionists once and for all'.[326] Chamberlain asked that the question of representative control through a majority of school managers should be kept open no more. And although at the meeting of his supporters a resolution condemning clause 7 was carried, he refused to countenance any attack either upon the clause or the government.

No concession to the Nonconformists was made in the remaining stages of the Bill, and, apart from the Kenyon-Slaney amendment, which merely confirmed Balfour's policy of vesting the control of religious education in the full board of managers, the alterations made were favourable to the denominationalists. Chamberlain did not nurse any sense of grievance against Balfour.

He did hold something against the Duke of Devonshire, as the man who had forced Morant's scheme upon the cabinet, and as a renegade Liberal Unionist. 'I told you that your Education Bill would destroy your own party', he wrote to the Duke on 22 September: 'It has done so. Our best friends are leaving us by scores and hundreds, and they will not come back.'[327]

Chamberlain was blind to the cardinal fact of the situation, that the Education Act of 1902 was essentially in tune with the spirit and the educational values of the time, while the shibboleths of the Nonconformists were not. He consequently feared a reversal of the measure, and genuinely wished that the whole thing had been left to the Liberals. It has been suggested that Chamberlain represented the 'rising spirit of "State socialism"' and was compelled to resist the Bill by a sectarian interest.[328] The exact opposite is the case. Chamberlain abhorred state socialism. Thus his objection to the Education Bill was fundamental—he saw no merit and much danger in the centralized control and uniformity of a state system: and while he could have conscientiously found grave objections to the whole approach of the Bill, he swallowed them to avoid breaking up the government.

The point is best illustrated by a comparison between Chamberlain's approach and that of the Fabians who were the true representatives of state socialism. In October 1902 Sidney Webb came out in favour of the Education Bill, thereby earning the suspicion and indeed active hostility of the London labour groups. 'All our political friends bitter or sullen', notes his wife.[329] There was a 'slump in Webbs'. When Morant began to negotiate with them over the London Education Act, a small 'clique' headed by Ramsay MacDonald advocated an *ad hoc* education authority for London instead of the London County Council, and got Sidney Webb defeated on the Technical Education Board. As Mrs Webb observed, 'So determined are they to "spite the government" and so anxious for a good battle cry that they are steering straight into a "water board" authority for education.'[330] The Webbs were thought to stand for too much secondary and university education at the expense of primary provision, and for ignoring the religious issue. They believed, in Beatrice Webb's words, in 'expenditure on services which will benefit other classes beside the working class, and which will open the way to working men to become fit to govern, not simply to represent, their class'.[331] In brief, they believed, much more so than the contemporary Labour leaders, in a bureaucratic, hierarchical and state-promoted educational system. They quickly gained the confidence of Morant, and undertook to enlist the support of the London Progressives if the government would hand over the whole of London education and the complete control of the education committee to the London County council.[332] In this way London was given a 'collectivist' educational system, which was precisely what Chamberlain had striven hard to prevent. He and the Tory squire Walter Long were the only members of the cabinet who could seriously contemplate the alternative of handing over London's education to a patchwork of borough councils.

Chamberlain in fact was no longer a progressive in domestic affairs, and like most of his generation he had no idea of the shift of emphasis away from the old political issues until the scales fell from his eyes in 1906. And Beatrice Webb, who had been so much more a Spencerian individualist than he in the 1880's, was now in a different world of thought to whose qualities Chamberlain remained quite blind. In outlining her programme of Fabian objectives in 1902 Beatrice Webb provides one of the best descriptions of the emergent spirit of state socialism in Edwardian England:

Beatrice Webb's diary, 28 February 1902: We want to get rid of all the old ideals and enthusiasms, we want to stamp out the notion that the world can be bettered by abolition of some of the existing institutions; we want on the contrary to set people to work to build up new tissue which may in time take the place of the old.

In Ireland, for instance, we don't want to abolish the Union with England, but so to reconstruct the internal government that it will make the bond of union of secondary importance.

We do not want to abolish or remodel the House of Lords, but to build up precedents for their non-intervention in national expenditure —all Collectivism coming under this head.

We do not want to disestablish the Church, but to endow science and secular ethics and any other form of intellectual activity that may seem desirable.

We don't want to abolish or restrain the development of private enterprise, but by creating dykes and bulwarks to control its mischievous effect on the character of the race.

We do not want to unfetter the individual from the obligation of citizenship, we want on the contrary to stimulate and constrain him, by the unfelt pressure of a better social environment, to become a healthier nobler, and more efficient being.

To these ideals the old Liberalism of Leonard Courtney, Morley, Campbell-Bannerman and the bulk of Celtic members of Parliament is not only unsympathetic but really hostile.*[333]

It was this kind of constructive collectivism which triumphed in the Education Act: while the failure of the combined forces of Nonconformity and the older Liberalism to maintain the libertarianism of the 1870 settlement signified more than the mere decline of the political power of these particular sects. It was a defeat for sectarianism, Anglican as well as Nonconformist, but above all it was the first major legislative reversal of the statecraft of *laissez-faire* and *ad hoc* authorities which since 1832 had put a premium upon the wills and the consciences of individuals.

---

* Sidney Webb was introduced to Chamberlain on the terrace of the House of Commons in July 1900 by his wife as 'a former civil servant'. 'I think you were in my office, Mr Webb,' said the Colonial Secretary. 'That is hardly quite correct,' replied Sidney clumsily, 'when I was there you were not.' After lunching with Chamberlain in June 1904 Beatrice Webb observed: '. . . he detests the salaried expert, and . . . he tries to ignore the necessity for the *official* government of society . . . .'

CHAPTER TEN

Imperial Preference

. . . their whole way of looking at politics . . . appears to me to be entirely sordid and materialistic, not yet corrupt, but on the high-road to corruption.

Lord Robert Cecil commenting on the Chamberlainites,
25 January 1906

IN May 1903 Chamberlain startled the public and eclipsed other political controversies by committing himself to the policy of imperial preference, speaking to a meeting at Birmingham. Soon after, by explanations which he gave from his place on the front bench of the Commons, he appeared to commit the government also to this policy, and immediately a section of free trade members of the cabinet challenged this step in private but indignant representations to Balfour. The Unionist party-split over the fiscal question had materialized: which to men at the time as to later writers seemed to have been provoked by a rash and irresponsible departure by Chamberlain. Conjectural motives for such a departure were not hard to invent. Chamberlain himself announced that imperial preference would over-shadow at the coming general election the controversy over the Education Act which was proving so disastrous to his own section of the Liberal Unionist party. Was this move his answer to the Conservatives who had refused to contemplate his succession to the party leadership when Salisbury retired? Was it a bid to found a middle party of protectionists and imperialists? In the absence of more satisfactory explanations the public were left to speculate along these lines.

Chamberlain's true designs, which had a long background in the undisclosed discussions and dissensions of the Unionist cabinets of Salisbury and Balfour, could not be revealed because these cabinets had been hopelessly divided upon all the collateral questions raised by imperial preference. Unknown to the public or the parliamentary party, the Unionist government had failed to make up its mind on the cardinal question of how to find revenue for mounting expenditure in all spheres—for social reforms, education, old age pensions, rearmament, colonial development, war loans, and the like. Under Salisbury's unhurried and unworried régime the Chancellor of the Exchequer, Hicks Beach, was able to veto any constructive planning and to stand out for uncompromising free trade and economy in its traditional forms. But Beach was almost alone, and would have had to go but for the South African War. When Balfour became premier, Beach and his conventional notions were jettisoned and the cabinet adopted a much more flexible approach to fiscal policy. Without being agreed on the theoretical merits of imperial preference, the new ministry accepted a tentative application of it after hearing the arguments of the Colonial premiers who came for the coronation in the summer of 1902. It was decided to remit in Canada's favour the 1s. duty on corn which Hicks Beach had imposed, strictly for revenue purposes, in his budget earlier that year.

That the corn duty should have been imposed at all, and by Beach of all people, was proof that other means of indirect taxation had been exhausted, and would only yield a diminishing revenue. It was therefore Unionist policy to 'broaden the base' of indirect taxation, and this aim conspired with other considerations to dispose the government to adopt imperial preference. For the one remaining accessible area of indirect taxation was the sacred category of food and raw materials, which Peel had relieved of heavy tariffs in the 1840's, and which Cobdenite budgets had made a sector almost—but not quite—of free imports. This was precisely the sector in which alone Britain could give a preference to the Colonies, if she chose to impose the appropriate tariffs against foreign imports. Moreover, the self-governing Colonies, and especially Canada, were at this time caught up in a rapidly moving course of competition with the great protective trade blocs of the U.S.A. and the German Empire. These Colonies were themselves highly protectionist, and most of all in manufactured goods and machinery which Britain exported. In raising tariffs against foreign manufactures, Canada had given Britain a preference of 25 per cent in 1898 and 33⅓ per cent in 1900—while still levying a substantial duty on British goods. They had in 1897 rejected the idea of an Empire *Zollverein* which Chamberlain had publicly recommended to them—although this would have been an area only of relative free trade. They were essentially free to conclude unilateral trade treaties with foreign countries, and there was every prospect that they would be forced very speedily to do so.

Thus the gesture which the government decided to make in 1902 by the remission of the 1*s.* duty in the case of Canadian corn was by no means hasty or extravagant. Even so, it would, had it ever come before the Commons, have met with very formidable opposition. Beach's minimal 1*s.* duty was condemned as 'protective', and indeed had caused a crystallization of parliamentary forces into Cobdenites and anti-Cobdenites. The Cobdenites were not simple-minded believers in the doctrines of the Cobden Club, but Liberals who knew that many of their supporters and Labour allies preferred to raise the revenue for social reforms from the direct taxation of the 'idle rich', and who rightly assessed the electoral power of the free food cry. The anti-Cobdenites were Conservative agricultural protectionists or 'fair traders' or fiscal agnostics who would prefer to find the additional revenue from tariffs rather than from direct taxation. In a situation in which Britain stood alone in her adherence to the faith of free imports, while her domestic finance was poised in this state of uncertainty, the atmosphere had become explosive. Balfour's party agent informed him that the 1*s.* corn duty was proving electorally more disastrous than the Education Bill.[334] The Unionist cabinet did not draw back, but decided to accept the challenge and come out for imperial preference. Originally the preferential tariff scheme put forward by Hofmeyr in 1887 had envisaged a 2 per cent tariff imposed by Britain and the self-governing colonies which would yield £7 millions a year for an imperial defence fund. When Hicks Beach was at the Board of Trade, his permanent secretary Robert Giffen prepared a memorandum of the economic objections to the Hofmeyr plan. Much of Giffen's argument is extremely questionable. He believed that a 2 per cent tariff on foreign materials would reduce profits and wages correspondingly, and that this reduction would tend to fall on wages exclusively. By his arithmetic, not only would wages thus fall by 4 or 5 per cent, but their purchasing power would be reduced by a further 5 per cent owing to the 2 per cent preferential duty on foreign food. Such were the horrors of even a small general tariff to British Cobdenite officials. 'There is no need to discuss these points,' Giffen concludes. 'No one in England dare propose differential duties on food and raw materials. . . . The proposals are not seriously within the range of practical discussion.'[335]

But there were more telling arguments against imperial preference. Only one-third of British trade was with her colonies: while Britain was also the great entrepôt for world trade. Any duties on foreign imports would therefore entail a heavy sacrifice, and especially in the case of food and raw materials whose cheapness had been the basis of Britain's industrial supremacy. No preference which the colonies could give would be any equivalent for such a sacrifice. The colonies were dependent for their revenues upon tariffs raised on imported manufactures, which came almost exclusively from Britain, and the preference which they wanted to give consisted not in the remission of the heavy duties on British goods, but in laying even heavier duties on foreign goods. Thus they did not offer Britain a customs union with no internal tariffs, but invited the mother country to become a party to an extension of protection.

There was therefore some foundation for the scepticism with which Whitehall viewed the approaches of the colonies. When Chamberlain was about to set off for the United States to conduct the Fisheries negotiation in 1887, he was warned to beware of the fiscal overtures of the Canadians by Sir Thomas Farrer, Giffen's predecessor at the Board of Trade and author of a widely read book on 'Fair Trade':

Farrer–Chamberlain, 15 October 1887: In speaking of Canada, are you aware that Canada has already had a reciprocity treaty with the United States, favouring U.S. goods at the expense of British . . .? It is said that this is what they want again, and if they do, it is most certainly not worth our while to buy them off by promising to put differentiated duties on to foreign goods. . . . Imperial union is not to be had by these means, and the first step on this course would be a fatal one.

I dread and mistrust these Canadian politicians altogether. They will use us as a catspaw if they can, as they have already done in the matter of investments. Besides, in a larger sense, I believe the welfare of our race does not consist in setting up the Union Jack against the Stars and Stripes: but in a nearer approach amongst all English peoples.[336]

Chamberlain seems to have broached some idea of imperial preference to Farrer at this time, for Farrer writes again two days later to say 'I should agree with you if the sacrifices we make are not such as we shall afterwards repent'. 'There is no popular cry', he goes on, 'I fear more than imperial federation.'[337]

Already there were what Farrer and Giffen would regard as sinister interests at work on the British side, not only manufacturers who wished to use preference as a cloak for introducing protection, but the trade unions and working classes. It was feared that sooner or later the working classes would espouse protection to maintain their standard of living, with plausible grounds for doing so in a world which was becoming rapidly protectionist. 'Fair trade' had been a sweeping slogan at the 1885 elections, and was making way in the Conservative party. Lord Randolph Churchill was sympathetic, and was perceptive enough to discern how imperial preference could be turned to account to gain the support of the masses:

Randolph Churchill–Balfour, 19 March 1892: The new [trade] unionism which goes for eight hours has almost entirely broken down the old unionism which was in mortal hostility to Toryism.

Eight hours will I believe carry with it as a necessary consequence on some increased cost of production a return towards protection which may take the form of an inter-colonial customs union. A result agreeable to all our party traditions.[338]

The supposedly inevitable conversion of the trade unions to protection was destined, however, to prove a very slow business, and anyone suspected of protectionist designs was prone to attack from all sides while remaining quite unsupported by any significant section of the public. Imperial preference was the only approach to protection that was practicable.

Before he became Colonial Secretary, Chamberlain had arrived at a way of meeting the demands of the colonies for preference. He would impose a duty on foreign corn, sufficient to encourage the Canadian supply without raising the price of bread to any noticeable degree: and he would return the cost of this sacrifice to the working classes in good measure by using the revenue to finance old age pensions. When he sat as a member of the royal commission on the aged poor in 1894–5, he was asked by Herbert Maxwell how he proposed to find the £9 to £20 millions that might be needed to promote even a contributory scheme. 'By an import duty on wheat', Chamberlain replied: 'Nothing that I have ever said or written would prevent me advocating a tax on corn *for a specific purpose.*'339 This was said privately. Publicly any such announcement would be premature until the colonial premiers had agreed upon some preferential scheme. The opportunity arrived with the Colonial Conference of 1897. Chamberlain went so far as to prepare the ground for this by a speech delivered at the Canada Club early in 1896 in which he advocated an imperial *Zollverein*—a free trade area with a population of 300 million. He hoped to persuade the colonial governments to set up a Council of the Empire to deal with imperial defence and trade. But the 1897 Conference was a disappointment. The colonies did not want to contribute to the cost of the British navy nor to relinquish their protectionist policies towards other parts of the Empire, and on both these counts Chamberlain's proposals were suspect. Farrer's analysis of the position seemed to have been confirmed. The colonies seemed to have nothing to give, and little to take from the mother country.

Meanwhile the prospects for a government scheme for old age pensions were not good, partly because of its dependence upon some preferential corn duty, partly because of the hostility of members of the Unionist cabinet, most important among whom were Hicks Beach and the Prime Minister. Chamberlain could neither disclose his interdependent plans to the cabinet nor easily explain the delay to his supporters. The delay in announcing the government's plan was prolonged by the failure of the 1897 Colonial Conference, and when the Boer War commenced Chamberlain had made no progress even in converting the cabinet. With the heavy expenditure on the war, the pensions scheme might have been indefinitely shelved had Chamberlain not pressed it while the government were deciding their wartime financial policy. A long deferred conflict was sure to result between the two strongest wills in the ministry, Chamberlain and the redoubtable Hicks Beach.

The immediate occasion was trivial. After the outbreak of the war, Beach refused the Colonial Office some expenditure for a channel steamer mail service between Cape Town and Natal. Chamberlain thereupon attacked in cabinet the system of

'Treasury control', apparently with some degree of success, for Beach was provoked into offering his resignation. In doing so, Beach mentioned that 'in another important matter I fear that my opinions will be very difficult to reconcile with those of the majority of the cabinet'.[340] He was against old age pensions. Salisbury's reply reveals that he, too, belonged to the minority:

Salisbury–Beach, 18 October 1899: I will say nothing about old age pensions. I am sceptical of the possibility of any large measure: and I think any measure in favour of those who are not in real poverty will be very unjust. But I think some relaxation of the rigours of the Poor Law in favour of old people would be (within the limits of financial feasibility) both just and wise. But that is not urgent just yet.[341]

Such was the atmosphere in which Chamberlain, anxious to pre-empt a due share of the national revenues, was obliged to disclose his scheme for old age pensions. It was placed before the cabinet in a confidential print dated 17 November 1899, during the period of suspense and preoccupation following the Boer invasion of British South Africa.[342] It varied from that put forward by the informal committee of the House of Commons which he had sponsored nine years earlier in some important respects: namely, that a non-contributory old age pension, in no case to exceed 5s. per week, was to be made available only to those persons over sixty-five years of age who were unable to maintain themselves, without assistance, by their own labour. In other words, only those who would in any case have fallen on the Poor Law would get a non-contributory pension, and only on rigorous conditions. The cost of this reform of the existing Poor Law would fall on the local rates, aided by a small Treasury grant.

Thus far, the scheme was merely a rationalization of the existing commitments of the Poor Law authorities. But against this deterrent and almost penal background Chamberlain wished to offer the incentive of pensions for those who had contributed for twenty years to a Friendly Society; or supplementary grants to those who took advantage of a post office contribution scheme which he outlined as follows:

Contributory Old Age Pensions:
1. Any person (man or woman) may pay any sum at any time into a a post office savings bank and may receive a certificate for a deferred non-returnable annuity payable after he attains the age of 65.

2. The state shall add one half to the amount of such payments, providing that this contribution of the state does not in the whole
amount to more than an annuity of 2/6d per week.[343]

The scheme contradicted Salisbury's idea that pensions should
go only to those in real poverty: but at the same time it intended
to reverse the negative incentive to saving which the existing
Poor Law held out, and reduce the extent of real poverty among the
aged by giving a powerful incentive to thrift and providence. It
was a document written in the spirit of Edwin Chadwick and the
Poor Law Commissioners' Report of 1834 rather than a signpost
pointing to the welfare state.

When Lord Salisbury resigned in July 1902, Beach grasped the
occasion to relinquish his office, nor could he be persuaded by
Balfour that the differences between himself and Chamberlain
could be bridged over. The way was thus cleared for the acceptance of imperial preference, both by the Colonial Conference
then in progress, and by the new government. But the Colonial
Conference was again a deep a disappointment for Chamberlain.
His proposals for a Council of the Empire and for Colonial
contributions to imperial defence met with a cold response,
while serious snags in the way of preference were disclosed.
While preference might have been successfully recommended to
the British public as a step toward an imperial *Zollverein*, it looked
as if it would have to be advocated as a desperate expedient to
retain what trade remained after the Colonies had completed their
own protectionist systems. The Canadian officials demonstrated
that the $33\frac{1}{3}$ per cent preference given to British goods had
arrested a decline in British imports, but it had not prevented the
continued relative success of United States exporters in Canada.
Yet the Canadians could not lower the duties on British goods,
and were thinking in terms of further increases in those raised
against foreign countries. Thus they did not offer anything which
Chamberlain could regard as worth bargaining for.

The Liberal opposition were beginning to make much play
with the argument that preference meant food taxes, and Balfour
was left in no doubt of the serious opposition that preference
would meet with. Sandars reported to him the alarm of the party
agent, Middleton, at the country's reaction to the newly-imposed
corn tax and the suspicion that it heralded a fiscal revolution:

Sandars–Balfour, 21 September 1902: [Middleton] takes a much more serious view of the Corn Tax [than of the Education Bill]. He says that of course if the tax be the precursor of a general scheme of fiscal reform in the direction of protection, well and good and it is worth keeping. But, if not, he asserts that it cannot be worth our while to maintain the tax. . . . He speaks of it as a millstone round our necks. . . .[344]

In spite of this warning the cabinet went ahead with a discussion of the plan to retain the corn tax while remitting it in favour of the Empire. After the first discussion on 21 October, Balfour reported to the King that there was a great deal to be said for this preference, 'But', he observed, 'it raises very big questions indeed—colonial and fiscal—and the Government which embarks upon it provokes a big fight. On the whole Mr Balfour leans towards it; but it behoves us to walk warily'.[345] The only serious dissentient was Ritchie, who came out strongly against it with all the familiar arguments of the mandarins of the Treasury and Board of Trade. His memorandum was in vain—the decision being taken on 19 November to implement the preference on corn in the 1903 budget, which Ritchie would prepare.[346]

Ritchie was able, however, to ensure that the decision was only tentative, and that his power to deal otherwise with the corn tax in any unforeseen alteration of circumstances was reserved. His own account of the transaction, given to Beach confidentially in a letter of May 1903, makes it plain that he had first refused a personal request from Chamberlain to give Canada preferential treatment, and that the cabinet decision had thereupon been pressed by the latter. Further, Ritchie admitted that the cabinet had decided affirmatively, 'the minority consisting of myself and one other'. 'Nothing more was said or done until a fortnight before Chamberlain was due home, when I spoke to Balfour on the subject, and told him that it was useless for me to proceed with the budget arrangements if the previous decision of the cabinet was to be adhered to, as I declined to be responsible for it. He then asked whether by that I meant to leave the government. I replied that I certainly meant that, and that nothing would induce me to stay.'[347] In this extraordinary way Ritchie was able to destroy the plan. He had been careful to avoid the mistake of Lord Randolph Churchill, who resigned over an undisclosed budget at Christmas. He never had the slightest intention of carrying out the decision of November, but by concealing this till the last moment he got the upper hand. The corn duty was abolished altogether. As Ritchie pointed out, 'It is really a contest between free trade and protection'.

In the spring of 1903 Chamberlain returned from his South African tour, 'rather ill, rather irritable, and very tired'.[348] For some weeks he sat on the Treasury bench taking little part in the debates. All the designs for which he had worked and waited within the cabinet had come to nothing, and his party in the country, whose leadership he had virtually abdicated while loyally serving the government, was now going to pieces. On more than one occasion he had announced that the end of his active political life was approaching, and he felt that if he were to launch his great scheme of fiscal and social reform, it must be without further delay. Ritchie's action had prevented the overt move towards preference which would have placed the fiscal question in the forefront of home politics. Chamberlain resolved to counter Ritchie's move and 'free food' arguments by coming out in public for the preference scheme.

His Birmingham speech of 15 May was at once recognized as a counterblast to Beach and Ritchie. In the context of the repeal of the corn duty it produced an enormous sensation. The main plea was for imperial union through preferential tariffs, but this was reinforced by a further plea for a power of negotiation and if necessary of retaliation against foreign countries who raised hostile tariffs against this country while enjoying the complete freedom of the British market. Such, it was suggested, would be 'the issues on which we shall take the opinion of the country'. Within the next fortnight this momentous declaration was followed up by parliamentary explanations which seemed to commit the government. On 22 May a debate on old age pensions drew from Chamberlain a condemnation of the scheme supported by some sections of the opposition for universal old age pensions at the expense of the state. Such a scheme, said Chamberlain, was impossible and also undesirable, 'because the promise of universal pensions to everyone, without reference to previous character, would be the greatest blow ever struck at thrift in this country'. But he did not say his own scheme was dead; it might be possible to find the funds for a contributory scheme, 'but that, no doubt, will involve a review of that fiscal system which I have indicated as necessary and desirable at an early date'.

The opposition were quick to seize upon this statement, which, as Sir Charles Dilke remarked in raising the question on 28 May, could mean only the taxation of food and a revolution in the country's fiscal system. Balfour and Chamberlain rose successively to meet this challenge.

Balfour spoke hypothetically—the Colonial Conference had asked for preference, and it had to be investigated. Chamberlain spoke of the actual situation. The colonies should have a reply from the electorate, and if the reply were 'no', the electors must give up all hope of closer fiscal relations and therefore of closer political relations with their kinsmen overseas. If the government did get a mandate, they could then produce a plan for the approval of the colonies. Meanwhile much investigation was needed. He admitted that the working class might have to pay three-quarters of the cost of preference, but they should get this, or indeed all the value of the tariffs, repaid to them in the form of social reforms. For 'while it would be absolute confiscation to put the cost of social reform wholly on the shoulders of one class . . . the richer class . . . yet on the other hand it is fair and right that they should make a contribution in return for the indirect advantages they gain from the great prosperity and contentment of the country'. The doctrine of 'ransom' had re-emerged, allied to a scrupulously conservative fiscal revolution.

Chamberlain had gone too far. Anticipating an early election, he could not await the results of a cabinet enquiry but was set on an immediate propaganda campaign in the country. At once the free trade section of the cabinet were up in arms. Ritchie sent a protest to the Prime Minister:

Ritchie–Balfour, 30 May 1903: He seems to have set himself the task of making it impossible for anyone who does not share his views to remain a member of the government. He has not merely given expression to his own views, but has sketched out a plan upon which he declares the government will at the next election take the opinion of the country, and in the meantime he proposes to advocate the policy throughout the constituencies. . . .

I believe his policy to be disastrous both to the country and the party, but, if he had limited his speech to a proposal for an examination into the subject, I would have said nothing.[349]

The same day, Ritchie wrote to Devonshire suggesting that Chamberlain's opponents should 'consult together with a view of taking common action'.[350] Devonshire seemed to concur, for he also wrote to Balfour repeating the doubt about the cabinet continuing, and warning him that he could not allow himself to be committed to a policy which he did not expect to be able to accept. Goschen and Balfour of Burleigh took the same line. Lansdowne, however, took a more tolerant view of the situation:

Lansdowne–Devonshire, 1 June 1903: I read the speech to indicate that so far as the immediate future is concerned, we are asked to admit only that there is a case for inquiry. Such inquiry would be made:

(a.) in regard to the attitude of people connected with commerce in this country.

(b.) in regard to the possibility of devising a scheme which the colonies would accept, and

(c.) as to the readiness of the working classes to pay more for bread and meat, in consideration of a corresponding increase of wages, and perhaps old age pensions. . . .

My impression is that, even if Chamberlain succeeds in 'educating' the working classes as to (c.), we are unlikely to come to terms with those most concerned as to (a.) and (b.) . . . But, until we know more, can we rule the whole scheme out of order?[351]

Was there any sense in breaking up the government before the fiscal question became an immediate issue? Balfour's reply to Devonshire pleaded in this sense, asking for a self-denying ordinance on both sides. No action on the matter could be taken until after a general election, which by all indications the Unionists were going to lose. Selborne also put this consideration to the fore on being sounded about his fiscal views by Devonshire. It was obviously much better to break up the government than the party: and equally evident, whatever one's fiscal leanings, that it was not possible to 'rush' a great party on a major question.

From June until September the cabinet held together on the basis of 'inquiring' into the fiscal question. This did not prevent both sides of the divided Unionist party from entering upon a 'raging, tearing propaganda' in the country. Chamberlain boldly advocated food taxes as indispensable to preference, adding that 'even if the price of food is raised, the rate of wages will certainly be raised in greater proportion'. The free trade Unionists entered the lists with free food literature. Only in the House of Commons was controversy stifled by a stern application of the government's procedural powers. Nevertheless even here an ominous party split was developing. While still in the cabinet, Ritchie concerted his moves with Hicks Beach, who started a Unionist free trade movement in the parliamentary party. The elements of this were somewhat diverse, consisting chiefly of a cautious wing of free trade purists like Beach himself, and a more adventurous group of 'Hughligans' led by the *frondeur*, Lord Hugh Cecil, who spoke of Chamberlain as an 'alien immigrant' among Conservatives.

Lord Hugh Cecil and Winston Churchill had suspected and opposed Chamberlain from the first manifestations of the new fiscal policy, and they were convinced that he would form a protectionist front which would dissolve the old party alignments. Consequently they were prepared to oppose him even to the extent of coalescing with the Liberals. They misjudged Chamberlain's intentions, although they assessed more accurately the character of those who joined Chamberlain's movement. To some degree they were responsible for driving Chamberlain in a more protectionist direction. Chamberlain realized the latent power of a protectionist cry, but there is no reason to disbelieve his denials of protectionist intentions, of which the following reported conversation with a Treasury official is an example:

Sir E. Hamilton's diary, 30 June 1903: We talked for half an hour; and very pleasant he was, as he always is, though I think he regarded me as a hopelessly prejudiced person.

. . . in his inmost soul he had always been an economic agnostic. He disclaimed strongly the idea that he had taken up an anti-free trade line as an electioneering cry. If he had, he certainly would not have raised the question while times were on the whole good. He thought it only fair that the country should consider the question quietly, whereas in bad times he had not a doubt that he could have swept the country with a protectionist cry. As matters were, he had no idea what the result of the electoral fight would be. . . . He had, he admitted, no plan whatever of a cut and dried sort.[352]

To oppose Chamberlain the free trade section took their stand on 'free food', a somewhat hypocritical position since food taxes

existed and they had themselves supported the corn tax. While
the bulk of the Unionist M.P.s supported the official embargo
on fiscal debates, the 'Hughligans' pressed for parliamentary
discussion. They aimed to secure the support of Devonshire,
under whose aegis many waverers might have gathered. 'I want
to urge you', Churchill wrote to the Duke, 'that the conditions
of fairness and impartiality in this controversy will be altogether
destroyed if procedure is construed and used to prevent all
unprejudiced debate in the House of Commons . . . inactivity
and silence would most certainly be interpreted in the country
as weakness and indecision.'[353] Lord Hugh Cecil appealed for
the Duke's support, while rumours circulated that Devonshire
might be called for, should the ministry break up, to form a free
trade administration in conjunction with Rosebery.

Devonshire was loyally trying to follow the cabinet decision
to pursue a fiscal inquiry, but he had followed suit with Chamberlain and was backing the free trade propaganda issued by his
side of the Liberal Unionist organization. His refusal to place
himself at the head of the free trade Unionists did not appear
very determined, when he wrote to Cecil:

Devonshire–Lord Hugh Cecil, 18 July 1903: We have a small committee
who are engaged in preparing and issuing leaflets on the free trade
side of the question. . . . Could you not start some similar action in the
Conservative Association? . . .

As to the leadership of free trade Unionists, it seems to me that
you need not at present look beyond Sir Michael Hicks Beach.[354]

Balfour attempted to persuade the Duke that fiscal reform would
not mean duties for protective purposes, or duties which would
increase the average cost of living for the working man. Devonshire accepted the policy of retaliation against hostile tariffs, but
as then advised he did not accept the continental style of retaliation
'to which', he wrote, 'Chamberlain at one time, I think, had
leanings'; that of starting with heavy protective duties and
bargaining for reciprocal reductions. What the Duke really feared,
with some reason, was that Balfour's moderate scheme would
be swept away in favour of pure protection at the first gust of
favourable opinion. Then, towards the end of August, the Duke
received a long letter from Chamberlain which convinced him

that Chamberlain was indeed fast moving 'in the direction of protection pure and simple'.[355]

Chamberlain wrote to explain a change of front which he thought would counter the free food cry. His original proposal, he said, was that the small duties necessary to give the colonies a preference should be treated as a revenue tax, and the profits 'used for the promotion of those social reforms which are certain to come in the future, and which ought in my opinion to be provided for by indirect, and not by an increase in direct taxation'. This proposal might have been studied without party conflict. 'But the Opposition thought the chance too good to be lost. They have raised the free food cry, and we must meet them on their own grounds.' He was therefore prepared to modify his plan so that any duties imposed on food should be balanced by corresponding reductions in existing food taxes. He continued in a vein which confirmed the Duke's worst apprehensions about the tendency of his policy:

Chamberlain–Devonshire, 25 August 1903: The question is, how much will the new taxation on food amount to? . . . I think it would be possible . . . not to tax corn at all. In that case we should tax dairy produce including butter and eggs, and all meat including pork, ham, etc. . . . According to some calculations of Gerald Balfour's this would enable us to give a preference of a larger amount than corn and meat alone would provide, and compensation could be found in a reduction on tea and sugar. . . .

I gather that you think that we must reckon the cost to the working man as equal to the whole amount of the duty. . . . Personally I am convinced that this is a mistake . . . [But] if you . . . think it necessary to return an amount equivalent to the duty . . . it may be necessary . . . to take into account some tax on manufactured goods. But this we are certain to gain in any case by the adoption of the second and more popular part of tariff reform, namely retaliation.[356]

Chamberlain did not expect that the tariff reductions granted by foreign countries through fear of retaliation would be in all cases 'enough to justify us in allowing an absolutely free market', and he supported tariffs to protect the standard of living:

In this connection I think we ought to take into account the burden of taxation on home production, and the extra cost involved in our regulations for the protection of the workmen.

If, owing to this, the cost of production is greater in this country than, say, in Germany, we are surely entitled to treat that as unfair competition, and to put on some duty which would roughly be equivalent to the extra charge our home manufacturers have to bear.[357]

Did Chamberlain foresee the degree of protection implied in this principle—to save Lancashire cotton, for instance, from the cheap labour of Japan? In theory it could be just 'fair trade', but in practice the line would be very difficult to draw: especially since he was bent on giving to the electorate the ultimate power of deciding the shape of the scheme. He intended to allow the scheme to be formed by the wishes of the electors and of colonial and foreign governments:

If, as I have always desired, we could get a general mandate to carry our inquiries further, it would be our first business to communicate both with our colonies and with foreign countries, and until we have done that, it seems to me impossible to come to a final conclusion as to what would be the exact alterations which we should subsequently propose for the consideration of Parliament.[358]

It must have appeared to the Duke as if the fiscal policy of the world's great free trade emporium was to be settled by a conclave of protectionist powers. He had not sufficient faith in the democratic process to believe that the outcome would represent the collective wisdom of the country, and not its collective interests playing upon the misguided notions of the working class. Chamberlain's letter convinced him that retaliation was too dangerous a policy to be admitted, and he wrote to Balfour dissenting from the retaliatory doctrine which Balfour himself had advocated in his cabinet paper 'Economic Notes upon Insular Free Trade'. If Balfour's paper were accepted, it would give official countenance to the autumn campaign which Chamberlain was planning, and a general election would follow on the simple issue of free trade versus protection. The Duke did not believe there could be any fiscal *via media*.

Everything really depended on whether Devonshire remained in the government or not. The cabinet was due to meet on 14 September, and it was clear that at least three ministers—Ritchie, Balfour of Burleigh, and Lord George Hamilton—intended to resign if Chamberlain's autumn campaign were not called off. Balfour wrote long and persuasive appeals to the Duke to abide by the original preference policy. On the other side, Ritchie pleaded the impossibility of compromise:

Ritchie–Devonshire, 3 September 1903: I confess I do not see my way to any compromise which would not mean an abandonment of principle either by Chamberlain or by those who fundamentally differ from him. It might be found in a royal commission, but this would have to be accompanied by an abandonment of the autumn campaign, which I suspect Chamberlain will not assent to.[359]

Viewed politically, the situation seemed to demand a choice between two clear-cut policies, and there was much to be said for taking an uncompromising stand behind the Free Food League and the Cobden Club. The Duke's natural inclination in this direction was being supplemented by, among many others, his close confidant, Lord James of Hereford, who appealed to the Duke's sense of dignity and against any sitting on the fence. He ought not, James told him, to accede to any *modus vivendi* on 14 September. 'It will not do, and will be destructive to us as a party, and also make us ridiculous nationally. We must stick to Free Trade, or become Protectionists.'[360]

But from the point of view of economic and fiscal exigencies, there was a lot to be said for compromise, as Balfour stressed, writing to Devonshire a week before the cabinet meeting. Was free trade so sacred that it came before Unionism and the unity of the party? Free trade according to the definitions of the Cobden Club meant illegitimate as well as legitimate competition, and if this were to become the party's line, the nation would repudiate it in the first great crisis of trade. Some answer had to be given to the menace of 'dumping' and unfair trade methods. Simply to oppose any compromise with Chamberlain 'will not merely break up the Unionist party; it will shatter each separate wing . . . dividing Tory from Tory, and Liberal from Liberal. This is dynamite with a vengeance! I still hope for better things.'[361]

The Duke spent the day before the cabinet consulting with the three dissentient ministers. They understood from him that he would resign with them, not grasping the exact nature of the reserves which the Duke made. When the cabinet met on 14 September, Chamberlain made it clear that he would himself resign if colonial preference were not accepted as government policy, and since it was apparent that the cabinet were not prepared to go that far, he announced his decision to resign. Actually Balfour had Chamberlain's letter of resignation in his pocket, expressing his desire to relinquish office as the most advantageous course for the furtherance of his movement, and hence little fuss or explanation followed Chamberlain's casual statement. Some understood his announcement as final, others (including Devonshire) did not—understandably, since Balfour made no mention of the written resignation. Moreover, the meeting witnessed Balfour's 'summary and decisive dismissal' of two dissentient ministers who had submitted minutes which showed them to be irreconcileable—Ritchie and Balfour of Burleigh. It was thus not at all clear, failing the production of Chamberlain's letter, why Chamberlain should want to persevere in resignation.

After the cabinet the three dissentient ministers went to consult with Devonshire at the India Office, after which the Duke himself went to Downing Street to tender his own resignation, and to ask on behalf of the dissentients whether the two who had been given 'notice to quit' should attend the cabinet on the following day.* Again there was a misunderstanding. 'I told him quite distinctly', Balfour later noted of his interview with the Duke, 'that preferential tariffs would be impracticable, and that, therefore, Chamberlain, as he had said at cabinet, would go.' The Duke only gathered a hint that Chamberlain *might* go. Hence he met the dissentients the next day (15 September) at the Council Office after the meeting of the cabinet, and 'finally settled to go'. A letter of resignation was written by Devonshire, while the others agreed to send in their resignations that afternoon. Devonshire, before sending his, went at 6.30 P.M. again to see Balfour at Downing Street, and at last understood that Chamberlain was almost certain to resign. Balfour also explained that the two dismissed ministers could not be retained. Devonshire left still resolved to resign, and his letter was dispatched to Balfour late in the evening.

The following day was a gloomy one for the Duke, who had

---

* The episode of Chamberlain and Devonshire's resignations has never been correctly recounted. The following reconstruction is based on the diaries of Balfour's secretary, Sandars (printed extracts in P.R.O. Cab. 1/2) and of Devonshire's secretary, John Dunville. (Devonshire PP. 2992A)

resigned out of solidarity and who still hoped that Balfour's answer would afford a loophole to avoid leaving the government. In the evening, Balfour arrived at Devonshire House, informed the Duke that Chamberlain had actually resigned, showed him the correspondence, and asked him to reconsider. The Duke consented to remain, even after Balfour had made it quite clear that the three dissentient ministers, whose letters of resignation he now had, could not possibly be reprieved. There was some discussion of the important policy pronouncement which Balfour was due to make in a speech at Sheffield, and Devonshire agreed to accept a declaration that taxation might be imposed for other than revenue purposes, though he gathered no definite idea of what kind of taxation was intended. After Balfour had left, the Duke wrote to Ritchie informing him of these developments.

On Thursday, 17 September, Ritchie turned up at Devonshire House, not having got the Duke's letter. He was bitterly aggrieved to learn what had happened, and bore some grudge against the Duke. In the afternoon the Duke went to call on Sandars to refresh his memory by re-reading the Chamberlain correspondence, and to discuss again the Sheffield speech. He was worried about the position the dissentients had got him into, and Sandars recorded:

He said with emphasis how lately he had become deaf and inattentive, and what a mistake he had made throughout the recent controversy in allying himself with Ritchie and Balfour of Burleigh. He said he ought never to have had anything to do with them, that he ought to have left them to take their own course, but by degrees he had been led into the position of giving them advice.[362]

Balfour himself had gone to Scotland, where he saw the King at Balmoral and was proceeding in the process of reconstituting the cabinet on the assumption that Devonshire would stay.

Balfour had gone a long way to meet the Duke. He was prepared to indicate that food taxes were not within the range of practical politics, and that any departure from strict free trade would be solely for the purpose of retaliation. But the Duke's mind was dwelling on the personal aspect of recent events, and slowly ruminating on a decision to leave the government for the very reason that Balfour wished him to stay—that his continuation in office would reassure doubtful people. He himself was full of doubts. On 27 September he saw Sandars again, and 'became fidgety about the Sheffield speech'. Then he received an unpleasant letter from Ritchie, alleging that when they separated on 15 September the Duke had virtually promised to go out with the dissentients. 'You . . . said that there was no chance of him [Balfour] altering your determination, but that if he did we should, of course, have an opportunity of reconsidering the matter.' Ritchie also accused Balfour of unfair collusion with Chamberlain. 'The dates of the letters of resignation and acceptance', he wrote, 'make it quite clear that there was preconcerted action between them to get us . . . out of the Cabinet, and get you to remain.'[363] In fact, as the Duke well knew, Ritchie himself had led the way in forming a 'cabinet within a cabinet' and in conspiring to form plans of preconcerted resignation, and it was exactly for this reason that Balfour had decided to dismiss him at all hazards. Nevertheless Ritchie's allegations were bound to prey on the Duke's mind, and tip the scales towards resignation. At Newmarket, before the Sheffield speech was delivered, Devonshire penned a letter to Balfour, but was persuaded by 'Eddy' Stanley to tear it up. He confessed 'that he literally could not sleep at night for the feeling that in the minds of the three secessionists he had treated them badly'.[364] The Sheffield speech was merely a public justification for a decision which Devonshire had slowly arrived at on more general grounds.

What really drove many Unionists, including Devonshire, to decide that Chamberlain had to be opposed actively was the manifest success of Chamberlain's bid to convert the constituencies to tariff reform. Not only was the Liberal Unionist Association, wherever Chamberlain controlled it, turned into a propaganda machine, but through the Tariff Reform League with its constituency branches leverage was exerted even on Conservative sitting members.* Thus it was no consolation to know that the Unionist

---

* The circumstances of the Tariff Reform League's foundation are related by J. L. Garvin (*Tariff or Budget*, 1909, p.164): 'A petition . . . requested him to form a League like the Anti-Corn Law League, but for the counter purpose. He acted with that terrible promptitude of his. . . . A dinner was held in his house. A meeting followed on a June afternoon of 1903 in a committee room of the House of Commons. The Tariff Reform League was founded out of hand. . . . The League was to be open to men of all parties. It attracted from the first Liberals like Mr Samuel Story and Mr Candlish in the North. . . .'

party would in any case be defeated and that tariff reform could not be implemented in the foreseeable future. Chamberlain was evidently aiming at subverting the traditional basis of the Unionist party by the elimination of all who did not agree with him. The Tariff Reform League appeared to be supported by many Radical protectionists. Moreover the tariff reformers very early began to create their own policy-forming instruments, which had little to do with Unionism. In June 1903 Chamberlain met Professor W. A. S. Hewins, an imperialist who was soon to quit his post as Director of the London School of Economics to become the economic adviser of the tariff reformers. In Bernard Shaw's opinion, Hewins was a 'fanatic'. He was an authoritarian, a 'born manipulator' with a mind 'full of energy and faith' who later became a convert to the Catholic Church. Beatrice Webb, who lunched with him weekly at the School, noted that he was 'a great admirer of Chamberlain' before the promulgation of tariff reform.[365] In June 1903 Hewins undertook for *The Times* to write a series of articles on Chamberlain's new policy, and thereby made his acquaintance. Under his direction the tariff reform movement assumed massive dimensions. He became the Secretary of the Tariff Commission, an unofficial 'royal commission' permanently in session, taking evidence from every kind of industry and publishing periodical reports and statistical accounts. Such a body was bound to become the sounding board of every protectionist interest in the country. Hewins always affected to despise Chamberlain's grasp of economics: and Chamberlain was content to leave him a free hand in point of doctrine so long as he supplied enough ammunition in the form of striking arguments.

In order to protect their seats and their position in the country, the 'free fooders' (as the free trade Unionists were called) formed the short-lived Free Food League, and later were driven into a negotiation with the Liberals. On their own they were very weak in the constituencies and shaky in the Commons—as Hicks Beach explained to Harcourt after Chamberlain's resignation had become known:

Beach–Harcourt, 19 September 1903: I am not at all clear as to the future of the Free Food League; and think it may not impossibly dissolve if the Sheffield speech is of the nature I have indicated. As you know, it is a very weak organization in point of numbers and means, and very many of its members are by no means prepared to oppose the principle of duties for the purpose of retaliation or bargaining.[366]

After Devonshire's final resignation early in October the free fooders could afford to act more independently of the official leadership. Their position was, however, precarious. Lord George Hamilton found 'that Chamberlain has captured the machine, and inoculated the Unionist constituencies to a greater extent than I had anticipated. My election committee are almost to a man against me upon the fiscal question.'[367] James was afraid that the headquarters of the Liberal Unionist Association was about to be taken over, and this impression was endorsed by an exultant letter from Chamberlain's representative:

Powell Williams–Lord James, 22 October 1903: Chamberlain is going to carry all before him with the country; and, if the Liberal Unionist party do not recognize that fact, so much the worse for the Liberal Unionist party. I have not been in political life for twenty-five years without being able to spot the winning horse.[368]

The writing was on the wall for the free fooders, at least in the Liberal Unionist section. A dramatic confirmation of Williams' impression appeared at a conference of north-country Liberal Unionist Associations at Newcastle in October, which ignored an appeal from Devonshire for fiscal neutrality and accepted the full Chamberlain programme by a sweeping majority. Up to that time the Duke had resisted the pressure from James and Goschen to put himself at the head of the Free Food League, fearing that this might compromise his position as president of the Liberal Unionist Association. Of the latter, Goschen's advice to the Duke was 'better break it up than let the whole of the free trade Unionists be left without your leadership'.[369] Devonshire was persuaded, accepted the presidency of the Free Food League, and wrote to Chamberlain asking that the Liberal Unionist Association be disbanded.

When he thus accepted the leadership of the free fooders, Devonshire was warned by Lord James that they might have to oppose Balfour and the government as well as Chamberlain. James believed 'that we shall have to deal with a forward movement headed by Winston Churchill, and that he and some others wish to come into the open as complete free traders and as opponents of Balfour's retaliatory policy'.[370] Together with Lord Hugh Cecil, who was determined to make Balfour's 'manœuvre of general meaningless reunion' appear absurd, Churchill was ready to act with the Liberals. Cecil explained the 'Hughligan' attitude, shared by Churchill, E. Vincent, J. Seely and Ivor Guest:

Lord Hugh Cecil–Devonshire, 2 December 1903: It seems clear that, except in exceptional circumstances, no free trade Unionist is likely to be returned to the next Parliament unless by the help of the Opposition. . . .

We can vote with them and (probably) against the government in an important and not impossibly a critical division. . . . We shall have quarrelled almost beyond reconciliation with Chamberlain and even with Arthur Balfour. Before we take so serious . . . a step, is it not wise to ascertain what assurance the Opposition will give in respect to our seats?[371]

Devonshire took up Cecil's suggestion of writing to Spencer, and also communicated with Rosebery and (in Rosebery's absence) with Asquith and the 'imperialist Liberals'. He met with little success. Rosebery protested that he had no influence with the 'official' Liberals, and passed the Duke's letter on to Asquith. Asquith stayed at James' house near Salisbury on the night of 21–22 December, and expressed the opinion that a working compact *vis-à-vis* seats presented 'insuperable' difficulties. But, according to James' report of the conversation, he delicately hinted that he would support a Devonshire government:

James–Devonshire, 22 December 1903: We then discussed parliamentary leaders. To Asquith Rosebery is incomprehensible. He does not wish Spencer to form a government, and will not do so himself.

I said 'What then?', and a shrug of his shoulders was the only reply. I said 'The Duke?' 'I hope so' was the answer.[372]

Devonshire's proposal was formally considered by 'nine or ten ex-official Liberals' on 5 January 1904, but with no definite or satisfactory result.[373]

Meanwhile Devonshire had burned the free fooders' boats before alternative transports were arranged. Within the Liberal Unionist Association, he had declared what Chamberlain called 'war to the knife' on the tariff reformers in his own party. Actually the Duke was the victim of another misunderstanding. Having failed to persuade Chamberlain to disband the Liberal Unionist Association, he had then made a proposal through Selborne that the Association should remain neutral, supporting all local associations in their choice of parliamentary candidates so long as their actions did not involve 'an attack upon the position of sitting Liberal Unionist members'. From Selborne Chamberlain gathered an entirely different idea, namely that the local associations were to be precluded from receiving central funds if they supported either tariff reformers or free fooders. Chamberlain did not reply to this 'one sided' offer, and in mid-December 1903 the Duke lent his name to a published letter which encouraged Unionists in a by-election at Lewisham to vote for the Liberal candidate and against a Unionist tariff reformer. This was the first overt sign of the split in the Liberal Unionist leadership, and was generally recognized as heralding the break-up of the party. In fact it led on to another triumph for Chamberlain, who challenged the Duke's right to dispense the funds which had been raised in his name, and overthrew the oligarchical structure of the party by summoning representative Liberal Unionists to London. In May 1904 the Duke retired from the presidency of the Liberal Unionist Association, and was replaced in that office by Chamberlain, who gave the party a 'democratic' constitution and turned it into an efficient engine for the tariff reform cause.

After the failure of Devonshire's approach to the Liberal leaders, the free food Unionists reverted to a policy of following Balfour, sometimes being, as the Prime Minister complained, 'more Balfour than Balfour himself'. They clung to the Sheffield speech as a security against further advances toward tariff reform of Chamberlain's variety, and exerted all their influence to keep Balfour to it. According to a calculation of John Morley in January 1904, there were 53 Unionist free traders in the Commons, but probably not more than 6 of these would, in Morley's opinion, dare to vote against Balfour. Many were afraid to declare their opinions, for fear of their local committees, and the few who did dare to quarrel with their committees were not prepared to be beholden to the Liberals for the retention of their seats. The only important exception to this was Winston Churchill, who believed that if a compact over the education question could be arranged between Lloyd George and Lord Hugh Cecil under Rosebery's auspices, this might be made the basis for a Rosebery–Devonshire government. The snag was that Rosebery stood aloof from the 'official' Liberals, who, as Churchill explained, were prepared only for a piecemeal accommodation:

Winston Churchill–Devonshire, 13 January 1904: While staying with Ivor Guest in Northamptonshire I went over to see Lord Spencer, and had a long talk with him. He thinks that time will be a great factor in an educational concordat; and he said that already in many parts of the country settlements were being effected. He seemed very unhappy about Rosebery, who will not play. . . .

Lord Spencer was most friendly to me, and would like to help our people, but he dwells a great deal on the obvious difficulties. Some people could be arranged for, others no. I said we should certainly stand together; and then quite suddenly came across me the explanation of Lord Rosebery's attitude. He said to me at Mentmore 'that he could be more useful in bringing people together if he were independent'. I thought this a mistake then—but if he were making his cooperation contingent on a suitable combination of Whigs and Unionist free traders, his plan would have a different complexion. At any rate it is certain that his aloofness causes the Liberal leaders the utmost anxiety and disgust.

I lunched with Herbert Gladstone yesterday, and talked to him a great deal about seats. There is no doubt that he will try his very best to save the seats of Unionist free traders who are sincere. About fifteen could be settled quite easily; but there are some very hard cases which would require more pressure. Several Liberal constituencies have approached me, and I think I could make my own terms as a Unionist. . . .[374]

For some months Churchill declined Liberal offers of a safe seat and remained prospective candidate for Sheffield in order to avoid severing his connection with the Free Food League and, as he told the Duke, 'your guidance'.[375]* Then, in April, after hope of even a limited compact had died, he received an invitation from the Liberals of the central division of Manchester too

---

* At this point Churchill was proposing to stand as candidate for Sheffield. 'Apparently', he told the Duke, 'they will employ the whole force of the Liberal Association on my behalf, although I stand as a Unionist free trader.'

tempting to reject. It was, he wrote to Devonshire, the constituency in which the Free Trade Hall stood, and the premier constituency in Lancashire. 'The return of a free trade candidate pure and simple—not a Liberal or a Home Ruler—for that division would be a considerable event in that part of the world.'[376] On this new footing Churchill severed his connection with the Unionist free fooders, who lost in him the only man capable of building them up into a viable independent force.

CHAPTER ELEVEN

Balfourism and Betrayal

He [Balfour] used his defeats, his doubts, his indecision, his charm—and left his heart out. That was the real business stroke—That did for me. . . . I liked him: he knew it. Whether he ever liked me, to this day, I don't know—for certain.

Imaginary comment by Chamberlain in
Laurence Housman's *Dethronements*

CHAMBERLAIN had resigned from the government with feelings of resentment against Devonshire for his 'indifference to a great policy' and his caballing with Ritchie and others who were not Liberal Unionists. Against Balfour no such feelings were entertained. Chamberlain appreciated that as leader of the Conservatives Balfour's first duty was to keep his party together, and part of the reason for his resignation was to be free to drive the parliamentary following forward. His idea was to support Balfour's leadership from the outside, while Austen Chamberlain succeeded Ritchie as Chancellor of the Exchequer and maintained sufficient liaison with the cabinet. There was no notion of a divergence of policy, as may be seen from the terms in which Mrs Chamberlain wrote about her husband's resignation in a letter to Betty Balfour: 'From the moment it was seriously suggested, I have been quite clear that it was right—both from Mr Balfour's point of view and Joe's, and I have no fear that they will not be able to work together, one from within, the other from without. . . .'377 Constitutionally the idea was somewhat anomalous, but Balfour accepted that the fiscal question was an 'open' one on which everyone could agree to differ, and that the constituencies should be left entirely free to impose whatever fiscal pledges or conditions they pleased upon parliamentary candidates.

Thus far the two leaders agreed. But in the spirit and emphasis with which they treated the policy of tariff reform, they were utterly different. For Chamberlain tariff reform was an inspiring crusade for Empire and social reconstruction, and any Unionist who was not for it was to be accounted an enemy and eliminated from the party. He saw that if Unionism was to offer an attractive alternative to socialism it must acquire a dynamic creed, a constructive ideal to match the vision of the socialists: nor was he particularly concerned to find room in this creed for the traditional Conservative values. Balfour on the other hand was blind to the urgency of the need for a party appeal which might strike the imagination of the people. If he approved of imperial preference, it was only as a fiscal or administrative reform no more important than the other projects which he was efficiently and unobtrusively furthering. While he was prepared to tolerate any form of fiscal heterodoxy, he was not willing to allow the free fooders to be driven to the wall. His tactics were defensive, and his policy of fiscal 'comprehension' was concerned chiefly with anaesthetizing the party where any disturbance of the equilibrium between the various sections of his followers was threatened.

Balfour did not pretend to give the Unionists a lead in the fiscal controversy. He merely expressed his own personal views, which amounted to a mild agnosticism with one salient point, retaliation. Retaliation did not require food taxes nor necessarily involve protection. It was a very satisfactory *via media*, which, however, Balfour had only formulated in his attempt to reconcile Chamberlain and Devonshire. After losing these ministers, he gave up the attempt to find a policy for the party. He soon discovered, however, that his party would not allow him to preserve an enigmatic silence on a matter which the fratricidal strife in the constituencies made of vital concern to every Unionist member. His Sheffield speech of October 1903 was laid hold upon by the free fooders, who pressed him to allow it to be construed as an *ex cathedra* pronouncement. The young Lord Salisbury, in congratulating Balfour on his 'dexterity, patience and courage', added 'I accept the Sheffield speech and . . . I do not think you should go beyond that position. . . . Owing to the Duke's deplorable defection the cabinet is overweighted with Joe's friends. . . . Joe, who has gone rank protectionist, must in effect denounce it.'[378] Sandars likewise took Sheffield as a definitive utterance and similarly forecast from 'the large following which Joe has on his side' a demand that Balfour should go further: '. . . they will not see that nothing is more foolish than to force the pace for the good free fooders, who taking Sheffield now, are certain to move towards that of Glasgow all in good time.'[379] At Glasgow Chamberlain had placed his standard far in the protectionist van of the party's march, undertaking to save the 'dying' industries of the country. Balfour never denounced this speech, and never accepted it.

The disunity of the party was emphasized by a continuing series of defeats at by-elections. If the Unionists were to enjoy the positive advantages of a popular tariff reform policy and not merely suffer the damage of fiscal disunity, some officially accepted party line seemed called for. Balfour had virtually dropped imperial preference, not seeing his way to accepting food taxes. He never grasped this nettle, even although Chamberlain had supplied an answer to the free food cry by proposing a transfer, without any overall increase, of food taxes. When it became apparent that the free fooders were to be accommodated, Chamberlain, observing the political scene from his hotel at Cairo, began to despair of getting anywhere in collaboration with Balfour: but rather than oppose his government, he preferred to retire from the struggle altogether:

Chamberlain–Austen Chamberlain, 11 March 1904: I gather from the telegrams first, that the elections (my dear Birmingham always excepted) have gone very much against us, second, that this has discouraged our friends very much and that they are in a jumpy and disorganized condition, third, that Balfour has plainly pledged himself to go to the country on retaliation and *nothing more*.

Well! I think he is wrong but I do not care. In the circumstances the best thing that can happen is that we should be beaten, whenever the general election does come, for *our* position would be intolerable if we won and then found that we were as far off our Imperial policy as ever. . . .

From my point of view it will be necessary at the next elections to get rid of the foes in our own household—the Churchills, Seelys, Bowles, etc. They attack us in the first place and they attack the government also. They ought to be excommunicated from the congregation and at all hazards got rid of entirely or sent to the other side.

In no case am I going to fight against Balfour's government. I would much rather go out of politics, and if things remain as they are I do not see any alternative. These are purely philosophical speculations and must not be considered as settled convictions. I should not think of communicating them to anyone but yourself.[380]

Chamberlain felt that the elections might have been more favourable 'if the Party and the machine had gone solid for the whole policy'.

The embargo on any parliamentary debates upon the future fiscal intentions of the government was maintained through the session of 1904. But although Balfour had no fiscal reforms to propose to the existing Parliament and knew that it was extremely unlikely that his party would be returned to propose anything in the next, he was obliged to decide what the party's attitude should be towards the next Colonial Conference. Turning over the problem, his inventive mind hit on a device which would allow the party to go to the polls with a preference policy while avoiding any controversy or pledges with respect to food taxes, or, for that matter, with respect to any fiscal propositions whatsoever. This was the idea of a 'free' Colonial Conference. All the governments attending should be untrammelled by any kind of pledges or pre-conditions, and he would promise the electorate that if the scheme of tariff reform agreed to by the Conference included food taxes, it would be submitted to the public at a second election before being put before Parliament.

Balfour discussed this idea with Austen Chamberlain in August. To Austen it seemed disastrous. It would relegate tariff reform to the distant future, success being dependent upon a fruitful conference and two successive electoral victories. Who would work and drudge for tariff reform under such a condition? The negotiation with the Colonies, Austen believed, needed to be pressed with a firm British plan, which when agreed should be ratified at once by Parliament. He dismissed Balfour's idea as no plan at all for the Unionists to fight the election on, and in the absence of an official fiscal policy 'each section will try . . . to make itself as strong as possible, by enforcing pledges and capturing associations and seats . . . if this is your last word', Austen concluded, 'I do not see how I can possibly come into line with you at the next election'.[381]

In resisting Austen's counter proposal, with its suggestion that he as leader should declare a 2s. corn duty and a 10 per cent general tariff as part of the official programme along with retaliation, Balfour had been supported by Lord Salisbury (son of the late prime minister), whom he had consulted. For Salisbury the double election idea was primarily a means of neutralizing the Chamberlains:

Salisbury–Balfour, 6 September 1904: I have read with the greatest care your box. I have no objection to offer to your programme. It is true that my suggestion was not a pledge that you would summon a conference, but that you would *consider* the summoning of a conference. But that I recognize is perhaps too divergent from Austen and his friends. . . .

If the Conference were allowed to cover all outstanding imperial problems, Salisbury believed that the food question would be 'diluted in a flood of imperialism', and went on:

So much the better. This advantage will of course be duly developed in your utterances. For the rest I have nothing to add to what I said at Hatfield. It is essential that Joe should publicly disapprove of your policy. It is important that in the autumn campaign your gun should go off before Joe's. . . .[382]

In further letters Salisbury showed no appreciation of Austen's point of view, and indeed wrote as if tariff reform could only be an electoral liability and had nothing to do with the proper programme of the party: 'The British elector believes in the motto *"noscitur a sociis"*. If we are associated with Joe the said elector will never believe we have a different policy.'[383] 'Austen writes as if we were going to win the next election. The Chamberlain family govern the country as if they were following hounds —where according to hunting conventions it is mean-spirited to look before you leap.'[384] How far Balfour concurred in these sentiments is not on record, but he certainly obeyed Salisbury's advice. Yielding nothing to Austen's strenuous pleading, he delivered his double election plan to the public by a speech at Edinburgh on 3 October, with momentous consequences for the future.

Like most of Balfour's public gestures, the Edinburgh speech raised more doubts than it settled. Did the second election apply to all tariff reform, or only to food taxes? Did the speech mean that Balfour had personally accepted food taxes? The free fooders were alarmed by the latter suggestion. Comparing his impressions with those of Beach, the Duke of Devonshire could not make out whether Balfour had spoken in collusion with Chamberlain, or whether the speech was 'intended to put a check on the tariff reform agitation'. He thought the Colonial Conference under whatever conditions formed 'a dangerous concession to Chamberlain, for it is difficult to see how any of us could go into such a conference unless we were prepared to consider food taxation'.[385] Balfour evidently had not disarmed the free fooders' suspicions. On the other side, the tariff reformers seized on the speech and hailed it as a sign of Balfour's conversion to food taxes. Chamberlain himself took it to mean this, and was genuinely incredulous when he heard that Balfour disagreed:

Chamberlain–Austen Chamberlain, 12 November 1904: I do not like to hear on Gerald [Balfour]'s authority that A. J. B[alfour] is inclined to 'wriggle' about the meaning of the Edinburgh speech. It is inconceivable to a plain man like myself that the Prime Minister can seriously contemplate a conference with the colonies without being prepared to give immediate effect to any proposals agreed to at such a conference. It is certain that if properly managed it would result in offers from all the colonies,

First, to give us a substantial preference against the foreigner which will enable us to increase—*and to keep*—our existing trade. The last is important, for we are certainly going to lose it if we do not get a preference.

But secondly, they will modify their general tariff in a sense favourable on the whole to British trade. They will not of course sacrifice their own principal industries, but they *may* be willing to give terms which will prevent their unnatural and artificial expansion to our detriment.

For their concessions they will require the taxation of food—or rather the transfer of food taxation which I propose. . . . Will A. J. B. accept and press such proposals? If not, it is inept to talk of a free conference, with a foregone conclusion not to accept its results. In that case the Edinburgh speech would merit all the evil things said of it by the Opposition. It would be a dodge to unite the party—our section of which must obviously be duped.

As to domestic policy, *we* know that retaliation is a farce. It is a word, a device on paper, a philosopher's romance—but it is not a practical commercial policy, as the Prime Minister will discover if ever he attempts to apply it.[386]

A serious misunderstanding still existed between the Chamberlains and Balfour. The rare pronouncements which Balfour made on fiscal matters seemed, like the Edinburgh speech, designed to conciliate opinion within the Unionists' ranks and, ultimately, to acknowledge that Balfour was prepared to follow the consensus of fiscal opinion within his party. Most of the party were going for tariff reform, and Chamberlain assumed that Balfour was sympathetic to this trend. In fact he was hardening in a secret hostility to it.

What Balfour particularly objected to was the manner in which tariff reform was being turned into a comprehensive and self-contained movement which threatened to swallow its parent the Unionist party. Chamberlain had no effective communication with him, and yet went on behaving as if he possessed the confidence of the government. Having democratized the Liberal Unionist Association and cut the ground from under the feet of the Conservative National Union by establishing branches of the Tariff Reform League in the constituencies, he appeared to be bidding fair to take over the Conservative Central Office, the last retreat of the Cecils and the 'old gang'. Later in 1904 he suggested that a representative of the Tariff Reform League should be placed in the Central Office, so that the two organizations might be kept in touch. Rebutting this idea, Salisbury pleaded the case against identification with Chamberlain:

Salisbury–Balfour, 23 December 1904: I agree you are between the devil and the deep sea; . . . I think that your dexterous policy must lean rather to including both the loyal free fooders and the loyal tariff reformers than to excluding either. But comprehension does not mean identification.

Either Joe is a member of the Government or he is not. If he is, then the country ought to know it, then the members of the Government would be aware that they are responsible for all the folly he talks and all the misfortunes which his recklessness is bringing upon us. If on the other hand he is *not*, then he is not entitled to any special position in the Head Office.[387]

Balfour himself was prepared to admit that a doctrinal difference had emerged. 'Joe', he observed in a letter at this time, 'has run a policy which his enemies describe as "protection", and which certainly is of the nature of an appeal to particular interests, in double harness with his Imperial propaganda. Personally I think it a mistake: and, so far as I am concerned, I play for the big ideal in its simplicity and nothing else.'[388] There was an even more important difference separating the two leaders. Chamberlain was working to enable the party to formulate and accept a fiscal policy for itself. Balfour would never admit the party's right to do this.

At last Chamberlain was beginning to realize that Balfour was not working cordially with him. Before the session of 1905 he wrote to suggest a private conference. They had had but one 'serious talk', said Chamberlain, since his resignation, and without a mutual understanding they would 'insensibly drift apart'. He now invited Balfour to a 'quiet dinner' and a discussion 'absolutely free from interruption'.[389] They met on 17 February, and the discussion turned on Balfour's double election scheme. As might have been expected, Balfour was not talked out of it, and the meeting was only the prelude to a duel by correspondence. 'Let me begin', Balfour wrote the next day, 'by admitting that your arguments against this plan have great weight.' Chamberlain had stressed the impossible dilemma of the second election: that if it came soon after the Colonial Conference it would be unpopular with the new members, who would resist it, while if it was delayed for a year or more the government would in all probability, through the swing of electoral opinion, lose it. Balfour countered this by arguing that any preferential scheme agreed with the colonies would be safe from party attacks by the opposition. Also the double election would ensure that the conference really was free: 'Just as a free conference requires the Canadians to go into it unpledged on the subject of Canadian protection, so it requires the British representatives to go into it unpledged on the subject of food taxation.' Only the safeguard of a second election would enable Unionist M.P.s to avoid having to pledge themselves against food taxes. Thus, Balfour concluded, '. . . if we could secure a free conference on your terms, *your* scheme is the best. But in order to obtain a free conference, *my* scheme is best.'[390]

Once again Balfour had disclosed to Chamberlain only the tactical objections he had to the tariff reformers' alternative. They were not the real ones, as Salisbury, who again was consulted and shown the correspondence, pointed out:

Salisbury–Balfour, 20 February 1905: The arguments in your letter to

Joe . . . seem admirable, but they only deal with one aspect of the situation. Here is the whole of it in brief:

1. You are a Preferentialist, *if it be possible*. Joe has no doubts.
2. You are a free trader. Joe is a protectionist in effect.
3. You are a Retaliationist, which you consider of great importance. Joe considers it insignificant unless it involves a scientific tariff, and not very important then.
4. You desire on behalf of other issues to keep the Party together. Joe cares for none of these issues, and is pursuing a course in the constituencies which in your opinion will go far to destroy it.

. . . What will happen in the constituencies if we do not check or at any rate completely dissociate ourselves from Joe's campaign against the free food seats? . . . a lot of moderate people who think such attacks unfair, un-English and un-Conservative [will join those who object to food taxes], and there will be fatal abstentions if not a split in the party in every constituency in England. Exit the Conservative party.[391]

Neither Salisbury nor Balfour were, however, very reliable authorities on the state of affairs in the constituencies. It was as much as anything the fatal uncertainty as to the official policy of the party which was encouraging the strife between free fooders and tariff reformers. The free fooders already claimed that Balfour was on their side. To have disowned the tariff reformers would not have silenced them. If Balfour had cared greatly for the electoral strength of the Unionists, he might have been convinced by the arguments which Chamberlain elaborated in his reply of 24 February. The present position, Chamberlain declared, was 'the worst of all that can be conceived'. Those candidates who had been persuaded through timidity to reject food taxes had lost the support of tariff reformers while failing to gain any free trade votes: for free trade electors were against retaliation, and would oppose any compromise and be unmoved by any concession. Meanwhile under the double election scheme the Unionist candidate was prevented from expounding the positive advantages of tariff reform:

Chamberlain–Balfour, 24 February 1905: He and his canvassers cannot point to the advantage of closer union with the colonies, or the gain to be secured by the concessions they are prepared to make, nor can he argue that what we propose is merely a transfer of taxation by which the poorest will gain in the balance. . . .

In my experience the ordinary voter never cares for detail. He seizes upon a principle or a large issue, and is quite willing to delegate to his representative all questions of detail and method. . . .

. . . while I believe that we should not gain anything by dilatory tactics, we should lose a great deal of the enthusiasm which can alone carry great political changes.[392]

But these considerations were beside the point, in Balfour's view of things. What Balfour dreaded was precisely the tariff reformer's popular appeal, which once sanctioned by the official leaders would quickly transform the Unionist party into a democratic organization run by protectionist squires and manufacturers.

The 1905 parliamentary session—the last that Balfour was destined to preside over as premier—witnessed a determined effort on the part of the tariff reformers to commit the party to their policy. Not only did Balfour stick to his double election plan, but he continued to give parity of esteem to the free fooders whom the Chamberlainites regarded as an intransigent minority. Matters came to a head when Hicks Beach put down some free food resolutions for 22 March and the government, feeling that their free food followers had been strained to the limit by being pressed to resist a similar motion by Churchill the week before, was disposed to allow a free vote. Chamberlain pressed Balfour to resist Beach's motion by the previous question on the accepted principle that the matter was not a practical one in that Parliament. His request was sent on to Balfour by Sandars with a note advising him not to comply with it.[393] But Austen in support of his father's line was prepared to resign, and told Balfour that 'our only chance is to put on all the pressure we can and dare our men to turn us out'.[394]

Curiously enough Balfour was also advised to make it a vote of confidence by his golfing friend Iwan-Muller, though for the opposite reason. 'I would far sooner risk defeat in that form', Muller wrote, 'than confess I could not carry on without Highbury patronage. *That* I dread and shrink from more than any disaster that could befall us.'[395] But Balfour had a trick of his own up his sleeve, and on the crucial night he led his supporters out of the House and ignored the debate. Once more he had dodged the claims of the tariff reformers to impose a majority decision on the party. It was only after much heart searching that Austen could bring himself to remain in office. Chamberlain endorsed his son's decision while severely condemning Balfour: 'I agree with you', he wrote on 22 March, 'that the decision of tonight involves us all in a great humiliation, but that is the fault of people who will not look beyond their noses, and who have not courage enough to take a bold decision in time to avert a crisis.'[396] This remark epitomized his view of Balfour's whole course of proceeding.

At this point the mass of the tariff reformers began to press for a clarification of the official fiscal policy of the party, and Chamberlain was prepared to come forward and lead them. He presided over a meeting held on 13 April at which a large number of tariff reformer M.P.s adopted a memorandum of demands to be presented to Balfour. This document began by demonstrating the numerical preponderance of tariff reformers by the following analysis of Unionist parliamentary strength:

1. Preferentialists who have publicly expressed their support of the whole policy 172
2. Preferentialists who would support the whole policy if it were recognized as being the policy of the government . 73
3. Retaliationists, many of whom would support preference also, if adopted by the government, but some of whom would refuse in any case to go further 98
4. Members totally opposed to any change in our fiscal system—most of whom are retiring at the next election . 27
5. [Others] 4

374[397]

The memorandum then developed an argument distinctly menacing to Balfour's leadership. The first group, 'commonly known as tariff reformers', constituted with the second a two-thirds majority of the whole party. The tariff reformers desired to continue in support of the leadership of the Prime Minister, but they felt 'that the situation is critical, and that the prospects of the Party as a whole are seriously jeopardized by the unfortunate division of opinion on the fiscal question. . . .' Party supporters in the country had shown themselves 'overwhelmingly in favour of the views taken by tariff reformers' both at meetings of the central organizations and at meetings of local committees, but had been 'disheartened' by lack of a definite lead. It was becoming increasingly necessary to define the exact position of the party as the general election approached. Finally the memorandum demanded a 'general tariff' as adopted by all countries which had gone in for retaliation, and the abandonment of Balfour's double election condition. At the meeting Chamberlain urged the 'paramount need of an aggressive policy even at the sacrifice of much individual support',[398] and later he headed a deputation to present the memorandum to Balfour, signed by 142 tariff reform members.

After a delay over Easter, Balfour called a small conference consisting of Chamberlain and Herbert Maxwell, representing the tariff reformers, with himself and Lansdowne. Before the meeting on 16 May Maxwell asked Chamberlain what he expected to come of the negotiation. 'Precious little,' Chamberlain growled, 'I think things are going very badly.' But things turned out very differently. Balfour startled them by offering to accept a general tariff and colonial preference as the first article of the party programme. Maxwell then raised a point which Balfour had not considered before. The Colonial Conference of 1902 had adjourned itself to the summer of 1906, when it would meet 'automatically'. There need not be a general election until 1907. Could not the problem of the double election be avoided by making the conference of 1906 the 'free' conference, and going to the country on the results? Balfour sent for Sandars, who was instructed to discover if there was anything in the Prime Minister's speeches to rule out this idea. After an hour, Sandars returned and confirmed that there was 'nothing so explicit' as to prevent it.[399] It must have seemed to Chamberlain an unbelievable piece of good fortune. The way was now cleared to reunite the whole party on a basis of moderate tariff reform. But with his instinctive caution, Chamberlain compared notes with Maxwell after the meeting, and set out the concessions on paper for Balfour to accept before the discussion was resumed the next day:

Chamberlain–Balfour, 16 May 1905: After our talk this afternoon, Maxwell and I agreed on the enclosed notes, slightly altered by me for the sake of clearness, as being what *we* thought the most important results. I think you ought to see them before tomorrow's continuation of the discussion, in order that there may be no mistake.

We are agreed that we have made progress, and we are both hopeful on these lines of coming to a conclusion which will give entire satisfaction to the majority of the Unionist party—a majority sufficient to keep the government in office if it is willing to remain.[400]

The 'notes' stated that tariff reform must be 'the main, fighting, constructive issue' at the next election, including Preference 'as the question probably arousing most enthusiasm and being most urgent'. The train of events was envisaged thus:

Assuming that it would not be inconsistent with the Prime Minister's public utterances, he would not object to the following programme:

a. Dissolution not to be officially contemplated till autumn 1906.

b. Meanwhile conference with colonies to be held automatically in spring of 1906 and to be free as to subjects of discussion.

c. Report of proceedings and recommendations of conference with the views of H.M. Government on them to form important part of the reference to the constituencies, who will thus be asked for a mandate to carry out decisions arrived at. . . .

The Prime Minister has no objection in principle to a general tariff, although he would not pledge himself not to have recourse to special negotiations if that appeared to offer better chances of success in any particular cases.[401]

At the meeting held the next day this arrangement was confirmed, and Chamberlain offered to return to the government as minister without portfolio, giving up any separate advocacy of tariff reform.

It was not to be. Within ten days Balfour had caved in before the pressure of the free fooders in the cabinet and the party. The free fooders could not put him in a minority in the Commons merely by abstention, but they could do so by voting with the opposition. The strongest moral grounds were necessary to justify this, but the free fooders were able to persuade themselves that the automatic conference plan was a distinct breach of the pledge that Balfour had given in his Edinburgh speech, and the opposition obligingly put down a motion to that effect. Balfour had been too clever. On 26 May he sent Lyttelton and Gerald Balfour to inform Austen that the proposed arrangement was off. Austen sent a hurried note to his father mentioning 'a most serious hitch—I fear an absolute breakdown', and urgently summoning Chamberlain to meet Balfour that afternoon.[402]

Chamberlain and Austen accordingly met Balfour, Lansdowne

and Lyttelton at Downing Street at one, and were told that Balfour had only envisaged being still in office in 1906 as 'a possible, even probable, contingency' when Maxwell had raised the point a few days before. It now looked as if Balfour intended to resign before the 1906 Conference. This was a shattering blow for Chamberlain, who went away 'much depressed'. 'I sat with him in his little room in the House of Commons', recounts Maxwell, 'trying to persuade him that, after all, we have been engaged in negotiation and had carried two points out of three.'[403] The two points were to be conceded by a public statement by Balfour embodying tariff reform in the party programme, but nothing definite had been promised.

The next day (Saturday, 27 May) Chamberlain and some leading tariff reformers briefed Austen on the terms which they demanded in exchange for supporting Balfour in office. If the tariff reformers abstained on the motion of censure put down for Tuesday, 30 May, as Chamberlain was disposed to do, the government would have to resign. The terms were that Balfour should make a statement in the debate that he would put tariff reform, including colonial preference, in the front of his programme when he went to the country: and further, that while he would act on the opposition's interpretation of his Edinburgh speech during the present Parliament, he would not hold himself bound by it when he went to the country. Austen conveyed these terms to Lyttelton, who thought that Balfour could not get out of the double election pledge at the next election, but that the pledge would not survive a defeat at the election. This was reported back to Chamberlain by Austen, who after some discussion wrote an ultimatum to Balfour:

Austen Chamberlain–Balfour, 27 May 1905: This account of your views was, I think, a severe disappointment to them. They were, however, most anxious to continue their support of your government and to avoid a breach in the party. But they feel, and again I agree with them, that a simple statement on your part on Tuesday that in deference to the views of friends as to the meaning of your speech you could not allow even the automatic conference to discuss this question during the present Parliament or, if they discussed it, take any notice of the results when appealing to the country, and that therefore you had decided to postpone the conference—they and I think that this would be not merely a 'slap in the face' for us, but would do deep and lasting injury to the cause of tariff reform which no subsequent explanation of your intentions could remedy.[404]

Balfour received along with this letter a report from Lyttelton stating that 'Joe would be quite satisfied' with a statement putting fiscal reform including colonial preference as the 'first item' on Balfour's election programme. Lyttelton also reported that he had warned Austen that 'such a declaration might involve the resignation of several members of the cabinet', and that he had told Austen that 'I considered that the mere private assurance that this was your intention was an immense concession to the Colonial Preference party.'[405]

Balfour knew through Austen that Chamberlain had called a meeting of the tariff reformers on the eve of the Commons debate on the double election pledge, to decide on a course of action. Balfour was not prepared, however, to make the slightest concession. His mood was summed up in a remark he had made to Austen: 'The tariff reformers have not made much concession to me.' In an off-handed note written at 8.10 P.M. Balfour replied to Lyttelton's letter in a way which qualified out of existence the statement he was asked to make:

Balfour–Lyttelton, 27 May 1905: If by 'Colonial Preference' is meant (as I suppose it is) closer commercial union with colonies (as per 'half sheet of notepaper'), and if by 'first item in my programme' be meant (as I suppose it is) that I regard it as the most important part (though the most difficult) of fiscal reform, and fiscal reform itself as the most important part of the Unionist policy, why should I not give the assurance asked for?—and why should any colleagues resign?

I have always taken this view, and (I fancy) have said so in my speeches. 'First item' must not of course be understood as meaning necessarily *first carried out*, because preference requires a conference, while retaliation does not.[406]

It was left to Lyttelton to concoct a reply to the tariff reformers out of these casual reflections, and send it to Austen. Exhausted by the mental strain of the previous few days, Balfour had fallen ill and retired to bed.

What Chamberlain had been striving for was an opportunity to go to the country on a tariff reform programme which had received official countenance, either from the 1906 'automatic'

Colonial Conference or, failing that possibility, from some explicit declaration made by Balfour. While Balfour had been able to accept in principle the first alternative, he could not now adopt the second, and take it upon himself personally to declare boldly for a decided fiscal policy. The essence of his difficulty was not fear of revolt within the party, but sheer inability to convince himself. His mind could dissect and multiply objections to any policy, but it could not produce that synthesis of technical and human considerations from which are born the directives of great popular leaders. He could never see any virtue in a popular 'cry', only crudity and imposture. Hence it was simply not in his power to go along with Chamberlain. His public statements in the Commons and in an important speech at the Albert Hall did not appear to add anything to his previous declarations, and Chamberlain had himself to interpret publicly Balfour's meaning in the sense of the letter received from Lyttelton.

An interesting account of Chamberlain's attitude at this time was sent to Balfour's secretary, Sandars, by Iwan-Muller, who recorded his impressions after a 2½-hours' conversation on 10 June with Chamberlain, who had sent another ultimatum to Balfour. 'Joe', he wrote, 'was amicable enough as far as I was personally concerned, beginning with the admission that if things should come to a rupture between "Arthur" (*sic* throughout the interview) [and himself], he was well aware that I should cleave to "Arthur" and not stand by him. I assented, and he went on to say that there was no reason why "Arthur" and he should not work together "towards the one Divine event to which the whole Creation moves, to wit Colonial Preference and a general (average) tariff all round (with free entries in certain cases), which, however, might be wholly remitted in the event of any nation offering us free and open markets".' But, Chamberlain went on, he was disappointed that Balfour had not confirmed that they were in 'substantial agreement' or given any particular prominence to the fiscal question in his Albert Hall speech. He also had to complain of the Conservative Central Office, 'to him the spring of all abomination', which in its leaflet reporting the Albert Hall speech had omitted all reference to the fiscal question. 'I know', said Chamberlain, 'that I cannot win without Arthur, but he can hardly win without me.' Then, after talking 'a good deal about his sacrifices (e.g. the double election, immediate dissolution, abandonment immediate food tax, etc.)', Chamberlain came to what he wanted 'in order to put an end to the present "critical state" of things'. He demanded a written letter from Balfour expressing substantial agreement on colonial preference, and 'a desire that the Chief's supporters should not pledge themselves in favour of or against a duty on corn (or food) pending the decision (if any) of the Conference (if any)': and, finally, 'assent to the *principle* of a "moderate all round tariff" . . . .' The conversation left Iwan-Muller with the impression that Chamberlain was 'sincerely anxious to work with the Chief', but considered that he had already made 'enormous sacrifices'. The interview was inconclusive:

Iwan-Muller–Sandars, 10 June 1905: . . . his last words were characteristic. 'Arthur and I can win together, for each has the qualities the other lacks; Arthur can manage the House of Commons, and I think I can manage the electors.'

He wants a written concordat, some of the objections I pointed out to him, notably that it would look as if neither trusted the other. . . .

Joe is burning for peace, and really don't understand the seriousness of some of his terms.[407]

Balfour would not of course write any such concordat. And indeed, after his recent experiences, the Prime Minister was becoming more and more disposed to play down the fiscal question and fight the election on other issues.

As the election approached, the schism between the tariff reformers and the free fooders threatened to get out of hand. Expecting an electoral defeat, the Unionist party was engaged in internecine strife to settle its aims and character for the future. The one thing that held the party together was the convention accepted by both sides, that loyalty to Balfour should be the test of inclusion within the party fold. But the free fooders were becoming more intransigent than the tariff reformers. They blamed Balfour for not positively denouncing tariff reform. They regarded his double election plan as an insincere and unwarranted concession. Ritchie, who had been active in resisting the 'automatic' conference plan of Maxwell's, remarked after he had been assured that there would be no departure from Balfour's promise of two elections: 'To have departed from this would have been a triumph for J.C. To adhere to it is a deceit.'[408] The free fooders became more aggressive as their strength declined.

The Free Food League had died a natural death at the end of 1904. Its financial state was never sound, nor its members united in aims. As Hicks Beach observed to Devonshire in January 1905, it was 'no real use to keep up staff and offices merely for the purpose of assisting a parliamentary committee which, as you very justly observe, has never been able to agree on any definite action'. The League had been so inactive, Beach thought, that 'no one will notice its extinction'.[409] It was superseded by the Unionist Free Trade Club under the leadership of Devonshire. But the Unionist free traders were impotent in the country. They could not get leave to speak on Unionist platforms, and their more belligerent spirits such as Lord Hugh Cecil or Lord James spoke at meetings organized by the Liberals. Here was something which Balfour could not understand—how Unionists, faced with a most menacing combination of Liberal and Labour forces, could undermine their own party by attacking a policy which could not possibly receive any attention in the next Parliament.

Yet such was the case. In October, 1905, Balfour encountered Lord James at Balmoral, who gave him the impression that Devonshire was going to launch an autumn campaign against the tariff reformers, speaking from Liberal platforms. Against this project Balfour composed a long argumentative letter to the Duke. In this one may see how Balfour was veering away from the idea of fighting the election on the fiscal question:

Balfour–Devonshire, 27 October 1905: James was very anxious that I should make some public declaration against particular proposals of Chamberlain's, e.g. what James called his 'penal 10% duty on foreign manufactured goods'. I told him that in my judgment it was from every point of view inexpedient to deal with detailed schemes, whether fiscal or legislative, until the time for parliamentary action arrived.

Chamberlain may sometimes express his general aspirations in a concrete and highly elaborated scheme, which often raises unnecessary controversy, disguises his central thought, and commits him to impracticable expedients. This procedure I do not feel called upon to imitate, either by developing plans of my own, or criticizing the plans of other people. . . .

My proper function is to state as clearly as I can the principles on which (as it seems to me) fiscal policy should proceed; and to leave it to my friends, to whichever wing of the party they may belong, to say whether they agree with me or not. [410]

Did the danger to free trade, Balfour asked, justify the weakening of Unionism? It was quite possible that free trade might in the future be imperilled by protectionist forces, but these were chiefly on the Liberal side. The Irish nationalists were 'protectionist to a man', and Balfour had no confidence that 'the trade unions will permanently hold themselves aloof from the doctrines which commend themselves to their class in every part of the world'. But there was no danger whatever to free trade in the next Parliament, while there was a very real menace from the socialistic projects of the left:

Nevertheless it seems plain that with the Irish in undiminished strength, with the Welsh acting as a more or less independent party, with forty Labour members constituting a separate and powerful organization, a Radical administration will be forced to conciliate one section of its supporters after another by legislative projects of a most dangerous description. The unjust increase of direct taxation, the taxation of ground rents, a perilous diminution of our military strength, payment of members, home rule all round, Welsh disestablishment, and so forth, are all evils which we must contemplate as within the region of practical politics. [411]

In spite of this appeal, Devonshire replied that he still intended to oppose the return of Unionist candidates pledged to protection. 'The real danger', he wrote, 'seems to me to be not to free trade, but to the future of the Unionist party.' Devonshire was convinced that men would vote with the fiscal question in mind: 'I think', he concluded, 'you scarcely do yourself justice as leader in holding aloof from the discussion which Chamberlain has raised. It is not a question of criticizing a member of your party, but of guiding it on a very definite and practical issue.' [412]

What the free fooders were so afraid of was not, of course, simply the idea of protection: it was rather the use which Chamberlain was making of this policy in order to 'democratize' the Unionist party. Chamberlain appeared to have captured the Unionist local committees, the national organizations (both

Liberal Unionist and Conservative), and the Unionist press—indeed everything except the Central Office. His movement seemed to stand for the rule of caucuses and interest groups, controlling the party from below: and in opposing it the free fooders were concerned above all to maintain the traditional ideal of dispassionate patrician government. At the outset, in May 1903, Winston Churchill had perceptively accused Chamberlain of wishing to bring about the 'Americanization of English politics'. Lord Hugh Cecil, with his jibes at Chamberlain the 'alien immigrant', was ideologically a traditionalist who wished to preserve the Conservative party upon its basis of the established Church, the landed interest and House of Lords, and an authoritarian party structure. Devonshire, James, and Goschen had the mentality of nineteenth-century Whigs. Their view was still the prevailing one amongst the Unionist leadership, and in this respect they agreed with Balfour and the party whips and central officials. Balfour was spiritually on the side of the free fooders, and in his key position he was able to resist the 'democratic' movement within his party for several years, until, in the unsettled conditions following the Unionist surrender over the Parliament Act of 1911, the tariff reformers were able to eject him from the leadership.

On 2 November 1905 Balfour walked into the Travellers' Club for lunch, carrying a French novel. There he was intercepted by a tariff reformer, who sounded him on his intentions with respect to a parliamentary dissolution. Chamberlain and his followers had been pressing him for a speedy election ever since the collapse of negotiations in May. The substance of Balfour's reply explaining the delay in going to the country was reported to Austen Chamberlain as follows: 'A dissolution in July, impossible because of the Japanese treaty; in August and September, because of the holidays of our workers in the constituencies. In October, because of the results of my inquiries into the state of party feeling. In November the same reasons . . . and in addition there is the charge of sharp practice to avoid a new register. December is an impossible month for a general election. And this brings us to January. . . .'[413]

Possibly as a result of this conversation, Balfour wrote the same day to Chamberlain giving a full account of his intentions.

He thought that 'we should call Parliament together on the last Tuesday in January, or the first Tuesday in February, and take the earliest legitimate opportunity of resigning'. Resignation would oblige the Liberal government to declare its policy before the polls, and since it was not 'very easy to find an excuse for resigning while Parliament is prorogued', Balfour thought he must meet a new Parliament.[414] Chamberlain disagreed, and pressed for an immediate dissolution. 'Practically', he wrote, 'the general election has begun so far as speaking and canvassing are concerned.'[415] He had himself done much to begin it, having just declared a war of annihilation against the free fooders. It was in vain that Balfour pleaded for restraint and party unity at the annual conference of the National Union on 15 November. The conference adopted a provocative Chamberlainite resolution. Chamberlain himself ignored Balfour's appeal, and at Bristol on 21 November demanded a 'forward' policy, declaring that the march of an army ought not to be governed by the pace of the lamest troops. Balfour and Chamberlain were now seen to be in open conflict.

The conflict between the two leaders was real enough, but it was magnified enormously by the speculations of the Unionist press, which anticipated a struggle for power. Sandars was persuaded that the sooner the election was held the better. Iwan-Muller wrote on 10 November to tell Balfour that he had come round also to this view: 'Leo Maxse, Garvin, Amery, Gwynn, Goldman', he observed, enumerating Unionist editors, 'are all Radicals inoculated with fiscalitis. So that all the Unionist papers are for the time engaged in "denigrer"-ing you in the interest of Radical-fiscal reform-Unionism. And mark my words, this written crusade will be developed with increasing malignity *till* the election . . . even the futile *Saturday Review* is bolting.'[416] In one of his rare expressions of irritation, Balfour wrote to his brother of 'Joe's methods of bribing each class of the community in turn'.[417]

Chamberlain's Bristol challenge was in this inflamed atmosphere too direct to be ignored. Sandars thought it 'changed the situation', and that 'we cannot go on'. Hicks Beach gathered from Balfour, who was 'furious with Chamberlain', that he might resign from the leadership altogether.[418] It was certainly clear that Balfour could not wisely meet Parliament, and if he must quit office earlier, the sooner the better. After going through the official formalities Balfour resigned from the premiership on 4 December.

The general election of January 1906 was not primarily a contest over tariff reform, and where this issue loomed largest, as for instance in Lancashire, the prevailing conditions of relative prosperity induced the artisan to prefer the 'large loaf' argument of the Liberals to the 'more employment' argument of the protectionists. Over the whole country the Unionists sustained a catastrophic defeat, obtaining only a quarter of the parliamentary seats. The most important single cause of the overwhelming Radical victory was the complete and scientific organization of the Labour vote. Thus while the Unionists actually secured a greatly increased total of votes over their 1900 figure—2,463,606 in 1906 as against 1,676,020 in 1900—the combined total of Liberal and Labour votes was more than doubled, rising from 1,520,285 in 1900 to 3,111,929 in 1906. Such a shift of voting in an electorate which had only increased by $7\frac{1}{2}$ per cent in these years marks the operation of more fundamental agencies than party appeals and programmes: the mass electorate had found its feet. All electoral predictions were falsified, and among these Chamberlain's estimate of the result proved grotesquely wrong. As late as 13 January 1906 Chamberlain put on record privately the following prediction: '. . . before the dissolution I reckoned the majority would be 140 with the Irish. After the dissolution, which improved our position, and up to now, I put the majority against us as 80. I am curious to see how far these guesses prove correct.'[419] The majority was 356! Never had there been such a débâcle. There does not appear to be any reason for attributing any part of it to the unpopularity of tariff reform. In Birmingham Chamberlain's men held on to all seven seats, with huge majorities except in one of the divisions—a striking reversal of the national trend. Among the Unionists as a whole, 102 of the total of 157 members returned were tariff reformers, while Balfour's loss of his seat seemed to emphasize the precariousness of his claims to continue to lead his party. Now that an attack on Balfour no longer involved jeopardizing a Unionist government, serious trouble could be expected from the shattered remnants of the Unionist parliamentary force.

Immediately after the election results were known, Chamberlain wrote to Balfour, making it clear that he intended to call a party meeting and get a majority decision as to policy. The Unionist press were after blood, and Chamberlain's lieutenant, J. L. Garvin, called for an end of 'the Byzantine theory of Unionist leadership—the theory of speechless loyalty to an hereditary succession'. Chamberlain himself issued a circular to the Liberal Unionists dated 26 January, in which he stated that while he had no intention of 'setting up against' Balfour, he would not join him again 'without a more definite understanding as to policy'. His terms were moderate. He asked for an official policy, to be decided by a straight choice between his own views as expressed in his speeches, and those of Balfour—the personal element in the contest having been removed by couching the alternatives in sufficiently general terms. The minority would not be 'excommunicated', but would have to say that their fiscal opinions were 'personal' and not 'official': and thereafter the party organizations could proceed on the assumption that the official policy should receive wholehearted encouragement. Meeting with wily resistance from Balfour, Chamberlain even reduced the scope of the fiscal resolution to be put to the party meeting to a minimum which was hardly an advance on what Balfour had already accepted. But it became clear that Balfour was opposed to any official policy, and equally implacably opposed to decision by majority vote. He was unable to resist the calling of a party meeting on 15 February 1906, but, encouraged by the officials and Lord Lansdowne, he threatened to throw up his position if a fiscal resolution were put to his followers.

The struggle was therefore really about the method of party leadership, not about tariff reform. The tariff reformers were themselves well aware of this. One of them commented to Austen privately, after the election, that he thought the question of the party leadership 'cannot be settled in a hole-and-corner way—or in the Whips' room—*this* time, though I have no doubt that the attempt will be made'. He continued:

Arthur Lee–Austen Chamberlain, 2 February 1906: I am quite ready to follow A. J. B.'s lead, if he gives a wholehearted and vigorous one, but I am not prepared under *any* terms to be led by Sandars and Acland Hood. In my mind's eye I already see a sinister clique growing at the Carlton and plotting how to rehabilitate the old régime, but this simply cannot be tolerated.[420]

Although he was writing from the Alpes Maritimes, his imagination was uncannily close to the mark. Hood, Sandars and Akers-Douglas, together with Lansdowne—whose attitude was summed up in his advice that 'The generals cannot be expected to take their orders from the rank and file'—were the men that Balfour consulted. Like Gladstone in 1885, he could not bring himself to summon together all his ex-official colleagues to resolve the deadlock, fearing that the result might go against his personal inclinations: and like Gladstone he supported himself on the self-made assumption that his mediatory role was indispensable. But unlike Gladstone, he had no solution of his own.

Instead he was playing a purely defensive and Conservative game, resisting as Salisbury in similar circumstances had resisted Randolph Churchill's bid in the 1880's to democratize the party. The week-end before the meeting—while Chamberlain's pistol was still levelled at his head—Balfour stayed at Hatfield where his cousin Lord Hugh Cecil observed him at close quarters while not venturing to tackle him directly on behalf of the free fooders:

Lord Hugh Cecil–Devonshire, 11 February 1906: A. J. B. is here, but he has not talked much about politics. His physical tiredness is very great, and it has therefore seemed impossible to harass him very much.

What he has said is anti-Joe, and I don't think he will move in Joe's direction at all. But I doubt whether he will depart from the region of mist where he has lived so long. For one thing, his fatigue makes it almost out of the question that he should take a bold and decided line. But even if he were not tired out, I am afraid he would never do what is wanted—never give a strong and clear lead.

With all his immense ability, his mind is not that of a leader, but of a diplomatist. He is a free trader, but doubts that protection would be very injurious. He likes colonial preference, but believes that a tax on corn is impracticable. He dreads 'dumping', but does not believe a tariff is the right remedy. He thinks retaliation good, but does not pretend it would have a very great effect. . . .

Yet, being not weak for all his complaisance, he will not adapt his opinions either to Joe's or to ours, and is in his heart angry both with

Joe and with us for not conforming obediently to his strange leadership.[421]

But at least Cecil and Balfour had in common a wish 'to prevent Joe capturing the party'.

For his part, Chamberlain had resolved that in no circumstances would he be a rival to Balfour for the leadership, and consequently he had to give way. The dispute was patched up by the 'Valentine letters' which they exchanged on the eve of the meeting, Balfour avowing a mild degree of tariff reform as agreeable to himself personally and in principle, while Chamberlain offered Balfour his support. Once more Balfour had dodged the demand for an official policy. He also evaded Chamberlain's demand for the democratic reform of the Central Office, promising to overhaul it himself.

To some extent Balfour recognized the need for an efficient and responsive Central Office if only to win elections, and was moved by the defeat of 1906—as later by the defeats of 1910—to press his officials for some changes. But his officials resisted these changes with the argument that the arcana of electoral matters were not fit to be discussed in a representative committee. No progress having been made by May, Chamberlain began to despair of success in this, his last expedient for breaking the deadlock. He had offered to amalgamate with the Conservatives, if the latter would put their house in order, but Acland Hood, Balfour's Chief Whip, was unwilling to accept the bargain:

Chamberlain–Austen Chamberlain, 4 May 1906: Balfour's illness, of course, prevented another conference with him, or any attempt to deal with reorganization, which has been hanging fire. I wish we could have struck while the iron is hot. As far as my information goes the Central Office is as bad as ever, and in all negotiations between it and the country organizations it leans heavily against Tariff Reformers and in favour of the free food section.

When I saw Balfour after the holidays I had a preliminary talk with him upon the subject. I told him that I was afraid that Hood would not listen to our proposals for the representative element in the Central Conservative Committee, that I thought he was entirely wrong, and that if his view prevailed there would be no possibility of amalgamation with the Liberal Unionists. No one could settle the question but Balfour himself. . . .

Of course if he agreed with me, he could settle the matter in five minutes, but I am afraid he is opposed to our views, or at all events not eager to adopt them at the expense of a difference with Hood. It is a discouraging situation, and as long as it lasts I see no hope of union or of that better and more popular organization which is desirable in the interests of the Unionist Party.[422]

Further conferences with Balfour did not make him more hopeful of overcoming the 'opposition from the powers behind the throne', as he called them. The Conservative Central Office maintained that a central party committee could not properly deal with electoral matters—presumably as an excuse for retaining the gulf between itself and the National Union, which was Chamberlainite. Taking up the challenge, Chamberlain was prepared to prove that such a contention was unfounded, instancing the Liberal Unionist central committee. 'I want to show', he said, 'that we are perfectly frank with our committee, that we discuss and settle everything so that the committee has real power; and at the same time to point out that no harm has ever resulted from our frankness, and that no leakage in consequence has ever taken place.'[423] But it was in vain that Chamberlain tried to roll this particular stone up the hill.

He had not attempted to take over the Conservative party, as his opponents thought. His intentions in January, when he first joined issue with Balfour, are unambiguously explained in a letter of Mrs Chamberlain to her mother. On the question of Chamberlain taking the party lead, his wife writes: 'I feel as I always have done—that it is not possible, he should not get the unreserved support of the Conservatives.' The purpose of challenging conclusions at a party meeting was to secure Chamberlain's personal freedom to champion tariff reform, whether with the party or absolved from its restraints. 'If', continues Mrs Chamberlain, 'the Free Fooders are still to be pampered at every critical moment, he feels there is no use in his wasting time and strength in helping to bear the brunt of the battle, and he would prefer to be in an independent position.'[424] Conscious of the need to husband his energies if he hoped to sustain his movement against the force of the times, and determined not to allow the tariff reform cause to be obliterated in Parliament for five or six years, Chamberlain was now what Randolph Churchill had called Gladstone—an old man in a hurry. But fate was about to overtake him.

On 8 July 1906 Chamberlain attained his seventieth birthday. A great celebration was arranged in his honour by his city, such as had no parallel except perhaps that accorded to John Bright in 1883 after twenty-five years as member for Birmingham. Chamberlain had now represented the city for thirty years, and served it for longer. The eve of his birthday, a Saturday, was celebrated in recognition of his municipal services by a civic luncheon, while the day after, Monday, 9 July, was arranged to culminate in a huge political gathering in the Bingley Hall, which was fitted up to hold an audience of 10,000 people. Together the events were recognized as presenting a gruelling ordeal. But Chamberlain got through them. At the Saturday luncheon he was observed to speak with 'keen emotion', and to lapse into a prolonged pause after the first few words, which was relieved by the audience breaking into cheers. From 3.30 began a motor tour of Birmingham's six public parks, a seventeen-mile course punctuated by enthusiastic receptions from the crowds and civic dignitaries awaiting the arrival of Chamberlain's procession of eighty motor-cars. In the parks entertainments were given from four o'clock till dusk, when firework displays were lavished on hosts of spectators estimated to amount to 50,000 in each of the places. Returning from dinner at Highbury, Chamberlain witnessed a fire portrait of himself thirty feet square suspended from balloons and ignited at a height of 1,000 feet.

There was some solicitude as to the effects of these demands on Chamberlain, but inquiries made on Sunday morning were reassuring. On the Monday the Bingley Hall audience were not disappointed, and when the now aged statesman rose for the last time, he was 'received with wild delight'. 'Such a scene', *The Times* account continued, 'has never been witnessed in Bingley Hall, the great Gladstone demonstrations not excepted.' Chamberlain's speech was a moderate review of the past twenty years and an unprovocative vindication of his new 'unauthorized' programme. Though not composed as a valedictory address, it had much of that character, prompted by the special and unrepeatable nature of the occasion. When the proceedings were over, Chamberlain's route back to Highbury was illuminated by over 4,000 torchbearers, who fell into procession six abreast as he passed and accompanied him to the gates of his house. The gesture again overwhelmed him with emotion, and he had to confess he had never seen anything like it.

The next day Chamberlain took the five o'clock train to London, where a birthday dinner at the Nineteen-hundred Club was arranged for him by leading tariff reformers on the following evening. In noticing his journey, *The Times* observed that he 'has not suffered from the enthusiasm and excitement of Monday'. Once more Chamberlain was fêted at an enthusiastic gathering, and presented with an antique silver epergne amid a throng of ardent admirers. One of those present, Sir Herbert Maxwell, was aware of the additional hazard of Chamberlain's habitually generous consumption at such occasions. Always reckless about his own health, Chamberlain had more than once told Maxwell that 'the work would kill him'. 'His labour', observed Maxwell, 'was incessant, he neglected all dietary and other precautions.' 'I noted with anxiety', writes Maxwell of the dinner of 12 July, 'the freedom with which he ate, drank, and smoked large cigars. "My friend", I thought, "you will be lucky if you have not to pay smartly for this." '[425] And so it was. Immediately after this celebration, Chamberlain had the stroke which prostrated him for the rest of his life. It was many months before the public realized what had happened. A mass meeting arranged for 18 July was put off with the excuse that Chamberlain was confined to his room with 'an acute attack of gout'. His family—certainly Mrs Chamberlain—did not know at first that recovery was not to be hoped for.

CHAPTER TWELVE

Tariff or Budget?

You have an opportunity. You will not have it again. . . .
The character of an individual depends upon the greatness of the
ideals upon which it rests, and the character of the nation is the same.
The moral grandeur of a nation depends upon its being sometimes able
to forget itself, sometimes able to think of the future of the race for
which it stands. . . .
. . . we can draw closer the growing nations, the sister States; and
by a commercial union we can pave the way for that federation . . . of
free nations which will enable us to prolong in ages yet to come all the
glorious traditions of the British race.
Never yet in our history has the great democracy been unpatriotic. . . .
Chamberlain's election address, January 1910

FOR five weeks Chamberlain did not stir from his room.
Then his doctors began to prescribe attempts at walking,
and by September he had made progress which in the
circumstances was very satisfactory. His recovery is chronicled
in Mrs Chamberlain's letters to her mother:

Mrs Chamberlain–Mrs Endicott, 19 September 1906: . . . then Joe came
down about 1 o'clock and walked to the end of the terrace and back—
then as soon as he had had his lunch went into his new chair, which
proved very handy. . . . he stayed out till nearly 5 o'clock. He was
much interested in the shrubbery garden and its growth. . . .
    By 9.40 after his cigar with Austen and Neville he was quite ready
for bed. . . .
Mrs Chamberlain–Mrs Endicott, 21 September 1906: He walks up and
down the entire length of the terrace with a stick and only one person
holding on to his right side, and he has made a distinct advance in
the ease and confidence with which he does it.
    He also walks up and down stairs . . . going up and down the terrace
twice almost at his natural pace. . . .[426]

By the end of the year the grave impairment of sight and speech
was somewhat mitigated. But, owing to an ocular divergence,
reading remained painful, and the wide range of newspapers and

journals which he habitually devoured had to be read out to him. Speech was too laboured for him to wish to hold conversations with political friends, though he ultimately recovered a working facility in a rather abbreviated form of expression. All committee work had to be dropped, but through Austen, who took his place in the Liberal Unionist Council and Tariff Reform League and numerous other bodies, he remained in touch with affairs and continued to follow them closely. Austen, who had always followed precisely his father's line in fiscal affairs, took into his hands all the threads of Chamberlain's tariff reform movement and preserved its continuity. At the same time Chamberlain's name and authority and to a large extent his guiding influence still backed the movement.

By the beginning of 1907 the serious nature of Chamberlain's disability had become apparent to the discerning public. Sandars, for example, learnt from a doctor's comments on a photograph which had appeared in an illustrated paper that he 'must have had severe hemiplegia—and that, having regard to the length of time which has elapsed since the stroke, recovery must be *very, very* doubtful'.[427] The Unionist kingmaker was no more to be feared. Yet the immediate effect of Chamberlain's removal from active affairs was an increase of pressure from the wilder spirits among the tariff reformers, Arthur Lee, Bonar Law, Maxse and L. S. Amery. The Tariff Reform League embarked upon a 'forward' movement so menacing that even the Conservative Whip, Acland Hood, became convinced that unless Balfour did something to bring his policy up some way to meet the party vanguard his followers would melt away 'until anarchy is succeeded by a new authority'. Equally surprising was the manner in which Sandars, having consulted Hood, Akers-Douglas and Iwan-Muller, took it upon himself to plead the cause which he had hitherto done everything to obstruct. The most striking part of Hood's recantation, as reported by Sandars, was his recognition of the point which Chamberlain had made in 1903—that twentieth-century politics demanded dynamic party policies:

Sandars–Balfour, 22 January 1907: Hood tells me that times have changed, that he does not find it possible to satisfy the party with these precedents [the electoral appeals of 1874, 1886, and 1895], and the rank and file clamour for some broad line of policy to be adopted above and beyond the policy of resisting and denouncing a Government. . . .

He reports that at the county meetings . . . there is generally a majority who, while not sympathizing with the advanced programme of Fiscal Reform, are in favour of some kind of Fiscal Reform, and he believes—and I think he is right—that if the only fiscal guides are Austen and Arthur Lee and that group, they—these moderate men—will gradually drift away from us and become members of the Tariff Reform League branches.[428]

There were many instances of the successful subversive action of the Tariff Reform League. The Conservative National Union, which had just been remodelled on a democratic basis, had formed a new Council which was, said Sandars, 'in a fair way to be captured by the Tariff Reformers'. The League, moreover, had come into funds. '*On dit*', comments Sandars, 'that several Radical manufacturers have subscribed, being afraid of predatory socialism and being keen on the possible advantages of a tariff.' One of Hood's best party agents was being enticed to act as a League Secretary at £500 a year; money which formerly would have gone to the Chief Whip's fund was being diverted to the League; and 'many of our best local committee men' were defecting. Finally, with the exception of the *Daily Telegraph* there was 'not a single organ of the London Press which would support the orthodox party and its leader against this development'.

Sandars himself was converted so far as to support Hood's plea for Balfour to declare himself a tariff reformer. It was a delicate task, but after some face-saving remarks against detailed commitment and the 'fatuous folly of Joe at Glasgow', Sandars made bold to advise a tariff reform speech from Balfour when he spoke to the National Union on 15 February:

Sandars–Balfour, 22 January 1907: But they [the party] do want a statement on broad lines touching Fiscal Reform in its relation to finance, both imperial and local: they would like a sympathetic reference to closer commercial union with the Colonies; they would like a point made of the fact that schemes for social reform depending on public money cannot be accomplished without that elasticity of revenue which alone can be obtained from a wider basis of taxation, and, finally, that, until the fiscal question is tackled, the British manufacturer will never get better treatment for his wares abroad. A speech on these lines without refinement of argument but declaratory of your own personal belief would, in Hood's opinion, pull the party together.

The point is, are you disposed to make it? It may in your judgement be unwise to make it. Be it so—but then, says Hood, we shall practically lose our army. . . .

I do not fail to see the great difficulty of the position, in the same way that I see the egregious folly of those who with a splendid case against the enemy wish to sacrifice a proportion of their strength by making themselves responsible for a constructive policy which is just the target their opponents want. But you have to take men as you find them, and if they will choose the path of difficulty it still behoves you—their leader—to guide them: doesn't it?[429]

To this momentous appeal Balfour could only reply gruffly that he was already aware of all that Hood had conveyed to Sandars, and that he was thinking rather of telling his party 'the truth in love'—that if it went to pieces 'the disloyal Tariff Reformers have as much to lose as anybody else'.[430]

But even Balfour was about to weaken, not under the duress of party pressure but under the urbane and flexible influence of Professor Hewins, whom he was consulting at this time. It was very agreeable, wrote Balfour, to talk to a tariff reformer 'who really knows something about his case. He, broadly speaking, takes my view of the subject. . . .' In the first place, Hewins supplied Balfour with a definition of tariff reform which he could unreservedly accept:

Hewins–Balfour, 18 February 1907: I should define the new policy as the deliberate adoption of the Empire as distinguished from the United Kingdom as the basis of public policy, and, in particular, the substitution in our economic policy of Imperial interests for the interest of the consumer, those interests being measured not necessarily by the immediate or even the ultimate gain of a purely economic character arising from a particular line of policy, but by the greater political or social stability, or greater defensive power, of the Empire.[431]

It was in fact free trade on an imperial basis. But Balfour's idea— and also Chamberlain's—of an imperial *Zollverein* was shown by Hewins to be impracticable. Simple free trade within the Empire would necessarily involve an Imperial Exchequer and all the machinery for allocating revenue possessed by, for instance, the German Empire: although undoubtedly a large imperial 'free list' was certainly possible. Hewins also demonstrated that the trend of national sentiment in the self-governing colonies such as Canada was running contrary to anything like an Imperial Council or a contribution towards imperial defence. Canada was demanding the right of direct participation in international trade negotiations—indeed in 1903 Canadian ministers had been in direct negotiation with the German government through the German Consul-General in Montreal, without any intervention from the British Colonial or Foreign Office. Moreover, Canada was pressing for inter-colonial preference, and already had preferential arrangements with the West Indies, New Zealand, South Africa, India, Ceylon, and the Straits Settlements. For all these reasons the most that could be hoped for by Britain was mutual trade preferences with the colonies.

Finally, Hewins demolished Balfour's idea that food taxes could be avoided in any such preferential bargains. The corn duty was 'the most powerful engine for securing preference', and since the colonial corn supply was unlimited a duty on foreign corn would not raise the price. It was one of the few duties, perhaps the only one, which could raise revenue and not be protective: and it was on the revenue argument that Hewins laid the stress. A large war or an economic crisis, he said, would 'smash the present fiscal system'. He had Balfour's hearty concurrence when he claimed that direct taxation could not be resorted to for large increases of revenue, and he clinched his case for increasing indirect taxation by producing figures which showed that there was room for increasing the ratio of indirect to direct taxes. Since 1840 the country had been progressively transferring the burden on to direct taxes, and the Unionist governments holding office since 1895 had accelerated the process:

| | Revenue in £ millions from | |
Years	direct taxes	indirect taxes
1840–4	12·8	37·4
1850–4	16·4	37·8
1860–4	21·9	42·4
1870–4	20·3	44·9
1880–4	25·4	45·8
1890–4	33·0	49·3
1900–4	59·4	67·4[432]

Only tariff reform could reverse this trend: or, indeed, hold the existing balance, for the socialists had begun to propound a financial policy which would virtually abolish indirect taxation altogether.

With Austen as with the other leading tariff reformers Balfour continued to remain on fairly distant terms. He could do nothing, however, to prevent the attrition of Conservative branches since he accepted completely the doctrine that the Central Office should not interfere with the local selection of parliamentary candidates. 'From their point of view', he said of the Tariff Reform League, 'they are perfectly right, since the very essence of our Party organization is that the local associations are (within their own sphere) supreme, and the task of capture ought not to be very difficult seeing that a majority of the party, and I suspect the great majority of its local office-bearers, are Protectionists at heart. . . .'[433] So long as the tariff reformers worked through the local committees and did not set up unauthorized candidates of their own their activities were regarded as legitimate.

One body, the so-called 'Confederates', were sworn to eliminate the free fooders even at the cost of losing Unionist seats by three-cornered contests, and there is some evidence that Chamberlain gave this secret group some countenance in 1906.[434] Austen had nothing to do with the Confederates. 'I believe them to be a knot of men', he told Balfour, 'who are dissatisfied with the Tariff Reform League and with me and others of its leaders, because we have not been willing to engage in or countenance a general attack on Free-food Unionists. I have heard that Leo Maxse is one of them, but I have never been able to learn their names. . . . Maxse is my personal friend, as he is yours, but I have as little political influence with him as you have.'[435] The Confederates, notably Leo Maxse and J. L. Garvin, were destined to play a decisive role later, but through their influence over the Unionist press, not by direct action. They supported Chamberlain and the 'Chamberlain spirit', but some of them—if Garvin is any true example—did not wish to have Austen as leader.

Events were leading towards a healing of the Unionist schism, for the free food Unionists were beginning to realize that the socialist menace was much more real and imminent than they could have imagined before 1906. By 1911 even the Cecils were prepared to swallow tariff reform. In one sense Chamberlain had played his hand too soon, and might have easily converted his party after the full horror of 'socialist finance' had been disclosed. On the other hand the enormous movement which had grown from his initiative of 1903 gave the Unionists a far more comprehensive and informed controversial strength with which to oppose the doctrines of Philip Snowden and Lloyd George than could have been developed from scratch after 1906. Nor was it only the financial aspect of socialism which served to 'educate' the Unionists in tariff reform, but the broad ideological challenge which it presented. Chamberlain's imperial policy rose to a higher premium as an antidote to the gospel of social war. Such was the consideration which turned Balfour's friend and ex-Irish Secretary, George Wyndham, into a tariff reformer. Wyndham threw himself into the popular controversies and street-corner politics of the 1906 election, and from the throes of the struggle he made the following diagnosis:

Two ideals, and only two, emerge from the vortex:
1. Imperialism, which demands unity at home between classes, and unity throughout the Empire; and which *prescribes* fiscal reform to secure both.
2. Insular socialism, and class antagonism. . . .
    As for the 'Liberals' and 'Unionist Free Traders'—the 'Whigs' of our day— Well! Their day is over. It is they who are drowned.
    The Imperialists and Socialists emerge. That is the dividing line of future parties.[436]

On the same kind of reasoning Milner came out for tariff reform in 1907—though he believed that in imperial questions British public opinion was 'quite rotten'.

In 1907 there appeared a little red book by Philip Snowden called *The Socialist's Budget*. This plan for 'socialism by instalments' struck Unionists as infinitely more insidious and dangerous than the older varieties of insurrectionary socialism. Instead of being prepared, like the generation of William Morris, to fight at the barricades for their millennial society, the Edwardian socialists were proposing to foster a rapacious materialism and effect a comfortable revolution by act of Parliament. Snowden's simple phrases went straight to the point. 'The existence of a rich class, whose riches are the cause of the poverty of the masses, is the justification for the Socialist demand that the cost of bettering the condition of the people must be by the taxation of the rich.' Snowden maintained that the poor should pay no taxes, because in any case 'the workers pay the taxes which are levied upon the idle rich'. He therefore proposed to abolish all indirect taxation. This would involve taking off about £12 millions on sugar and tea, and in all some £29 millions on food, tobacco and drink. In addition Snowden proposed to axe away the burden of the local education and poor rates. Having thus freed the masses from indirect taxation, he proposed to add £72 millions to the income tax—mostly at the upper end on the 'thirtieth of the population who take one third of the national income'. This steeply graduated income tax would provide a surplus for state education, old age pensions, unemployment benefits, and the payment of M.P.s.

This kind of scheme reduced the tariff reformers' fiscal devices to the scale of molehills. At once many indications appeared that the Unionists would find tariff reform relatively innocuous and practically the only fighting alternative to socialist appeals. 'For the purposes of our time', Maxse warned his readers, 'what we shall have to grapple with is not the Utopian creed but the Budgetary method. Practical socialism . . . is a system of finance.' Austen Chamberlain was quick to sense the change in direction, and encouraged by receiving from Balfour a letter elaborating on the theme that 'A great change has manifested itself within the last year', he replied with an urgent appeal for a new programme:

Austen–Balfour, 24 October 1907: Labour-Socialism is making enormous strides among the working men, and especially the young men. No doubt when, if ever, it gets a majority, it will break down and be discredited. But when will that be, and how much mischief will it have accomplished in the meantime?[437]

The progress of socialism was attributed by Austen to the fact that it spoke with a steady and decided voice, and had a positive policy which aroused the hopes and enthusiasm of the masses. Why could not Balfour come out for a general tariff and a corn tax, and then for social reforms? On the subject of old age pensions, he observed that Asquith had committed himself to a 'universal non-contributory scheme'. 'I believe this to be vicious in principle and impossible on account of the cost. May we not say that we are prepared to propose a contributory scheme, somewhat on the German model—1/3rd from the workman, 1/3rd from the employer, 1/3rd from the state?' On the land question, Austen asked 'Ought we not to "crystallize" our policy . . . and definitely to propound purchase and ownership in opposition to hiring and tenancy as adopted by the government and the socialists? . . . It is to the land question that the Radicals are looking to destroy both us and the House of Lords. They avow it freely in conversation.' With the addition of other items dealing with housing, the sweated trades, etc., Austen believed that there were here 'the elements of a fine programme . . . popular and capable of rousing great enthusiasm'. Would Balfour 'rescue the party from chaos' and put forward a constructive alternative to the 'wildcat and predatory schemes of the present government and its socialist allies?'

If Balfour hesitated to take Austen's advice, he received confirmation of its diagnosis in the form of a very similar appeal from Wyndham four days later, containing much the same analysis of the situation. Sandars had inquired casually in a postscript what was Wyndham's impression of the attitude of Conservatives in the North. Wyndham replied:

Wyndham–Sandars, 28 October 1907: You ask for an impression of the attitude of our men. I have been to Scotland and Northumberland to the home of (a.) Individualism (b.) The export coal trade; and I say that our friends and any who might become our friends want:

1. *the Empire*; as the state which we must become if we are to vie with other Empires.

2. that they misdoubt a battle between Individualism (Lord Wemyss and the lower-middle class) and Socialism. They misdoubt both, because both ignore the state, i.e. the Empire, in constant competitition —at peace, by tariffs, or at war—with other states which are becoming Empires.

They see that if you 'run' Individualism you ignore the state except as a 'police' officer. And that, if you 'run' Socialism, you ignore the state except as a relieving officer. . . .

But a third fact has emerged, i.e. an active fourth party—the Labour

Party—inspired almost wholly by continental socialism. Now, whatever their ideals may be, their 'practical' policy is to pile up direct taxation (see Snowden's Budget).

Our case is that you cannot do that without (a.) *smashing credit*; necessary for any measure of social reform or Imperial Defence. (b.) *creating unemployment* by pinching the middle classes.

So, to go back to the chief's speech . . . you *must* have more *indirect* taxation and, if that is right, it is obviously right also

   1. to fight for fair play in foreign markets,

   2. to accept favours from Colonial markets,

   3. to safeguard *our labour*, with our Young England humanitarian restrictions, against (a.) sweated labour and (b.) dumped goods.[438]

The fact that the Liberal government were going ahead with their old age pensions scheme before they had disclosed where the funds were to be obtained made the situation more disturbing. Clearly Unionists could not hope to regain office without at once being able to maintain a greatly enhanced level of state expenditure. The Liberals might take it off defence spending—but could the Unionists?

In 1908 Lloyd George carried through the Liberal old age pensions Act, and in July he announced: 'Next year I shall have to rob somebody's hen-roost, and I must consider where I can get most eggs, and where I can get them easiest and where I shall be least punished.' In this spirit he framed the controversial 1909 Budget. Financially, the Budget departed from the traditional ratio of direct to indirect taxes, by adding over £6 millions to income tax and death duties, while leaving the sugar duty as it was after being halved by Asquith in 1908. But there were substantial increases in the duties on liquor and tobacco, while £1¾ millions were put on stamp duties and motor taxes, and half a million pounds on the new land and mineral taxes. The Budget was thus a palpable but not a reckless departure from the hitherto accepted canons of balance and justice as between classes. What made it so provocative was the declared attitude of its backers. Churchill spoke of abolishing all indirect taxes except those on tobacco and liquor, and remarked that in future the question would be not 'What have you got?', in considering direct taxation, but 'How did you get it?' Lloyd George talked of further demands for social reforms, while the socialist journals hailed the Budget as 'quite a Red Flag Budget'; or, 'almost as good a Budget as we could expect from a Socialist chancellor in his first year of office'. Above all the land taxes—the halfpenny in the pound on the capital value of undeveloped land or mineral resources—seemed to contain 'the minute but living and growing germ of complete confiscation'.

Lloyd George had set a trap for the Unionists, and one which they would see but still walk into with their eyes open. He aimed, in Garvin's words, at 'breaking the Parliamentary deadlock, reversing feeling in the country, side-tracking tariff reform, and solving simultaneously the financial, the electioneering, and the Constitutional problems'.439 The Budget pleased the Socialist allies of the Liberals, found money for old age pensions, revived the anti-Lords cry, and bolstered up the failing system of Cobdenite finance. Its provision for compulsory land registration was not strictly a financial item and was *pro tanto* an illegal 'tack': but it was admirably calculated to incense the House of Lords into throwing out the whole Bill. The only disadvantage of the Budget, from the Liberal point of view, was that it gravely offended both the traditional Conservatives and the tariff reformers, and was therefore sure to heal the quarrel between the rival Unionist factions and unite them under Balfour in a common opposition. If prudent counsels had prevailed among the Unionist leaders, the long struggle over the Bill in the Commons might have concluded with a unified opposition under Balfour and a final bowing before the inevitable. Lloyd George could not and seemingly did not count on the Budget being rejected, while the Unionists finally resolved to reject it for reasons ulterior to the measure itself. Ultimately the temptation to which they succumbed was a dual one—the tariff reformers wishing to fight a fiscal election, and Balfour wishing to lead into battle a united party.

The Unionist outcry against the tendencies of the 1909 Budget originated in Confederate circles. Chamberlain himself was among the first to declare for uncompromising resistance in May 1909, and the diehard line was taken up by Leo Maxse in the *National Review* and Garvin in *The Observer*. Balfour remained uncommitted until the latter part of the year. He might have resisted the tariff reformers' suggestion that the Budget was anethema to his party, had not Lloyd George in his celebrated Limehouse speech of July appeared to be declaring a class war, while later Asquith, travelling to Birmingham in a train called 'Erebus', declared to a Bingley Hall audience that the budget was an alternative to tariff reform. The Liberal leaders were courting a symbolic battle over socialist finance. The idea was taken up and developed by Garvin in an admirably contrived series of *Observer* articles designed to emphasize how sinister the intentions of the Budget promoters were. In Garvin's imagination the Budget became a gigantic conspiracy, a seductive and ensnaring device to demoralize and ultimately ruin the country. 'Capital and Labour would be ground between the upper and nether millstones of Socialistic taxation and foreign importation. . . . Capital with its employment-giving power will stream abroad. The free importation of foreign manufactured goods will enjoy the utmost facilities for displacing British labour at home.'[440] Here was a receipt for growing impoverishment and an exacerbation of class war until the country, its navy and imperial connections neglected and its industrial strength sapped, fell an easy prey in the conflict of nations. Even the details of the Budget were pregnant with mischief. Its high licensing duties were the means to 'force the rejected Licensing Bill into law over the heads of the Peers and the people', while the land registration provision was a Trojan horse to usher in land nationalization.

Balfour rose to this kind of suggestion. He agreed to speak at Birmingham on 22 September to answer Asquith and appear as a deputy for Chamberlain. Curiously enough a personal acquaintance and confidence grew up between Garvin and Sandars, hitherto fiscal opponents, so that Garvin's ideas were filtered through Sandars to Balfour at this critical stage. Nor does it appear that Sandars was merely cultivating Garvin to keep a hold on him or gain information. On the contrary, Sandars seems to have fallen equally a prey to Garvin's fixation about Lloyd George. The day before Balfour was due to speak at Birmingham, he was sent an account by Sandars of a conversation which Garvin had had with the editor of the *Daily Mail,* Kennedy Jones, the day before:

Sandars–Balfour, 21 September 1909: [Quoting Garvin's account] For the first time Kennedy Jones told me of his weekend with Lloyd George on Lipton's yacht. He said Lloyd George talked with a frankness not merely demented but useful.

He went out from the Port of London transaction, and talked like a man hypnotized by the facility with which things could be nationalized. He not only spoke of the railways, first to be cheapened by motor competition practically subsidized on the new state roads and then bought, but he went on to say that he meant to nationalize public houses, and to cheapen them also by repeated increases of taxation before taking them over. There has been no such demagogue as this. It is far meaner as well as more dangerous than a campaign for open confiscation. . . .

Kennedy Jones said shrewdly, if only Mr Balfour would show how it means Socialism, it would have immense authority coming from him, as follows:

That land nationalization is aimed at by the Land Clauses.

That railway nationalization is evidently sought by certain features of the Development Bill.

That public house nationalization is pointed out by the Liquor Clauses, and so on.

And that in all these cases covert, unfair, and dishonest methods are adopted to 'bleed white' each interest that it is intended to destroy.[441]

The Bingley Hall speech of the next day did indeed follow the general lines Garvin advocated. Balfour emphasized that the country stood at the parting of the ways—whether to go upward in 'the hopeful movement of tariff reform', or 'on that downward track which leads to the bottomless confusion of socialist legislation'. Point was given to this utterance by a message from Chamberlain read out to the meeting, observing that 'The Budget will supply us with money, but at the same time will deprive us of work', and expressing a hope that the House of Lords would see its way to force a general election. The total effect of the meeting was greeted by Sandars with real enthusiasm. 'It was a triumph!' he wrote to Balfour, adding that 'the boys' in the Whips' office were delighted, and that 'Garvin was enchanted with your speech and reports wholesale satisfaction among tariff reformers and active journalists'.[442]

At Highbury Chamberlain had listened to the Bingley Hall proceedings by means of an Electrophone, through which he could hear perfectly even the asides of the platform. After hearing Balfour's speech, he gave an interview to a journalist of the *Daily Mail*, 'talking wonderfully well . . . and telling him it was a speech which made history'. Balfour came to stay the night at Highbury, and remained till after lunch the next day, so that he and Chamberlain could have 'a good chat' in the conservatory. Balfour gave Mrs Chamberlain the impression that he was 'most anxious for Joe's approval', for among other things he had turned to her on the platform immediately after sitting down to ask 'Do you think Joe will be satisfied?' He was indeed. After a day or two Chamberlain came out with the remark: 'On thinking it over I have come to the conclusion that Balfour played up very well.'[443]

The stage was now being set for the rejection of the Budget. It seems clear that Balfour was by this time turning his mind to the prospect of a December or January election. In October he was again at Highbury, after receiving an honorary degree at Birmingham University. At dinner he discussed with Chamberlain 'various aspects of the political situation'. Mrs Chamberlain's account gives the plain impression that the chief topic was an imminent general election: 'Speculation is rife,' she continues, 'and even the King has not escaped from it. It is said the Bill will not reach the Lords before November 8th. . . . Mr Balfour is perturbed in his mind, for he cannot make out their game— whether they want an election at once or in January.'[444] Chamberlain was solidly behind the idea of rejecting the Budget as a matter of principle, and he moved to his London house in November to play as much of a part in affairs as possible. 'We have had frequent guests,' his wife recorded, 'and Joe has talked extremely well most of the time. . . . Joe is more optimistic of the result than most people.' It was not expected that the Unionists would win an election, if they forced one, although by-elections had been promising and there were signs of failing employment. The most hopeful calculations did not prognosticate a Unionist net gain of more than 150 seats, not enough to equalize the parties. Nevertheless Chamberlain felt that 'we should be in a very different position in the House'.[445]

Lord Lansdowne had grave misgivings about the expediency of moving the rejection of the Budget, forced on him, as a free trade unionist comments, by the 'clamour of the Unionist press and the apprehensions of Tariff Reformers'.[446] His party in the Upper House was by no means solid behind him, the free trade Unionist peers being generally against rejection. Hicks Beach called it 'the worst gamble I have ever known in politics'. The pressure came from Balfour, who supplied Lansdowne with the words of the rejecting amendment. Balfour's motives appear in a letter which his secretary wrote to Lansdowne, deprecating timidity and the squeamish approach of the 'Palace' circle, who regarded the refusal to pass the Budget as 'mad':

Sandars–Lansdowne, 6 November 1909: On Wednesday last I dined with Lord Knollys, Esher and Davidson (Equerry) at Brooks. . . .

They were all non-militant people, very anxious about the King's position, very anxious about what our estimate might be of the result of the election, querulous, rather unreasonable, strangely ignorant . . . they had no idea that Asquith had formidable dissents in his own party.

But . . . the burden of their conversation was that . . . a dead heat or a beating ought not to be risked, for the King would then be in a very difficult situation. That there was any question of principle at stake—anything beyond mere tactics—seemed to them a novel contention.[447]

Sandars goes on to enthuse about the tactics which 'our best Unionist Press Editors' intended to adopt to simplify and drive home the issue at stake. Garvin's rationale of the position had prevailed. The Budget was now a 'Parliamentary *coup d'état* against the House of Lords', an attempt to establish a 'Single-Chamber despotism'. To pass it would be a base surrender of the British Constitution.

After the rejection of the Budget by the House of Lords, on the grounds that it was 'not justified in giving its consent to this Bill until it has been submitted to the judgment of the country', the tariff reformers were the apparent dictators of their party's strategy. They had always called for an aggressive, constructive programme, and if the peers were to seem to represent anything more than mere rank and privilege, it had to be some conception of the common weal to which the Budget was supposedly inimical. Admittedly there was no logical necessity for the diehard peers—who in rejecting the Budget were inviting a struggle *à outrance* with the House of Commons—to pose as anything more than the upholders of the people's right to control the legislature. But practically such a move required a fighting spirit and a confidence in appealing to the public which was very much akin to the spirit of the tariff reformers.

This was the making of the 'diehard' party. Certainly from the tariff reformers' point of view, the House of Lords became the citadel of their cause, a symbol of the true British values and tradition to be defended to the last ditch against socialistic demagogues and chance majorities. Garvin took a very low view of the intelligence and political sophistication of the average elector, and at the same time observed that the great powers of the world all had two-chamber constitutions. For a great Empire to be governed by an institution so totally unchecked as the House of Commons would be, once the House of Lords was reduced to a nullity, seemed to him unthinkable. It would speedily be ruined by the destructive designs of Radicals like Lloyd George and Churchill.

Garvin's *Observer* articles, with some additions by Maxse, were got out in a campaign handbook for tariff reformers called *Tariff or Budget,* for which Chamberlain composed a preface. The terse reasoning of Chamberlain's contribution reveal him as solidly behind Garvin:

Highbury, 14 December 1909: Tariff Reform is the only alternative to the Budget. It is the only policy dreaded by the authors of the Budget. . . . Nothing would be more satisfactory to our opponents than to put this issue aside by raising new disputes to distract the mind of the electorate.

Consider the alternative. The supporters of the Government would sweep away all the constitutional usefulness of a second Chamber. Apparently they intend to attempt the practical destruction of the House of Lords, and not its genuine amendment. . . .

If a vote at the coming elections were given in favour of the Budget, not only would the new system of finance be accepted and extended in the future, but the House of Lords would be relegated to a position of impotence. . . .

. . . I believe that a House of Commons entirely uncontrolled would be a great public danger. It would be much worse than the House of Lords, which, just because it is a hereditary chamber, must depend for its whole strength and influence upon its success in interpreting the true mind of the people.

... The time has surely come for the Tariff policy, which would promote British trade and welfare, instead of the Budget policy which, in every respect, would surrender our interests and security to foreign rivals. It is better to abolish Cobdenism and not the Constitution; to pull down free imports and foreign privilege in our market and not the Second Chamber. ... Let the workers defend their work and stand by the Peers, who in this case are standing by them.

In spite of the strenuous propaganda of Garvin and others, however, the general election of January 1910 was not fought on the tariff issue, or even on that of a 'Second Chamber'. The plain man saw things in terms of landowning peers retaliating against a supposed invasion of the privileges of the upper House by the enormous counterstroke of throwing out a popular budget. As an electoral appeal, Garvin's attitude was quite unrealistic. It was also tactically a piece of folly—a folly in which almost all the Unionist party were involved.* For by greatly reducing the Liberal majority, they rendered Asquith dependent upon the goodwill of Redmond and the Irish, and the price of that good-will was a Parliament Bill to curtail the Lords' veto, with a Home Rule Bill to be introduced after the way for its passing had been cleared.

Immediately after the Budget had been reintroduced and passed by both Houses in the session of 1909, the new Liberal Government tabled resolutions for the reform of the House of Lords. The power to hold up money bills was entirely withdrawn, while the ability to hold up other legislation was to be restricted in practice to a period of two years. On this project Asquith would have gone to the country in the summer of 1910, but the death of King Edward VII made it desirable to postpone the controversy for some months.

---

* Chamberlain was likewise complacent about the risks of 'referring' the Budget. In a press interview given in January 1910 just after the results of the election were known, he said: 'I should think that Mr Asquith must have gone away very cross with his people. ... They told him they were going to sweep the country with the Budget, but now he is dependent on the Irish. He will find them hard taskmasters, but he won't give them Home Rule. He will get out of it somehow.'

On the risk of a pledge being extracted from the King to 'swamp' the Tory majority in the House of Lords, Chamberlain optimistically declared: 'The people are always on the side of the Crown, and such a step would mean disaster for the party that took it'—(cutting in Chamb. PP.).

From June until October 1910 the two major parties suspended hostilities while four of their leaders on either side were engaged in a 'Constitutional Conference' to find an agreed procedure for resolving deadlocks between the two Houses. Against recourse to the device of 'swamping' the predominantly Unionist House of Lords by a massive creation of four or five hundred Liberal peers there was much to be argued. The precedent of 1832 was not very convincing and Balfour took the view that a device could not be constitutional if it could not be repeated. The involvement of the King personally in what bade fair to become a ludicrous and discreditable episode was also highly undesirable. The Unionists advocated the counter-plan of a referendum to settle the fate of disputed measures of constitutional change. The Government seems to have objected to submitting a Home Rule Bill to a plebiscite, proposing as an alternative that 'if [the] general election, after [a] Home Rule Bill [was] rejected by [the] Lords, gave a majority to them, it should be treated as ordinary legislation' in the next Parliament.[448] It was the Redmond difficulty again, for the Irish could expect a massive vote in Great Britain against Home Rule as a single issue. On this difficulty the Constitutional Conference foundered.

At this point Balfour made another grave miscalculation. He failed to see that there was no escape from the dilemma which the Liberals posed him—a package bargain including some *ad hoc* arrangement over Home Rule, or *force majeure* and a swamping of the Upper House over the Parliament Bill. The only other course was an abject surrender, and as Garvin put it to him a little later, 'To have allowed the Conference to break down would appear a crime indeed if surrender followed now, when in consequence of a disastrous but irrevocable error only fighting can "save the face" of the Unionist party.'[449] Balfour should either have stuck to the line of 'no surrender', or reached a fair accommodation when it was possible.

Possibly the realities of the situation were obscured, as in the previous year, by the immediate prospect of another general election which might be won. But again there is evidence that Balfour did not expect to gain a majority in the December elections of 1910. He lunched with the Chamberlains late in November, and according to Mrs Chamberlain's account 'he and

Joe agreed that they did not see how we could win enough for a victory, though both were full of confidence in the ultimate issue. . . .'450 The main emphasis of the party's appeal was not placed upon the Parliament Bill. For it was realized, as Milner had observed earlier in the year, that 'A majority of the people are . . . against the House of Lords *in any form*. No doubt they are also against Single Chamber government. But they are too thick-headed to see that, unless they turn this Government out, they are in for it. . . .'451 Instead, tariff reform was placed to the front.

Garvin still retained his influence, and his advice was to clear away all other distracting questions and side-shows. He was even prepared to accept Home Rule. 'Would not an Ireland', he asked, with 'federal Home Rule under the Quebec model send a solid majority of Conservatives to help defend in the Imperial Parliament nearly all we care for?'452 Balfour, he suggested, should make it clear that in the approaching election 'we shall fight for a strong Second Chamber as the "only bulwark" against socialism and all destruction; but that we shall not close the door to a reconsideration of the Irish question. . . .'453 There was far less reason to fear that Home Rule would lead to separation, for the Irish were now dependent on Great Britain for their exports and their old age pensions, and the land grievance had been removed. Thus 'the moderates in Ireland would always come out on top in any showdown with Great Britain'.454

Balfour naturally found this too much to swallow at once. But he accepted Garvin's idea that food taxes—the 'free food' factor—could be eliminated from the election. Garvin wanted to reduce the tariff reform propaganda to the 'red-hot, brief, pungent' style of the Radicals. They had simplified things. Their 'dream ' was 'Socialism and the earthly paradise', their 'bogey' was landlords. 'Our dream Imperial Strength and Industrial Security based upon tariff reform; and our bogey must be the freely importing foreigner.'455 Hence Garvin suggested to Sandars on 14 November that the corn tax, 'now the fifth wheel of the Preference coach', should be dropped and an electoral appeal made with the cry that 'At *this* election your vote will tax the foreigner but will not tax your food'.

Balfour was swayed, and sent Garvin's letter to Austen Chamberlain. He might have known that Austen, like his father, never saw that anything was to be gained by this kind of concession. The reply was contemptuous:

Austen Chamberlain–Balfour, 15 November 1910: Food taxes may be, and indeed are, a handicap, but to drop Preference would be destruction. I wouldn't do it if I could, and (what Garvin doesn't see), we *can't do it if we would*.

Fancy going to the country on a policy which is to keep the counties by persuading them that we *will* and to win the towns by persuading them that we won't!

Let us win or lose with credit.[456]

At this Balfour abandoned the idea of dropping food taxes directly out of the Unionist programme. There was, however, another way of achieving the same result, namely a slight variation of Balfour's double election pledge of 1904.

Garvin and Sandars decided that Balfour ought to announce that tariff reform when first introduced would be submitted to a referendum. Garvin asserted that Lancashire could only be won by such a referendum pledge. 'Austen', he wrote to Sandars on 27 November, 'has already done us and himself much harm by the fossilized rigidity of his attitude in a crisis like this; and the decision to refer Tariff Reform is simply inevitable. Why did we insist on "referring" by existing means the Budget to the People? Because its finance involved a gigantic innovation. So does Tariff Reform finance.'[457] Confirmation of Garvin's argument came the next day from Lansdowne, who sent in a letter reporting that Lord Derby attached 'very great importance to the point so far as Lancashire is concerned'. Lansdowne added his own decided advice in favour of the referendum pledge.[458] But from Scotland Austen signalled frantic dissent from the new line:

Austen Chamberlain–Balfour, 28 November 1910: Garvin's proposal seems to me bad, and I don't believe that he has thought out the consequences.

1. The House of Lords guided by Lansdowne who acted after consultation with the leaders of our party, has just laid down a policy which includes special provisions for dealing with finance.

No sooner is this scheme adopted by the party and the House of Lords than Garvin proposes to knock a hole in it. . . .

2. Whose vote will you gain? I don't believe the plan is worth a hundred votes in any constituency. . . .[459]

Balfour, however, had to consider the broad consistency of his now somewhat complicated strategy. He had 'referred' to the people the 1909 Budget, and he hoped to 'refer' the impending Parliament Bill. Probably he considered the manifest vindication of his own fairness and consistency the chief point to be gained. And so, speaking at the Albert Hall, he gave the referendum pledge which was to be his death warrant in the eyes of the militant tariff reformers. To them he appeared to be wantonly plunging their policy 'fathoms deep in futurity' for the sake of a litter of votes in Lancashire.

The referendum pledge came as a great shock to Chamberlain. Mrs Chamberlain's account conveys the impact of it upon the hitherto cordial atmosphere at Highbury:

Mrs Chamberlain–Mrs Endicott, 2 December 1910: A bolt from the blue fell upon us on Tuesday night, and I could not believe my eyes when I saw what Mr Balfour had committed himself to at the Albert Hall. He took up the Radical challenge and agreed to submit Tariff Reform to a Referendum!!! I could have cried. Poor Joe! Poor Austen! Just when their efforts seemed ready to be crowned with success, and the whole party brought into line, Mr Balfour strong for the policy and all going well, the Free Fooders coming over in shoals still disliking Tariff Reform, but hating it less than the Government proposals, and prepared to support the whole policy if need be. . . .

Joe is his usual controlled self over it, but I felt it was the irony of fate that at lunch on Tuesday he should speak to Sir Savile Crossley more enthusiastically than I have ever heard him of Mr Balfour's attitude and leadership. He thought every move had been excellent— and then to have this sprung upon him.[460]

Austen wrote to Balfour to say that his decision was a 'great discouragement'. Yet the Chamberlains came into line with Balfour. Leo Maxse and his group did not, and openly condemned Balfour's move. The seeds of the diehard revolt had been sown.

While Balfour's referendum pledge split the tariff reformers, his as yet undisclosed attitude to the Parliament Bill was calculated to produce a very serious schism in his own section of the Unionist party. For already, just after the unfavourable result of the December election was known, he was contemplating surrender. On being informed of this by Sandars, Garvin was incredulous. 'From the early days of the Budget fight', he wrote to Sandars, 'you and I seemed to agree that there should be no yielding to a threat of "guarantees".' Surrender would take the life out of the party. 'There would be an open schism and then deadly lassitude.' Unionist leadership responsible for accepting the Veto policy without compelling the execution of the threatened or already obtained guarantees 'would never be trusted or followed again'.[461]

The diehards had to admit that by forcing a massive creation of Liberal peers the Unionists would throw away the advantage of a Tory House of Lords. But what was a two-year delaying power worth, if the moral authority of the Lords was forfeited? Garvin therefore concluded: 'If we fight to the last against the Parliament Bill as it stands we should keep our party in great heart and increasing strength even if the 500 [peers] were made, nay largely because of that, and we could fight them with tremendous effect to force a referendum on Home Rule. Otherwise we should be morally discomfited at the beginning of that struggle.'[462] Sandars was not convinced, but thought that there was time for reflection. He felt that to allow the Lords to be swamped would be selling the pass to Home Rule. Again Garvin pressed the advantages of the other course:

Garvin–Sandars, 2 January 1911: In the worst event there can be no ambiguous procedure leading to Unionist surrender in a way that while accentuating a ministerial triumph really won by guarantees would screen ministerial responsibility, place all the public ignominy on us, and make the Unionist half of the nation not only sick, sore and sullen within itself, but full of suspicion, misunderstanding and coldness towards the Crown. Above all plainness. Let the Crown, as the Germans say, 'Seek refuge in publicity'. . . . If the guarantees are given to satisfy one side they ought to be executed to satisfy the other.[463]

Other reasons in favour of forcing a creation of peers occurred to Garvin. Once this had happened, the House of Lords could hardly be attacked again by those who had thus strengthened it. Hence the new Liberal peers, chosen for their approval of the Parliament Bill, could thereafter take an independent line, and not all of them could be guaranteed to accept an undisclosed Home Rule Bill. A small divergence on the part of only a few, on a question such as Ulster, would be enough to force a referendum. Whereas the other course, of relying on 'a dilatory process prolonged by the House of Lords as it is' would be futile. Home Rule would be passed

after two years without any further election, the Liberals meanwhile 'working social reform for all it was worth'.

There was much in Garvin's point of view, although the die-
hard line ran a distinct risk that the swamped House of Lords
would forthwith pass the Home Rule Bill sent up to it in the following session. This risk, nevertheless, was probably not so great
as was generally feared by Unionists. Here, certainly, was the
essence of the matter. The remarkable thing is that Balfour did
not invite his colleagues to discuss it. Instead he left them to
commit themselves to attitudes of 'no surrender', in doing which
they naturally assumed that he meant to follow out this course:
whereas in December 1910 he distinctly envisaged surrender.

He could not see how he might form a government, since a
third dissolution was out of the question. Hence he accepted that
Asquith might at any time in the course of the session of 1911
demand and obtain guarantees from the King to create the
requisite number of peers to force the Parliament Bill through the
Upper House. Much as he deplored any such action, believing that
a massive creation of peers was unconstitutional, he had no plan
for countering it. The most he could hope for was a royal intervention, backed by public feeling, in favour of some compromise
at the eleventh hour, and doubtless with this in mind Lansdowne
introduced measures for Lords' reform into the Upper House
in the new session. But this was a speculation, another gamble by
a leader already over his ears in political gambling debts. He knew
it. But instead of facing up to the hard dilemma of surrender or
swamping, between the choice that, as Sandars put it, 'the Lords
should strike their flag without firing a shot', or alternatively
'that the Government should be involved in the laughter and
ridicule which would accompany the appearance of this vast
mass of puppets', Balfour had 'not yet made up his mind'.

Thus the Unionist party was thrown into the struggle against
the Parliament Bill and allowed to take up advanced positions
without any inkling that its commander was debating whether
to surrender its supplies and strongholds in the rear. Austen
Chamberlain, for one, had no idea that surrender was contemplated. When, therefore, in July 1911 the Government informed
Balfour that the King had in the previous November given
pledges to create peers if and when necessary to ensure the passing

of the Bill, the shadow cabinet was totally unprepared for the situation. Much has been made of the November pledges, but it is difficult to see how they made any difference to the position. A resolute and experienced monarch might have refused to give them, but Balfour's idea that he could have gone to the country on the question was chimerical. Had the King given no pledges, there would have been no justification for Balfour to have accepted office in November 1910 or to have raised the question in the country. Equally, if Asquith had obtained no pledges, he could still have advised the creation of peers at the last moment, and his advice would have had to be accepted. Certainly Balfour himself had not seen how the King could have escaped the pressure from his ministers, and under his direction the Unionist shadow cabinet decided to surrender before the exact nature or date of the pledges had been confirmed. The operative fact was that the King acted on the advice of his ministers, as he was bound to do, and no providential escape route, such as Balfour had hoped for, was presented to him.

Meanwhile the forward sections of the party were deeply committed to 'no surrender'. Austen had accepted Balfour's referendum pledge for the December elections, but held, with other tariff reformers, that it did not survive the party's defeat. The idea of using what Balfour called a 'poll of the people' to resolve legislative deadlocks or sanction measures of fundamental constitutional change was scouted by Asquith and the Liberals. It was too transparently a device adopted for tactical reasons by Balfour and Lansdowne, and indeed it was the keystone of their counter-proposals to the Parliament Bill, moved by the House of Lords in the form of amendments. Balfour and Lansdowne had in fact adopted the referendum pledge for ulterior motives. Even so, they could have retained the support of the tariff reformers if they had persevered in the Lords' amendments to the end. But Balfour's preference for surrender, confided privately to Garvin months before, made nonsense of the whole manœuvre, and Garvin was driven back into alliance with Austen Chamberlain.

From March 1911 *The Observer* espoused the die-hard cause in line with Maxse's *National Review*. No Unionist voice was raised in favour of accepting the Liberals' Parliament Bill, while Balfour, following what Garvin called his 'Mr Micawber' policy, kept his counsel. Even Austen remained entirely unsuspecting of his train of thought. When therefore in July Balfour opted for surrender, Austen was totally unprepared for it. 'I have discussed this matter with you', he wrote reprovingly to Balfour, 'in council of your colleagues and in conversation. Nothing that you have said on any of these occasions has prepared me for the line you have now taken up.'[464] The first intimation that the King had given pledges was received via Lord Esher on 5 July. And yet it was prior to this date that the first intimations of surrender wrung from Garvin another despairing protest:

Garvin–Sandars, 28 June 1911: I am entirely desolated by the prospect of a final fiasco on the Veto Bill. Last Saturday I could not write a word. . . .

Of course every strong word written now will be a boomerang if we let the thing through at the last. . . .

How after solemnly bringing forward amendments of such weight we can retreat from them, my dull head cannot conceive.

Infinitely better, were capitulation contemplated, to do it now immediately after the Coronation on a big dramatic plea of the King's interest. To push amendments, leading all our simple people to believe that a real fight is intended, and to surrender at the last, this means the very maximum of mischief, prolonging our ignominy and aggravating the injury to our cause and the sullen disgust of our supporters. . . .

No making of peers could give this Government a majority in the House of Lords on Home Rule. Yet our leaders would not be compromised. The threat to repeal the Bill would not then be a farce. . . .[465]

Thus the November pledges cannot be regarded as having altered the situation, and were not viewed by tariff reformers as of any consequence. Nor was it only the tariff reformers who took this unflinching line. The die-hard peers who followed Lord Halsbury had declared for 'no surrender' before July, and they were joined by the militant free-fooders, Lord Hugh and Lord Robert Cecil.

The split in the party was in fact one between the 'forward' active or militant elements, and the older, staider leaders. It was the kind of divergence which had emerged in earlier party squabbles over the respective merits of an 'aggressive' or a 'defensive' programme. Nor did the rift heal with the passing of the Parliament Act on 10 August, aided by the votes of 37 Unionist peers and many abstentions. Lansdowne, who first gave the public word to 'scuttle', came in for bitter denunciation in the Unionist press, especially for not condemning and disowning the 'Judas' group of Unionist peers who had gone into the Government lobby. The most virulent and distorted accounts of the 'great betrayal' were published by Leo Maxse. 'Any attempt to replace our heads under the Balfourian yoke', he wrote in one of his editorials, 'is doomed to failure. B.[alfour] M.[ust] G.[o].' The 'gross and base betrayal' had freed from their allegiance to Balfour all those who had 'fought for tariff reform in the Chamberlain spirit'. Some countenance to this kind of attitude had been given by Chamberlain, who in a message to the Halsbury group had written: 'I heartily support the object. The country owes a great debt to Lord Halsbury, since in the crisis of her fate he has refused to surrender his principles.' Austen, likewise, had commended Halsbury for saving 'our party from disgrace and our cause from disaster'. A very severe strain was placed on his loyalty, which was intensified after August by the anti-Balfour activities of the Halsbury group.

Early in October the forward elements in the party formed the Halsbury Club, a development of great importance and significance. Balfour, having been informed by his party organizer, Steel-Maitland, that the Club was not hostile, but 'muddleheaded', affected to ridicule its aims. But it was a challenge to him which, had he not already been bent on retiring, would have probably forced him to go. Lord Willoughby de Broke convened the first meeting of the Club for 12 October by a circular letter telling how some of the Halsbury group—including Milner, Amery, Selborne, Salisbury, Carson, Wyndham and F. E. Smith—had met and decided that the spirit of the die-hard movement should become a 'permanent force in the party': and to seek to keep together 'that mass of opinion both in and out of Parliament that is looking for a definite lead'.466 With the invitation sent to Austen Chamberlain went a message from his brother Neville saying that the diehards were 'ready and anxious' to follow his lead. Neville added on his own account: 'I feel that this is the crucial point of your career. . . . Of course I am not suggesting any open revolt at present, but no doubt a difference of opinion will arise sometime (if A.J.B. does not resign first) and you will get your way if you have the Die-hards solid behind you.'467 Austen, just returned from abroad, was briefed on 9 October by Wyndham. He was told that the group 'could go no further' without him, and he agreed to join them in pursuit of the following objectives:

They wished to speak more plainly about national dangers and National Defence; to give more definite form to the Unionist programme of Social Reform; and in all things to take a more vigorous fighting line; to act in common within the party and to speak in unison both in the House and out of it. They had decided to back Carson for all they were worth in his resistance to Home Rule. . . .

. . . neither Bob [Lord Robert Cecil] nor Hugh Cecil would give any more trouble about Tariff Reform. Hugh said he would never be a Tariff Reformer but that he wished now that we should carry Tariff Reform and that quickly. Bob he regarded as even more advanced.468

These were momentous decisions. The die-hards had been taught by a socialist budget to accept a tariff reform one—and they regarded themselves as now absolved from the referendum pledge. They had been taught by the cave-in of hereditary peers to accept the idea of elected ones in preference to the 'hanky-panky' of earlier Unionist projects for Lords' reform. The grave international situation convinced them that national service should be introduced. These ideas were powerfully advocated by Milner, whom Austen had tried to get admitted into the shadow cabinet; and it was Austen who persuaded Milner to adhere to the Club. Milner went further than the group, in his support for a completely elective second chamber and a Federal United Kingdom on the Canadian or South African models, but was persuaded to keep quiet on devolution. The Die-hards did not wish to strengthen the hands of the Irish separatists by any weakening of the traditional Unionist stance.

There was lively indignation in the Carlton at the formation of the Halsbury Club, seen as a threat to the Conservative sections of the party, and a counter-movement was promoted by Curzon. On 24 October a meeting was called at Devonshire House, attended by Lords St. Aldwyn, (Hicks Beach), Curzon, Midleton, Londonderry, Derby, and Chilston (Akers-Douglas), with Steel-Maitland, Lyttelton, Long, Chaplin, and Bonar Law, to discuss 'the situation as accentuated by the Halsbury Club, and the best means by which they could help Balfour'. The result was that

Bonar Law and Long were deputed to see Carson and obtain from the Halsbury group a declaration of loyalty to Balfour. Carson would do nothing without Austen, and Austen loyally undertook to make a graceful acknowledgment of Balfour's leadership at the Halsbury Club meeting of 6 November.

It had been with considerable reluctance that Austen had become involved in a distinct and overt break-away movement. He had done so not to challenge Balfour, but to concert action for the immediate future, with the imminent prospect of a very critical autumn session of Parliament. In the planning of concerted action Chamberlain played a not insignificant part, of which a glimpse appears in a letter by his wife:

Mrs Chamberlain–Mrs Endicott, 18 October 1911: . . . Joe has had some good talks with him [Austen] and has become very much interested in discussing with him all the difficulties and complexities of the present situation, and the immediate plan of campaign during the autumn session. 'I am very pleased with Austen, and approve his ideas', was his verdict one night [i.e. 13 October].[469]

Milner paid some visits to Highbury, and had 'much political talk'. He was 'not very keen about their having formed a Club', a misgiving shared by both Joe and Austen.

The truth was that Balfour had abdicated his functions. He had been 'much concerned at the differences of opinion' at the shadow cabinet in July which had debated the policy of surrender to the Veto Bill. One afternoon a little later he was told that Selborne had asked for a shadow cabinet to consider the question of payment of M.P.s and the Naval Prize Bill. Balfour answered promptly 'I do not mean to have another shadow cabinet'.[470] He had grown so unused to consulting his colleagues on matters of party action that the idea of calling shadow cabinets was now thoroughly distasteful to him. On the day of the final division over the Parliament Bill he had fled abroad to Bad Gastein, and on his return he allowed the party to go to pieces. He was told plainly by Steel-Maitland, on his return to Scotland early in September, of the 'dissatisfaction in the ranks of the party', and of the 'necessity of drastic efforts being made by Mr Balfour to bring his colleagues and the Party into line'. Instead, Balfour allowed the accumulating signs of discontent to form an excuse for retirement and for two months did nothing.

By the end of October he began to break the news of his decision to retire to his closest colleagues. Austen learnt of the decision on 2 November, and wrote a letter of protest. There was, he said, no obvious successor, and in the present situation of 'distorted perspectives' there would be only disputes and disunity. Besides which, there was the impending struggle over Home Rule. Balfour could 'take part in that struggle only as leader. To pretend that anyone else was leader whilst you still sat in the House and took an active part in the debates would be impossible.'[471] But Balfour's mind was quite made up, and it only remained for Austen to pay a respectful tribute, regretting that he had in the summer 'appeared in the public eye as taking a different course from yours':

Austen Chamberlain–Balfour, 5 November 1911: You have given me your confidence in most generous measure. In critical times I learned to know you and if I may say so to love you. My position between you and my father was not always an easy one, but I look back on those troubled years and feel that it is to him and to you that I owe all I am and that I was able, thanks to the confidence you both gave to me, to play the part of connecting link and perhaps save the Party from a disastrous split.[472]

In the light of the new development, the Halsbury Club meeting on 6 November partook of an unlooked-for character. Balfour's decision was not yet made public, and Austen and Lord Halsbury, who knew of it, were obliged to threaten resignation unless a pro-Balfour resolution were accepted. The proceedings were protracted, members objecting to the resolution 'because to register it now would appear to stultify their earlier existence as a body which was formed to keep Mr Balfour in touch with the forward movement in his party'.[473] Eventually, after Wyndham and F. E. Smith had been let into the secret, the resistance was overcome. Such was the nature of the die-hard spirit that Balfour was up against. Two days later the news was quietly broken to a small public meeting in the City, where Balfour covered his retreat with pleasantries about the danger of elderly statesmen becoming 'somewhat petrified' in old courses. Returning from the City, Balfour went to Buckingham Palace, and then came back to Carlton Gardens. 'After some further conversation' with his secretary, who had accompanied him, Balfour signed his letters, and, Sandars notes, 'I walked with him to his motor and said goodbye, and he left for his brother's house at Woking.' Thus quietly and unobtrusively the brilliant but aloof leader relinquished the reins.

Unluckily for Austen's personal fortunes, his recent association with the die-hard group presented his curiously suspicious and jealous rival, Walter Long, with an opportunity of heading the pro-Balfour section of the party and opposing his candidature for the leadership. Long succeeded in gaining the support of roughly half the parliamentary party in what was really an obstructive candidature—for all agreed that Long himself would be a disastrous choice—and hence Austen volunteered to stand down in favour of Bonar Law if Long did so too. Thus it was that a man who had never sat in a cabinet came to the front. Bonar Law was a hard-hitting, incisive speaker and a notable tariff reformer, but also acceptable to the Balfourite section as a Conservative who had prudently avoided taking any part in the internal party feuds of the summer. In some respects Bonar Law resembled the elder Chamberlain, and his ambition and aggressive qualities made him seem to some a better choice than Austen, who 'always played the game and always lost'. Austen was let down even by some of his own friends. 'I have heard various things from the inside', Mrs Chamberlain wrote to her mother shortly after the election of Bonar Law, 'of the action of individuals who one might have thought would be ranged among Austen's supporters, which I should not like the family to know, for their indignation would know no bounds.'[474]

Chamberlain took the disappointment of his son's defeat calmly: '. . . he received your news', Mrs Chamberlain wrote to Austen, 'as he always does, in his strong, firm way. "I do not see that under the circumstances he could do otherwise." That is his verdict.' But it is clear from other observations of Mrs Chamberlain that the disappointment was not a transitory one:

Mrs Chamberlain–Mrs Endicott, 18 November 1911: Joe has been so strong about it. Of course he regrets it and perhaps wonders whether the course of things could have been altered—but he is reconciled by the thought that on those terms Austen could not have done justice either to the cause or himself.

At all events harmony is secured, and a strong and militant Tariff Reformer is at the head of affairs.

Mrs Chamberlain–Mrs Endicott, 22 November 1911: I do not believe, feeling as he did, he [Austen] could have overcome the patent hostility which permeated the rank and file, who cared more for the preservation of the old Tory traditions than for the policy and cause.[475]

The position of tariff reform was indeed worse than the Chamberlains realized. The cause was bound to be eclipsed by the Home Rule crisis leading up to what seemed an inevitable civil war over the fate of Ulster. But other strange and incalculable factors were seemingly steering the course of affairs to the brink of immeasurable disaster—suffragettes and syndicalists at home, and grave developments in international relations abroad. The landmarks of 1903 had largely disappeared, and much of Chamberlain's original scheme of tariff reform needed revision. Yet the Unionists were still to spend much energy in sterile disputes over food taxes. Like Balfour, the tariff reformers themselves had become somewhat fossilized.

The original inspiration of Chamberlain's movement had been a compounding of the ideals of imperialism and social reform. The practical policy of tariff reform was an adaptation of this to the fighting position of the Unionist party at the beginning of the century, and in particular to its requirement of a dynamic programme capable of progressive development. Under the banner of tariff reform the Unionist party had undergone a revolutionary change in its organization and its approach to political warfare. The progress which it had already made along these lines by 1909 enabled it to preserve some faith in its future and some rallying point for its militant spirits through the most shattering defeats which any British party has ever suffered. Mere traditional Conservatism or a purely defensive philosophy would not have served for this purpose, as the conversion of men like Lord Hugh Cecil testified. In the conditions of the twentieth century there had to be some constructive ideal such as Chamberlain had provided. From this point of view, tariff reform had achieved its essential object by 1911. It was a cause with a future. But it had already transformed the Unionist party, which was able in 1912 to abandon the distinction between Liberal Unionist and Conservative, the party having been revitalized from its base upwards.

In 1914 Chamberlain resigned his seat, and died a few months later. He did not quite live to see how the tangled deadlocks of party strife were resolved in the cauldron of the Great War, nor could he have imagined the sea-change which the war would effect in the whole political system. His death closes an era, and the direct legacies of his tariff reform and other campaigns to the post-war future cannot be regarded as of signal importance. It is only in the most comprehensive sense that his approach, his spirit and style can be said to have left their mark on other men in different circumstances. In this broad view Chamberlain stands as the prophet and architect of British democracy at the close of the patrician era, and as happens almost always with English statesmen of the first rank, it is not his theories or policies but his style and method which have proved of most lasting significance.

Source Notes

[1] *Physics and Politics,* chap.1, pp.8–9, which first appeared in a *Fortnightly Review* article of November 1867.

[2] For details of the League's development see *The Educational Reporter* (Birmingham), October 1869–January 1870, *passim.* Also *Birmingham Daily Post,* 6 January 1870, summarizing the League's *Monthly Paper.*

[3] Chamberlain papers, University of Birmingham.

[4] *Ibid.*

[5] *Ibid.* Chamberlain–Dixon, 16 July 1870.

[6] Chamb. PP.

[7] *Ibid.* To Morley, 13 September 1873.

[8] 26 June 1873, quoted in *National Review,* February 1933, p.249.

[9] Chamb. PP., Wright–J. T. Bruce, (telegram), 9 August 1873, summarizing what he had reported to Chamberlain.

[10] Chamb. PP., to Bunce, 10 August 1873, regretting that Bunce could not join the deputation to Bright the next day.

[11] Chamb. PP., 19 August 1873. Cf. J. L. Garvin, *Chamberlain* I, p.161.

[12] Chamb. PP.

[13] *Ibid.*

[14] *Ibid.*

[15] Morley's phrase in *Fortnightly Review,* January 1876.

[16] Entry in a commonplace book, Morley library, Ashburne Hall, Manchester.

[17] F. W. Hirst, *Early Life and Letters of John Morley,* I, pp.178 and 183.

[18] *Fortnightly Review,* September, 1876, p.398.

[19] *Ibid.,* August 1876, p.261.

[20] Speech by Chamberlain of 9 April 1877.

[21] Garvin, *op. cit.,* I, p.243. 10 May 1877.

[22] Speech of 9 April 1877.

[23] Reports in *Manchester Guardian* of 14–17 January 1878, and 13 September 1879.

[24] Chamb. PP., 25 January 1880.

[25] H. M. Hyndman, *Record of an Adventurous Life,* p.247.

[26] To Dilke, quoted in Garvin, *op. cit.,* I, p.326.

[27] Chamb. PP.

[28] To R. J. Page Hopps, 21 December 1881, quoted in C. H. D. Howard, *A Political Memoir,* p.20.

[29] Quoted in C. H. D. Howard, *op. cit.,* pp.18–20.

[30] Garvin, *op. cit.,* I, p.345.

[31] C. H. D. Howard, *op. cit.,* p.17, note.

[32] Chamb. PP.

[33] Chamb. PP., Chamberlain–Spencer, 26 May 1882.

[34] *Ibid.*

[35] Chamb. PP.

[36] *Ibid.*

[37] *Ibid.,* 31 August 1882.

[38] *Ibid.*

[39] *Ibid.,* 23 July 1883.

[40] Helen Taylor PP., London School of Economics.

[41] Chamb. PP.

[42] *Ibid.,* Memo. on Land Nationalization by Chamberlain and Arthur Chamberlain, which appeared in the *Pall Mall Gazette* of 24 and 29 January 1883.

[43] Chamb. PP., 31 December 1882. Chamberlain adds: 'I am strongly inclined to believe that something much more drastic than free trade in land is looming in the near future, and I am told that the London working men are buying George and Wallace's books on land nationalization by thousands.'

[44] *Fortnightly Review,* December 1884, pp.724–5.

[45] Henry Broadhurst PP., London School of Economics.

[46] Broadhurst PP. Letter to Broadhurst cited above.

[47] Speech at Birmingham of 5 January 1885. Cf. Garvin, *op. cit.,* I, p.549.

[48] Speech at Ipswich, 14 January 1885.

[49] Speech of 28 April (*Times* report of 29 April).

[50] Speech at Ipswich, 14 January 1885.

[51] Chamb. PP., 28 December 1883.

[52] Chamb. PP. 29 November 1883.

[53] Chamb. PP., Labouchere–Chamberlain, 18 September 1883.

[54] Chamb. PP., 22 December 1883.

[55] *Ibid.,* 18 December 1883.

[56] Speech at Devonshire Club, 23 July 1884.

[57] *Ibid.*

[58] Speech of 7 October 1884.

[59] Chamb. PP., 20 December 1884.

[60] Chamb. PP.

[61] *Ibid.*

[62] *Ibid.,* Trevelyan–Chamberlain, 27 December 1883.

[63] Chamb. PP., quoted in C. H. D. Howard, *op. cit.,* p.141.

[64] Chamb. PP.

[65] Cabinet paper of 25 March quoted above.

[66] Quoted in Ramm, *Correspondence of Gladstone and Granville*, II, pp.366–7.

[67] *Ibid.*

[68] *Ibid.*

[69] Chamb. PP.

[70] *Ibid.*, 18 June 1885.

[71] Gladstone–Derby, 17 July and reply of 19 July 1885, quoted and summarized in John Morley, *Gladstone*, III, p.215.

[72] *Times* leader, 19 September 1885.

[73] Chamb. PP., Chamberlain–Harcourt, 25 September 1885.

[74] 20 September 1885, quoted in Garvin, *op. cit.*, II, p.94.

[75] The documents bearing on this meeting are quoted in C. H. D. Howard, *op. cit.*, and Ramm, *op. cit.*

[76] B. M. Add. MS. 46015. Card from Labouchere–Herbert Gladstone of 10 October, sent with Healy's letter of 7 October.

[77] Letter quoted in full in J. L. Hammond, *Gladstone and the Irish Nation*, p.416.

[78] Add. MS. 46015. 6 October 1885.

[79] T. M. Healy–Labouchere from Dublin, 15 October 1885, quoted in full in Thorold, *Labouchere*, pp.235–7.

[80] Add. MS. 46015.

[81] *Ibid.*, Labouchere–Herbert Gladstone, 20 October.

[82] Passages quoted in this para. are from Garvin, *op. cit.*, II, pp.118, 113–14.

[83] Add. MS. 46015. Cf. with Gladstone's letter of 14 November to his son quoted in Hammond, *op. cit.*, pp.447–8. Hammond makes no mention of Herbert Gladstone's transmission of the substance of his father's letter.

[84] Chamb. PP.

[85] Add. MS. 46015. Labouchere–Herbert Gladstone, 3 December 1885, reporting a conversation with Lord Randolph Churchill.

[86] *Ibid.*

[87] *Ibid.*, 12 December 1885.

[88] *Ibid.*, Herbert Gladstone–Labouchere, 9 December 1885.

[89] Chamb. PP., 6 December 1885.

[90] For the report of Dilke's speech sent by Lyon Playfair to Herbert Gladstone see letter in Add. MS. 44280 f.208.

[91] Add. MS. 46015. Labouchere–Herbert Gladstone, 17 December 1885.

[92] *Ibid.*, same letter.

[93] *Ibid.,* Labouchere–Herbert Gladstone, 22 December 1885.

[94] Granville–Gladstone, 21 October 1885, quoted in Ramm, *op. cit.,* II, p.410.

[95] Add. MS. 46015. Letter quoted above. Hammond's contention (*op. cit.,* p.442) that Gladstone did not know of the Conservative decision is difficult to sustain in the light of this letter.

[96] Granville–Gladstone, 27 December 1885, in Ramm, *op. cit.,* II, p.419.

[97] Quoted in *Hammond, op. cit.,* pp.451–4.

[98] See esp. Labouchere–Herbert Gladstone, 19 December 1885 (Add. MS. 46015).

[99] Granville–Gladstone, 28 December 1885, in Ramm, *op. cit.,* II, p.420.

[100] To Harcourt, 6 January 1886, quoted in Garvin, *op. cit.,* II, p.162.

[101] e.g. Garvin, *op. cit.,* II, p.175.

[102] Chamb. PP., Maxse–Chamberlain, 12 June 1887.

[103] Chamb. PP.

[104] Cf. Garvin, *op. cit.,* II, pp.147–8, quoting other sections of this letter.

[105] Chamb. PP.

[106] 3 January 1886, in Ramm, *op. cit.,* II, p.422.

[107] Chamberlain–Harcourt, 6 January 1886, in Garvin, *op. cit.,* II, p.162.

[108] The letter is given in full in C. H. D. Howard, *op. cit.,* pp.187–8.

[109] Morley, *Recollections,* I, p.215.

[110] Chamb. PP.

[111] Morley, *Recollections,* I, p.216.

[112] Chamb. PP.

[113] Morley, *Gladstone,* III, p.305.

[114] To Gladstone, 12 April 1886, in Ramm, *op. cit.,* II, p.441.

[115] To Chamberlain, 3 May 1886, quoted in Garvin, *op. cit.,* II, p.224.

[116] Ramm, *op. cit.,* II, p.447.

[117] Chamb. PP., Gladstone–Rev. R. W. Dale, 29 April 1886.

[118] Chamb. PP.

[119] *Ibid.*

[120] Labouchere–Chamberlain, 1 May 1886, quoting Morley's words: in Thorold, *Labouchere,* p.300.

[121] Garvin, *op. cit.,* II, p.231.

[122] Morley, *Recollections,* I, p.208.

[123] Chamb. PP.

[124] Dale–Gladstone, 26 April 1886, quoted in A. W. W. Dale, *Life of R. W. Dale,* pp. 455–7.

[125] Chamb. PP.

[126] Dale–Morley, 9 May 1886, quoted in A. W. W. Dale. *Life of R. W. Dale,* pp.457–8.

[127] 10 May 1886, quoted in Garvin, *op. cit.,* II, p.228.

[128] Chamb. PP.

[129] P. W. Clayden, *England under Coalition,* pp.73–4.

[130] Chamb. PP.

[131] To Gladstone, 21 May 1886, in Ramm, *op. cit.,* II, p.449.

[132] Chamb. PP.

[133] 29 May 1886, quoted in Garvin, *op. cit.,* II, p.241.

[134] Chamb. PP.

[135] *Ibid.*

[136] Chamb. PP., Caine–Chamberlain, 30 May 1886, from which the figures in this and the following para. have been derived.

[137] Chamb. PP.

[138] *Pall Mall Gazette,* 3 June 1886.

[139] *Ibid.,* 2 June 1886, p.8.

[140] *Birmingham Daily Post,* 3 June 1886, p.8.

[141] *Ibid.,* 5 June 1886.

[142] *Ibid.,* 7 June 1886.

[143] *Ibid.,* 8 June, p.8.

[144] Taken from an analysis of the division in *The Times,* 9 June 1886.

[145] Ramm, *op. cit.,* II, p.451, footnotes 1 and 2.

[146] Morley, *Gladstone,* III, p.342.

[147] *Birmingham Daily Post,* 5 June 1886.

[148] *Pall Mall Gazette,* 10 June 1886. Article by 'A sanguine Conservative'.

[149] Chamb. PP.

[150] *Ibid.,* Chamberlain–Arthur Chamberlain, 7 June 1886.

[151] *Ibid.,* same–same, 9 June (two letters).

[152] Chamb. PP.

[153] 9 July 1886, in Ramm, *op. cit.,* II, p.458.

[154] Chamb. PP.

[155] Ramm, *op. cit.,* II, pp.455–6, Gladstone–Granville, 6 July 1886: 'I apprehend we must now give up all idea of getting a majority for our Irish Bill. . . .' (and of the Liberal Unionists): 'I take it that most of the followers, or many of them, may still be our followers except upon this question.'

[156] Ramm, *op. cit.,* II, p.458. Gladstone–Granville, 9 July 1886, paraphrasing a possibility which, as he tells Granville, 'you justly bring into view'.

[157] *Ibid.,* p.459. Gladstone–Granville, 12 July 1886.

[158] A. G. Gardiner, *Harcourt,* I, pp.594–5.

159 Chamb. PP.

160 Gardiner, *op. cit.*, II, p.3, 20 July 1886.

161 Chamb. PP., Chamberlain–Harcourt, 21 July 1886.

162 Blanche E. C. Dugdale, *Balfour*, I, pp.103-4.

163 Chamb. PP.

164 Beatrice Webb, *My Apprenticeship*, p.107.

165 Cf. *Diaries of Beatrice Webb*, 1924–32, ed. Margaret Cole, Appx. p.312, which quotes the first sentences of this extract.

166 *Ibid.*, pp.314-15, which quotes this extract but with altered tenses and slight discrepancies.

167 *Ibid.*, p.316.

168 Beatrice Webb's diary (Passfield Trust PP.), 12 January 1884.

169 *Ibid.*, quoted in *My Apprenticeship*, pp.107-8.

170 Beatrice Webb's diary.

171 *Ibid.*, 24 January 1884. The diary entries were made at irregular intervals of days or weeks, and the date cited is usually some time after the event described, but can also be before.

172 Beatrice Webb's diary.

173 *Ibid.* (Post), 24 January 1884.

174 *Ibid.*,

175 Beatrice Webb, *My Apprenticeship*, pp. 108-9.

176 Beatrice Webb's diary.

177 *Ibid.* (Post), 24 January 1884.

178 *Ibid.*, 28 July 1884.

179 *Ibid.* (Post), 24 January 1884.

180 *Ibid.*, 22 April 1884.

181 *Ibid.*

182 *Ibid.*, 16 March 1884.

183 *Ibid.*, 12 May 1886, describing the previous July.

184 *Ibid.*, 16 October 1886, describing an episode of 'last winter'.

185 This and other letters of Chamberlain are interleaved in the diary.

186 Chamb. PP., Beatrice Potter–Chamberlain, 27 February 1886.

187 Beatrice Webb PP.

188 Chamb. PP.

189 Beatrice Webb PP.

190 *Ibid.*

191 Beatrice Webb's diary, 8 August 1887.

192 Copy of note in Beatrice Webb's diary.

193 Beatrice Webb PP.

194 Beatrice Webb's diary, 1 January 1901.

195 *Ibid.*, same date.

196 *Ibid.*, same date.

[197] Beatrice Webb's diary, 1 January 1901.

[198] A. W. W. Dale, *op. cit.*, p.468. Dale–Guinness Rogers, 8 July 1886.

[199] Chamb. PP., 27 December 1886.

[200] Gardiner, *Harcourt,* II, p.26. 7 January 1887.

[201] Ramm, *op. cit.,* II, p.421. Granville–Gladstone, 2 January 1887, wrongly ascribed to 1886.

[202] Gardiner, *Harcourt,* II, p.24. 3 January 1886.

[203] Chamb. PP.

[204] Chamb. PP., Bright–Arthur Chamberlain, 11 February 1887, declining to write a preface for a collection of Chamberlain's speeches on the Irish question. Also Chamberlain–Arthur Chamberlain, 18 February, mentioning Bright's remark about the 'piece of impudence' and commenting: 'This old man is not friendly!'

[205] Chamb. PP., Trevelyan–Chamberlain, 17 February 1887, quoted below.

[206] Chamb. PP.

[207] *Ibid.*

[208] *Ibid.,* 3 March 1887.

[209] *Ibid.*

[210] *Ibid.,* 3 April 1889.

[211] *Ibid.,* 3 May 1891.

[212] *Ibid.*

[213] *Ibid.,* 29 April 1891.

[214] Chamb. PP.

[215] *Ibid.*

[216] *Ibid.,* A. V. Dicey–Chamberlain, 1 May 1893.

[217] *Ibid.,* memo. by Chamberlain, 13 November 1894.

[218] *Ibid.*

[219] *Ibid.,* memo of 13 November quoted above.

[220] *Ibid.*

[221] Speech at Queen's Hall, 8 November 1894.

[222] A. G. Gardiner, *John Benn and the Progressive Movement,* pp.205-7.

[223] Beatrice Webb's diary, March 1895.

[224] *Ibid.,* 13 March 1896, quoted in Sir G. Gibbon and R. W. Bell, *History of the London County Council,* p.96.

[225] Chamb. PP.

[226] *Ibid.*

[227] *Ibid.*

[228] *Ibid.*

[229] *Ibid.*

[230] *Ibid.*

[231] *Ibid.*

[232] *Ibid.*

[233] *Ibid.*

[234] *Ibid.*

[235] *Ibid.*

[236] *Ibid.* Cf. Auberon Herbert, *A politician in trouble about his Soul* (1884) p.184, on socialists and deliverance from 'this universal sloppiness'.

[237] Chamb. PP.

[238] Speech of 23 May 1895.

[239] Chamb. PP.

[240] Balfour PP., Add. MS. 49773. Chamberlain–Balfour, 3 February 1898.

[241] *Ibid.*, Add. MS. 49707. Selborne–Balfour, 7 July 1898.

[242] Public Record Office, Cab. 1/2. Memo. by Balfour, 5 September 1898.

[243] Chamb. PP., minute by Chamberlain.

[244] *Ibid.*, comments by officials. Frederick Graham was Chief Clerk, Sir Edward Wingfield, Permanent Under-Secretary, at the Colonial Office.

[245] P.R.O. Colonial Office files, 417/279. Minute by Chamberlain addressed to Graham.

[246] Chamb. PP.

[247] C.O. 417/279. Minute by Chamberlain, 28 April 1899.

[248] C.O. 417/261. Minute of 23 May 1899.

[249] *Ibid.*, 25 May 1899.

[250] C.O. 417/261. 27 May No. 3. Last sentence quoted in Wilde, *Chamberlain and the South African Republic*, p.106.

[251] C.O. 417/262. Typed minutes of the Conference.

[252] C. Headlam, *Milner Papers*, pp.445-6. 25 June 1899.

[253] C.O. 417/279.

[254] C.O. 417/262.

[255] C.O. 417/279. Tel. to Milner, 16 June 1899.

[256] C.O. 417/262. 2 June No. 2.

[257] *Ibid.*

[258] *Ibid.*

[259] *Ibid.*

[260] *Ibid.*

[261] C.O. 417/262. 30 June 1899.

[262] Balfour PP., B.M. Add. MS. 49746. Lord Rothschild–Balfour, 6 July 1899.

[263] C.O. 417/279. Chamberlain–Milner, 6 July 1899, quoted in Wilde, *op. cit.*, p.117.

[264] *Ibid.*

[265] Headlam, *op. cit.,* I, p.468. Chamberlain–Milner, 18 July 1899.

[266] *Ibid.,* I, p.471.

[267] Balfour PP., Add. MSS. 49707, 49773. 20–21 July 1899.

[268] C.O. 417/264.

[269] *Ibid.* Cf. J. S. Marais, *Fall of Kruger's Republic,* p.303 (where commission is misquoted as 'conference').

[270] C.O. 417/264. Milner–Chamberlain, 10 August No. 3.

[271] *Ibid.,* minute of 13 August, quoted in Wilde, *op. cit.,* p.129.

[272] C.O. 417/264. Milner–Chamberlain, 7 August No. 2.

[273] Letter to Milner of 11 May 1899.

[274] C.O. 417/264. Milner–Chamberlain, 15 August No. 1, quoting two telegrams from Greene of which shortened versions were printed in a Blue Book.

[275] Personal details are taken from Mrs Chamberlain's letters to her mother (Chamb. PP.).

[276] Headlam, *op. cit.,* I, pp. 489–90. Also C.O. 417/264, Chamberlain–Milner 16 August No. 6.

[277] C.O. 417/264.

[278] Garvin, *op cit.,* III, pp.435-6.

[279] C.O. 417/265

[280] *Ibid.*

[281] *Ibid.*

[282] *Ibid.*

[283] *Ibid.,* Milner–Chamberlain, 20 August No. 2.

[284] *Ibid.,* Milner–Chamberlain, 22 August No. 3.

[285] *Ibid.,* Selborne–Chamberlain, 23 August 1899.

[286] *Ibid.*

[287] *Ibid.* The last sentences are quoted in Wilde, *op. cit.,* 134, and Marais, *op. cit.,* p.312.

[288] C.O. 417/265. Milner–Chamberlain, 26 August No. 2, received in London 6.40 P.M. same day.

[289] *Ibid.*

[290] *Ibid.*

[291] *Ibid.* Sent as telegram the next day, omitting the comment on Milner.

[292] B(ritish) P(arliamentary) P(apers). Vol. LXIV, 1899, pp.714 *seq.*

[293] Chamb. PP.

[294] C.O. 417/266.

[295] *Ibid.*

[296] B.P.P. 1899, Vol LXIV.

[297] C.O. 417/266.

[298] Chamb. PP.

[299] C.O. 417/267.

[300] C.O. 417/280.

[301] Hicks Beach PP., Lord Salisbury–Beach, 29 March 1902.

[302] Balfour PP., B.M. Add. MS. 49773.

[303] Balfour PP., Add. MS. 49853. Balfour–Rt. Hon. H. Hobhouse, 12 September 1899.

[304] *Ibid.*

[305] For the opposition's attitudes and criticisms, and Chamberlain's self-justification, see *Hansard,* debate of 19 October 1899.

[306] Chamb. PP. Cf. Garvin, *op. cit.,* III, p.520.

[307] C.O. 417/280.

[308] Chamb. PP., Chamberlain–Balfour, 4 August 1902.

[309] Beatrice Webb PP.

[310] Beatrice Webb's diary, 4 May 1902.

[311] Chamb. PP.

[312] Add. MS. 49769. Devonshire–Balfour, 6 December 1901.

[313] Add. MS. 49787.

[314] Add. MS. 49787. Cf. B. M. Allen, *Morant,* pp.166-9, quoting from this memo. but also freely paraphrasing and distorting the wording. Morant, for instance, never told Chamberlain '. . . your war has made further recourse to State grants impossible', as in Allen's version (quoted by Julian Amery, *Chamberlain,* IV, p.484), but asked: 'Can *you* safely say that your war stops us from doing what you think *ought* otherwise to be done for education?'

[315] *Ibid.*

[316] Chamb PP.

[317] P.R.O. Cab. 1/2. Paper by Devonshire, 4 February 1902.

[318] Sir Almeric FitzRoy, *Memoirs,* I, p.80. FitzRoy was Clerk of the Council and had been Devonshire's secretary.

[319] Balfour PP., Add. MS. 49761.

[320] *Idem.,* Add. MS. 49787. Memo. of 14 March 1902.

[321] FitzRoy, *Memoirs,* I, p.81.

[322] Chamb. PP.

[323] Balfour PP., Add. MS. 49787.

[324] Balfour PP., Add. MS. 49761.

[325] *Ibid.*

[326] Chamberlain–Sandars, 9 October 1902, quoted in Amery, *op. cit.,* p.500.

[327] Bernard Holland, *Life of Devonshire,* II, p.284.

[328] Amery, *op. cit.,* p.510.

[329] Beatrice Webb's diary, 14 October 1902.

[330] *Ibid.*, 14 March 1903.

[331] *Ibid.*, 15 March 1903.

[332] *Ibid.*, 27 May 1902.

[333] Beatrice Webb PP.

[334] Balfour PP., Add. MS. 49761. Sandars–Balfour, 21 September 1902.

[335] P.R.O. Cab. 1/2. 'Commercial Union between the U.K. and the Colonies' by Robert Giffen, 9 February 1891.

[336] Chamb. PP.

[337] Chamb. PP., 17 October 1887.

[338] Balfour PP., Add. MS. 49695.

[339] Sir Herbert Maxwell, *Evening Memories*, p.245.

[340] Lady Hicks Beach, *Life of Sir Michael Hicks Beach*, II, pp.109-10. Beach–Salisbury, 17 October 1899.

[341] Hicks Beach PP., Colne St. Aldwyn.

[342] Chamb. PP.

[343] *Ibid.*

[344] Balfour PP.

[345] Amery, *op. cit.*, p.518.

[346] *Ibid.*, p.523.

[347] Lady Hicks Beach, *op. cit.*, II, pp.188-9, 7 May 1903.

[348] Balfour PP., Add. MS. 49770. Balfour–Devonshire, 27 August 1903.

[349] Devonshire PP. (copy).

[350] *Ibid.*

[351] *Ibid.*

[352] Add. MS. 48681.

[353] Devonshire PP., 13 July 1903.

[354] Devonshire PP.

[355] The correspondence between Balfour and Devonshire was printed in a cabinet document after the latter's resignation. P.R.O. Cab. 1/2.

[356] Devonshire PP.

[357] *Ibid.*

[358] *Ibid.*

[359] *Ibid.*

[360] Devonshire PP., Lord James–Devonshire, 8 September 1903.

[361] P.R.O. Cab. 1/2. 7 September 1903.

[362] Balfour PP., Add. MS. 49761. f. 196. Undated memo. by Sandars.

[363] Devonshire PP., Ritchie–Devonshire, 28 September 1903.

[364] Reported by Stanley to Sandars on 30 October (Balfour PP., Add. MS. 49761 *loc. cit.*).

[365] Beatrice Webb's diary, 2 January 1902.

[366] Hicks Beach PP.

[367] Devonshire PP., Hamilton–Devonshire, 6 October 1903.

[368] Devonshire PP.

[369] *Ibid.*, Goschen–Devonshire, 11 October 1903.

[370] Hicks Beach PP., Devonshire–Beach, 27 October 1903, describing James' views.

[371] Devonshire PP.

[372] *Ibid.*

[373] *Ibid.*, Lord Spencer–Devonshire, 7 January 1904.

[374] Devonshire PP.

[375] Devonshire PP., Churchill–Devonshire, 8 February 1904.

[376] *Ibid.*, 12 April 1904.

[377] Balfour PP., Add. MS. 49831. 21 September 1903.

[378] *Ibid.*, Add. MS. 49757. 10 October 1903.

[379] *Ibid.*, Add. MS. 49761. Sandars–Balfour, 24 December 1903.

[380] Chamb. PP.

[381] Austen Chamberlain, *Politics from Inside,* p.32 and generally pp.22-34.

[382] Balfour PP., Add. MS. 49757.

[383] *Ibid.*, 21 September 1904.

[384] *Ibid.*, 24 September 1904.

[385] Hicks Beach PP., Devonshire–Beach, 10 October 1904.

[386] Chamb. PP.

[387] Balfour PP., Add. MS. 49757.

[388] *Ibid.*, Add. MS. 49697. To H. Northcote, 1 January 1905.

[389] *Ibid.*, Add. MS. 49774. 12 February 1905.

[390] *Ibid.*, 18 February 1905.

[391] *Ibid.*, Add. MS. 49758.

[392] *Ibid.*, Add. MS. 49774.

[393] *Ibid.*, Chamberlain–Balfour, 17 March 1905. If the tariff reformers were left in the lurch, he warned, they would refuse to support Balfour's 'retaliation' group in later divisions and the government would be defeated. Also Add. MS. 49763, Sandars–Balfour, 18 March 1905, suggesting that these fiscal motions might be treated as 'purely academic'.

[394] Chamb. PP., Austen Chamberlain–his father, 20 March 1905.

[395] Balfour PP., Add. MS. 49796. E. B. Iwan-Muller–Sandars, 20 March 1905.

[396] Chamb. PP., Chamberlain–Austen Chamberlain, 22 March 1905.

[397] Balfour PP., Add. MS. 49780.

398 *Ibid.,* Add. MS. 49857. James F. Hope–Balfour, 17 April 1905, reporting the substance of the meeting. See also H. Maxwell, *op. cit.,* p.249.

399 H. Maxwell, *op. cit.,* pp.250-1.

400 Balfour PP., Add. MS. 49774.

401 Balfour PP.

402 Chamb. PP.

403 H. Maxwell, *op. cit.,* p.252.

404 Balfour PP., Add. MS. 49735.

405 *Ibid.,* Add. MS. 49775.

406 *Ibid.*

407 *Ibid.,* Add. MS. 49796.

408 Devonshire PP., Ritchie–Devonshire, 1 June 1905.

409 Hicks Beach PP., Beach–Devonshire, 14 June 1905.

410 Devonshire PP.

411 *Ibid.*

412 *Ibid.,* Devonshire–Balfour, 8 November 1905.

413 Chamb. PP., G. H. D[uckworth]–Austen Chamberlain, 2 November 1905.

414 Balfour PP., Add. MS. 49774.

415 *Ibid.* To Balfour, 4 November 1905.

416 *Ibid.,* Add. MS. 49796.

417 *Ibid.,* Add. MS. 49831. 10 November 1905.

418 Devonshire PP., Balfour of Burleigh–Devonshire, 26 November 1905, reporting separate conversations he had had the day before with Sandars and with Hicks Beach.

419 Chamb. PP., Chamberlain–John Boraston, 13 January 1906.

420 Chamb. PP.

421 Devonshire PP.

422 Chamb. PP.

423 *Ibid.,* Chamberlain–Boraston, 18 May 1906.

424 Chamb. PP., Mrs Chamberlain–Mrs Endicott, 27 January 1906.

425 H. Maxwell, *op. cit.,* p.255.

426 Chamb. PP.

427 Balfour PP., Add. MS. 49765. Sandars–W. M. Short, 4 March 1907.

428 *Ibid.*

429 *Ibid.*

430 *Ibid.,* Balfour–Sandars, 24 January 1907.

431 *Ibid.,* Add. MS. 49779.

432 *Ibid.,* W. A. S. Hewins–Balfour, 11 February 1907.

433 *Ibid.,* Add. MS. 49765. Balfour–Sandars, 5 April 1907.

434 Henry Page Croft, Lord Croft, *My Life of Strife,* pp.41-5.

[435] Balfour PP., Add. MS. 49736. 24 October 1907.

[436] J. W. Mackail and Guy Wyndham, *Life and Letters of George Wyndham*, II, p.540. Add. MS. 49806.

[437] Balfour PP., Add. MS. 49736.

[438] *Ibid.*, Add. MS. 49806.

[439] J. L. Garvin, *Tariff or Budget*, p.14.

[440] *Ibid.*, p.20.

[441] Balfour PP., Add. MS. 49766.

[442] *Ibid.*, 24 September 1909.

[443] Chamb. PP., Mrs Chamberlain–Mrs Endicott, 25 September 1909.

[444] *Ibid.*, 22 October 1909.

[445] *Ibid.*, 17 November 1909.

[446] Sir Almeric FitzRoy, *Memoirs,* I, p.386.

[447] Balfour PP., Add. MS. 49730.

[448] Note in Hicks Beach PP.

[449] Balfour PP., Add. MS. 49795. Garvin–Sandars, 21 December 1910.

[450] Chamb. PP. To Mrs Endicott, 2 December 1910.

[451] Balfour PP., Add. MS. 49697. Milner–Balfour, 17 April 1910.

[452] Garvin–Balfour, 17 October 1910, quoted in A. M. Gollin, *The Observer and J. L. Garvin*, p.215.

[453] Balfour PP., Add. MS. 49795. Garvin–Balfour, 17 October 1910.

[454] *Ibid.*, Garvin–Balfour, 25 October 1910.

[455] *Ibid.* Undated memo. criticizing Unionist campaign literature.

[456] Add. MS. 39736.

[457] Balfour PP., Add. MS. 49795.

[458] *Ibid.*, Add. MS. 49730. Lord Cromer–Lansdowne, 28 November 1910, and Lansdowne–Balfour of same date.

[459] *Ibid.*, Add. MS. 49736.

[460] Chamb. PP.

[461] Balfour PP., Add. MS. 49795.

[462] *Ibid.*

[463] *Ibid.*

[464] Austen Chamberlain, *Politics from Inside*, pp.348–9, 26 July 1911.

[465] Balfour PP., Add. MS. 49795.

[466] A. Wilson Fox, *Lord Halsbury*, p.286.

[467] Sir Charles Petrie, *Austen Chamberlain*, I. p.293.

[468] Austen Chamberlain, *op. cit.*, pp.358-9.

[469] Chamb. PP.

[470] Balfour PP., Add. MS. 49767. Note on events leading to Mr Balfour's retirement, by J. S. Sandars.

471 *Ibid.*, Add. MS. 49736.
472 *Ibid.*
473 *Ibid.*, Add. MS. 49767. Sandars' note cited above.
474 Chamb. PP., 22 November 1911.
475 Chamb. PP.

Bibliography

A. MANUSCRIPT SOURCES:

Hicks Beach papers at Colne St Aldwyn.
Balfour papers, British Museum. References in the text range between
   Add. MS. 49691 and Add. MS. 49857.
Chamberlain papers, University Library, Birmingham.
Devonshire papers at Chatsworth.
Herbert Gladstone papers, British Museum, Add. MS. 46015.
Henry Broadhurst papers, London School of Economics.
Passfield papers, London School of Economics.
Colonial Office files, Public Record Office. C.O. 417/261–7, 279–80.
Fitzjames Stephen PP., Cambridge University Library.
Helen Taylor papers, London School of Economics.

B. ARTICLES BY JOSEPH CHAMBERLAIN:

'The Manufacture of Iron Wood Screws', in *The Resources Products and
   Industrial History of Birmingham* . . . (ed. Samuel Timmins), 1866.
'The Liberal Party and its Leaders', *Fortnightly Review*, September 1873.
'The Next Page of the Liberal Programme', *Fortnightly Review*, Octo-
   ber 1874.
'The Right Method with Publicans', *Fortnightly Review*, May 1876.
'A Visit to Lapland, with Notes on Swedish Licensing', *Fortnightly
   Review*, December 1876.
'Free Schools', *Fortnightly Review*, January 1877.
'Municipal Public Houses', *Fortnightly Review*, February 1877.
'A New Political Organization', *Fortnightly Review*, July 1877.
'The Caucus', *Fortnightly Review*, November 1878.
'Land Nationalization', *Pall Mall Gazette*, 24, 29 January 1882.
'Labourers' and Artisans' Dwellings', *Fortnightly Review*, December
   1883.
'A Radical View of the Irish Crisis', *Fortnightly Review*, February 1886.
'Shall we Americanize our Institutions?', *Nineteenth Century*, Decem-
   ber 1890.
'Favourable Aspects of State Socialism', *North American Review*, May
   1891.
'Old Age Pensions', *National Review*, February 1892.
'Municipal Institutions in America and England', *Forum*, November
   1892 (New York).
'The Labour Question', *Nineteenth Century*, November 1892.

'A Bill for the Weakening of Great Britain', *Nineteenth Century*, April 1893.

'The Case against Home Rule', *Pall Mall Gazette*, 8 August 1893.

'The Home Rule Campaign', *National Review*, May 1894.

'Municipal Government', *New Review*, June 1894.

'Old Age Pensions and Friendly Societies', *National Review*, January 1895.

'The Policy of the United States', *Scribner's Magazine*, December 1898.

'Nelson's Year and National Duty', *Outlook*, 11 March 1905.

C. COLLECTED SPEECHES BY JOSEPH CHAMBERLAIN:

Henry W. Lucy, *Speeches of J. Chamberlain* (1885).

C. W. Boyd, *Mr. Chamberlain's Speeches*, 2 vols., 1914.

The Radical Platform. Speeches—Autumn. 1885.

Home Rule and the Irish Question. Speeches—1881–7 (1887).

Speeches on Irish Question—1887–90 (1890).

Foreign and Colonial Speeches (1897).

Imperial Union and Tariff Reform. Speeches—May–November 1903.

Chamberlain papers, extensive collection of newspaper cuttings in several volumes.

D. BIOGRAPHICAL AND GENERAL STUDIES OF CHAMBERLAIN'S CAREER:

Creswicke, Louis, *Life of Joseph Chamberlain* (1904).

Filon, A., *Profils anglais—Joseph Chamberlain*, etc. (1893).

Garvin, James L., *Life of Joseph Chamberlain*: vol. 1, *Chamberlain and Democracy, 1836–1885*; vol. 2, *Disruption and Combat, 1885–1895*; vol. 3, *Empire and World Policy, 1895–1900.*

(Continued by Julian Amery) vol. 4, *At the Height of his Powers, 1901–1903.*

Gulley, Elsie C., *Joseph Chamberlain and English Social Politics* (Columbia University, U.S.A. 1926).

Jeyes, Samuel H., *Joseph Chamberlain* (1903).

Mackintosh, Sir Alexander, *Joseph Chamberlain* (1906).

Marris, N. M., *Joseph Chamberlain: the man and the statesman* (1900).

Pedder, H. C., *Joseph Chamberlain* (1902).

Petrie, Sir Charles A., *The Chamberlain Tradition* (1938).

— *Joseph Chamberlain* (1940).

Robertson, Rt. Hon. John M., *Chamberlain: a study* (1905).

Skottowe, B. C., *Life of Joseph Chamberlain* (1885).

Stead, W. T., *Joseph Chamberlain: conspirator or statesman?* (1900).

Life of Joseph Chamberlain. By Viscount Milner, J. A. Spender, Sir H. Lucy, J. Ramsay MacDonald, Harold Cox, and L. S. Amery (1912).

E. BASIC PERIODICAL SOURCES:

Hansard.

B[ritish] P[arliamentary] P[apers] (complete file in the State Paper room, British Museum, and on Readex Microprint.

Public Record Office. Cabinet papers 1880–1914 on microfilm.

The Annual Register.

The Times (with Palmer's Index).

The *Manchester Guardian* (manuscript index in the Central Library, Manchester).

The *Birmingham Daily Post.*

The Nonconformist.

The *Pall Mall Gazette.*

The Liberal Unionist.

The Speaker.

The Daily News.

The Fortnightly Review.

F. BIBLIOGRAPHY TO CHAPTERS:

1. *The 'Party of Progress'*

Adams, Francis, *History of the Elementary School Contest* (1882).

Arch, Joseph, *Story of his Life, told by himself* (1898).

Bodelsen, C. A. G., *Studies in Mid-Victorian Imperialism* (1924).

Briggs, Asa, *History of Birmingham* (1952).

Bright, John, *Speeches* (ed. J. E. Thorold Rogers).

Bruce, J. T. and Vince, C. A., *History of the Corporation of Birmingham* (1878–85).

Collings, Jesse and Green, J. L., *Life of Jesse Collings* (1920).

Cowen, Joseph, *Speeches on Near Eastern Question* (1909).

Cowling, Maurice, *Mill and Liberalism* (1963).

Crosskey, H. W., *The Liberal Association—the '600'—of Birmingham* (1877).

Dilke, Sir Charles W., *Greater Britain* (1868).

Dolman, F., 'Joseph Chamberlain's Municipal Career', *Fortnightly Review,* June 1895.

Eisen, Sydney, 'Huxley and the Positivists', *Victorian Studies,* June 1964.

Everett, Edwin M., *The Party of Humanity: the Fortnightly Review and its Contributors* (1939).

Gladstone, William Ewart, *Speeches in Scotland* (2 vols. 1879 and 1880).

Hanham, H. J., *Elections and Party Management* (1959).
Harrison, Frederick, *Autobiographical Memoirs* (1911).
Hirst, F. W., *The Early Life and Letters of John Morley* (2 vols. 1927).
Kelly, Robert, 'Midlothian', *Victorian Studies,* December 1960.
Knickerbocker, F. W., *Free Minds. John Morley and his friends* (Harvard, 1943).
McGill, Barry, 'Francis Schnadhorst and Liberal Party Organization', *Journal of Modern History,* March 1962.
Mill, John Stuart, *Dissertations and Discussions* (4 vols. 1859–1875).
Morley, John, *Life of Richard Cobden* (2 vols. 1881).
— *The Struggle for National Education* (1873).
— *On Compromise* (1874).
Roach, John, 'Liberalism and the Victorian Intelligentsia' (Cambridge), *Historical Journal,* XIII, 1957.
Shannon, R. T., *Gladstone and the Bulgarian Agitation,* 1876 (1960).
Southgate, Donald, *The Passing of the Whigs* (1962).
Staebler, Warren, *The Liberal Mind of John Morley* (1943).
Vincent, John, *Formation of Liberal Party 1857–68* (1966).

2. *Separatists and Socialists*
Cox, Harold, *Land Nationalization* (1892).
Crofts, W. C., *Municipal Socialism* (1885).
Bramwell, Lord, *Laissez faire* (1884).
Elton, Godfrey, *'England Arise!'* (1931).
Escott, T. H. S., *England: her People, Polity and Pursuits* (1885).
George, Henry, *Progress and Poverty* (1880).
Gwynn, S. and Tuckwell, G. M., *Life of Sir Charles Dilke* (2 vols., 1917).
Harrison, Henry, *Parnell, Joseph Chamberlain and Mr Garvin* (1938).
Howard, C. H. D., 'Joseph Chamberlain and the Unauthorised Programme', *English Historical Review,* LXV, 1950.
Hyndman, H. M., 'The Dawn of a Revolutionary Epoch', *Nineteenth Century,* January 1881.
— *The Text-Book of Democracy: England for All* (1881).
— *The Record of an Adventurous Life* (1911).
— *Justice.*
Liberty and Property Defence League. Reports and publications.
Lynd, Helen M., *England in the Eighteen-Eighties* (1945).
Maccoby, S., *English Radicalism, 1853–86* (1938).
Marriott, W. T., *The Liberal Party and Mr Chamberlain* (1884).
Mill, John Stuart, *Chapters on Socialism.* (Reprinted from *Fortnightly Review,* 1879.)
Palmer, N. B., *The Irish Land League Crisis* (New Haven, 1940).

Pembroke, Earl of, *Liberty versus Socialism* (1885).
The Radical Programme (1885).
Rae, John, *Contemporary Socialism* (1884).
Robinson, Edward S., *Communism* (1884).
Tsuzuki, C., *H. M. Hyndman and British Socialism* (1961).
Wallace, Alfred Russel, 'How to Nationalize the Land', *Contemporary Review*, November 1880.

3. *Hawarden is Willin'*
Curtis, L. P., *Coercion and Conciliation in Ireland, 1880–1892* (1963).
Dicey, A. V., *England's Case against Home Rule* (1886).
Hammond, J. L., *Gladstone and the Irish Nation* (1938).
Howard, C. H. D., 'Joseph Chamberlain, Parnell and the Irish Central Board Scheme', *Irish Historical Studies*, VIII, September 1953.
Gladstone, Herbert, *After Thirty Years* (1928).
Jenkins, Roy, *Sir Charles Dilke: A Victorian Tragedy* (1958).
Longford, J. A., *The Old Liberals and the New* (1886).
O'Brien, R. B., *Life of Parnell* (1898).
O'Brien, D. C. C., *Parnell and his Party, 1880–90* (1953).

4. *The Home Rule Struggle*
Dale, A. W. W., *Life of R. W. Dale* (1899).
Chamberlain, Joseph, *A Political Memoir* (ed. C. H. D. Howard 1953).
Magnus, Sir P., *Gladstone* (1954).
Morley, John, *Life of Gladstone* (3 vols., 1903).
— *Recollections* (2 vols., 1917).
Newton, John, *W. S. Caine, M.P.* (1907).
Ramm, Agatha (ed.), *The Political Correspondence of Gladstone and Granville 1876–86* (2 vols., 1962).
Thorold, A. L., *Life of Henry Labouchere* (1913).
Trevelyan, G. M., *Life of John Bright* (1913).
Watson, R. Spence, *The National Liberal Federation* (1907).

5. *Chamberlain and Beatrice Webb*
Webb, Beatrice, *My Apprenticeship* (1926).
— *Diaries*, ed. M. I. Cole: *1912–24* (1952), *1924–32* (1956).
Spencer, Herbert, *Autobiography* (2 vols., 1904).
— *Man versus the State* (1884).

6. *The Making of Unionism*
Cocks, H. F. Lovell, *The Nonconformist Conscience* (1943).
Dicey, A. V., *Law and Public Opinion in England* (1905).

Ensor, R. C. K. 'Some Political and Economic Interactions in Later Victorian England', *Transactions of Royal Historical Society*, 1949.

Fraser, Peter, 'The Liberal Unionist Alliance', *English Historical Review*, Jan. 1962.

Gardiner, A. G., *Life of Harcourt* (2 vols., 1923).

Goodman, G. L., 'Liberal Unionism and the revolt of the Whigs', *Victorian Studies,* Dec. 1959.

Herbert, Auberon, *A Politician in trouble about his Soul.*

Hurst, M. C., 'Joseph Chamberlain and West Midland politics 1865-95' (Dugdale Society, 1963).

Hyndman–Labouchere debate, 'Will Socialism benefit the English People?' (1884).

Kidd, Benjamin, *Social Evolution* (1894).

Koebner, R., and Schmidt, H. D., *Imperialism* (1964).

Maycock, Sir Willoughby W., *Mr Chamberlain in the U.S. and Canada* (1914).

Ritchie, David G., *Darwinism and Politics* (1889).

Semmel, B., *Imperialism and Social Reform* (1960).

Somervell, D. C., *English Thought in the Nineteenth Century* (1929).

Stephen, Leslie, *The Science of Ethics* (1882).

7. The New Radicalism

Beer, Max, *History of British Socialism* (1921).

Cornford, James, 'The transformation of Conservatism in the late Nineteenth Century', *Victorian Studies,* September 1963.

Lord Crewe, *Life of Rosebery* (2 vols., 1931).

Gibbon, Sir I. G. and Bell, R. W., *History of the London County Council* (1939).

Mallalieu, W. C., 'Joseph Chamberlain and Workmen's Compensation', *Journal of Economics History,* X, 1950.

Milne, A. J. M., *The Social Philosophy of English Idealism* (1962).

Trade Union Congress. Annual Reports.

Webb, Sidney J., *Socialism in England* (1890).

— *The London Programme* (1891).

Fabian Essays in Socialism (1889).

8. The Struggle for South Africa

Cambridge History of British Empire, vol. 8 (South Africa).

Curtis, L. G., *With Milner in South Africa* (1951).

Drus, E., 'Select Documents . . . concerning Anglo-Transvaal Relations, 1896–99', *Bulletin of Institute of Historical Research,* XXVII.

— 'Question of Imperial complicity in the Jameson Raid', *English Historical Review,* October 1953.

Fitzpatrick, Sir J. W., *The Transvaal from Within* (1889).
Gollin, A. M., *Proconsul in Politics. Milner* (1964).
Hall, H. L., *The Colonial Office* (1937).
Halperin, V., *Lord Milner and the Empire* (1952).
Headlam, C., *The Milner Papers* (2 vols., 1931).
Hensman, Howard, *Cecil Rhodes* (1901).
Hobson, J. A., *The War in South Africa* (1900).
— *Imperialism* (1902).
Iwan-Muller, E. B., *Lord Milner and South Africa* (1902).
Marais, J. S., *The Fall of Kruger's Republic* (1961).
Pakenham, E., *The Jameson Raid* (1960).
Ponsonby, A., *Democracy and Diplomacy* (1915).
Robinson, R. E. and Gallagher, J., *Africa and the Victorians* (1961).
Stokes, Eric, 'Milnerism', *Historical Journal*, V, 1, 1962.
Strauss, William, 'Joseph Chamberlain and the theory of Imperialism', Public Affairs (U.S.A.), 1942.
Thornton, A. W., *The Imperial Idea and its Enemies* (1959).
Walker, E. A., *Lord Milner in South Africa* (1942).
Wilde, R. H., *Joseph Chamberlain and the South African Republic, 1895-99* (Archives Year Book for South African History, 1956, vol. 1, Cape Town.)
Wrench, Sir John E., *Milner* (1958).

9. *State Education*
Adamson, J. W., *English Education 1789-1914* (1930).
Allen, Bernard M., *Sir Robert Morant* (1934).
FitzRoy, Sir Almeric, *Memoirs* (2 vols., 1925).
Halévy, E., *History of the English People*, Epilogue, vol. 1 (1929).
Kekewich, Sir G. W., *The Education Department* (1920).
McBriar, A. M., *Fabian Socialism and English Politics, 1884–1918* (1962).
Roberts, David, *Victorian Origins of the British Welfare State* (1960).
Webb, Sidney J., *London Education* (1904).

10. *Imperial Preference*
Askwith, G. R. A., *Lord James of Hereford* (1930).
Brown, Benjamin H., *The Tariff Reform Movement, 1881-95* (New York, 1943).
Dowding, W. E., *The Tariff Reform Mirage* (1911).
Farrer, T. H., *The Neo-Protectionist Scheme of Joseph Chamberlain* (1896).
Gallagher, J. and Robinson R., 'The Imperialism of Free Trade', *Economic History Review*, VI (2nd ser. 1953).
Giffen, Sir Robert, *Economic Inquiries and Studies* (1904).

Hewins, W. A. S., *Apologia of an Imperialist* (2 vols., 1929).
Hicks Beach, Lady Victoria, *Life of Hicks Beach* (2 vols. 1932).
Hoffman, R. J. S., *Great Britain and German Trade Rivalry, 1895-1914.*
Holland, Bernard, *Life of Devonshire* (2 vols., 1911).
MacGoun, A., *A Revenue Tariff within the Empire.* Canadian Chapters on Mr Chamberlain's Policy (1904).
Parkin, G. R., *Imperial Federation* (1892).
Tyler, J. E., *The Struggle for Imperial Unity, 1868–1895.*
Williams, E. E., *Made in Germany* (1896).
Zebel, G. H., 'Fair Trade', *Journal of Modern History,* XII, 1940.

11. *Balfourism and Betrayal*

Chilston, Eric Alexander, Viscount, *Chief Whip. Political Life and Times of Aretas Akers-Douglas, Viscount Chilston* (1961).
Dugdale, Blanche, E. C., *Balfour* (2 vols., 1936).
Fraser, Peter, 'Unionism and Tariff Reform: the Crisis of 1906', *Historical Journal,* V, 2, 1962.
Gollin, A. M., *Balfour's Burden* (1965).
Maxwell, Sir Herbert, *Evening Memories* (1932).
Morgan-Browne, H., *Balfourism* (1907).
Peel, Arthur G. V., *The Tariff Reformers* (1913).
Sandars, J. S., *Studies of Yesterday* (1928).
Outlook
Literature of the Tariff Reform League, Free Food League, Free Trade Union, etc.

12. *Tariff or Budget?*

Amery, L. S., *My Political Life* (2 vols., 1953).
Blake, Robert, *The Unknown Prime Minister* (1955).
Chamberlain, Austen, *Politics from Inside* (1936).
Croft, Henry Page, *My Life of Strife* (1948).
Fox, A. Wilson, *Lord Halsbury* (1929).
Fraser, Peter, 'The Unionist Debacle of 1911 and Mr Balfour's Retirement', *Journal of Modern History,* December 1963.
Garvin, J. L., *Tariff or Budget* (1909).
Gollin, A. M., *The Observer and J. L. Garvin* (1960).
Jenkins, Roy, *Mr Balfour's Poodle* (1954).
— *Asquith* (1964).
Mackail, J. W. and Guy Wyndham, *Life and Letters of George Wyndham* (2 vols., 1925).
Newton, Lord, *Lansdowne* (1929).
Nicolson, Sir Harold G., *George V* (1952).

Petrie, Sir Charles, *Walter Long* (1936).
— *Life and Letters of Sir Austen Chamberlain* (2 vols., 1939).
Robertson, Rt. Hon. John M., *The Collapse of Tariff Reform* (1911).
Snowden, Philip, Viscount, *The Socialists' Budget* (1907).
— *An Autobiography*, vol. I, 1864–1919 (1934).

Index

Conservative National Union: 258, 272, 277, 282

Conservative Party (*see also* Tories *and* Unionist Party): xiii, 4, 9, 10, 30, 166, 219, 276, 310; Parnell supports, 74; rejects Home Rule, 78; and Unionist Liberals, 105; J.C. and, 144–5; and amalgamation with Liberal Unionists, 276–7; in the North, 288–9

Constitutional Conference (1910): 297 *bis*

'Continuation-in-Office Bill': 97

Convention with South African Republic (1884): 179, 181, 185, 192

Corn Laws, repeal of: 1, 4, 235

Corn tax (*see also* Imperial preference): 234, 235, 239, 268, 284, 298

Council of the Empire: 231, 233

County councils: democratic, 144; as local education authorities, 210

County Councils Act (1888): 209

Courtney, Leonard: 24, 55, 56, 150, 206, 225

Cowper-Temple, Rt. Hon. William Francis (later Lord Mount-Temple): 8–9

Cowper-Temple principle of state education: 218, 220

Crimes Act, Irish: 60, 62

Crimes Bill (1882): 40, 59, 61

Crown, the: and the people: 296 *n*

Curzon, George Nathaniel (Marquess): 306

Daily Mail: 291

Daily News: 66 *n*; *quoted*, 13–14

Daily Telegraph: 66 *n*, 282

Dale, Rev. Dr R. W.: 11–12, 93–4, 130, 139, 144; *quoted*, 130

Darwin, Charles: 3

Darwinism, social: xiii, 123

Deadlock between two Houses of Parliament, resolving: 297

Delagoa Bay: 174, 175

Demagogues: 154

Democracy: 2, 4; J.C.'s main preoccupation, xii–xiii, xiv; evils of, 154

Democratic Federation (Hyndman's, 1881): 36, 38, 46

Derby, Earl of: 66, 78, 299, 306

Devonshire, 8th duke of (*formerly* Lord Hartington, *q.v.*): and Radicalism,

150, 166; and state education, 208–19 *passim*, 223; and Imperial preference and tariff reform, 237–49 *passim*; tenders resignation, 243–4; resigns office, 247; resigns Presidency of Liberal Unionist Association, 249; and party policies, 252–71 *passim*; *quoted*, 211, 239

Devonshire House, meetings at: 14 May 1886, 95; 24 Oct. 1911, 306

Dicey, Professor A. V.: 150; *quoted*, 150

'Die-hard' party (*see also* Halsbury Club): 295, 300, 301, 304, 305, 308

Dilke, Sir Charles: xiv, 236; and social reform, 23, 26, 28; and Irish problem, 34, 48, 54, 55 *bis*, 56, 58, 59, 61, 63, 68, 76, 79, 81, 86

Dillon, John, M.P.: 71

'Diplomacy, the new': 175 *and n*

Disestablishment: of Church of England, 14, 132, 138, 139 *bis*; Welsh, 135, 136

Disraeli, Benjamin (Prime Minister, 1868, 1874–80, *later* Earl of Beaconsfield): xiv, 2; his oriental (Near Eastern) foreign policy, 27–8; *quoted*, 50

Dissenters: *see* Nonconformists

Dissentient ministers, 1903: 241–5 *passim*

Dixon, George: 7, 8, 18, 23

Double election scheme, Balfour's: 255, 256 *bis*, 259, 261, 263, 266, 268–9, 299

'Dublin Castle' administration: 62, 63

Dublin Parliament: 32, 34, 73, 76, 79, 88

'Dynamic party politics' needed: 281

'Economic Notes upon Insular Free Trade' (Balfour's cabinet paper): 241

Edinburgh: 57, 256–7, 258, 264, 265

Editors of newspapers, Unionist: 272, 294

Education Acts: *1870*, 4–11, 147, 225; *1902*, 208–25, 226, 228

Education, Board of: 210, 216, 217

Education Department: 209, 210

Education, State: 2 *bis*, 3 *bis*, 6, 7, 48, 49, 138, 144, 208–25; local education authorities, 210–20 *passim*; conversation on (J.C. and Morant, 12 Dec. 1901), 214, 215; 'collectivist' system for London, 224

JOSEPH CHAMBERLAIN